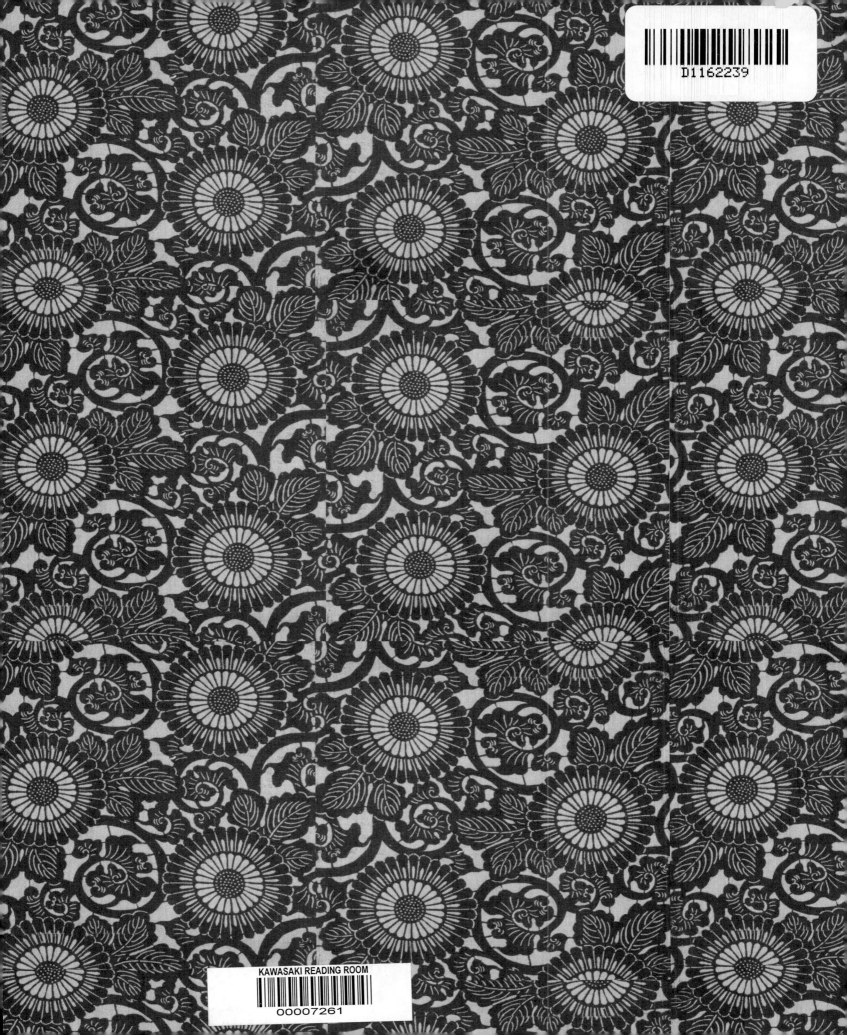

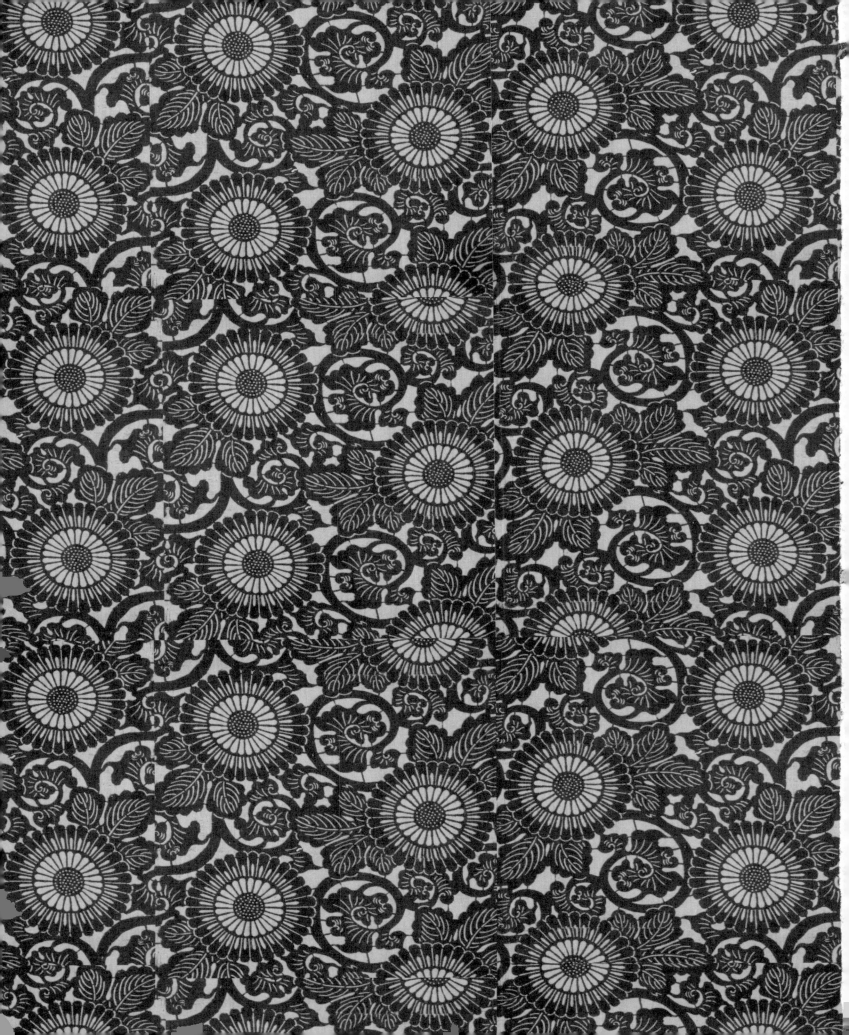

ONE THOUSAND YEARS OF
MANGA

To Kévin and Hélène-Flore

ACKNOWLEDGEMENTS

This book, for me, symbolizes Franco-Japanese friendship.

I am glad to able to express my warm gratitude to the individuals and organizations listed below for their advice, enthusiasm, and support in the course of writing.
(Japanese names are cited in the traditional order with the surname preceding the forename).

Paule Adamy, Geneviève Aitken, Ando Chieko, Harada Noriko, Hatakeyama Yutaka, Kamiyama Fumiko, Kashiwabara Junta, Kawamura Hiroshi, Kawanabe Kusumi, Kikuchi Makiko, Kobayashi Kunihisa, Kôno Minoru, Kotoku Minoru, Geneviève Lacambre, Maki Miyako, Makino Kyôko, Christophe Marquet, Matsukubo Yoriko, Matsumoto Hiroyuki, Matsumoto Leiji, Matsuo Tomoko, Mizuki Shigeru, Mura Yukio, Nakajô Masataka, Nakayarna Meguri, Nishimura Junko, Michelle-Esther Nissato, Ochiai Noriko, Ôki Hiroshi, Ôki Yukiko, Okuda Atsuko, Ozawa Hiromu, Isabelle Philippe, Corinne Quentin, Saitô Akiko, Sakamoto Naoki, Satô Hiroko, Sekiguchi Shun, Shimizu Isao, Suzuki Hiroko, Suzuki Michiko, Suzuki Sôichirô, Takahata Isao, Takeda Aya, Takeda Mikiko, Takeda Toshihiro, Tanaka Atsushi, Tanaka Haruko, Tanaka Yasuhiko, Taniguchi Jirô, Uchiyama Takeshi, Ueno Akio, Usui Noriaki, Watanabe Asako, Yamada Tomoko, Yamanashi Emiko, Yamazaki Emi, Yasuno Kôji, Yokoe Fuminori, Yukari Tai, Yumoto Gôichi.

Adachi Foundation for the Preservation of Woodcut Printing, Chiba City Museum of Art, Communications Museum Tokyo, Edo-Tokyo Museum, Idemitsu Museum of Arts, Ikeda Riyoko Production, Japan Foundation, Kawanabe Kyôsai Memorial Museum, Kobe City Museum, Kumon Research Institute, Kyoto International Manga Museum, Machida City Museum, Machida City Museum of Graphic Arts, Mizuki Shigeru Production, Musée de la Bande Dessinée at Angoulême, Ôta Memorial Museum of Art, Saitama Municipal Cartoon Art Museum, Studio Ghibli, Suntory Museum of Art, Tezuka Productions, Tokyo Bunkazai Kenkyuijo (Independent Administrative Institution, National Research Institute for Cultural Properties, Tokyo), Tokyo National Museum, University of Tokyo, Waseda University, as well as the Temples of Chôgosonshiji, Hôryûji, and Kôzanji.

I would also like to thank my parents, family, and friends.

Distributed in North America by Rizzoli International Publications, Inc.

Simultaneously published in French as *Mille Ans de Manga*

English-language edition

Flammarion
87, quai Panhard et Levassor
75647 Paris Cedex 13

www.editions.flammarion.com

ISBN: 978-2-0803-0029-4

ONE THOUSAND YEARS OF
MANGA

BRIGITTE KOYAMA-RICHARD

Flammarion

Contents

Editor's notes

Japanese names are cited in the traditional order
with the surname preceding the forename.
Japanese terms followed by an asterisk (*) in the text
are explained in the glossary.

The origins of manga

All over the world, the manga phenomenon is gripping an increasingly large audience. In Japan, everyone reads these graphic works for both fun and education, and they form an integral part of everyday life. But how have they reached such a pinnacle of success? What makes manga so different, and so attractive, when compared to American, European, or other comics? When and how they did they start? What is the origin of the word *manga*, and what does it signify? The answers to these questions find their roots in the ancestral culture of Japan, in which art often bore the marks of good humor.

In fact, profound pictorial similarities seem to exist between manga such as we know them today and ancient caricatures, extending from illuminated scrolls and brocade prints down to the birth of the modern comic strip. Thus Japanese traditions remain tangible in mangaka drawings by talents such as Mizuki Shigeru and in the splendid animations of Miyazaki Hayao and Takahata Isao, presented by Studio Ghibli.

The word *manga* was coined by Hokusai in the nineteenth century as the title for collections of drawings intended both for his disciples and for art lovers generally. The term is composed of two ideograms: *man* (meaning *executed rapidly, thrown off*) and *ga* (meaning *drawing*). Subsequently, the word was adopted by artists of that period to refer to such sketches, and only in the twentieth century was it employed in reference to comic strips. The Kôjien, the Japanese-language dictionary, defines *manga* as: "Simple, humorous, and exaggerated drawing. Caricature or social satire. A series of pictures telling a story; 'comics'."

In our own time, the word *manga* has changed to the point that it is hardly used in Japan other than by people born before World War II, who generally would use the word to refer to satirical or critical political comic strips published in the press. For succeeding generations, the word might call to mind Edo-era prints—and not cartoons at all. For these younger generations of Japanese, publishers and booksellers employ the term *comic*, which covers mangas of all kinds.

So it is a paradox that the West has chosen a word, *manga*, that Japan no longer uses. This book attempts to retrace the cultural and visual origins of manga and to study how this art form has progressed through time.

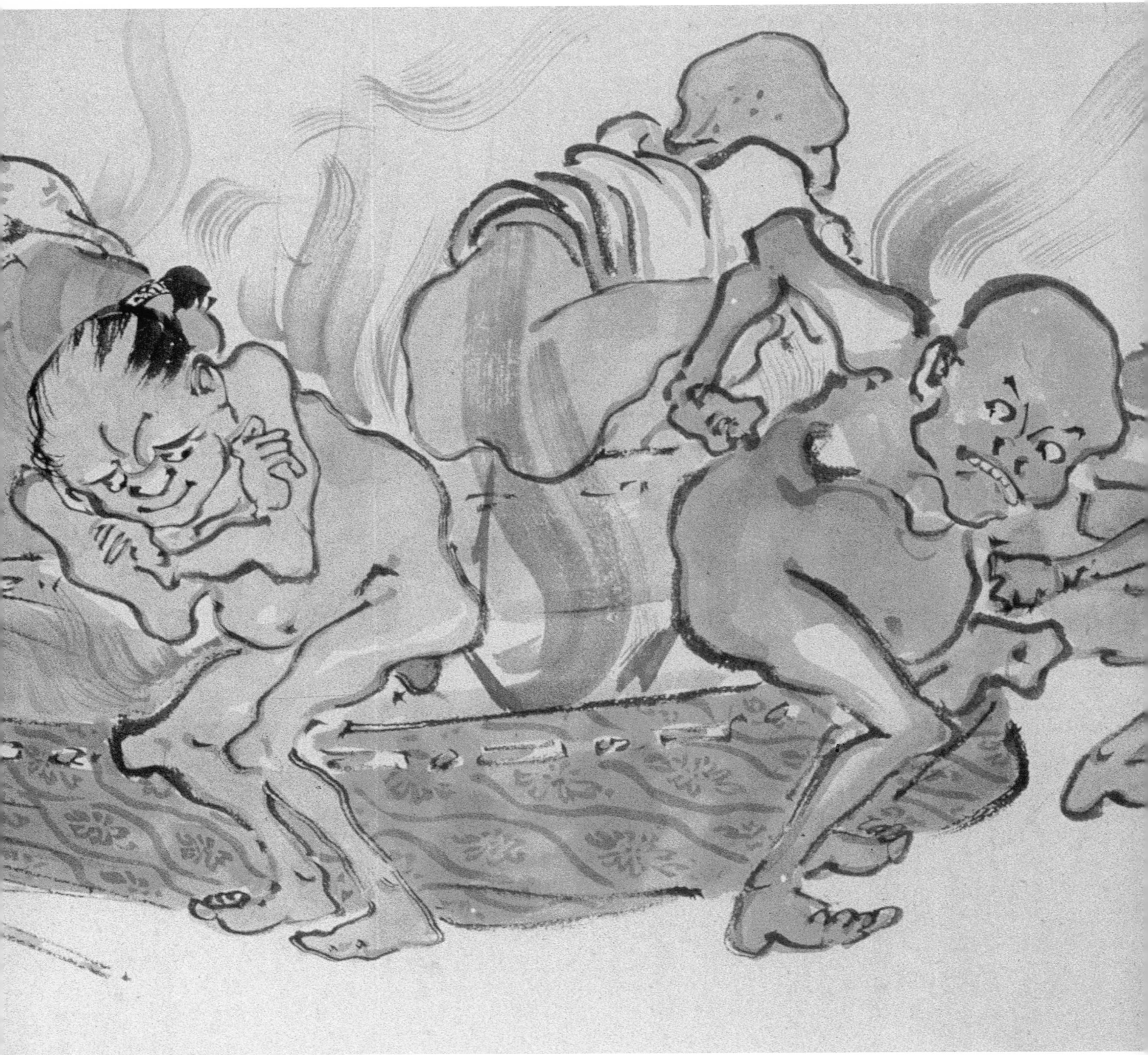

Fig. 47 (detail)

THE MAGIC OF THE SCROLL: FROM THE EARLIEST CARICATURES TO THE ONSET OF THE COMIC STRIP

Throughout the ages, man has drawn in caves, on walls, and on pottery, often evoking the sacred world and caricaturing forms from the physical one. This was true in Japan, where some of most beautiful examples ever discovered date back to the end of the seventh century, most notably in the Hôryûji Temple. There, irreverent drawings were etched on the Figs. 1–2 back of the temple's ceiling planks—probably by the craftsmen who built the edifice—and they remained long hidden from public view.

Japanese painting came into its own during the Nara period in the eighth century and, subsequently, became a perfect reflection of the esthetics and life of the court in the Heian era, from the late eighth through twelfth centuries. At the same time, illuminated scrolls, the *emakimono**, were produced by artists who vied with each other in virtuosity.

Originating in China, but magnificently adapted and transformed in accordance with the Japanese esthetic, these scrolls remain fascinating today. The Chinese and, in their wake, the Japanese chose not to confine the image within a frame or panel, but to present its multiple facets, allowing the viewer's eye to roam and take in a succession of scenes—outside or within temples or palaces—viewed from below or from high above, and from every conceivable angle, as if viewing the image through the lens of a movie camera.

Intended for an aristocratic or religious elite, the scroll became a precious object in its own right; it is fragile and demands the greatest care in handling. The scroll is a long strip of paper that can reach about 49 ft. (15 m) in length and is wrapped around a stick, unrolling from right to left in sections measuring 20 to 24 in. (50 to 60 cm). The viewer can thus take in each scene as it segues into the following segment. A single work can even extend over several scrolls. Unlike a mural fresco of limited dimensions, such scrolls allow very long stories to be told and often combine painted scenes with calligraphied texts. After being perused by a lucky few, this precious object is delicately rolled back up and carefully stored away. The roll is reinforced with brocade and secured by a ribbon.

The majority of these scrolls illustrate religious events or scenes from literature. By commemorating the foundation of a temple or sanctuary, or describing hell as portrayed in Buddhist scripture, or else depicting spirits or recalling diseases, they are intended as a vade mecum of human behavior. In their accounts of great battles or episodes from history, or satires of manners, they constituted a valuable storehouse of the past for future generations. Many have disappeared today, but among those preserved, four have been classified as a "National Treasure": the *Genji monogatari emaki (The "Tale of Genji" Scroll)*, *Shigisan engi emaki (The Legends of Mount Shigi)*, Figs. 9–10 *Chôjû jinbutsu giga (Frolicking Animals and People)*, and *Ban Dainagon* Figs. 5–8 *emaki (Scroll of the Illustrated Narrative of the Grand Counselor Ban* Figs. 11–14 *Dainagon)*.

In Western culture, wall hangings such as the renowned Bayeux Fig. 15 tapestries may be likened to these Japanese scrolls, which recorded historical events and sometimes were produced over successive centuries. With its divisions and scenes of everyday life, this extraordinary work, embroidered between about 1070–80, shortly after the conquest of England by William, Duke of Normandy, in 1066, can also be seen as a kind of 2,756-in. (7,000-cm) long by 20-in. (50-cm) broad "comic strip." It is divided into three parts, and the most important zone runs along the middle. The upper and lower bands comprise figures that have little to do with the main narrative: a decor of more or less fantastic animals from the Romanesque bestiary—comparable to, although different from, those offered by Japanese imagery—together with foliage and vegetal ornaments. Even if there was any putative reciprocal influence that has not to date been proved, it is interesting to note how, at different periods and in regions so distant from one another, artists and craftsmen shared a need to record historical episodes on strips of paper or bolts of fabric, showing the selfsame desire to explain and transcribe the events, as well as to depict the customs of the time.

Even before the advent of the Japanese print, painters frequently represented the everyday lives of their contemporaries. If scrolls and folding-screens foregrounded aristocratic existence, there were exceptions, in particular when the material was derived from folktales or fiction. The roll *Fujibukuro-sôshi emaki (The* Figs. 16–17 *Wisteria Basket Story)* provides an interesting example. Japanese artists always excelled in the depiction of animals. Although they were often the favorites, the members of the Chinese zodiac (the rat, ox, tiger, rabbit, dragon, snake, horse, sheep, monkey, bird, dog, and wild boar) were not alone. Many painters, such as Utagawa Kuniyoshi and Kawanabe Kyôsai, took cats or frogs as a subject. Thus, the scroll *Nezumi-Soshi emaki (Scroll of a Tale of Rats)* shows rodents acting like humans and making preparations for a wedding reception.

Certain scrolls, which to Western eyes might seem coarse, present genital or farting contests. Considered comic, such scenes became very popular in the Edo* period in illustrated prints and books.

There are also numerous scrolls evoking the supernatural world and the *yôkai**, beneficent or malicious monsters which had since ancient times formed a preponderant part of Japanese literature. In the beginning, the *yôkai* were representations of the *oni**, equivalents of our demons, and the *tengu**, sorts of devils, as well as foxes and snakes to which all kinds of magic powers were ascribed. The earliest pictorial compositions showing *yôkai* appeared in the twelfth century. At this time, it was thought that objects, on attaining their hundredth "birthday," possessed the ability to change shape: a good reason to dispose of them before they attained that dangerous age. Legend had it that, in spite of every precaution, some objects did manage to undergo their metamorphosis and wreaked their vengeance on humans so as to force them to repent and devote their lives to Buddhism. In painting, these ill-disciplined articles were comically represented in the shape of a nocturnal procession of one hundred demons.

Astonishing similarities exist between these ancient illustrated scrolls and today's manga* and anime*, as explained by the celebrated filmmaker and producer of the Studio Ghibli, Takahata Isao, in his work, *Jûni seiki no anime-shon, kokuhô emakimono ni miru eigateki animeteki narumono* (Cartoons in the Twelfth Century. Aspects Evocative of the Cinema and Animation in Twelfth-century Painting Scrolls Listed as National Treasures). According to this author, the *emaki* that is gradually unrolled to reveal the successive scenes produces an impression of time flow and of progression in the action, as a manga divides the story into a series of boxes—and of course as in animation generally.

Figs. 37–42
Figs. 61–66
Fig. 18

Fig. 47

Figs. 43–45

Figs. 19–20

Figs. 21–36

Emaki scrolls were aimed at privileged individuals; the people had no access to their pictorial richness—indeed they possessed no form of art representative of their lives. At the beginning of the seventeenth century, though, this situation was about to change.

1–2
Temple ceiling, late seventh century, Hôryûji. © Hôryûji, photo Shogakukan

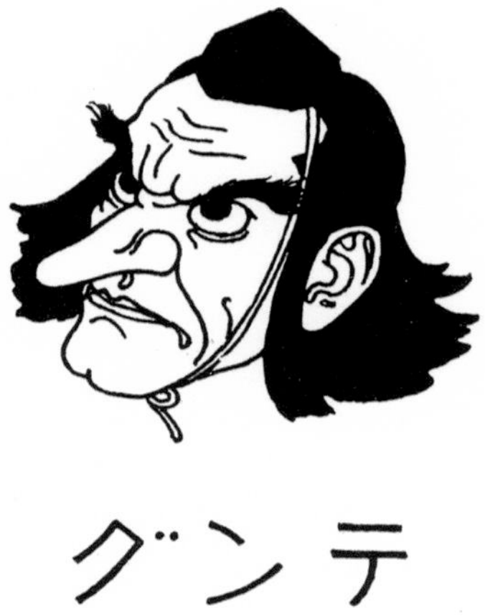
テング

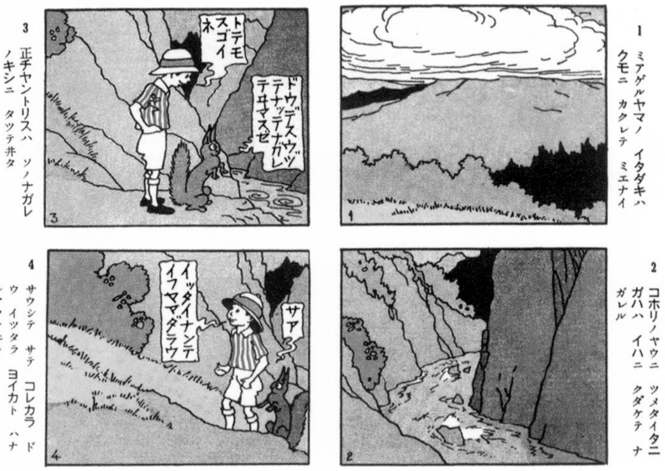
1
ミアゲルヤマノ イタダキハ クモニ カクレテ ミエナイ
2
コホリノヤウニ ツメタイタニガハハ イハニ クダケテ ナガレル
3
トテモスゴイネ
ドウデスウヅテナッテナガレテヰマスゼ
正チヤントリスハ ソノナガレノキシニ タッテヰタ
4
サア
イッタイナンテイフヤマダラウ
サウシテ サテ コレカラ ドウ イッタラ ヨイカト ハナシアッテヰル

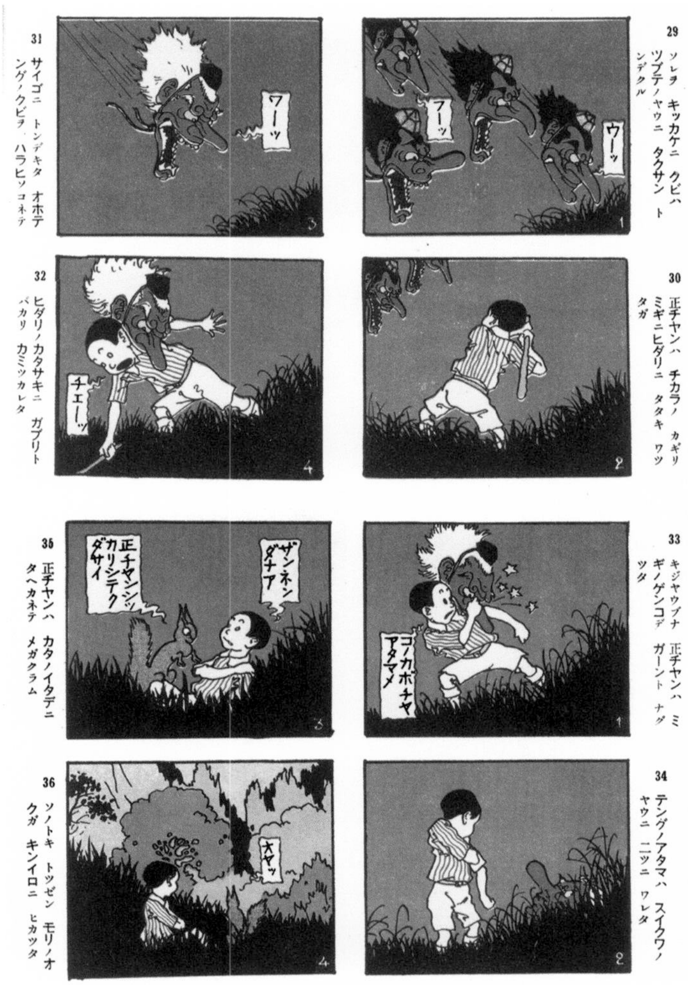
29
ソレヲ キッカケニ クビハ ツブテノヤウニ タクサン トンデクル
ウーッ
フーッ
30
正チヤンハ チカラノ カギリ ミギニヒダリニ タタキ ワッタガ
31
サイゴニ トンデキタ オホテングノクビヲ ハラヒソコネテ
ワーッ
32
ヒダリノカタサキニ ガブリト バカリ カミツカレタ
チエーッ
33
キジヤウブナ 正チヤンハ ミギノゲンコデ ガーンと ナグッタ
コノカボチヤアタマメ
34
テングノアタマハ スイクワノヤウニ 二ツニ ワレタ
35
正チヤンハ カタノイタデニ タヘカネテ メガクラム
ザンネンダナア
正チヤンシッカリシテクダサイ
36
ソノトキ トツゼン モリノオクガ キンイロニ ヒカッタ
オヤッ

3–4

Kabashima Katuchi, Oda Shôsei, *The Adventures of Shôchan*, taken from Vol. 4, 1925, ed. Ashishinburska (reprint, Shogakukan Creative, 2003). © Kabashima Katuchi, Oda Shôsei

This long-nosed *tengu* flying above Shôchan, the hero of the manga, *The Adventures of Shôchan*, is strangely redolent of that of Hôryûji. The two caricatures are, however, separated by some thirteen centuries.

Chôjû jinbutsu giga, "National Treasure," attributed to Toba Sôjô (Kakuyû, 1053–1140), composed of four scrolls in Chinese ink from 30 to 40 ft. (9 to 12 m) long. © Kôzanji

The two last scrolls are reputed to have been executed a century later by a painter whose name remains unrecorded. The most amusing scroll, that of the birds and animals, is particularly daring in its structure and irreverence, since some of its scenes portray the dissolute life of monks. Rabbits, frogs, monkeys, and foxes appear among the protagonists of the first scroll, while monks and imaginary animals feature in the following rolls. Unique of its type, the significance of this masterpiece has been much discussed by experts: is it a critique of the behavior of the devout, a parody of the staging of the great annual festival of *Nenjûgyôji**, or a satire on contemporary society?

Replacing the modeling found in Western painting, effects of depth are here conveyed by gradations of gray ink. In certain scenes, the painter made use of the speedlines that Hokusai was to employ again later with such brio.

The scene presents a sumo* tournament. According to legend, sumo was a fight between two *kami** (divinities) to seize Japan. Of shamanic and Shinto origin, a version of these battles had been held in the presence of the emperor—*sechie-zumô**—since the Nara period, but the rules of sumo such as we currently know it were fixed only in the Edo period. All the scenes in this scroll occur outside.

(Fig. 5) In these stories it is not always the strongest who carries the day; a tiny frog has thrown a rabbit to the ground, to the immense joy of his companions, one of whom, in tears of laughter, has fallen over, while steam (representing the animal's exertions) hisses out of the winner's mouth.

The painter captures the personality of each figure with an energetic line. The scroll is extremely rare in presenting no fewer than seven different sports.

(Fig. 6) Various animals with "rosaries" attend a religious ceremony.

(Fig. 7) This scene is one of most amusing in the entire roll. A monkey, sporting the monastic habit, reads *sûtra kyô** before what should be a Buddhist statue but which is here replaced by a live frog squatting on a lotus leaf. The monkey makes a heartfelt recitation of his prayer, as depicted on a kind of white word balloon. The tree in the front and the foothills in the mid-ground create a perspective effect. Indifferent to the scene, an owl peers at the viewer, pointing up the painter's ironic vision.

(Fig. 8) The monkey has finished his prayers. A rabbit brings him some watermelon, a luxury fruit at the time. Another waits to engage in conversation with the self-satisfied-looking old monk, whose heavy jowl is an indication of a healthy appetite. He brings a superb tiger skin as an offering to the monkey. Behind him, a frog prepares a splendid string of prayer beads. In what is surely another of the painter's little jokes, the last character on the left delicately holds in his arms a painted scroll, perhaps illustrated with stories from the life of this very monk. Throughout a story that unfolds seamlessly but with singular dynamism, human characteristics and defects are pointed out with finesse and exactitude.

Editor's note

Different sections of the scroll have been attributed distinct figure numbers in the captions. The sections are reproduced here as a continuous image. When an explanation of a particular section occurs in the text, a figure number appears beneath the appropriate section for ease of reference.

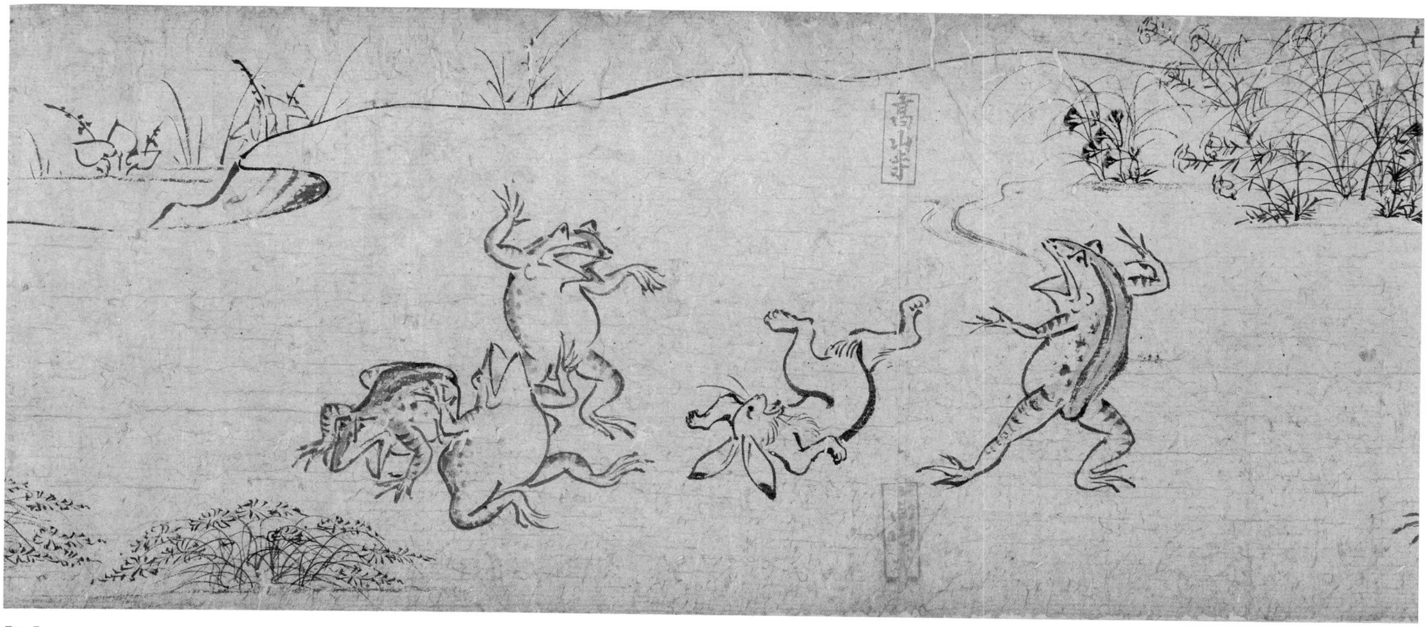

Fig. 5

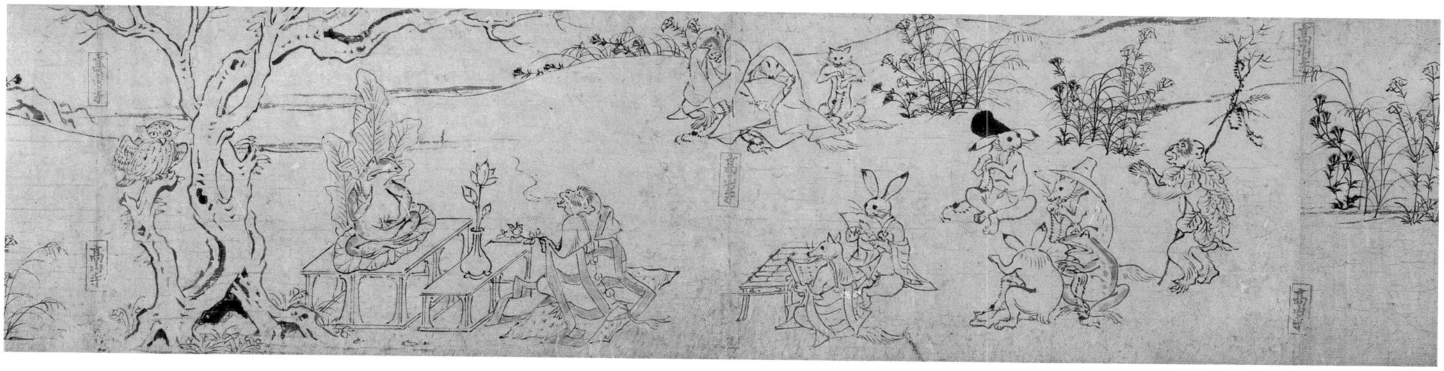

Fig. 7

Fig. 6

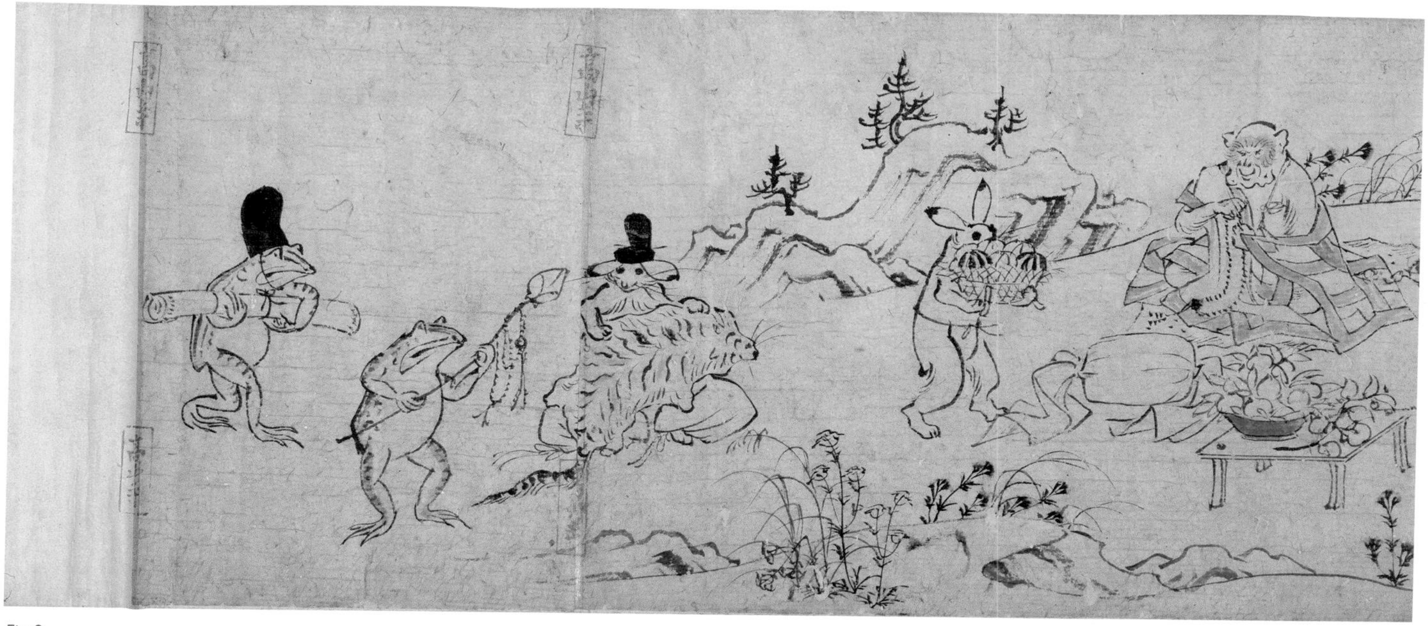

Fig. 8

9–10

Anonymous, *Shigisan engi emaki (The Legends of Mount Shigi)*, National Treasure, twelfth century, composed of three scrolls 117 ft. 9 ½ in. long in total by 12 ½ in. wide (35.9 m x 31.5 cm). © Temple of the Chôgosonshiji

The scroll of *The Legends of Mount Shigi* records the foundation of the temple and the miracles performed by its founder, Myôren, in the tenth century.

Amusing and lively, the first scroll narrates the story of a covetous landowner to whom Myôren had sent his gold begging bowl with a request for a little rice as alms. Instead of giving him an offering, however, the miser decides to keep the precious object. With a wave of his hand, Myôren orders the cup to leave its hiding place and fly off, tearing the house from the ground and thus carrying off all the rice balls. The astonished populace gazes on as the cup speeds away, while the miser pursues it in vain.

In the second scroll, Myôren is summoned to the sick emperor's bedside. In his stead, he dispatches a messenger who soars into the air and lands in the palace. The painter describes his lengthy voyage through the sky and, in a manner analogous to a "flashback" in a film, deliberately arranges the action from left to right to show that it unfolds prior to the messenger's arrival in the palace.

Dressed in a garment studded with sharp swords, the messenger travels across the sky pushing in front of him a wheel, the symbol of the law of Buddha. The ideas of time, speed, and movement—the rotating wheel in particular—are all admirably conveyed. The scene setting and layout, the expressions of the figures and the overall dynamism of this scroll all mark it out as a masterpiece.

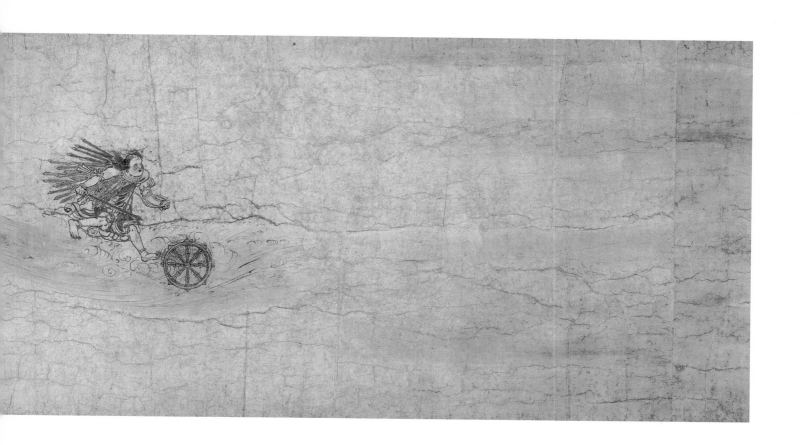

Ban Dainagon ekotoba (Scroll of the Illustrated Narrative of the Grand Counselor Ban Dainagon),
National Treasure, attributed to Tokiwa Mitsunaga, end of the twelfth century, comprising three scrolls.
© Idemitsu Museum of Art

The *Illustrated Narrative of the Grand Counselor Ban Dainagon* is the only one of the four "National Treasure" scrolls to take as its starting point a real event that occurred in Kyoto on March 10, 866. The *dainagon** Tomo no Yoshio set fire to one of the doors of the palace but contrived to divert the blame onto one of his enemies, Minamoto no Makoto. A year later, however, the truth came out. Two children were quarreling in a Kyoto street; one was the son of the servant of Yoshio, the other that of Makoto, who had actually seen the *dainagon* running off shortly before the conflagration broke out. The parents interceded in the children's squabble. Faced by the arrogance of Yoshio's servant, Makoto's man, who, because of the gravity of the case, had previously kept the secret to himself, decided to break his silence. Due to his exalted rank, Yoshio escaped the death penalty but was condemned to exile.

This exceptionally beautiful scroll depicts the rise and fall of the scheming courtier. In the tiny area that shows the two children arguing, one can make out an adult coming to the aid of one and kicking out at the other. The boy is about to tumble over, the fall being depicted as in a film in which the camera freezes on a figure for a split second. A woman pulls the other child away by the arm. The boiling intensity of the scene—borne up in a circular movement—the violence of the gestures, and the time-lapse between fracas and separation are all rendered with striking realism.

Employing the most precious pigments, the painting contains nearly four hundred figures. The expression on each face, pushed almost to caricature, translates the emotion of the moment: one can feel the terror in the eyes when the fire starts to blaze, followed by the bafflement as to its cause; then the anger of the squabbling kids, and so on.

Far from seeking to prettify his figures, the artist was intent on capturing the characteristics of the feelings each expresses. This scroll is reminiscent of a storyboard, in which a sequence of drawings allows the director to visualize each shot in the film; the course of the action culminates steadily, the climax being attained in a quarrel that must have seemed banal at first, but which led to the culprit's confession.

Several centuries separate the events from the time the scroll was made. The painter chose a dramatic version that unfolds seamlessly right up to the banishment of the guilty party.

Fig. 11–14

15

The Bayeux Tapestry, end of eleventh century, embroidery on linen, 20 x 276 in. (50 x 700 cm), Musée de la Tapisserie, Bayeux. Depiction of the conquest of England by the Normans (1064–66): feast given by William the Conqueror in the presence of Bishop Odon. © akg-images

These valiant soldiers are about to cook some poultry. They have taken off their coats of mail, laid down their helmets and shields, and seem to take visible delight in the festivities. The unexceptional gestures of everyday life are represented with great exactitude.

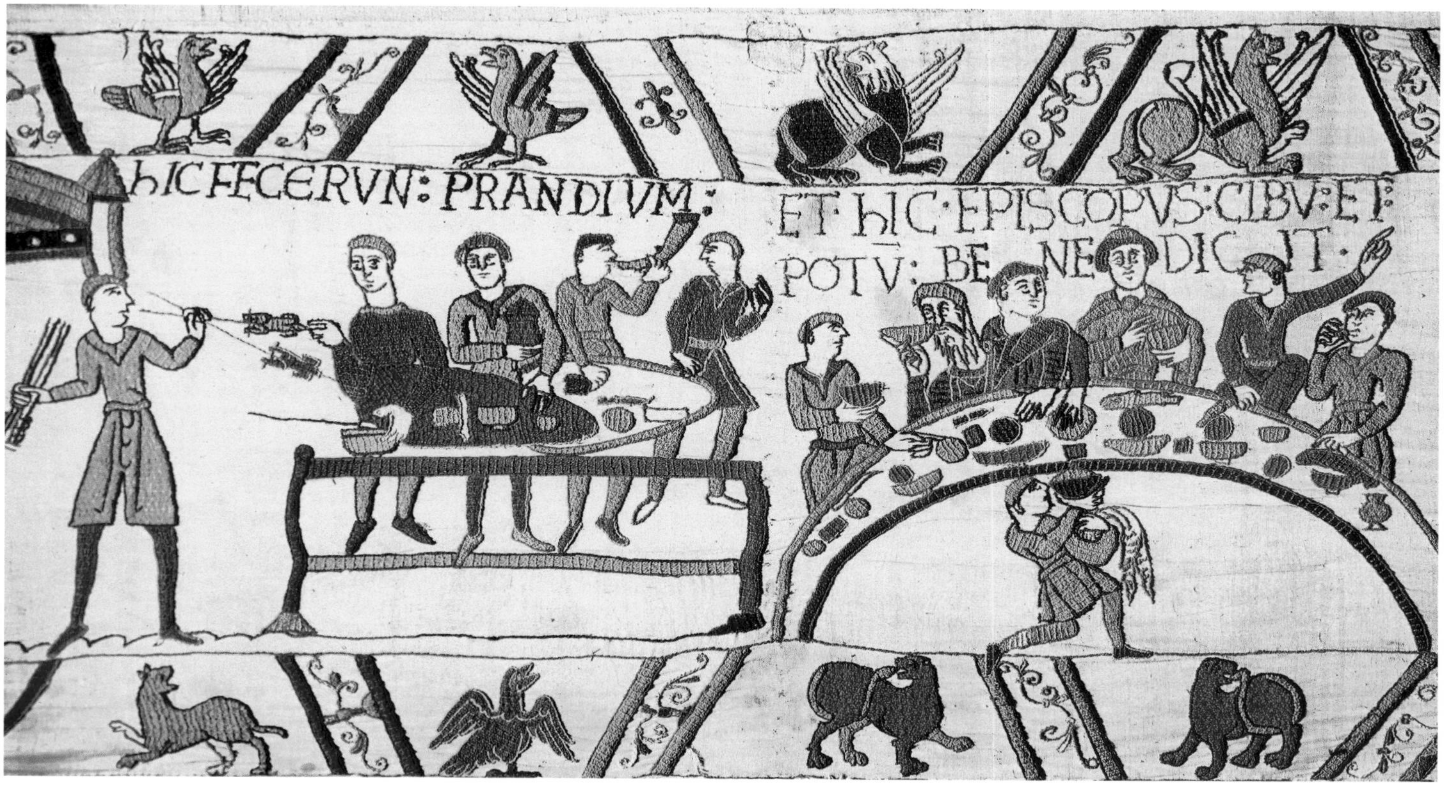
HIC FECERVN: PRANDIVM:
ET HIC·EPISCOPVS·CIBV·ET·
POTV: BE NE DIC IT·

READING FROM RIGHT TO LEFT

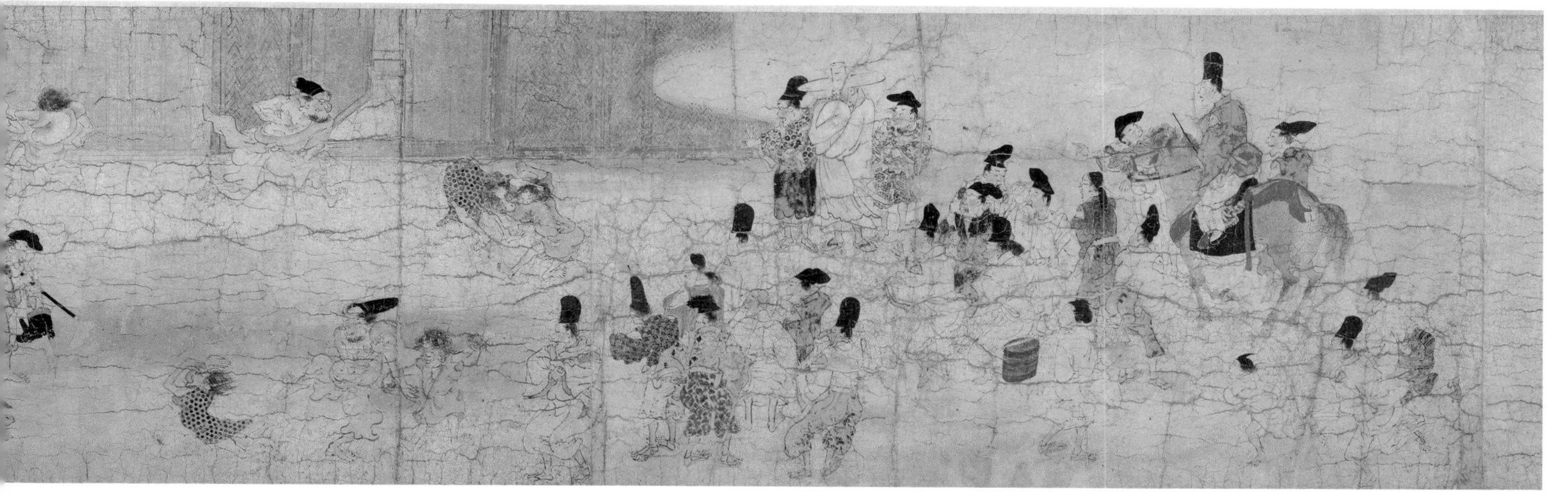

Anonymous, *Fujibukuro-sôshi emaki (The Wisteria Basket Story)*,
sixteenth century, 2 ¾ x 7 ¾ in. (7 meters x 19.7 cm). © Suntory Museum

In this tale from *The Wisteria Basket Story*, an old man, exhausted by years of toiling in the fields, murmurs under his breath that he is ready to give his daughter in marriage to any who agrees to take his place. A monkey, hearing the offer, jumps at the chance, and starts plowing the fields. Obliged to keep his promise, the peasant has to offer the ape his daughter's hand. The unhappy girl follows the animal, who stuffs her in a bag braided from wisteria and tries to hang her from a tree so she cannot escape. As luck has it, a huntsman passes by and witnesses the cruel scene. Freeing the girl, they are soon married—not without first punishing the cheeky monkey.

The scroll features monkeys which do not actually appear in the narrative; their attitudes and expressions show how close they are humans.

← READING FROM RIGHT TO LEFT

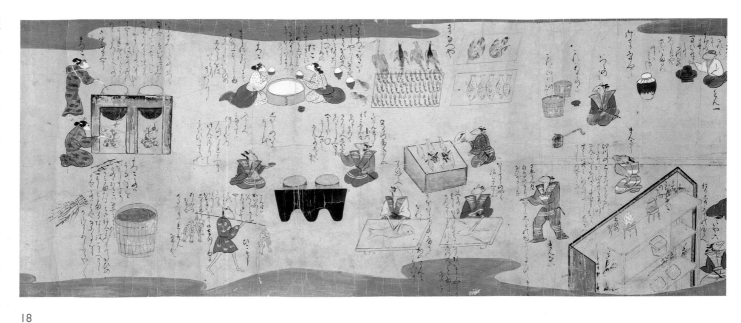

18

Anonymous, *Nezumi-Soshi emaki (Scroll of a Tale of Rats)*,
sixteenth century, comprising five scrolls ranging from
13 ¼ x 185 in. to 13 ¼ x 220 ½ in. (33.8 x 470 cm to 33.8 x 560 cm).
© Suntory Museum

The vice-governor of the mice has set off to ask the *kannon** of
Kiyomizu to find him a wife so that he can have human offspring. He meets a beautiful princess whom he marries. The
couple lives happily until the day the husband discovers his wife
is just another mouse. The unhappy mouse-girl cuts her hair as
a sign that she has renounced earthly life and goes off to pray on
Mount Koya, the site of a Buddhist temple complex belonging
to the Shingon-shu sect founded in 816 by Kukai. This sad love
story was to become extremely famous.

In this scene, the mice are busying themselves getting the
wedding banquet ready and discussing how to season the dishes.

19
Anonymous, *Kegon shû soshie den (Scroll of the Legend of the Sect of Kegon)*, National Treasure of the Kôzanji, thirteenth century, composed of seven scrolls. © Kôzanji

This *Scroll of the Legend of the Sect of Kegon* outlines how two Korean monks, Gishô and Gengyô, who had traveled to study in China, introduce the sect of Kegon-shu into Korea. Gengyô chooses to go back home, leaving Gishô to his own devices. During his journey, the latter meets a Chinese girl who falls in love with him. Gishô refuses to marry her, however, and prefers to return to Korea to teach Buddhism. In an attempt to protect her beloved beyond life and death, the besotted girl throws herself into the stormy sea as soon as Gishô embarks. She is promptly transformed into a powerful dragon that is reminiscent of both Edo period prints and today's manga, with green bristles and huge eyes ringed in red and blue. The animal, which fears the wrath of neither sky nor ocean, protects the ship and keeps the young man safe and sound until he regains his native land.

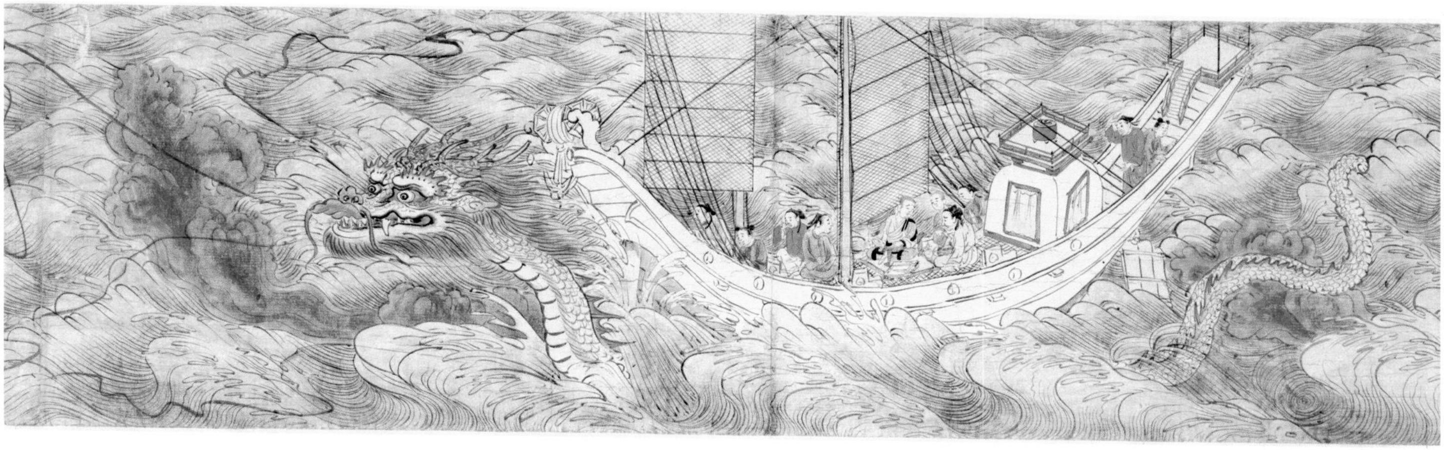

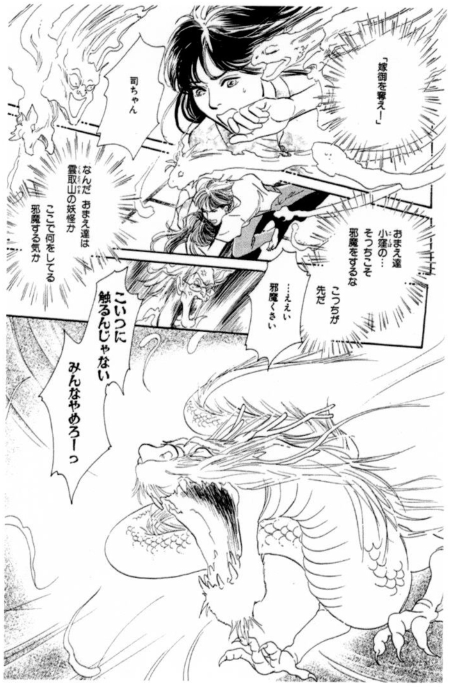
「嫁御を奪え!」
司ちゃん
おまえ達 小窪の… そっちこそ 邪魔をするな
こっちが 先だ
…ええい 邪魔くさい
なんだ おまえ達は 雲取山の妖怪か ここで何をしてる 邪魔する気か
こいつに 触るんじゃない
みんなやめろーっ

20
Ima Ichiko, Ashai Sonorama, *Hyakki yagyô emaki (Parade of a Hundred Demons)*, © Ima Ichiko, Ashai Sonorama, Tokyo, 2005

The title of this manga is taken directly from the past; the procession of one hundred demons *(hyakki yagyô*)* is a theme in hand scrolls.

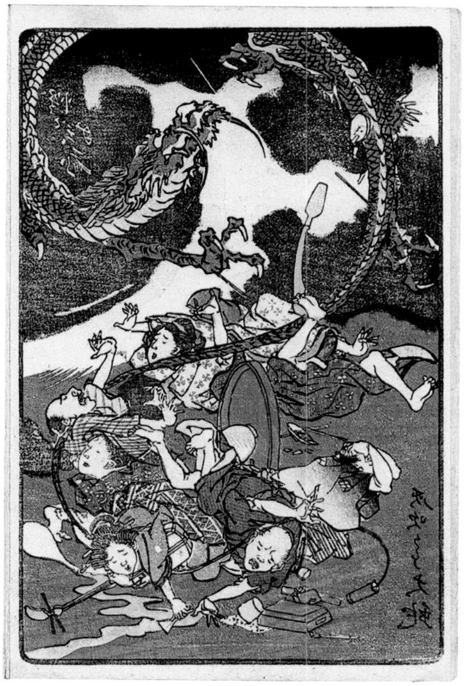

Detail of fig. 84, see page 57
Kawanabe Kyôsai, *Kyôsai Hyaku zu*, published between 1863 and 1866, © Kawanabe Kyôsai Memorial Museum

21–36

Momotarô, hand scroll on paper, Kô Sûkoku, end of the eighteenth century, 519 ¾ × 11 ½ in. (1,320 × 29 cm). © Kumon Institute of Education

Lacking text calligraphy, this scroll is entirely painted. The *emaki* illustrates one of the most popular tales in Japan: after many a long year, a couple, saddened by their lack of children, are amazed to see their dream realized. One day, when the old woman is going to the river to wash her linen, she finds a large peach on the path and brings it home. When she cuts it in two, she is astonished to see it contains a baby boy. Overcome with joy at this unexpected turn of events, the couple hastens to prepare the child for his first bath. They are then dumbfounded to see their offspring clamber to his feet and stand up.

Momotarô, whose extraordinary strength then surprises everyone, soon decides to sally forth from his home to vanquish various demons that have been terrorizing all and sundry. On his

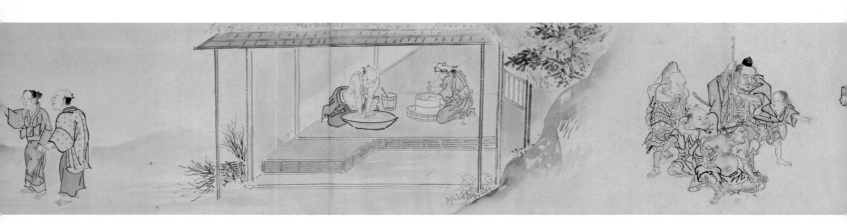

way, he comes across a monkey, a dog, and a pheasant; they together decide to assist him in his noble deeds. They all dress, take up their sabers, and head off in the direction of the island of demons. Hardly have they landed than battle is joined. They fight doughtily and manage to cut down all the demons, which are forced to abandon their treasure to them. Momotarô and his companions then regain the village, whose inhabitants can henceforth live in peace, while Momotarô gives all the booty to his parents.

The story of Momotarô (in Japanese, *momo* means "peach") appeared in the Edo era and proved such a success that it features in countless prints, and then in children's books and finally in manga. It remains the subject of a steady stream of publications even today.

READING FROM RIGHT TO LEFT ←

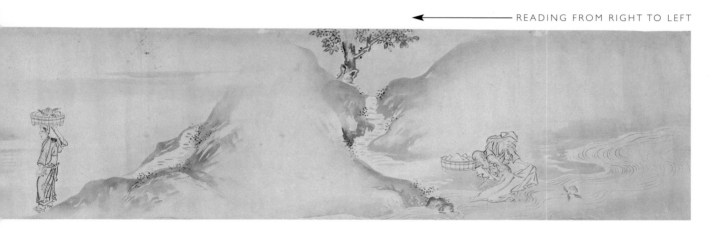

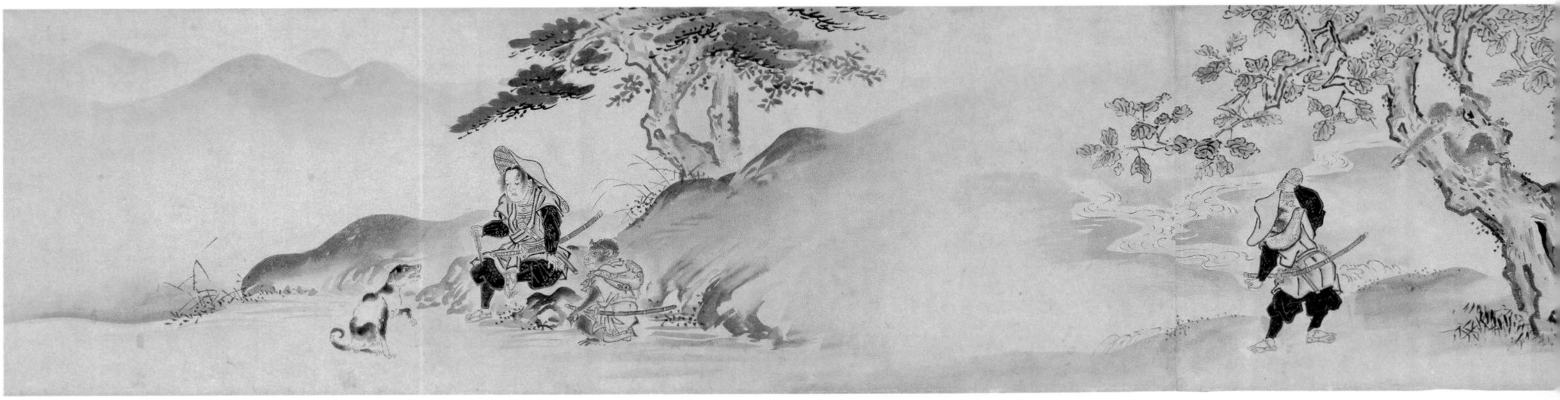

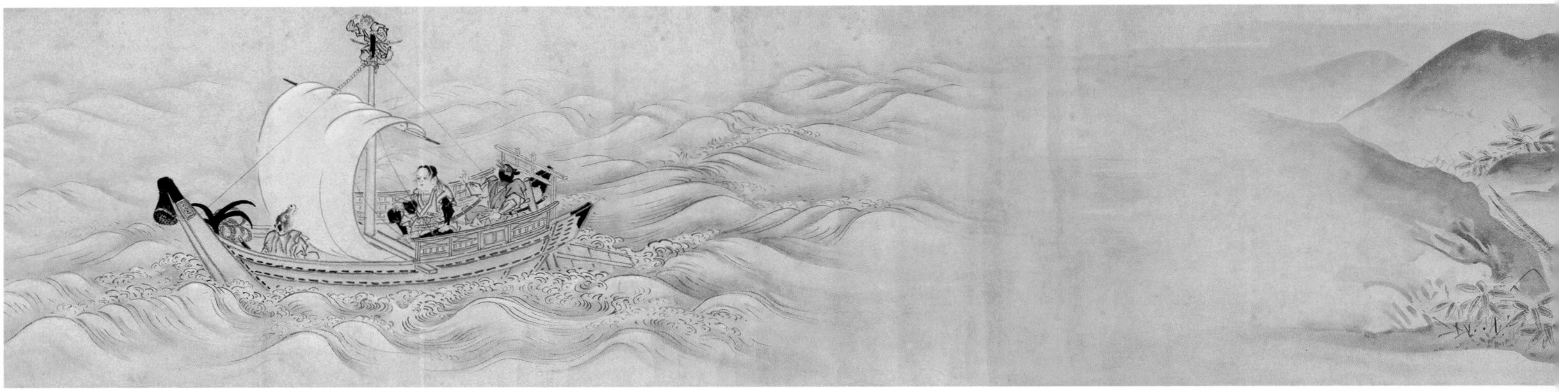

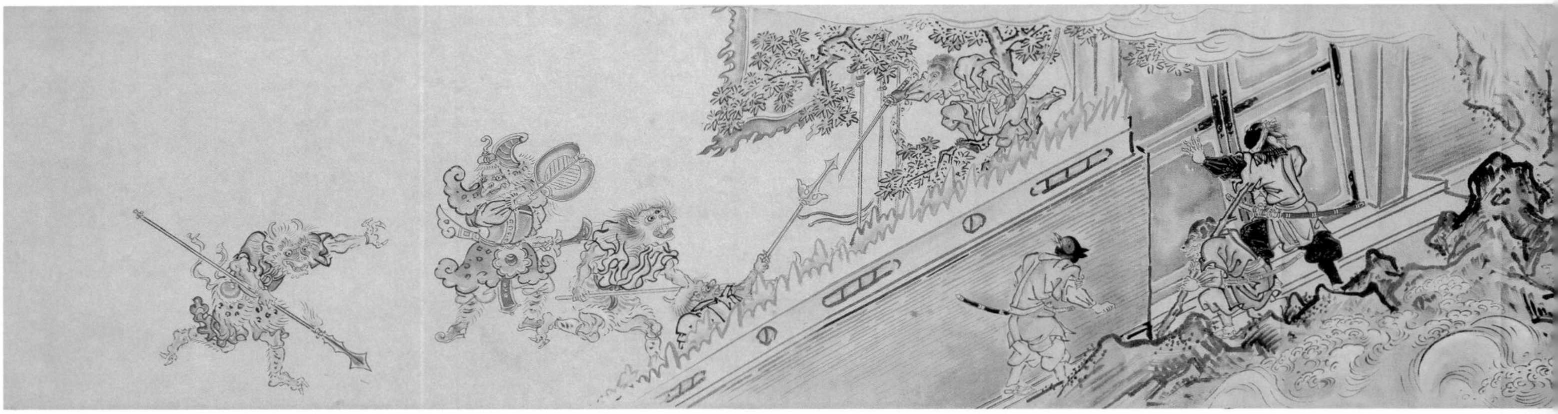

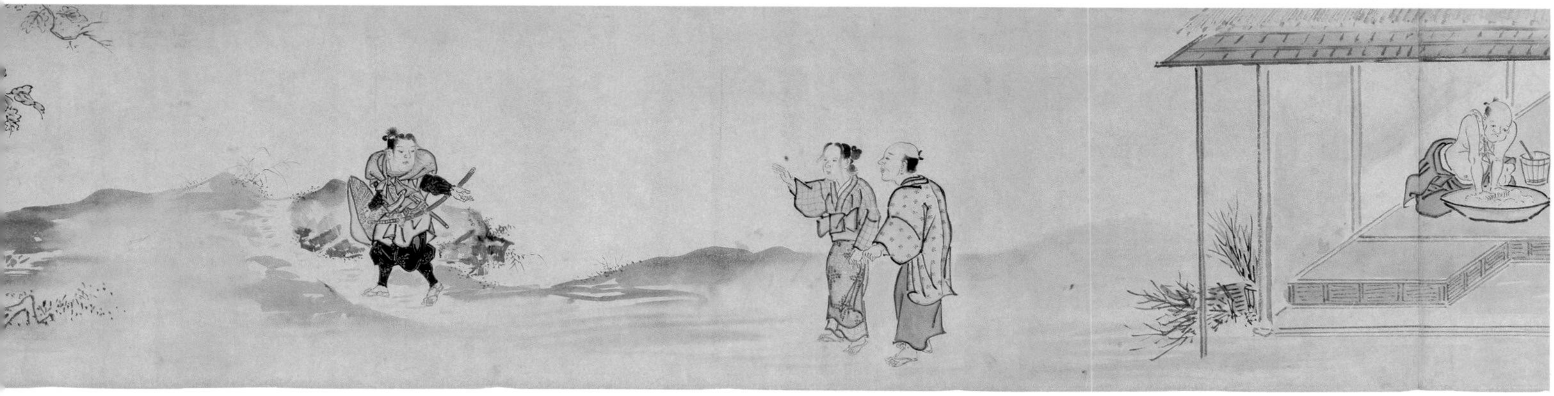

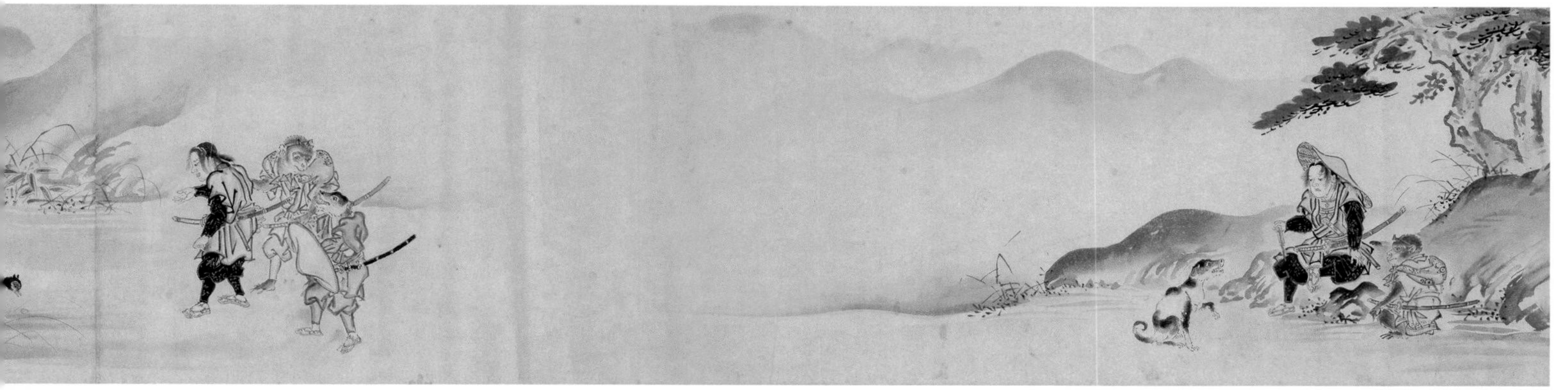

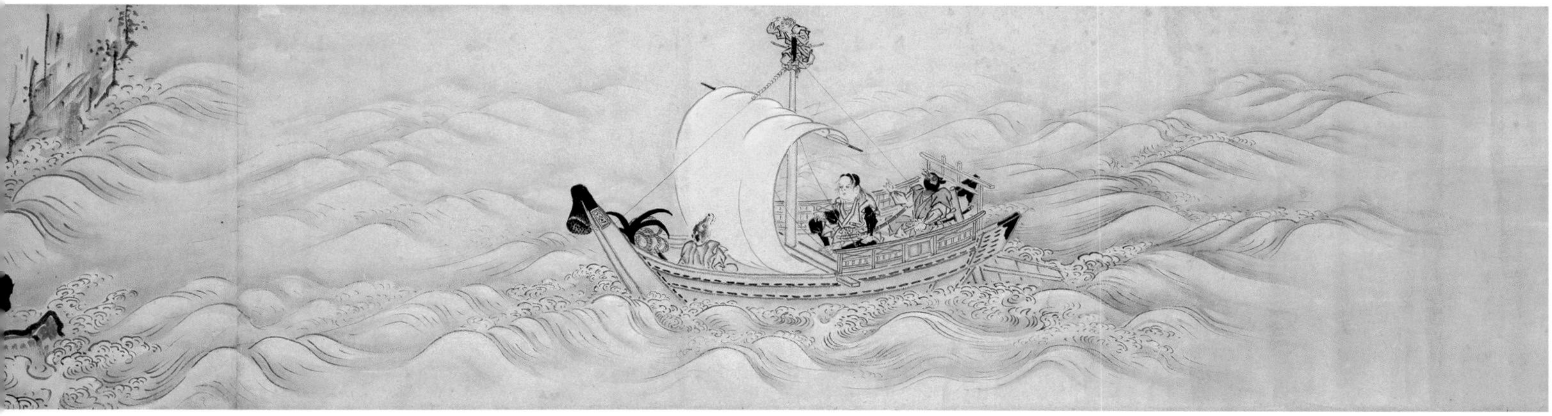

← READING FROM RIGHT TO LEFT

Fig. 37

Fig. 38

Fig. 39

Fig. 40

Fig. 41

Fig. 42

37–42
Sumiyoshi Jôkei, *Tamamushi monogatari (Tale of the Jewel-Beetles)*,
extract from a hand scroll, seventeenth century, 450 ¾ × 8 in. (1,145 × 20.4 cm).
© Kumon Institute of Education

This scroll, which once again turns to the world of animals to portray human life, tells the story of a beetle princess of unequaled beauty (jewel-beetles—*Buprestidae*—are iridescent winged insects that live in the trees in summer). All wish her every happiness—and a husband. Yet no love letter seems to satisfy her expectations. The prime minister then addresses an epistle to her in the language of the old tales, and the beauty, touched by the style, receives his demand in marriage favorably. During their engagement, the suitor offers a gift known as a *yuinô* to the fiancée's family: this may, depending on the period concerned, take the form of a keg of *sake*.

At the time of the wedding, the princess receives, not a dowry, but clothes and furniture, which she has transported to her husband's home with all due ceremony (fig. 37). The families, friends, and neighbors then come to offer their congratulations to the couple (fig. 38). In accordance with their rank, the princess and the ladies of her entourage are dressed in *jûni-hitoe**, consisting of several kimonos of different colors overlaid, beneath which they wear a *hakama**, a kind of long divided skirt with pleats. This luxurious garment in heavy silk was worn in the Heian and Kamakura epochs. At that time, women kept their long hair loose. The husband too sports a costume worthy of a man in an exalted position, while the servants keep to the simple kimono. The wedding is followed by a feast (fig. 39), prepared by a large staff; another jewel-beetle dances while the musicians play. Their happiness is unfortunately of short duration as the princess soon falls seriously ill. Her husband calls a *miko** to her bed-side. Wearing a white kimono, she prays to the *kami* gods to restore the princess to health (fig. 41). She is cured and soon gives birth to her first child (fig. 40). Then we are shown the first rite that follows every birth: the newborn (jewel-beetle) baby's *ubuyu** or bath. While the husband holds the infant proudly in his arms, his mother looks on tenderly (fig. 42).

READING FROM RIGHT TO LEFT

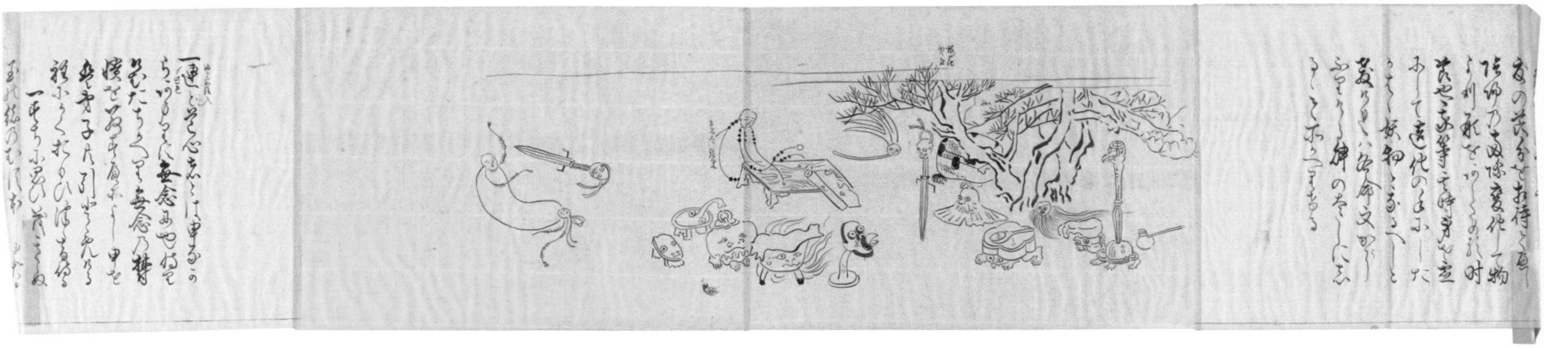

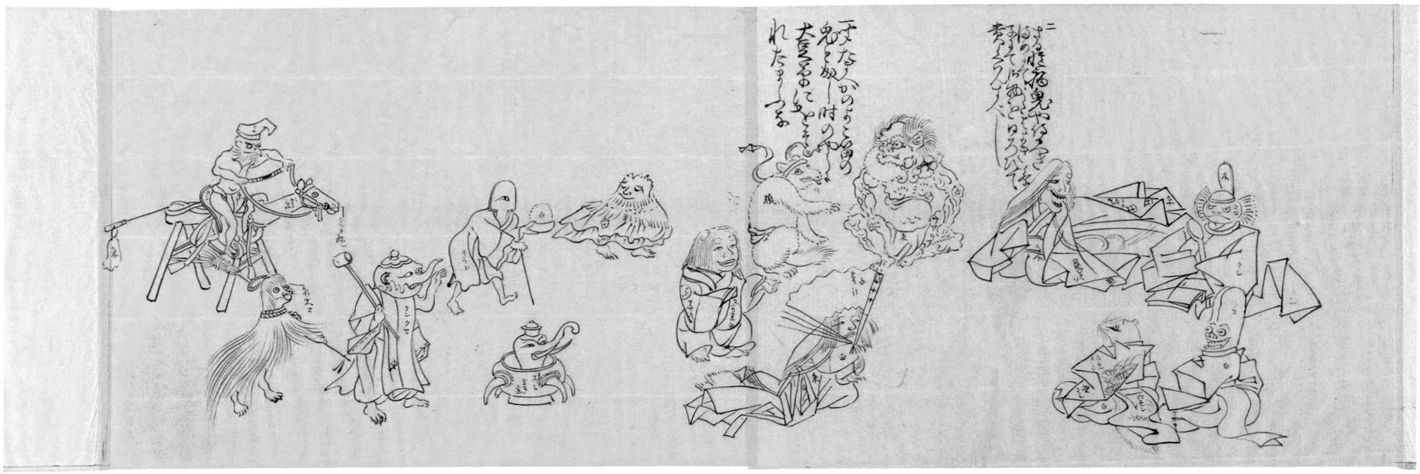

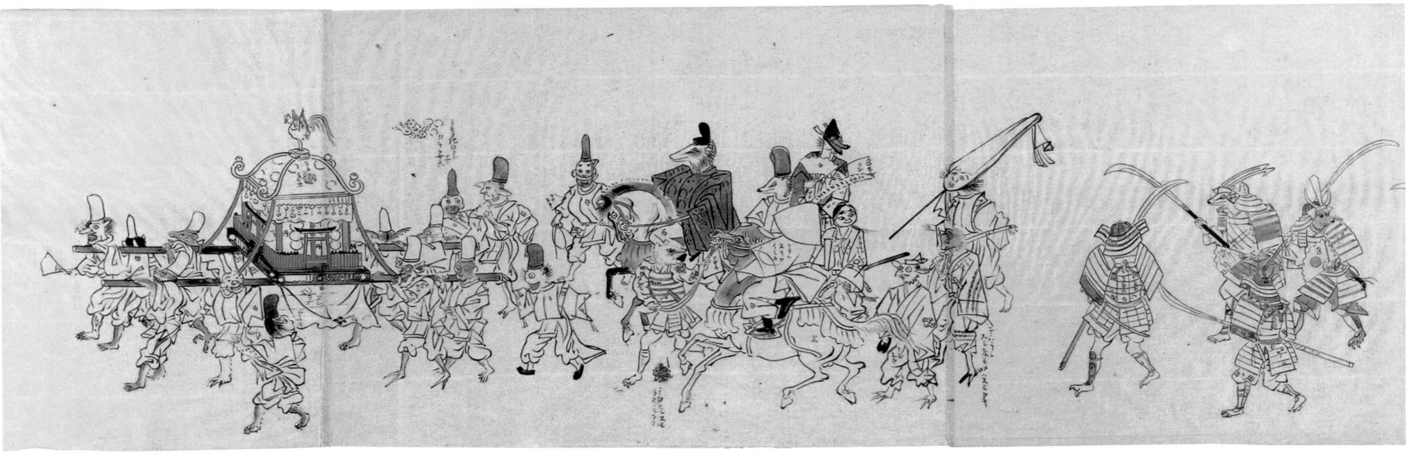

43–45

Anonymous, *Tsukumogami e kotoba (Illustrated Record of the Tsukumogami)*, painted scroll, no date. © Waseda University Library

Once night falls, the *tsukumogami**, the "spirits of old objects," come out to disport themselves in the company of other demons. Such spirits have undergone something of a revival in manga, with Mizuki Shigeru exploiting their wealth of imagery with singular success.

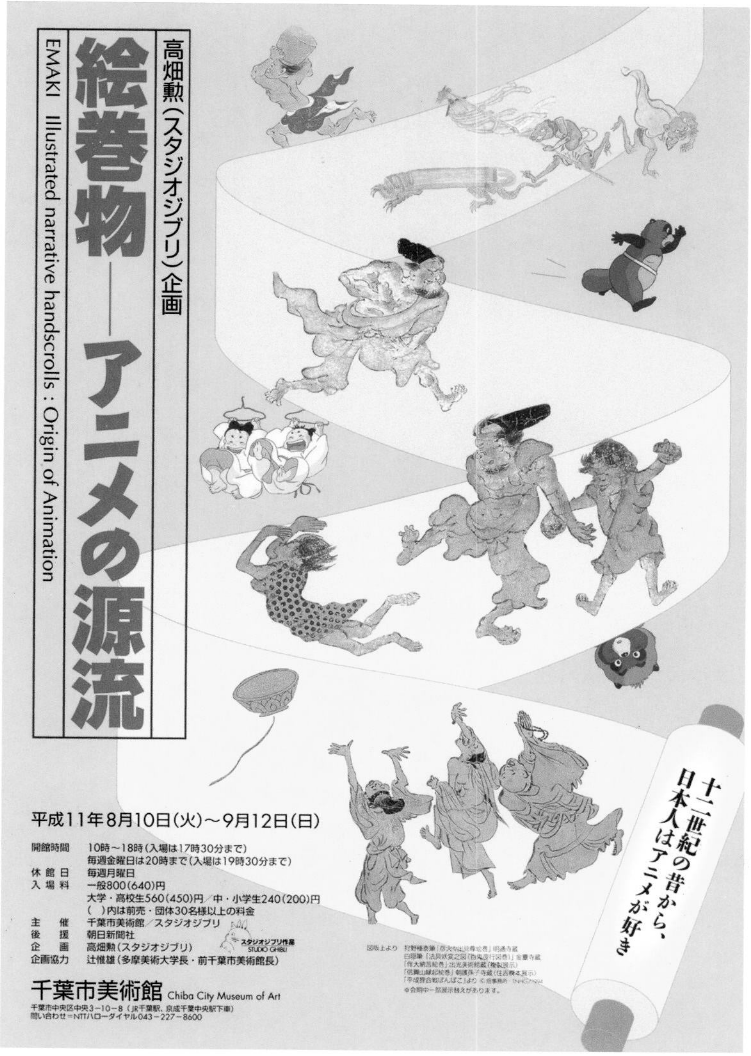
高畑勲（スタジオジブリ）企画
絵巻物——アニメの源流
EMAKI Illustrated narrative handscrolls : Origin of Animation
十二世紀の昔から、
日本人はアニメが好き
平成11年8月10日(火)～9月12日(日)
開館時間 10時～18時(入場は17時30分まで)
毎週金曜日は20時まで(入場は19時30分まで)
休館日 毎週月曜日
入場料 一般800(640)円
大学・高校生560(450)円／中・小学生240(200)円
( )内は前売・団体30名様以上の料金
主催 千葉市美術館／スタジオジブリ
後援 朝日新聞社
企画 高畑勲(スタジオジブリ)
スタジオジブリ作品
STUDIO GHIBLI
企画協力 辻惟雄(多摩美術大学長・前千葉市美術館長)
千葉市美術館 Chiba City Museum of Art
千葉市中央区中央3-10-8 (JR千葉駅、京成千葉中央駅下車)
問い合わせ＝NTTハローダイヤル043-227-8600

46

Poster for the exhibition "The Painted Scroll, *emakimono,* or the Origin of Cartoon Drawings" © Chiba City Museum of Art © Takahata Jimusho. TNHG/1994, Design Takahata Naho

This poster for the exhibition "The Painted Scroll, *emakimono*, or the Origin of Cartoon Drawings," organized in 1999 in the Chiba City Museum of Art, clearly testifies to the affinities between the figures to be found in these two pictorial genres. It features several figures from various famous *emaki*. At the top, what could be a figure from the scroll by Kanô Taneyasu Hiko, *Hohodemi no Mikoto emaki (Scroll of Hiko, Hohodemi no Mikoto*, Myôtsûji Temple, c. seventeenth century) and *yôkai* escapees from the scroll *Hyakki yagyô emaki (Parade of a Hundred Demons*, Kontaiji Temple). In the middle, one recognizes the quarrel scene from the *Ban Dainagon* scroll (Idemitsu Museum of Art) and men from the *Shigisan engi emaki (The Legends of Mount Shigi*, Temple of the Chôgosonshiji), running after the gold begging-bowl as it flies off. Among these all characters mingle *tanuki** (raccoon-dogs), heroes of the film *Heisei tanuki gassen Pompoko* (Battle of the Tanuki of the Heisei era, released as *The Raccoon War)* by Takahata Isao of Studio Ghibli.

47

Kawanabe Kyôsai, *Farting Contest*, 1867, illustrated paper hand scroll,
349 ¼ x 11 in. (887 x 28.2 cm). © Kawanabe Kyôsai Memorial Museum

In early 2007, the Mori Museum in Tokyo exhibited this *emaki*
with a screen above it showing a film of the entire scroll that had
been photographed beforehand. A great many visitors came to
admire a work presented in a way that emphasized its resemblance to an animated film.

← READING FROM RIGHT TO LEFT

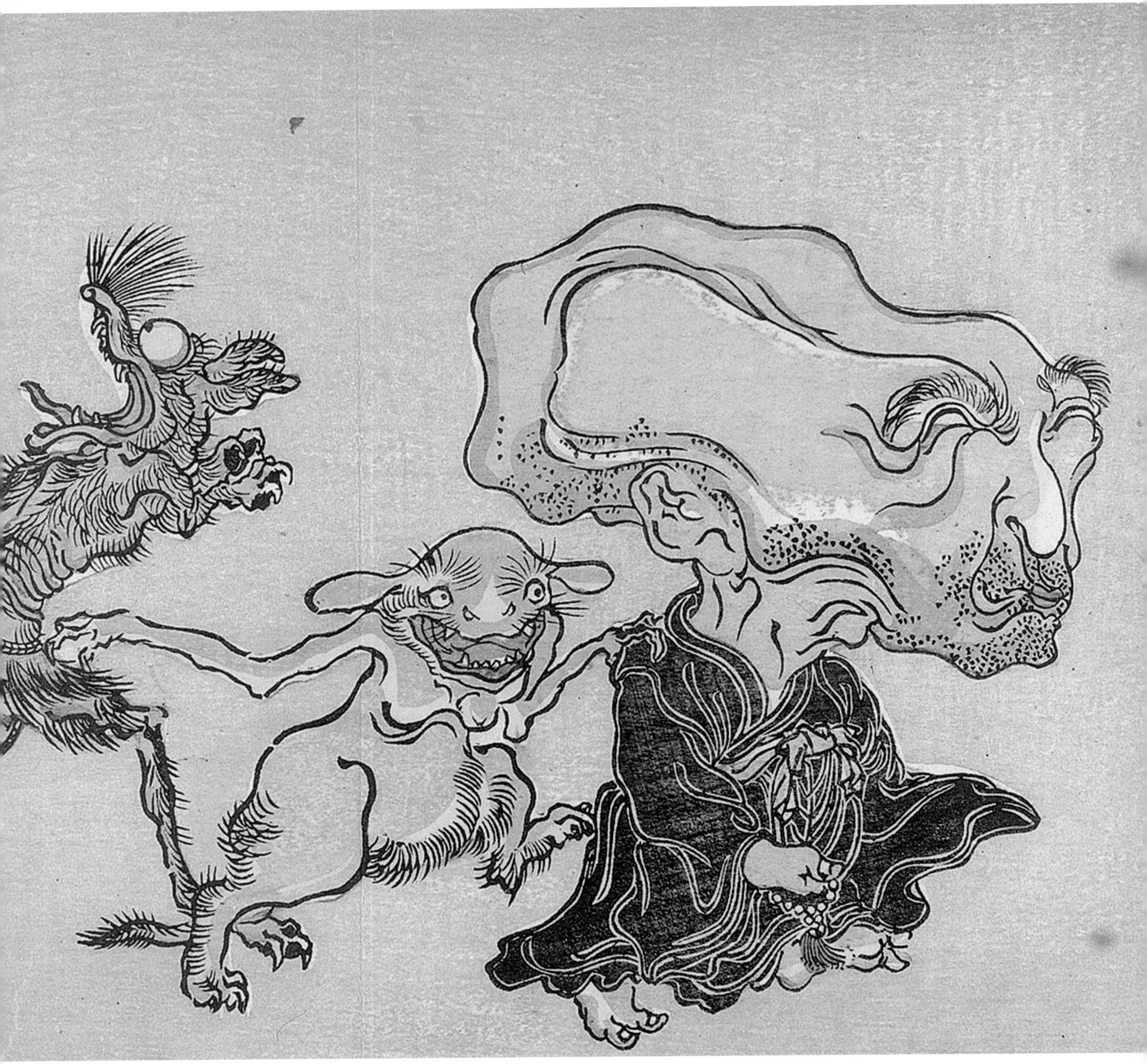

Fig. 67 (detail)

Edo: the meteoric rise of a new capital

When, in 1603, the emperor conferred the title of supreme chief, *sei-i-tai shôgun**, on Tokugawa Ieyasu (1542–1616), he chose to set up his government at Edo* (today, Tokyo). The city went on to grow rapidly, spiraling out from the stronghold at its center. It was not long before it was competing with Kyoto, which remained the imperial capital, and with Osaka, the major commercial hub, before surpassing them and becoming the largest conurbation in the whole archipelago. By the eighteenth century, Edo had swelled into an agglomeration of more than a million inhabitants.

The spectacular explosion of the new capital had its roots in the political system known as *sankin kôtai** imposed by Tokugawa's Shogun* regime. It was based on a form of alternating feudal service that obliged the headmen, or *daimyô**, to stay in Edo for long periods, together with their wives, children, and domestics. When they returned to their estates on which other members of their family lived, their household would remain behind in Edo as hostages. This peripatetic residence, whose itinerary was strictly regulated and which called for a considerable escort, proved a great burden on the budgets of *daimyô* from remoter areas.

Society had been divided into four classes, *shinôkôshô**, by the ruling powers: warriors, farmers, artisans, and merchants. Monks, physicians, and people of marginal status were not included. This hierarchy was, however, far from being a reflection of reality. Indeed, if power centered on the warriors, their incomes were in freefall, whereas merchants and craftsmen, who formed the *chônin**, or (middle-class) townsmen, grew ever richer as demands from the warrior class grew ever greater.

It was a period of peace, so the warriors could idle away their time and indulge in a life of luxury; the craftsmen therefore deployed all their expertise and dexterity in dressing them in sumptuous silks, or in designing objects in lacquer, ivory, ceramics, and bronze—all of remarkable beauty. As it was compulsory to carry two sabers, the warriors employed blacksmiths, who attained perfection in sword-making. Soon crippled by debt, the *daimyô* had recourse to merchants and in turn those too grew wealthy through moneylending.

Naturally, this merchant and artisan class wanted to enjoy the fruits of their labors too, and fostered a cultural flowering in which art, literature, and performance arts were created to satisfy their growing appetite. If the wealthiest among them, whose fortune sometimes exceeded that of the *daimyô*, could purchase folding-screens and scrolls or paintings by the masters of the Kanô* school, those less fortunate also wanted to decorate the *tokonoma** of their house or simply have access to books and pictures at reasonable prices.

It was in this context that the *ukiyo-e**, the Japanese print, was born; soon great advances were being made in the technique. The term "*ukiyo-e*" encompasses both paintings and prints. Created at the beginning of the 1650s, the term actually means "images of the Floating World," and denotes, according to Buddhism, an "earthly domain governed by changeability and fleeting pleasure."

Appearing first of all in the shape of *kakemono** (vertical scrolls), these works later took the form of prints on separate sheets. Monochrome and then retouched by hand, they attained their apogee in the middle of the eighteenth century, when the invention of the *kentô**—the notch preventing the sheet from slipping, which improves registration—made it possible to carry out multicolor woodblock prints of great beauty for a modest outlay (see the chapter Figs. 395–40 on the prints of Mizuki Shigeru, p. 212–225). Today, their splendor, scarcity, and sometimes exorbitant price mean that such prints are regarded as works of art. In the Edo period, however, they were considered merely as an amusing diversion that could be thrown away when they had served their purpose. Some of the finest have been preserved, though, and were collected by the middle classes and overlords alike.

Prints fulfilled many roles. Used as advertising, they allowed silk stores, beauty products, or restaurants to be publicized, or else they might praise the charms of a pleasure-house courtesan. Long before the Figs. 48–50 invention of photography, a print made it possible to possess a portrait of a fashionable *kabuki** actor or of the most beautiful courtesans, those who popularized the latest fashions in hairstyle, make-up, or kimono.

As a means of communication, prints could deliver the news or provide recipes to cure disease. For teaching, they were used to train children to write and read: a kind of color "encyclopedia," these

48–50

Utagawa Toyokuni, *Parody of Merchants of the Four Classes*,
triptych *nishiki-e* print, 1857. © Ota Memorial Museum of Art

The painter here turns his interest to some pretty women in a print-shop. In the middle, a girl seems delighted to have found a print of her favorite actor. On the right a little child on his mother's back grasps the picture she has just bought for him. In the Edo era, *nishiki-e* prints were treated in the same way as posters today. They were not framed, and if they sometimes decorated walls in houses, they were thrown out as soon as they yellowed. The "upright" prints, *hashira-e**("pillar print"), were often used to hide stains on pillars in Japanese dwellings.

Fig. 51
The young woman wanders about the sky
in search of her husband.

illustrations—accompanied with words transcribed in *kana* (syllabary) or *kanji* (ideogram)—inculcated the names of plants, animals, everyday items, etc. More playful incarnations provided considerable scope for amusement, including "spot the person" parodied in a caricature or rebus. There were also prints that children could cut out and make into toy models or dolls to dress up. Something like Edo period "postcards," they might depict landscapes or famous places in the capital or the provinces. Through its convenience and price, the print became a highly prized gift for tourists, who bought them in considerable quantities.

It was the Edo era that saw the development of publishing generally. Two types were then distinguished: *shomotsu**, considered as useful articles, including collections of erudition and religion; and *sôshi**, books for entertainment that also incorporated prints—these were sold out of specialist outlets called *ezôshiya**. The publisher could be a formidable businessman: depending on the subject, he would carefully choose the artist from whom he would order his prints. This aspect of publishing concentrated in this period on single-sheet prints.

Eager to sell them off rapidly to make a profit, a publisher was ever on the lookout for new material in keeping with the taste of the day, and would attract customers with colorful and prettily decorated shopfronts. The prints were hung in a line on a wire, their bright colors and varied themes covering the entire length of the store. The *surimono**, purely artistic prints which employed the most sophisticated techniques, were executed to special order and were aimed at a limited circle of privileged clients. Printed on paper of finest quality called *hôshôgami**, these were beautifully embossed and spangled with gold, silver, and bronze of astonishing delicacy.

The book in the Edo period

Art and literature are closely linked in Japan. From the very first scrolls, and then on folding-screens, prose and poetry in calligraphy often intermingled with painting. In the Edo era, illuminated books of great beauty aimed at a very wealthy class began to appear.

The book began to be democratized towards the end of the seventeenth century. In the Edo period, two movable-type printing

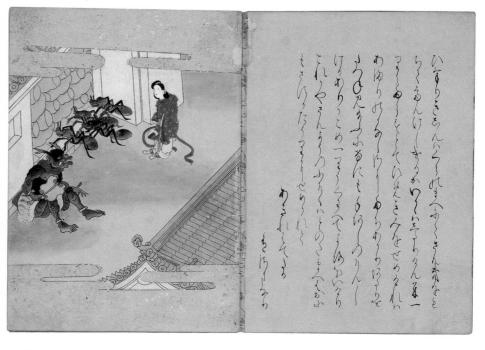

Fig. 52
She discovers that her father-in-law is a devil.

Fig. 53
He keeps her captive and orders her to carry more than a ton of rice without spilling a grain.

あーーーーっ
きゃあ……っ
やっ
あの
女の子の
ひめいが
まてーっ
えいっ!!

54
Tezuka Osamu, *Astro Boy*, 1964.
© Tezuka Osamu, Tezuka production

It is interesting to compare the imagery in Figures 51–53 with Tezuka Osamu's style, even though the latter, a keen insect lover, was influenced primarily by "B" science-fiction films with their "giant ant robots," etc.

51–53
Anonymous, *Nara ehon* (Illustrated Book of Nara: the Festival of Tanabata*)*,
Edo period, 9 x 6 ¾ in. (23.3 cm x 16.9 cm), three volumes.
© Kumon Institute of Education

Of great refinement, the illustrated books known as *nara* were created toward the beginning of the seventeenth century by Buddhist painter monks. Decorated with silver or gold powder, these precious works dealt with famous stories or novels, such as the *Tale of Genji*.

There survive many versions of this legend of Chinese origin that celebrates the annual meeting of the Weaver and the Herdsman on July 7. The author tells the story of three girls who were washing their linen when they were surprised to see a snake bearing a letter for them from his master. The serpent demanded that one of them follow him; though terrified, the youngest acquiesced and was ordered to cut off the reptile's head. A fine young man climbed out of the body of the animal and married her. A few days later, however, her beloved vanished. The father-in-law of the young woman ordered her to search for him in the sky, but, revealing himself to be a demon, he subjected her to many ordeals. The two were finally transformed into stars, condemned to meeting but once a year in the Milky Way.

This kind of luxury work already shows characteristics of the graphics of today's *mangaka**. The representation of the figures, both human and demonic, and the insects chosen are very close to some manga.

processes were introduced into Japan. The first arrived in 1590 through the intermediary of the Jesuits, who imported the Gutenberg technique (invented about 1445), and published Japanese texts in Latin transcription, followed by Chinese and Japanese movable characters. Its spread was halted by the prohibition of Christianity.

The second procedure was brought back after military expeditions to Korea in 1592–93. But printing in movable characters was not suited to all processes of impression. Moreover, typography meant that the composition had to be reset when the characters were reused, while engraved boards allowed prints to be pulled numerous times, keeping the costs of reissuing classic books down. In the seventeenth century, the Japanese technique of xylography (woodblock), which had originated in China and had been employed for a long time, supplanted these two processes, and the Western technique of movable type did not return to favor until the Meiji Restoration.

The Shogunate* of Tokugawa, which lasted from 1603 to 1868, developed an education policy that favored publishing. Up to that time, books on Buddhism, medical science, and philosophy were published with only intellectuals in mind. From this period, however, booksellers began to accelerate production and increase the number of pullings, employing more master engravers and printers to turn out popular illustrated works.

*Jihon donya**, or non-specialized publishers, brought out *kusa-zôshi**, written in a colloquial style and with large-size illustrations. Various types of *kusa-zôshi* can be recognized by the color of their covers: the "red books," *aka-hon**, containing tales and legends, published from 1673 on, were especially aimed at children; "black books," *kuro-hon**, appeared between 1744 and 1751; "green books," *ao-hon**, from 1745 on, retold dramas from kabuki theater; while the "yellow books," *kibyôshi**, appearing around 1775, remained very popular until 1818 and offered cards, tales, etc. Intended for the people, these inexpensive works covered ten pages and had simple texts crammed with illustrations. The stories were sometimes presented in the form of a serial.

There were also the *sharebon**, "books for men about town," *kokkeibon**, whose material was comic, and *ninjôbon**, which contained romantic stories and moral tales. A successful *kibyôshi* could run to anything between one and two thousand copies, a figure sustained through many borrowing outlets (*kashihonya*).

Though censorship was strict, the print-masters took delight in circumventing it. Books, which had once been limited to the upper echelons, to monks, and then to the warrior class, could now reach the entire population. Often illustrated by great painters such as Katsushika Hokusai and Kitagawa Utamaro, they were issued complete with woodblock prints (see p. 79).

An art of entertainment

Numerous prints reflect the way of life in Edo, whose inhabitants never seemed to pass up an opportunity for amusement. The precariousness and harshness of everyday existence, the frequent fires and countless earth tremors encouraged a free-and-easy lifestyle that reveled in the present moment. In conveying this atmosphere, the masters of the print deployed considerable ingenuity and humor.

"Assembled" faces

Figs. 55–57 Like many of the more playful *ukiyo-e*, the strange faces that Utagawa Kuniyoshi's brush (1797–1861) was one of the first to produce were painted simply to divert. Artists vied in imagination to execute ever more original prints. Although there is to date no proof of this, the resemblance is sometimes so striking that it seems that some of them might have been inspired by the paintings of

Figs. 58–59 Giuseppe Arcimboldo, whose compositions are very similar. Kuniyoshi, for one, might well have come across reproductions of the Italian artist's works.

Prophylactics against natural disasters

Residing in one of the most seismically active regions in the world, the Japanese have always lived in fear of earthquakes. Long ago, they tried to forestall them by invoking a protecting deity or purchasing a print depicting it. According to one legend, tremors were caused by an enormous catfish trapped under a large stone by a divinity near the Shinto sanctuary of Kashima. Full of humor and imagina-

Figs. 60–61 tion, such prints were much vaunted.

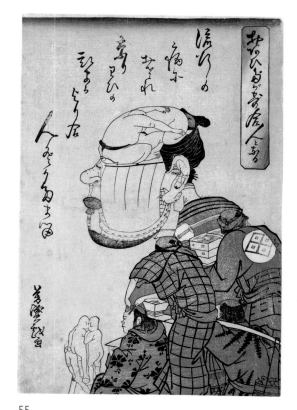

55
Utagawa Yoshimori, *They are Blue But, Recombined, They Form a Man*, no date.
© Edo-Tokyo Museum

This strange personage is composed of a group of unemployed merchants together with a customer-less courtesan to form the neck: a personification of a period of crisis following a serious epidemic. At that time, it was thought that, in the event of infectious diseases breaking out, certain fruits or vegetables (the figure's mouth is a watermelon), and certain fish (the base of the face in the shape of a boat refers to fishing) could be harmful. Pallid, unoccupied—and blue: everyone is waiting for work to resume. Firmly convinced that disease was propagated by Yakubyogami, believers tried to placate the god by hanging a print showing him, together with the illness they hoped to be spared, at the entrance to their houses. Sold at low prices, these prints dispensed medical advice and explained how to avoid contracting various maladies, or how to treat them.

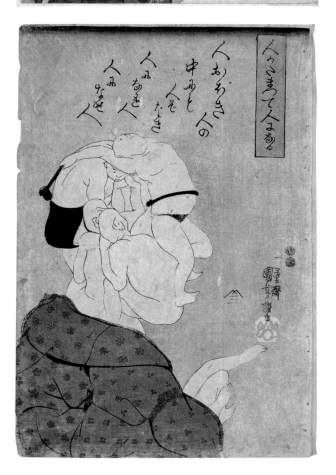

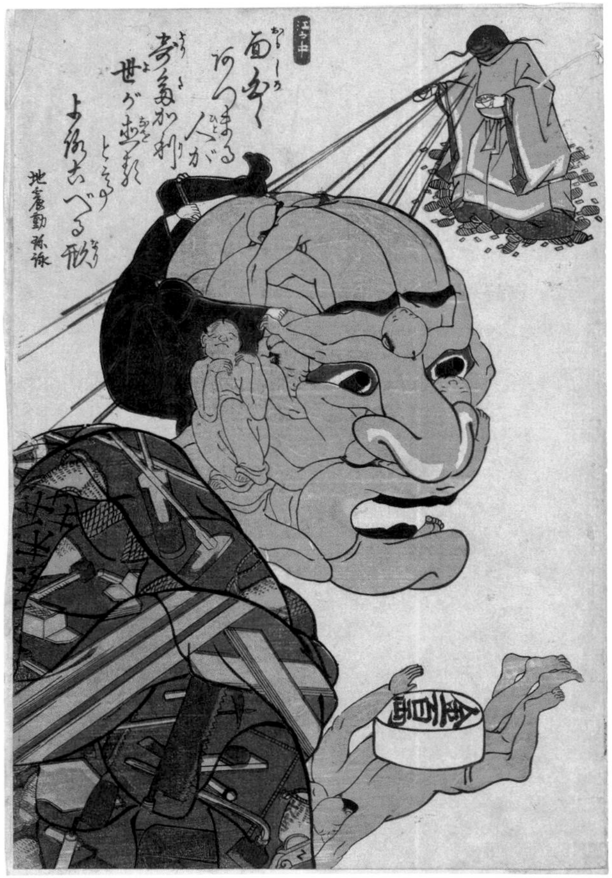

56

Anonymous, *People Assembled in an Original Manner*, *namazu-e* catfish print, probably by Utagawa Kuniyoshi, who signed an identical print without the catfish (prints showing catfish are never signed), after 1855. © Edo-Tokyo Museum

The fearsome catfish dressed in a kimono top right seems to foretell of some catastrophe. The figure in the foreground, however, holds in his hand a large gold coin. His kimono features the carpenter's tools that will be needed to rebuild the city. It's an ill wind…. One game consists in counting how many figures appear in the print—don't forget the hand!

57

Utagawa Kuniyoshi, *Men Assembled into the Shape of Another Figure*, *nishiki-e* prints, no date. © Waseda University Library

In the same style, Kuniyoshi once again deploys a wealth of talent. He was often imitated, but no other painter managed to compose faces with as many figures and with such humor and exactitude in the details.

A taste for anthropomorphism

Figs. 5–8 *Frolicking Animals and People* testifies to the adroitness of Japanese artists when it came to representing animals in human form. This conceit was exploited wholesale by the masters of *ukiyo-e*, who composed—often in three parts but just as well on broadsheets—drawings of animals that look so alive they might step off the paper. One of

Figs. 62–66 most gifted in this area was incontestably Kawanabe Kyôsai (1831–89). Born in a period of transition, he witnessed the enforced Westernization of his country, and his output of drawings and prints was huge. A master of traditional Kanô* painting, he never forgot that in his youth he had been a disciple of the *ukiyo-e* painter Utagawa Kuniyoshi, whose humor and imagination he had inherited.

Monsters of all stripes

More present than ever in the folklore and imagination of the Japanese in the Edo period, monsters invaded art and literature. *The*

Figs. 67–84 *Parade of a Hundred Demons*, so richly painted in illustrated scrolls, enjoyed still greater success in the print form. Kawanabe Kyôsai used this theme as a basis for many drawings

Scenes from everyday life: school and its depiction

The Edo epoch saw the setting up of a traditional education system that remained in force until the modernizing measures taken by the government of Meiji during the 1870s. In the seventeenth century, learning (until then the preserve of the aristocracy and the warrior class) percolated down to the people, thanks to the creation of *terakoya** (from *tera**, "Buddhist temple")—schools placed within the grounds of a temple.

At the outset teaching provision, which was not obligatory, was ensured by monks and literati, with female assistants making an appearance later. The new need for knowing how to read, write, and count was part and parcel of economic growth. Children—primarily boys at first, but increasingly girls too—entered the *terakoya* at around six and stayed there until they were about ten or twelve. All pupils studied in a relaxed atmosphere in the same room, squatting

Fig. 83 on their heels and writing on a low table.

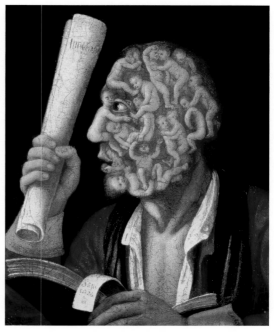

58–59
Giuseppe Arcimboldo, *Portraits of Adam and Eve*, 1578, oil on canvas, private collection, Switzerland.
© Private Collection, Switzerland/The Bridgeman Art Library

60
The Manga of Kyôsai: a Catfish Flying above Mount Fuji, extract from
an illustrated book signed by Kawanabe Tôiku, 1881.
© Kawanabe Kyôsai Memorial Museum

The catfish flying above Mount Fuji here represents the members of the government, and the cat playing the *shamisen** refers
to the geishas who control them. They sit higher than their
clients; indeed, they can even soar above Mount Fuji!

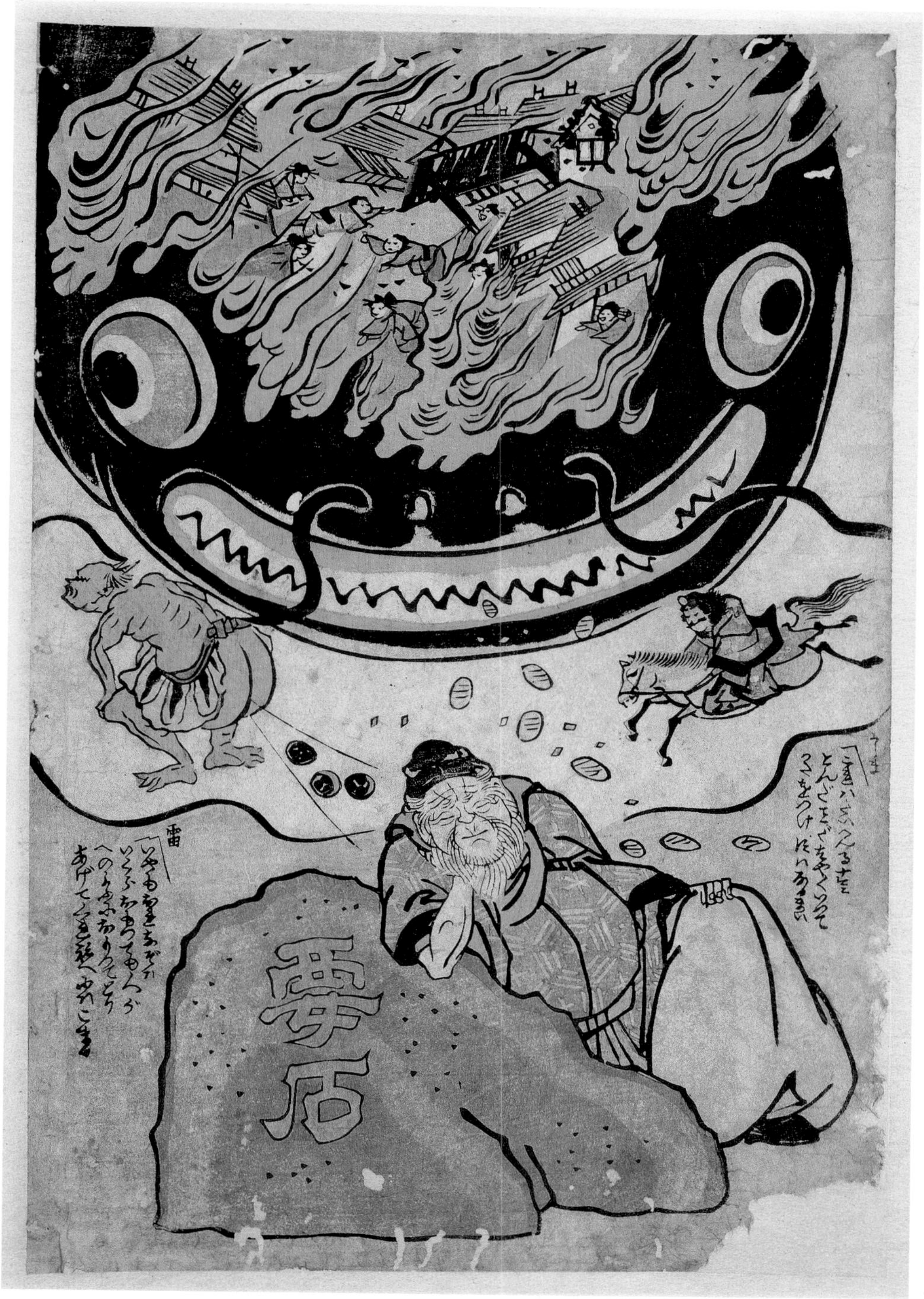
雷
要石

61
Anonymous, *Nishiki-e* print of the *namazu-e* category (print representing a catfish), no date. © Edo-Tokyo Museum

In 1855, a terrible earthquake devastated the city of Edo, killing thousands. Following this tragic event, many unsigned prints bearing catfish appeared; these were supposed to offer protection from earth tremors. The divinity lounging on the rock fondly imagines the consequences of the catastrophe. In the bubble containing his thoughts, the enormous catfish seems to be smiling at the prospect of the horrors he is about to cause, especially the violent fires. However, *koban** (a currency of the time) are pouring out of his maw—the sign of the riches that some will gain from events, carpenters in particular.

62
Kawanabe Kyôsai, *Picture of a Great Frog Battle*, triptych *nishiki-e*
print in *ôban* format, signed Ôju Kyôja, 1864.
© Kawanabe Kyôsai Memorial Museum

In this work, Kawanabe Kyôsai depicts the activities of his
favorite animal, the frog. These charming amphibians were not
painted solely to amuse, however, and they are not illustrations
to a tale or fable either. The piece is in fact a satirical triptych
dealing with the government, describing the violent confronta-
tions that preceded the restoration of the Meiji emperor in 1868.
This coded image was readily comprehensible for contemporary
Japanese people. In the foreground on the right, the broad leaf
seemingly stuck over the cannon wheel is an emblem of the
Shogun family of Tokugawa. On the left on the green hanging,
where the shell has just fallen, appears the insignia of the Môri
family. This scene thus symbolizes the battle between the clan of
the Tokugawas and Môri Takachika (1819–1871), head of the
Chôshû clan. Readers loved this kind of drawing and had fun
guessing the names of the politicians concealed behind the faces
of the frogs.

63
Kawanabe Kyôsai, *The Capture of a Snake by Frogs*, *nishiki-e* print,
signed Seisei Kyôsai, after 1871.
© Kawanabe Kyôsai Memorial Museum

Kawanabe Kyôsai's frogs have no fear! They easily get the
better of this giant serpent that seems distraught at being
immobilized. With one foot on the reptile's head, one of the
frogs struts his stuff, a gingko leaf in his paw.

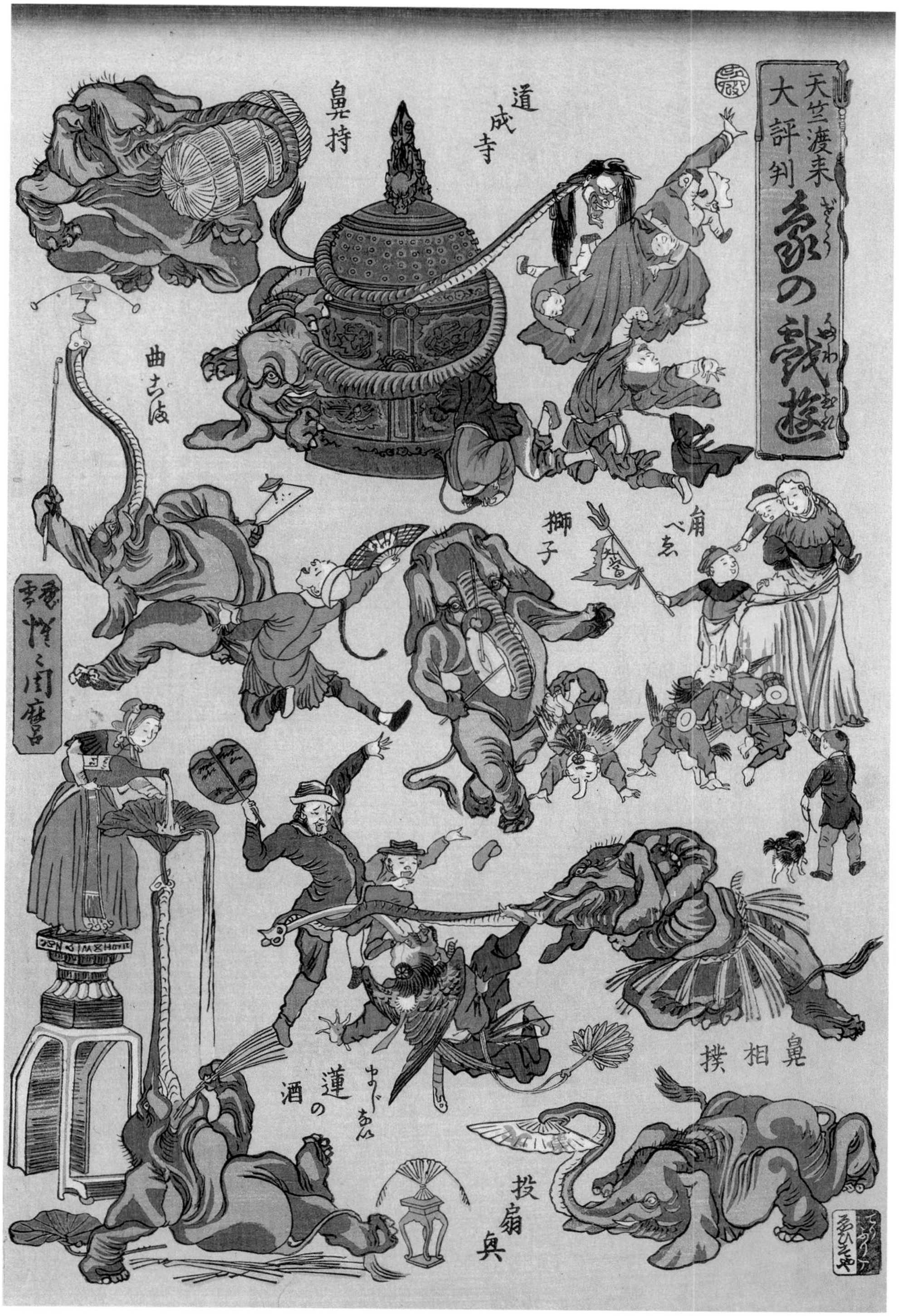
天竺渡来
大評判
象の戯遊
道成寺
獅子
鼻相撲
蓮の酒
投扇興

64
Kawanabe Kyôsai, *Games of the Celebrated Elephant from Abroad, nishiki-e* print in *ôban* format, signed by Ôjû Seisei Shûmaro, 1863. © Kawanabe Kyôsai Memorial Museum

The arrival of an elephant in Japan in 1863 proved a welcome attraction. Fascinated by the animal, Kawanabe Kyôsai, together with his publisher, studied it closely, precisely noting the animal's attitudes. He carried out a series of compositions based on it which proved a hit with children. It showed the great beast in all kinds of poses, transforming it into a diverting and extremely sympathetic caricature. The graphic style is such that one would only have to cut out the various elephantine adventures and arrange them one beside the other to make a comic strip.

65

Kawanabe Kyôsai, *A Cat Exterminated by Mice*, prints signed Seisei Kyôsai, book illustration, from 1871. © Kawanabe Kyôsai Memorial Museum

The mouse, one of the twelve signs of the Chinese zodiac, was often portrayed in Japan. As an anthropomorphic subject, he is one of the favorite animals among painters, who show him as a sly-boots who always gets the better of the cat—indeed of any animal. There can then be no hope of escape for this poor feline....

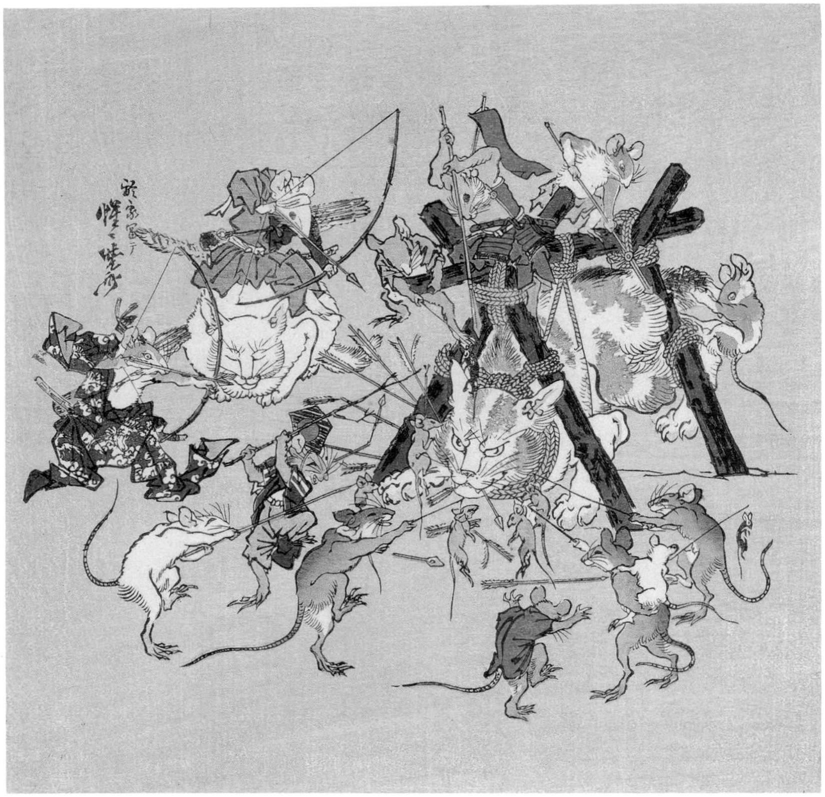

66

Utagawa Kuniteru, *The Mice of the Hidden Village*, *nishiki-e* print, 1866. © Kumon Institute of Education

This shows a parody of a famous folktale, *The Hidden Village*, which exists in many versions. Here, the mice, which act just like human beings, live in a village hidden from the eyes of men. By chance, every so often, a human stumbles across this fairytale world concealed in the heart of the mountain and discovers with amazement fields of vegetables and fruit that extend as far as the eye can see. In certain versions, a divinity intervenes, making the person who has discovered the hideaway lose their sense of time; he is offered a blissful life, though he will finally reject this, so as to return to his own kind.

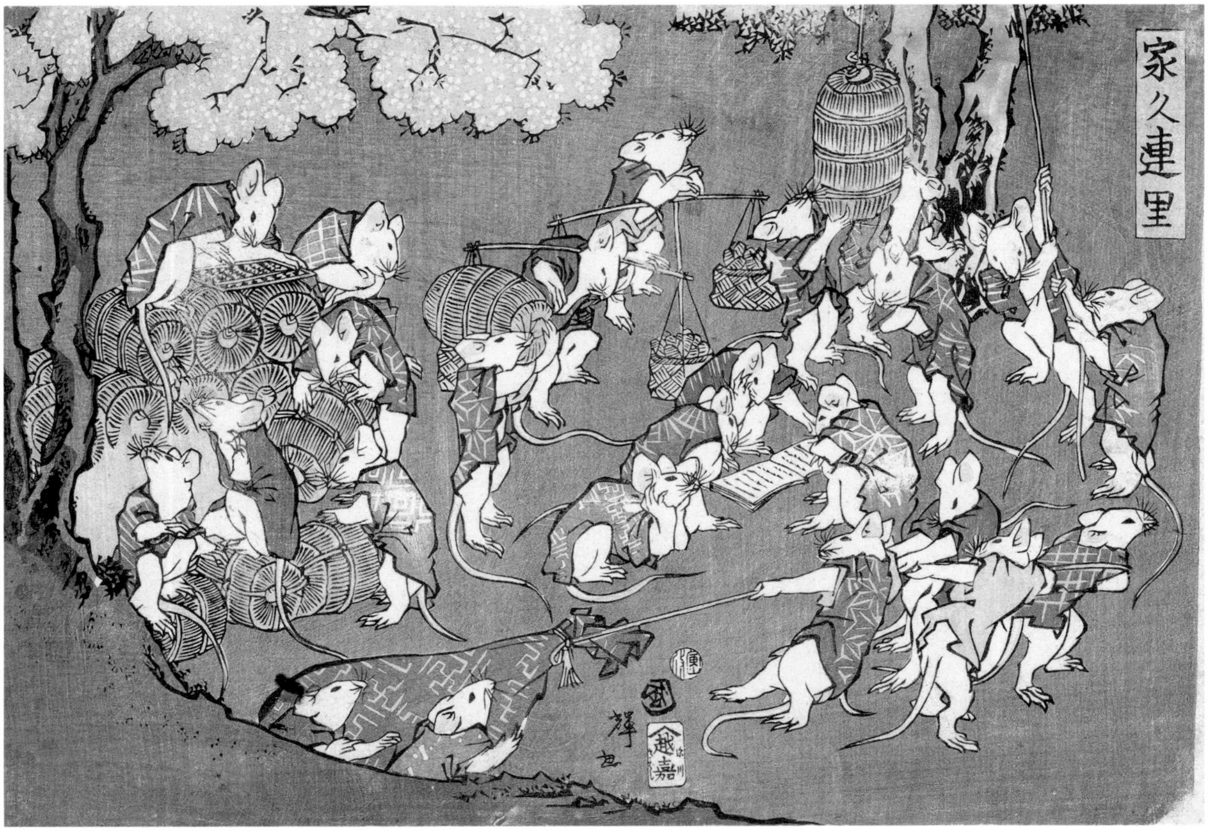
家久連里

67
Kawanabe Kyôsai, *The Night Parade of a Hundred Demons*, extract
from *Pandemonium Kyôsai Hyakki gadan*, illustrated book signed Kawanabe Tôiku, 1889.
© Kawanabe Kyôsai Memorial Museum

68
Mizuki Shigeru, *Yokai Nurarikyon of the Night Procession of the Hundred Demons*,
© Mizuki Shigeru Production

Fig. 69

Fig. 72

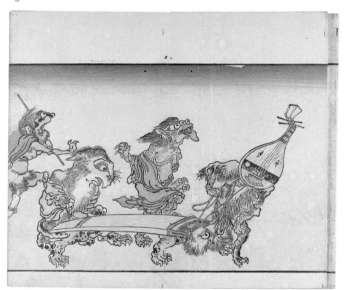

Fig. 70

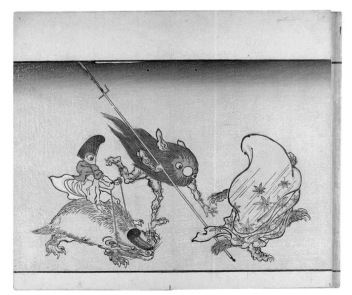

Fig. 71

67 and 69–72

**Kawanabe Kyôsai, *The Night Parade of One Hundred Demons*
from *Pandemonium Kyôsai Hyakki gadan* (illustrated book, 1889,
signed by Kawanabe Tôiku). © Kawanabe Kyôsai Memorial Museum**

In company of all species of *yôkai**, various monsters and dis-
carded objects form a merry procession. Since time immemorial
in Japan there has always been a great diversity of supernatural
creatures, and today they are experiencing a renewal of interest
through manga. In the chapter on Mizuki Shigeru, we will see
how that artist helped publicize and give fresh impetus to the
study of *yôkai* (see p. 212–215).

Any human encountering this nightly procession was sure to die
in short order unless he or she was protected by certain *sutra kyô**.
It was then best to avoid going abroad at night on certain days of
the month. Here, a female demon, still running, tries to apply her
make-up using the head of another *yôkai* as a looking-glass.

People would gather at night—under dim light and their
heads covered with sheets—to tell these hundred *yôkai* tales. At
the end of the one hundredth tale, the monsters are actually
meant to appear. Very popular in the Edo period, countless versions of these tales were published at that time.

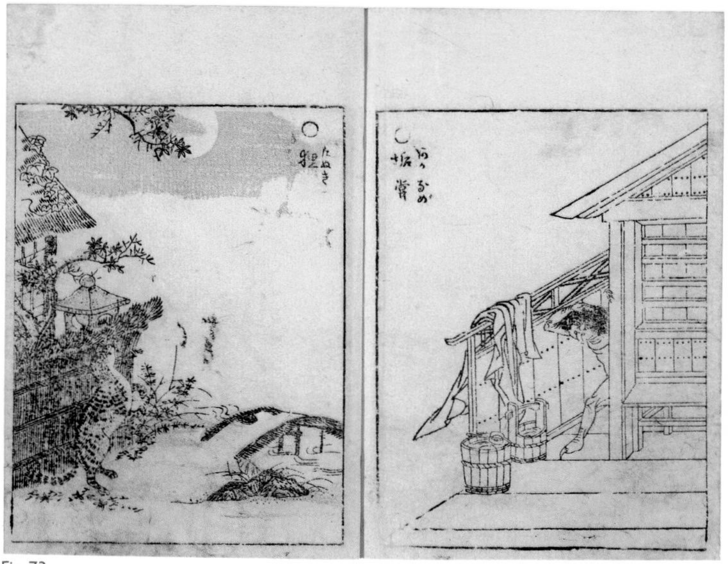

Fig. 73

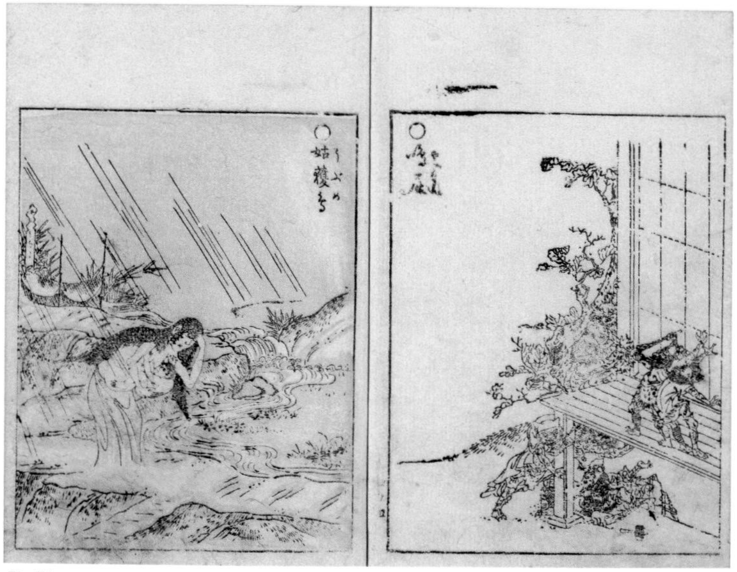

Fig. 74

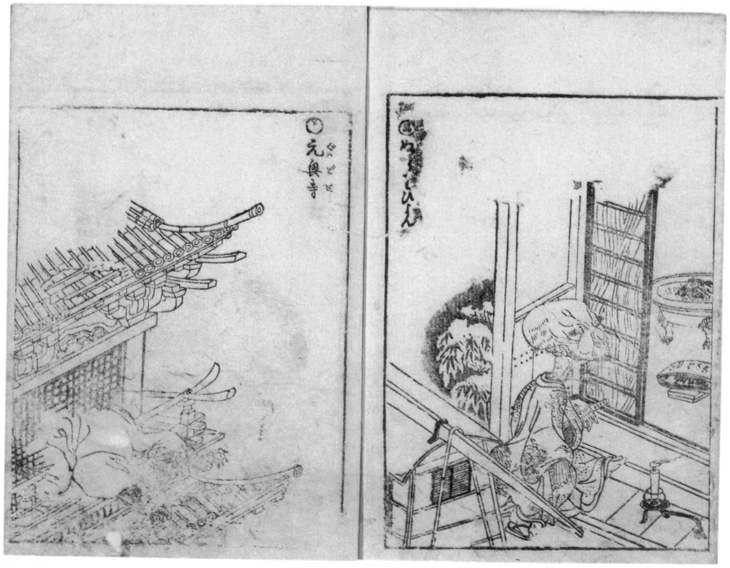

Fig. 75

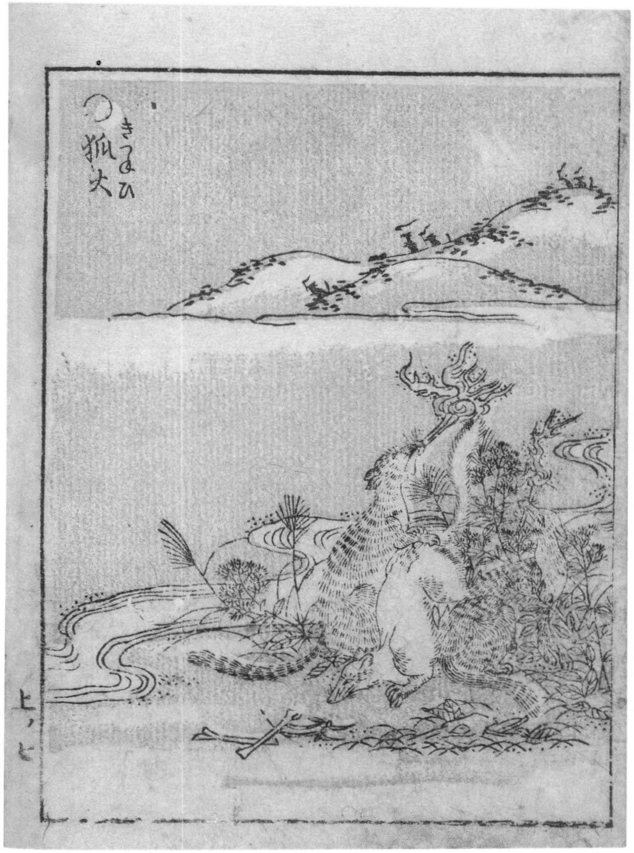

Fig. 76

73–76

Toriyama Sekien, *Hyakki Yagyô*, book in three volumes, 1805.

In this other version of *The Night Parade of a Hundred Demons*, one finds the *yôkai* Nurarihyon (fig. 75), who was also drawn by Kawanabe Kyôsai and Mizuki Shigeru. The character is immediately identifiable, even if each artist, employing different techniques, provides his own personal twist. Unlike the masters of the Edo era, Mizuki Shigeru would draw in ink-pen before painting the figures with seven natural pigments that he mixed to obtain the desired hue; he then handed the finished drawing over to his publisher (fig. 68).

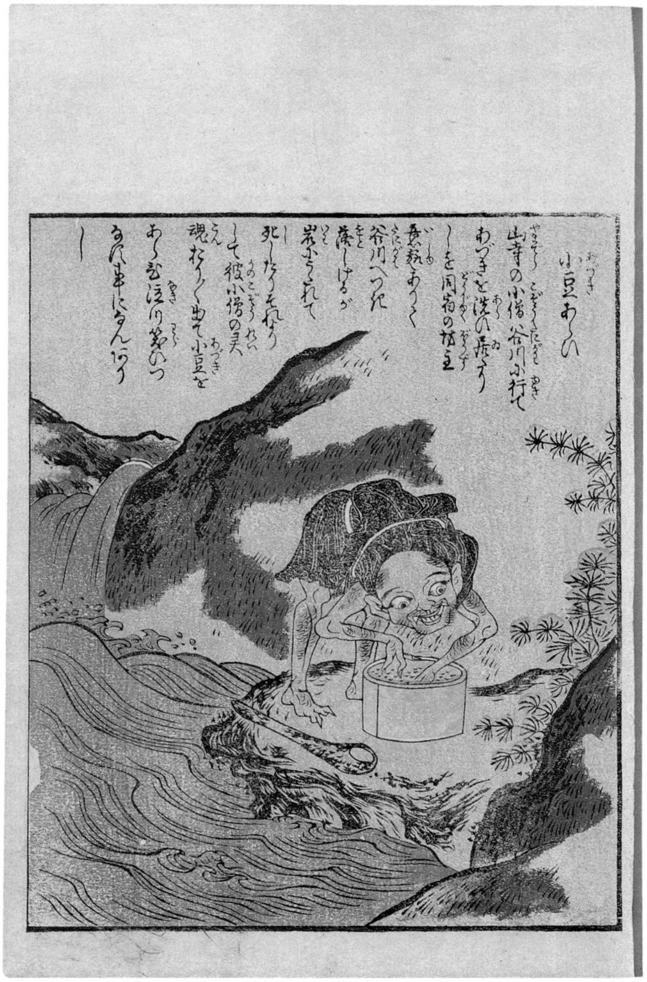
小豆あらひ

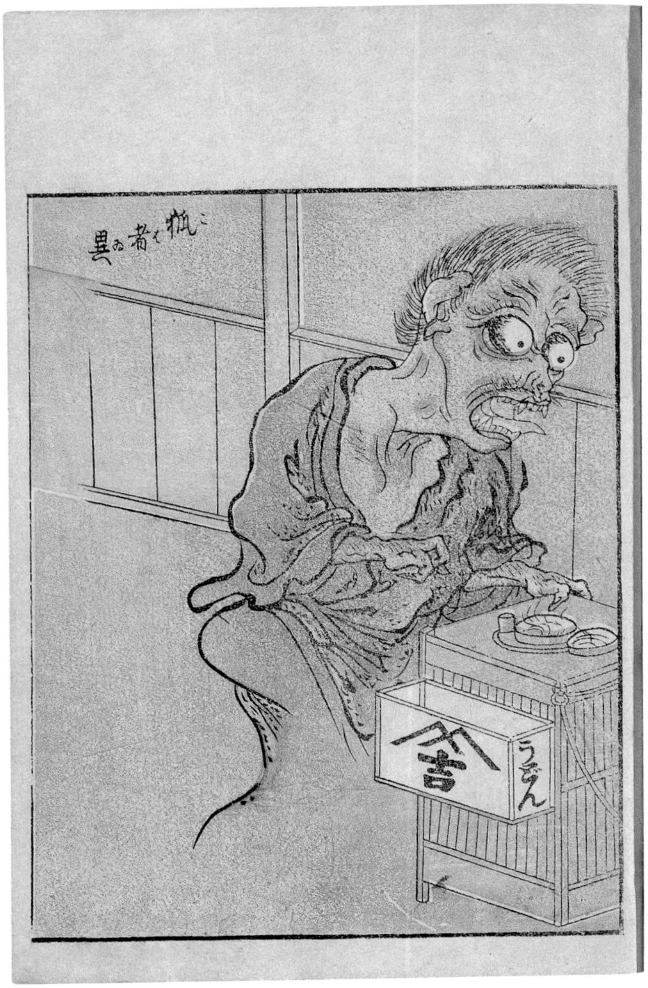
うどん

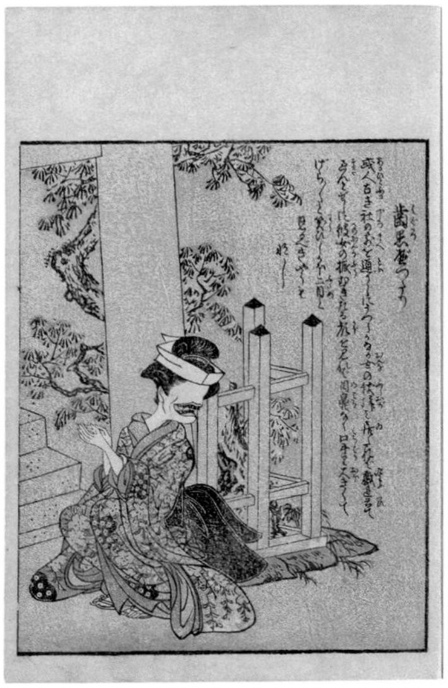

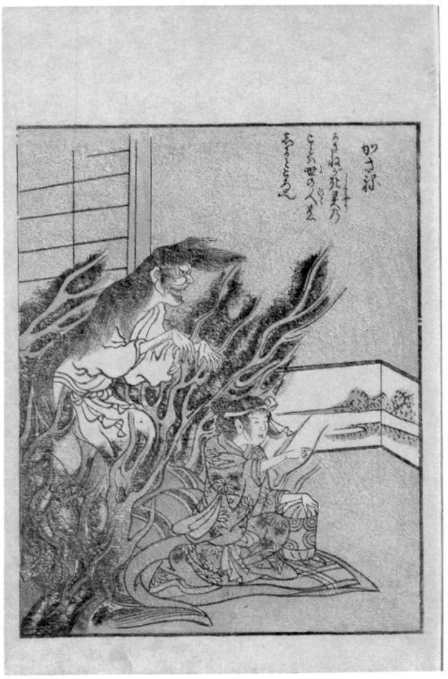

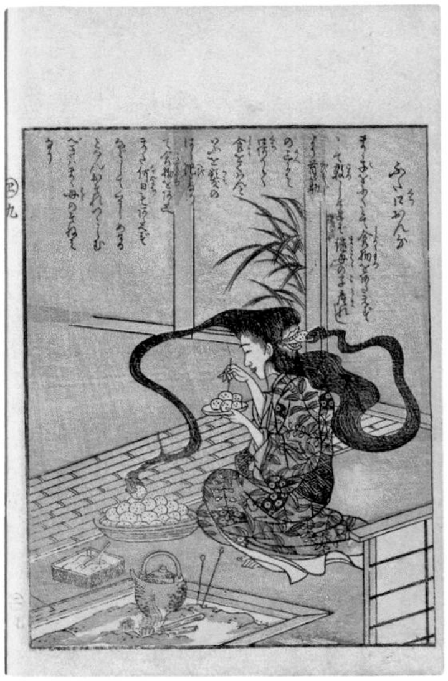

77–81
Takehara Shunsen, *Hyaku monogatari (The Hundred Tales)*, book with *yôkai* tales, no date. © Waseda University Library

The custom was that, in the evenings as the light faded, people would gather round and, their heads draped in a cloth, retell *yôkai* stories. At the end of the hundredth tale, the monsters were supposed to make an appearance.

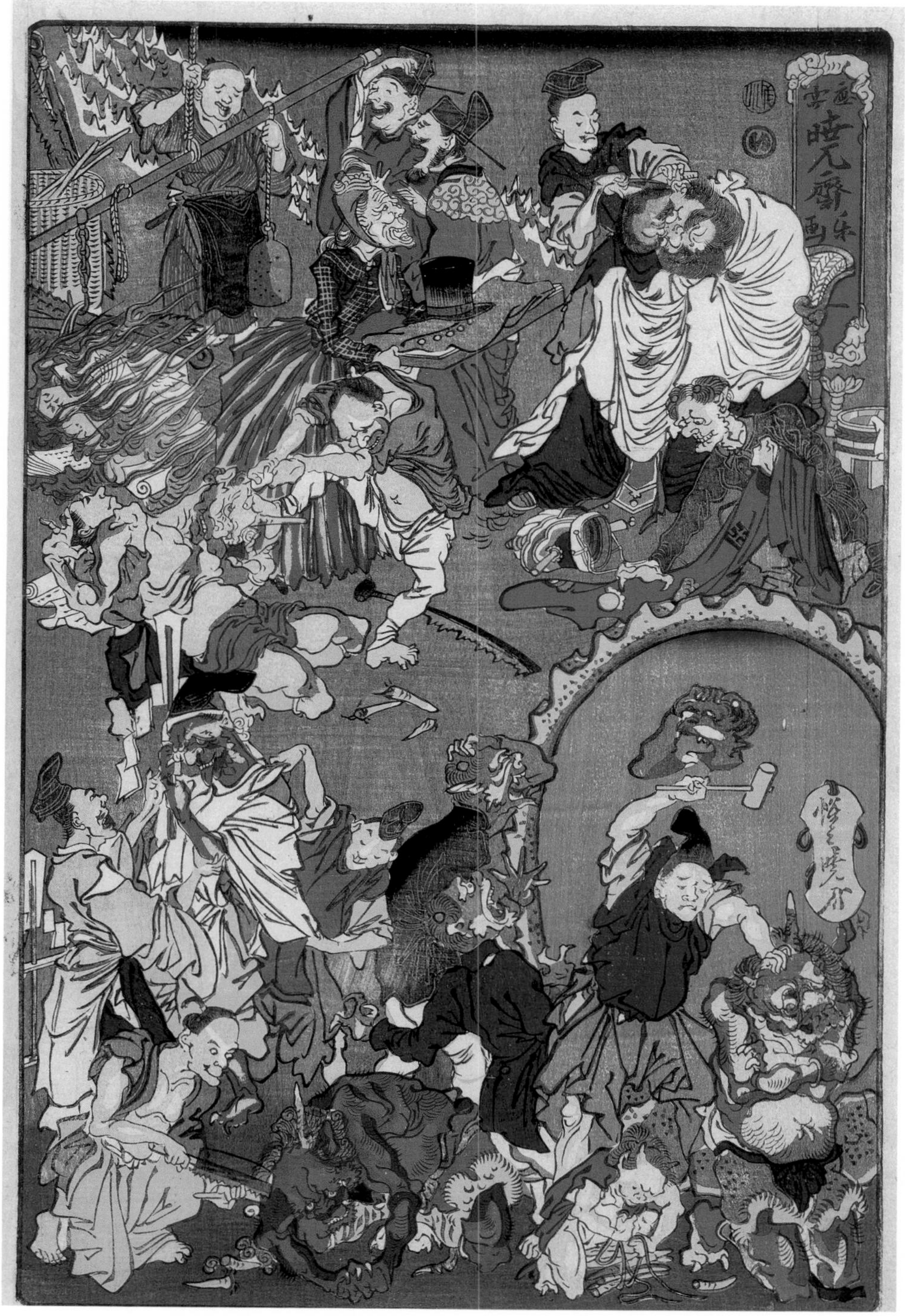

82
Kawanabe Kyôsai, *Kyôsai rakuga I (The Hellish Opening Up of the Country to Civilization)*, *nishiki-e* print, 1874.
© Kawanabe Kyôsai Memorial Museum

With his usual wit, Kawanabe Kyôsai here illustrates new habits introduced by Western civilization. He replaces human beings by monsters, enabling him to obliquely criticize some of the more recent laws, such as the one which, in 1871, forced the Japanese to abandon their *chonmage** topknot, or another that in 1876 prohibited the wearing of swords, except by soldiers and police officers.

In this print, the god of hell, Emma, is forced to have his hair cut and to don the costume handed to him. It was not that the painter was necessarily opposed to the changes, but he found them excessive and rushed.

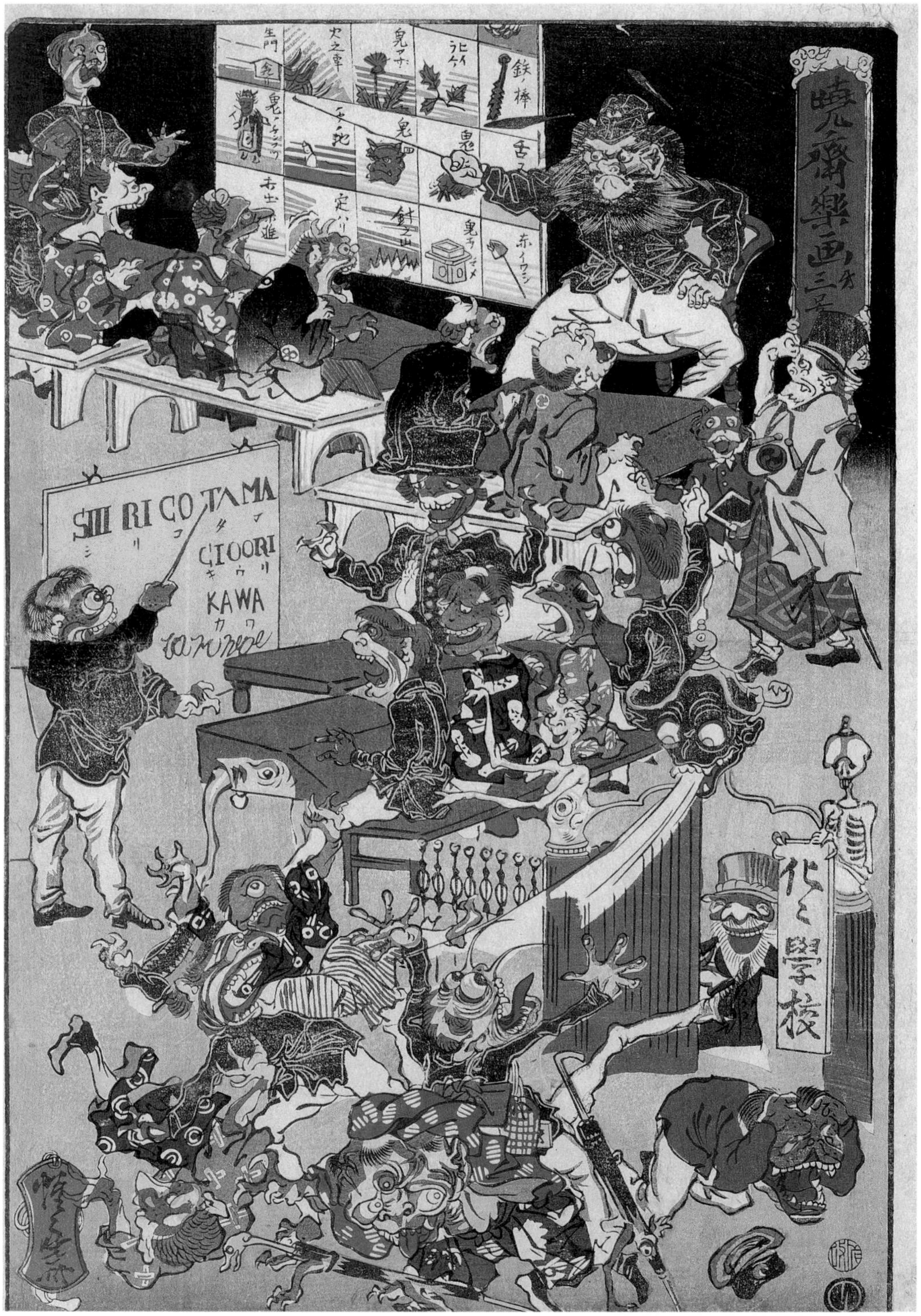
KAWA
學校

83
Kawanabe Kyôsai, *School for Monsters*, *nishiki-e* print in the *ôban* format, signed by Seisei Kyôsai, 1874. © Kawanabe Kyôsai Memorial Museum

These little monsters lack discipline! The government had instituted a new education system: traditional schools, the *terakoya*, were ousted by establishments on the Western model, complete with benches, tables, and training in the alphabet, in addition to Japanese syllabaries and ideograms.

84
Kawanabe Kyôsai, *Kyôsai Hyaku zu*, published between 1863 and 1866. © Kawanabe Kyôsai Memorial Museum

85

Anonymous, *Demon Playing the Shamisen*, Edo period.
© Machida City Museum

One of the favorite subjects of the Ôtsu pictures
is the *oni** (demon).

Popular images from Otsu (Ôtsu-e)

Monsters and animals were also represented in popular imagery.

As well known as prints, the naïve images from the town of Otsu, painted with Chinese ink and hand-colored with natural, vegetable, or mineral pigments mixed with water, were sold out of shophouses throughout the Tokaido* between Otsu and the Temple of Mii. In the Edo period, the Tokaido was the road connecting Edo and Kyoto. Strictly monitored by the government, it comprised fifty-three stopping-places that are magnificently depicted in the famous series of prints by Utagawa Hiroshige, *The Fifty-three Stations of the Tokaido*. The route would be taken by processions of *daimyô* and by common people traveling or going on pilgrimages.

The history of the *Ôtsu-e** lasted some two hundred years, between the mid-seventeenth and the end of the nineteenth century, with their zenith in the middle of the eighteenth century. At the beginning, they took inspiration from Buddhism; at the time when Christianity was prohibited, it was considered good form to possess a number of them in order to prove one was untainted by that faith. Then, under the influence of the print, numerous caricatures and cartoons of demons, animals, etc., made an appearance.

Figs. 85–88

Speech bubbles and word balloons

The balloons or bubbles we now see in comic strips appeared in Japan at the beginning of the twentieth century, but could they not already have existed, in a somewhat different but related form, in the twelfth century, and perhaps even before? An initial avatar of the word balloon is already clearly identifiable in the twelfth-century *Frolicking Animals and People*, as well as in certain prints.

Figs. 5–8
and 90–93

In the Edo and Meiji eras, these "bubbles" were not drawn in line with the mouth or head but the neck. This was an important part of the body, as it was there that the soul was believed to enter the human body—as well as the demons responsible for illnesses or death. Japanese children, notoriously mollycoddled by their mothers, would never have their hair shaved at that point. A little tuft of hair would be kept to protect the nape of the neck, poking out from under the clothing.

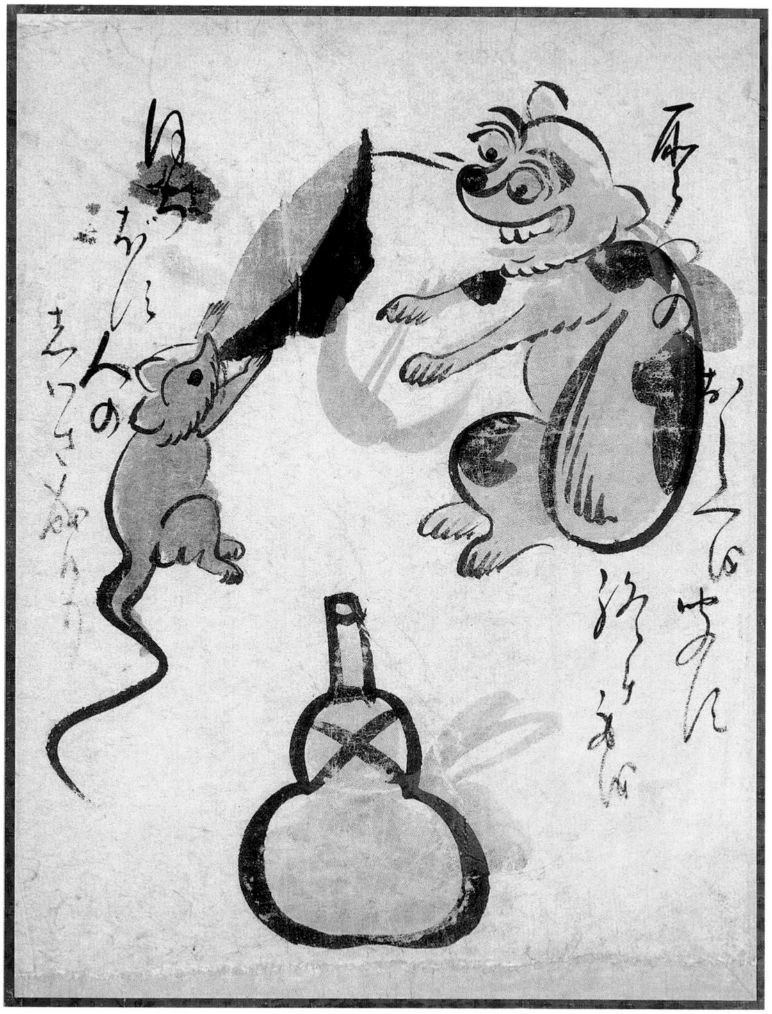

86
Anonymous, *The Cat and the Mouse*, Edo period.
© Machida City Museum

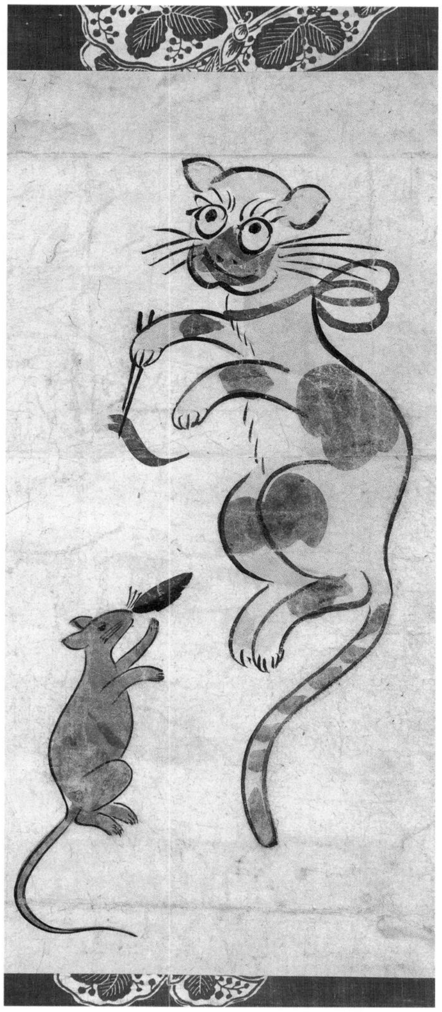

87
Anonymous, *The Cat and the Mouse*, Edo period.
© Machida City Museum

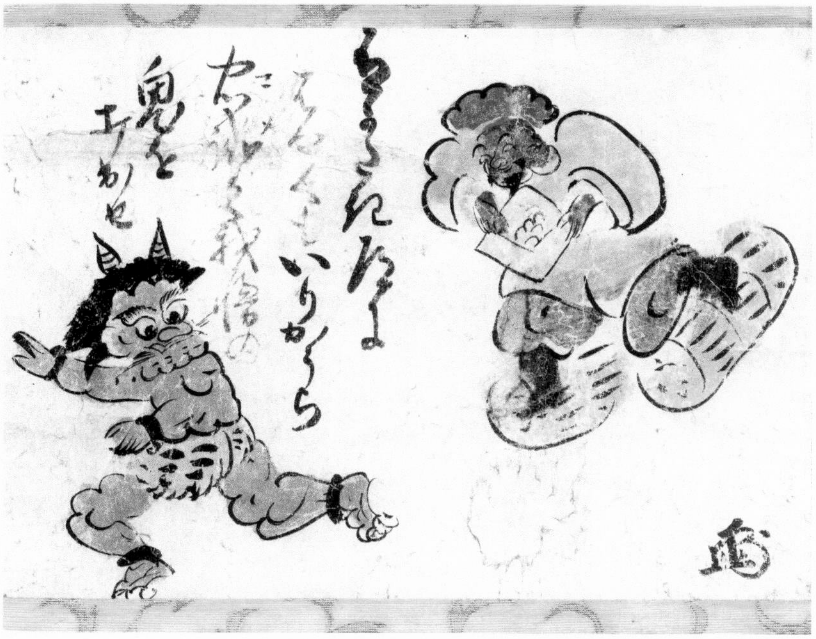

88
Anonymous, *Daikoku and a Demon*, Edo period.
© Machida City Museum

Daikoku, one of the seven divinities of happiness, throws seeds on to a demon to drive him out. The demon makes his getaway, running off as fast as he can. At the time of the festivals celebrating these divinities, it is still traditional to shout "Away with the demons! Let happiness reign in this house!"

89

Anonymous, *Dragon and Bamboo*, Edo period.
© Machida City Museum

An extremely rare subject in images of Ôtsu, a dragon curls round a bamboo stem. A link between the earth and the waters, the dragon is an omnipresent motif in Asia and an animal considered positive—contrary to Christian iconography, which sees it as a fire-breathing leviathan. In Japan, it is encountered in all periods in painting, ceramics, and in manga.

Pictures that speak: the rebus

All the rage at the beginning of the Edo era, rebuses were sold by the sheet, with the solution usually inscribed on the verso. As here, a text supplying some clues accompanies the drawing.

Figs. 94–95 and 98

From box to box: board games and "comic strips"

Very close to manga* in the way they are divided into "panels," certain illustrated tales or "roll-and-move" board games (like "snakes and ladders") are very ancient. The first *sugoroku**, which appeared in the guise of a variant of backgammon, arrived in Japan from China in the seventh century. The *e-sugoroku** or "picture roll-and-move-game," made its appearance in the Edo period. Originally used to teach Buddhism to young monks, they were drawn in Chinese ink; after the creation of the brocade print, *nishiki-e**, they were more and more often colored. With very simple rules, these *e-sugoroku* were also used as educational aids for children who, by playing them, might learn the secrets of social ascendancy, the rules of good conduct, or simply famous place-names. All types existed aimed at every age. The one showing the most famous sites in the capital made an ideal gift for visitors from the provinces, of course. Certain prints divided into squares presented children with various trades or other subjects. With hints from the title and clues inside the squares, they could readily understand the content of each image.

Figs. 98–107

Towards the end of the Edo era and the beginning of the Meiji, illustrated prints featuring tales and stories began to be published in the form of prints in which the narrative unfolds in boxes, as manga was to do.

Figs. 100, 103

The illusion of cinema: magic lanterns

With the introduction of Western science, the Japanese became obsessed with optical instruments, telescopes, stereoscopes, etc., from Holland and from China. This fad is recorded in many prints. As during the Edo, in the Meiji era children had even more fun with prints with which they could make a magic lantern. The lantern and elements for the "film" were printed on a sheet of paper, ready to be cut up and put together. The lanterns took the form of a cylinder on

Figs. 107–111

Figs. 112–115

Kitagawa Utamaro, *A Child Pestered by a Nightmare with his Mother*, nishiki-e print in the *ôban* format, c. 1800–01. © Kumon Institute of Education

A mother tries to comfort her child who is terrified of the demons disturbing his dreams. The child's words are given in the text and picture in the balloon.

91

Journey to the West: the Hundred Demons, triptych *nishiki-e* print signed by Gyokuen, end of the Edo period. © Kumon Institute of Education

Songokû (a character famous in the West thanks to a modern version of his adventures, *Dragon Ball*) is here getting ready to come to grips with the hundred demons confronting him.

92
Anonymous, *The Insects*, nishiki-e print, no date.
© Kumon Institute of Education

In the Edo era, children adored insects, which they would catch outside in the grass—or even buy.

Here, the men and women talk together while the insects identify themselves in the "bubbles": "I am the insect that scratches in a horse's mane," says the first. "Me, I'm the cricket," retorts a second. "And me, a cicada," chirrups the third. In this way, they call out to the customers, hoping to attract their attention.

93
Tale: the Sparrow Whose Tongue Was Cut Out, triptych *nishiki-e* print, signed Utagawa Yoshimori, 1864.
© Kumon Institute of Education

An old man who loved animals befriended the wounded little sparrow he looked after. He gave him rice to peck at, but his miserly wife cut out the wretched bird's tongue, and the bird returned to his parents. Determined to beg forgiveness for his wife's cruelty, the old man set off to look for the sparrow. Finding him, the bird received him well and he was offered one of two boxes as a present. Choosing the smaller, he was astonished to find that it contained treasure. His covetous wife in her turn went off to see the sparrow, but she opted for the larger box, convinced it would have gold inside. Her spite was rightly punished when she raised the lid: demons poured out, each one more terrifying than the last, forcing the woman to repent her ways.

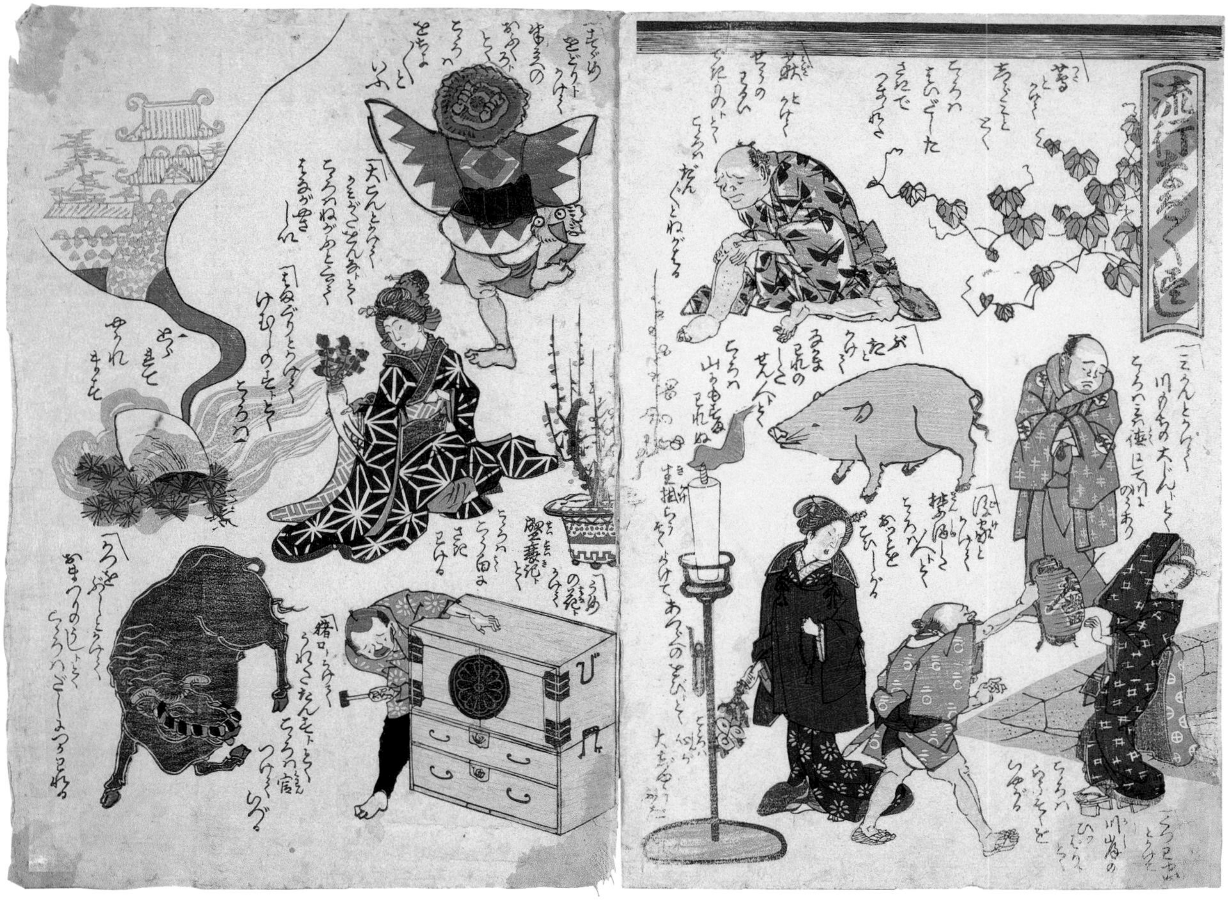

94
Anonymous, *Fashionable Print*: *the Rebus*, *nishiki-e* print, no date. © Waseda University Library

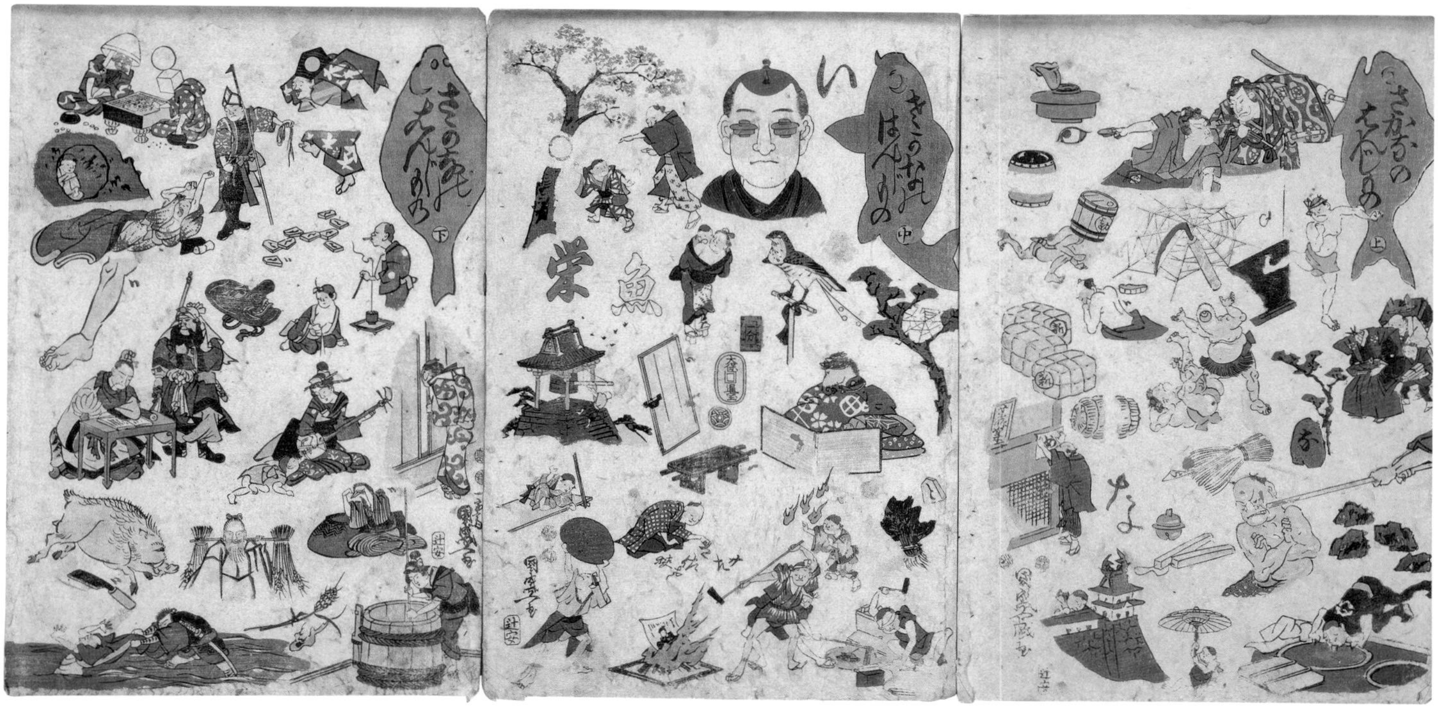

95
Utagawa Kunimori, *Fish Rebuses*, triptych *nishiki-e* print, no date. © Waseda University Library

which the pictures were printed and which would move due to the warmth produced by a candle placed in the center of the tube.

Incredibly popular in the Edo period, the subject was often provided by the theater. By seeing them in such pictures, children would soon learn about all the most famous actors of the day. Staging little plays, they would use figures cut out of specially produced prints and move them about the theater. In the following decades, subjects increasingly close to those in the West were to appear. Figs. 116–117

Katsushika Hokusai: the painter of *Manga*

Hokusai can be regarded as the first direct ancestor of manga, since it was with him that the term as currently used first appeared: then employed in the feminine, at the beginning it designated a group of drawings intended to serve as models for the master's pupils. It was only at the end of the nineteenth century that it started to mean "caricature," and then comic strip.

Katsushika Hokusai (1760–1849) is one of the most talented of all Japanese artists. Entering the studio of the print painter Katsukawa Shunshô (1726–1792) aged eighteen, he began with a series of portraits of actors. The famous publisher, Tsutaya Jûzaburô, then discovered his genius and supplied him with work. Experimenting with numerous styles and techniques, Hokusai excelled in all fields and fulfilled a dazzling variety of commissions—not only for paintings and prints, but also for technical manuals and albums. Among his many nicknames, the most memorable is surely *Gakyôjin Hokusai* ("Hokusai, mad about painting"). Tireless and ever eager to transmit his passion for drawing to his many disciples and admirers, not even age blunted his enthusiasm and perfectionism. His series of *Thirty-Six Views of Mount Fuji* is famous throughout the world.

The Great Wave off Kanagawa represents the quintessence of Hokusai's art. Japanese scientists have studied it in detail and demonstrated that the drawing reflects exactly the position and precise form of a real wave to one hundredth of second. As accurate as a camera lens then, Hokusai's eye captured the fleeting moment just before the breaker crashes over the frail-looking boats. In drawing it, the artist put himself in the place of the people in the boats as they gaze up from below at Mount Fuji and the towering wave.

96
Anonymous, *Working the Fields*, *nishiki-e* print, 1898.
© Edo-Tokyo Museum

This print showed children various types of agricultural work. The arrangement in boxes is reminiscent of manga layout.

97
Taniguchi Jirô, *Aruku Hito (The Man Who Walks)*, 1992.
© Taniguchi Jirô

98
Utagawa Yoshikazu (Ichijusai), *The Acrobats*, *nishiki-e* print, 1858.
© Edo-Tokyo Museum

The inhabitants of the city of Edo liked to venture into the popular districts of Asakusa and Ryogoku and to enjoy the *misemono**, or attractions. Crowds would pour over the Sumida Bridge, which led to the one of the most bustling quarters in the capital. Countless boats plied the river, which was bordered by teahouses, and in summer breathtaking firework displays were put on. To the delight of children, various treats and inexpensive toys were sold and, together with their parents, they would cluster round the fairground huts to watch jugglers and acrobats. The latter were among the best in the world and, at the end of the nineteenth century, a number of Japanese troupes successfully toured the West.

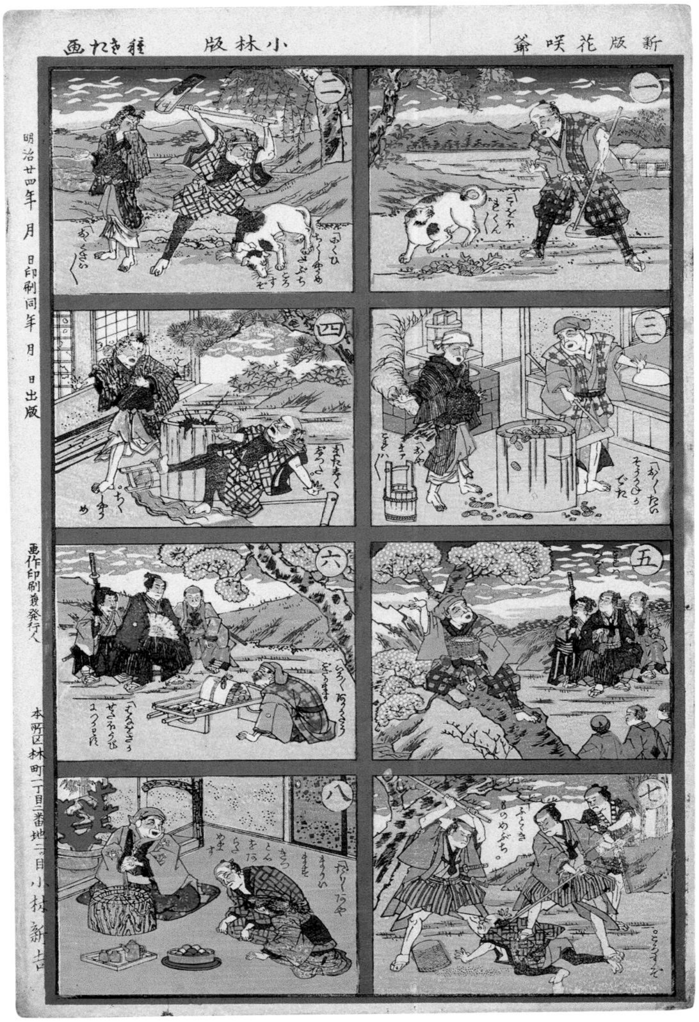
新版花咲爺

99

Utagawa Tanesada, *Hana saka jijii (The Man Who Made the Trees Flower)*, *nishiki-e* print, 1891. © Kumon Institute of Education

This print tells a story from the end of the Muromachi period or beginning of the Edo era in pictures arranged in boxes in a manner that will reappear in later cartoons. Thanks to his dog, a kindly old man discovers treasure at the foot of a tree. A covetous and jealous neighbor then kills the poor animal. The old man digs him a grave in the shade of a tree, which he later cuts down to make a mortar. Each time he crushes his rice in it, it changes into gold coin. The malicious neighbor, having borrowed the mortar to make some gold of his own, cannot get it to work and, in a rage, burns it. The old man then spreads the mortar's ashes around some dead trees, which promptly burst into flower.

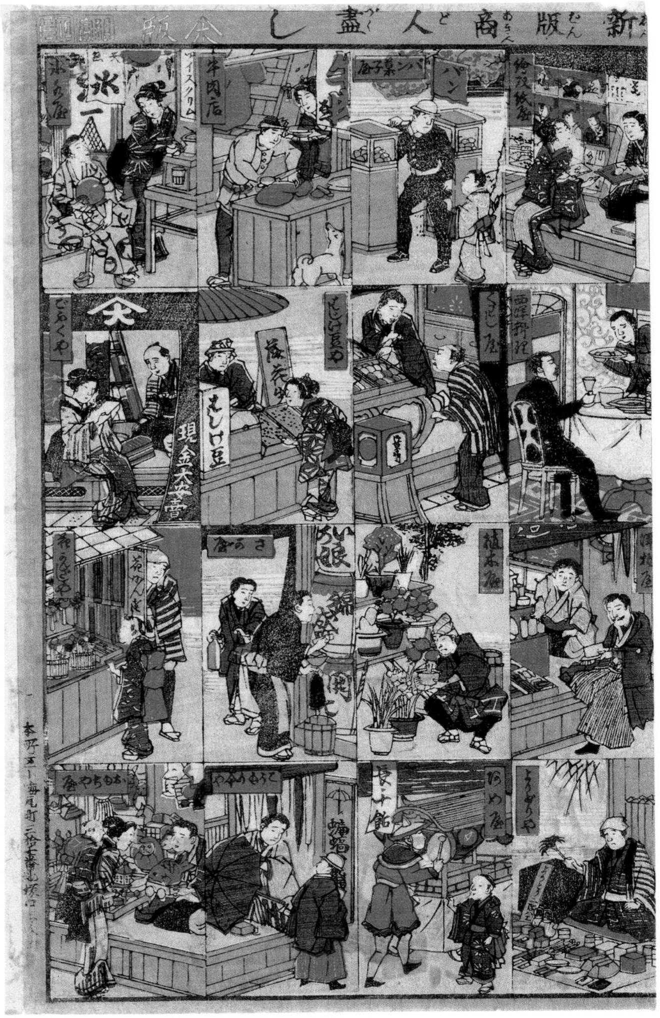

100

Anonymous, *A New Print of Tradesmen*, *nishiki-e* print, no date. © Edo-Tokyo Museum

Various trades are represented here: sorbet-, ice-cream- and cake-sellers, a butcher, etc. Both tradesmen and customers seem very busy. In the second column, extreme right, one can see a man, wearing a suit and seated at a table, being served a meal in a Western restaurant.

Here both the changing manners and habits are highlighted. Both the gestures of the figures and the succession of images create an impression of movement.

101

Shimada Nobukazu, *Sugoroku: the Kindergarten*,
Meiji period. ©Waseda University Library

Various activities for children are depicted here.
After two years in kindergarten, the children are
awarded a diploma (top left).

102

Anonymous, *Japanese Revenge*, Meiji period. ©Waseda University Library

Some famous acts of revenge—in particular that of the *Forty-seven
Rônin**, who restored the honor of their lord, reproduced at the top
in the middle of the print—are arranged in various compartments.
These adopt various shapes that hold the reader's attention, struc-
turing and pacing the layout in the way of a modern manga.

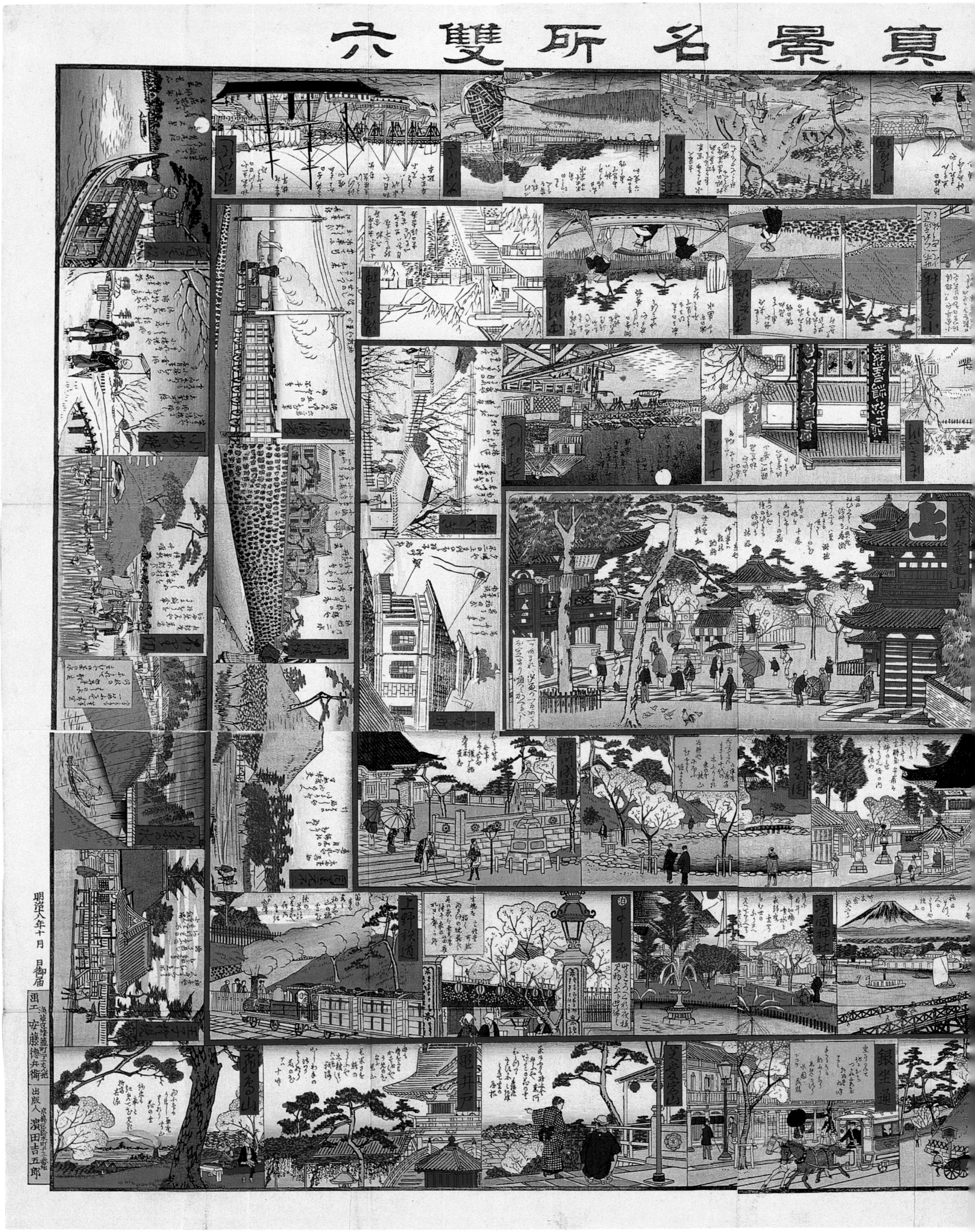
眞景名所雙六
明治八年十月　日御届
画工　安藤徳兵衛
出版人　濱田吉五郎
上野
亀井戸
銀座通

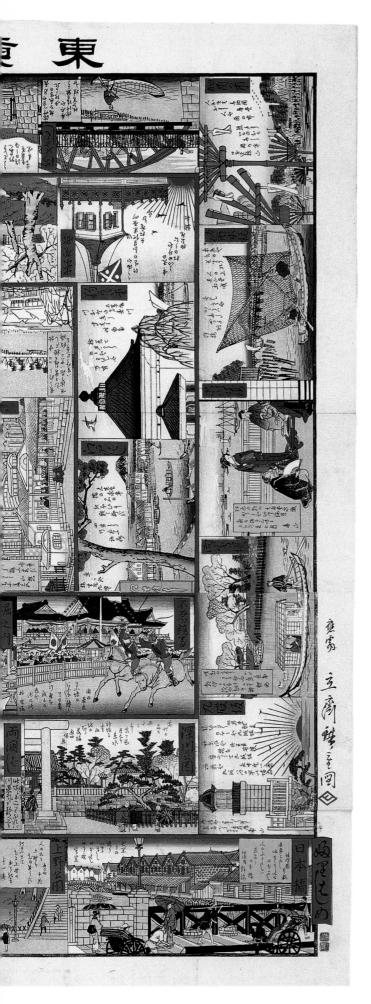

Utagawa Hiroshige, *True Views of Tokyo*, 1885.
© Waseda University Library

One of the famous print-master's successors depicted landscapes in this roll-and-move game as a way of improving the players' knowledge of geography and history.

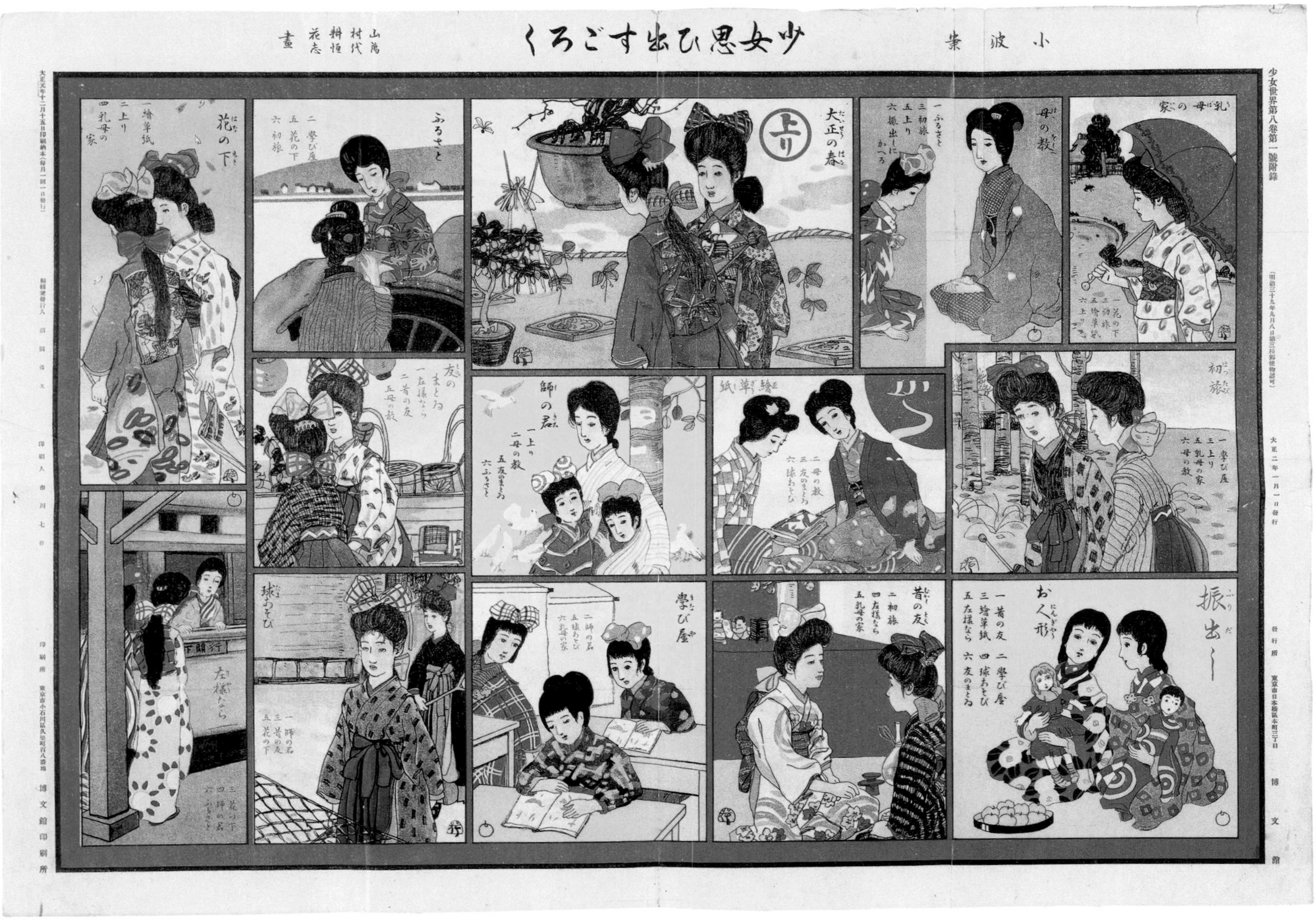
少女思ひ出すごろく
小波案
大正の春
上り
花の下
ふるさと
母の教
乳母の家
初旅
師の君
學び屋
昔の友
振出し
お人形
球あそび
左様なら

104
Imaya Sazanami, Yamamura Kôka, Bandai Tsuneshi, *Sugoroku: Memories of Young Girls*, lithograph, 1913. © Waseda University Library

Dressed in a *hakama** or else in a kimono, and sporting a large ribbon in their hair in keeping with the latest fashion, the girls are shown playing, studying, doing sport, etc.

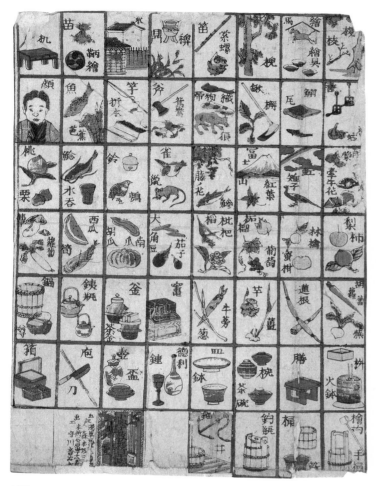

105

Morikawa Otojirô, *Encyclopedic Print for Teachers in Primary Schools*, nishiki-e print, c. 1870–80. © Edo-Tokyo Museum

Moderate in price, these "encyclopedic" prints, which consisted in accumulating the greatest number of elements on the same theme, were also very popular. Colorful and attractive, they were a playful teaching aid that helped children learn the names of flowers, animals, plants, utensils, famous places, etc., as well as the numerous difficult ideograms of Japanese script.

106

Anonymous, *Sugoroku of Ponchi of Foreigners Allowed to Live Where They Want*, 1899. © Waseda University Library

With their long noses, blue eyes and light-colored hair, these foreigners, though got up partly in the Japanese style, are finding it hard-going fitting in with Japanese life!

107

Katsushika Hokusai, *Fûryû nakute nanakuse*
(Series of Seven Fashionable Prints), *nishiki-e* print,
Edo period, c. 1789–1804. © Kobe City Museum

This print combines two of Hokusai's finest portraits. The woman with the sunshade is married, as indicated by her deliberately blackened teeth. Her attire shows she belongs to the upper echelons of society. The girl in the foreground is looking at something through a field glass, a highly prized article at the time.

It was not the first time the painter had devoted a work to this subject: about thirty years previously, he had already produced a few similar pieces, though they did not attain the same level of intensity.

The French man of letters, Edmond de Goncourt, who was the first European to dedicate a work to the Japanese painter in 1896, has given a fine account of just how the artist came to compose his famous manga from which so many Western artists took inspiration in the vogue of *japonisme*. The Hokusai specialist Nagata Seiji has since added to this biography (*see* Nagata Seiji, *Katsushika Hokusai*, Tokyo: Yoshikawa Kôbunkan, 2000).

In 1812, Hokusai had visited one of his disciples, the painter Maki Bokusen (1775–1824), in Nagoya. He remained with him for many months, during which he executed approximately three hundred drawings in response to a request from Bokusen and the publisher Eirakuya Tôshirô. These drawings were the origin of a first volume of manga, which appeared in 1814; in the end there were to be no fewer than fifteen. Published under the title *Edehon Hokusai manga (Hokusai's Manga Drawing Manual)*, this collection was thus intended, not only for his many adepts, but also for all those who wanted to learn how to draw (any drawing executed with the brush in Chinese ink).

In the foreword to the fourth volume, the master explains how he devised his *Manga* to advance his pupils' progress. The sketches the painter gathered together are then not caricatures at all. Far from being his first go at producing such a handbook, Hokusai had already issued pattern-books with motifs for combs or *kiseru* (long pipes) made for craftsmen that had proved a great success. Already fifty-three when the first volume came out, he continued working on them right up until his death, while never ceasing to paint. His *Manga* was imitated by many other artists but never equaled.

Hokusai's output in the field of illustrated books was considerable too. The very detailed manga bibliography that Ishinomori Shôtarô (1938–1998) devoted to the matter runs to almost six hundred pages. The artist demonstrates his mastery of drawing on all types of support—from a grain of rice to absolutely vast surfaces. On several occasions, he offered proof of his genius in the open air before astounded onlookers. In 1804, he painted a *Daruma** (an

effigy of the first Zen "patriarch") of huge size, and in 1817 repeated the feat before the Nishigakejo Temple during a sojourn at Nagoya. Edmond de Goncourt records the event: "A length of paper measuring 194 meters [636 feet] had been set up. Regularly spaced struts of wood kept it taut. Enormous brushes were placed at the painter's disposal. First of all, Hokousaï [sic] took up a brush the size of a bundle of hay and, having soaked it in ink, drew the nose and then the left eye of the *Daruma*: then, he strode off and drew the mouth and the ear […]. The *Daruma* was only totally finished by nightfall when the great painted 'machine' could be lifted up with pulleys […]. This was not the only outsized painting Hokousaï made. Later, in Honjo, he painted a colossal horse, and subsequently in Ryogoku a giant *Hotei* that he signed *Kintaisga Hokousai*, that is to say 'Hokousaï of the house with the bag of brocade'—an allusion to the cloth bag that is the god's invariable accessory. The day he painted
Fig. 121 the horse the size of an elephant, it is said that he placed his brush on a grain of rice. When this was later examined under a magnifying glass, one had the illusion of seeing, in the microscopic spot left
Figs. 118–120 and 125 by the brush, a pair of sparrows in flight" (Edmond de Goncourt, *Hokousaï*, Paris: 10/18 ["Fin de siècle"], 1986, p. 220–221).

Hokusai was probably the painter who most influenced Western artists, starting with the Impressionists. The discovery of Japanese culture provided an opportunity of engaging with an art totally unlike the academism that prevailed at that time. The compositions, the flat tints, the bird's-eye views, the broad planes characteristic of the Japanese print provided a spur to a revival in Western painting. The Impressionists were the first to absorb this inspiration, but they were soon followed by Neo-Impressionists, the Nabis, and by Art Nouveau, Art Deco, Modern Style, as well as by creators of posters and advertising. The comic strips of the beginning of the century—those of Benjamin Rabier in France, or George McManus *(Bringing up Father)* and Winsor McCay *(Little Nemo in Slumberland)* in the United States—were thus created under the influence of Japanese
Figs. 125–127 art, which, impregnated by Western animation, imitated it in its turn and spawned today's manga.

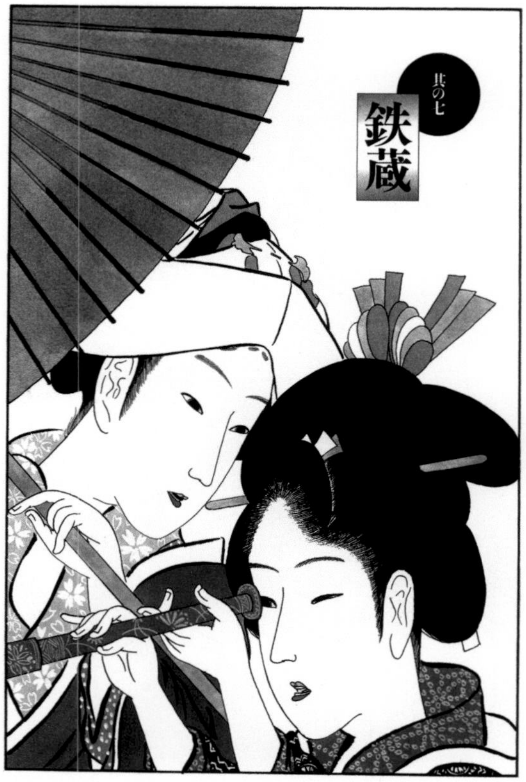
其の七
鉄蔵

108
Sugiura Hinako, *Sarusuberi (Lagerstroemia).*
© Suzuki Michiko, *The Complete Works of Sugiura Hinako*, vol. 3, Tokyo: Chikuma Shobô, 1995
In reference to his illustrious forebear, Sugiura Hinako reutilized this print as an illustration for the seventh chapter of his manga, *Sarusuberi*.

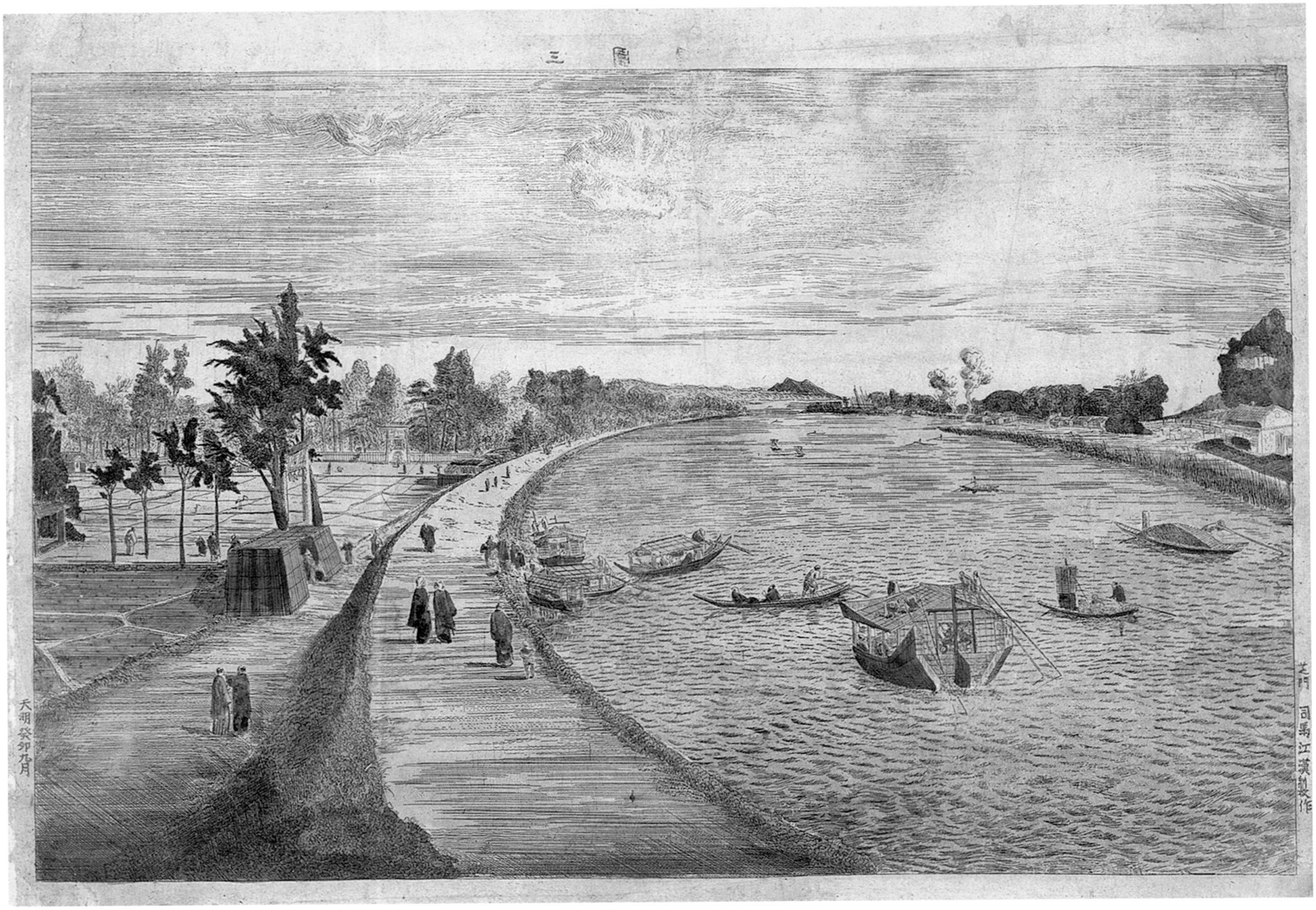
芝門 司馬江漢製作
天明癸卯九月

109

Shiba Kôkan, *View of the Mimeguri Temple*, 1783. © Kobe City Museum

This is the first etching executed in accordance with Western perspective and designed to be looked at in a magic box, the *nozoki karakuri**. From the 1720s, the date at which foreign books, save for religious works, were authorized, many scientific anthologies became available, fostering the "Dutch studies" (*Rangaku**) of specialists, the *rangakusha**. Shiba Kôkan (1747–1818), who had first learned the art of the *ukiyo-e* print with the celebrated Suzuki Harunobu (1725–1770), was to turn to decidedly Western techniques and perspective. Eager, like other pioneers in this field, to encourage progress in his country, he painted in oils, depicting landscapes in conformity with rules of perspective born in the Renaissance.

110

Nozoki karakuri; a stereoscope providing images with an impression of relief and depth, between 1764 and 1781, 11 x 15 ½ in. (27.7 x 39.2 cm). © Kobe City Museum

Imported from Holland, the stereoscope was modified by the Japanese and turned into an instrument of smaller size. Various alternatives were designed. Six engravings were placed one behind the other on the top of a box into which, by pulling on the strings, one could lower the images as required, observing them through a lens fitted at the front. Artists composed engravings especially for this apparatus, which, providing the illusion of images in three dimensions, became hugely popular.

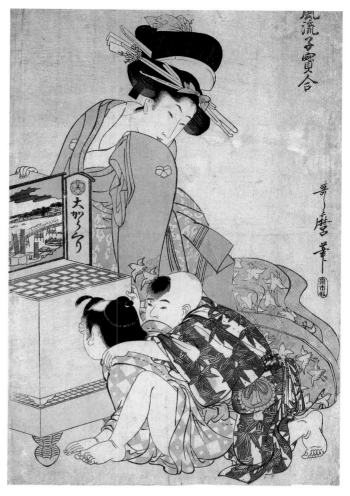

111

Kitagawa Utamaro, *Children Are Such a Treasure: the Magic Box*, *nishiki-e* print, 1802. © Kumon Institute of Education

With his characteristic gentleness and elegance, the great print-master has here captured the wonder of children as they peer at the three-dimensional pictures depicted in the optical box.

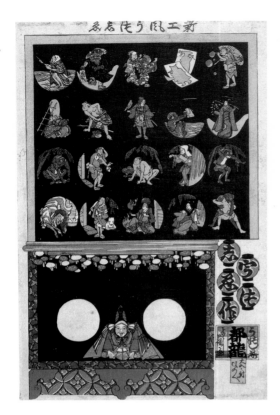

113
Utagawa Yoshifuji, *New Print to Cut Out and Reassemble: Magic Lantern*, *nishiki-e* print, c. 1860. © Kumon Institute of Education

112
Utagawa Yoshifuji, *New Print to Cut Out and Reassemble: Magic Lantern*, *nishiki-e* print, c. 1860. © Kumon Institute of Education

Originally inspired by a play entitled *Sambasô Sticking Out His Tongue*, this magic box comprises two disks to each side of the main figure that can be cut out so that children can insert the other figures in the holes and tell stories with them. It is thus a readymade paper theater. Sambasô is the character who raises the curtain in a *kabuki* theater.

114
Ishikawa Toyomasa, *Children's Games: the Month of December*, *nishiki-e* print, no date © Kumon Institute of Education

Children adored magic lanterns. Made out of Japanese paper, they comprised a cylinder on which pictures were printed. In the center of the cylinder, a candle was placed whose heat made the device turn slowly. These ancestors of the cinema are extremely rare nowadays.

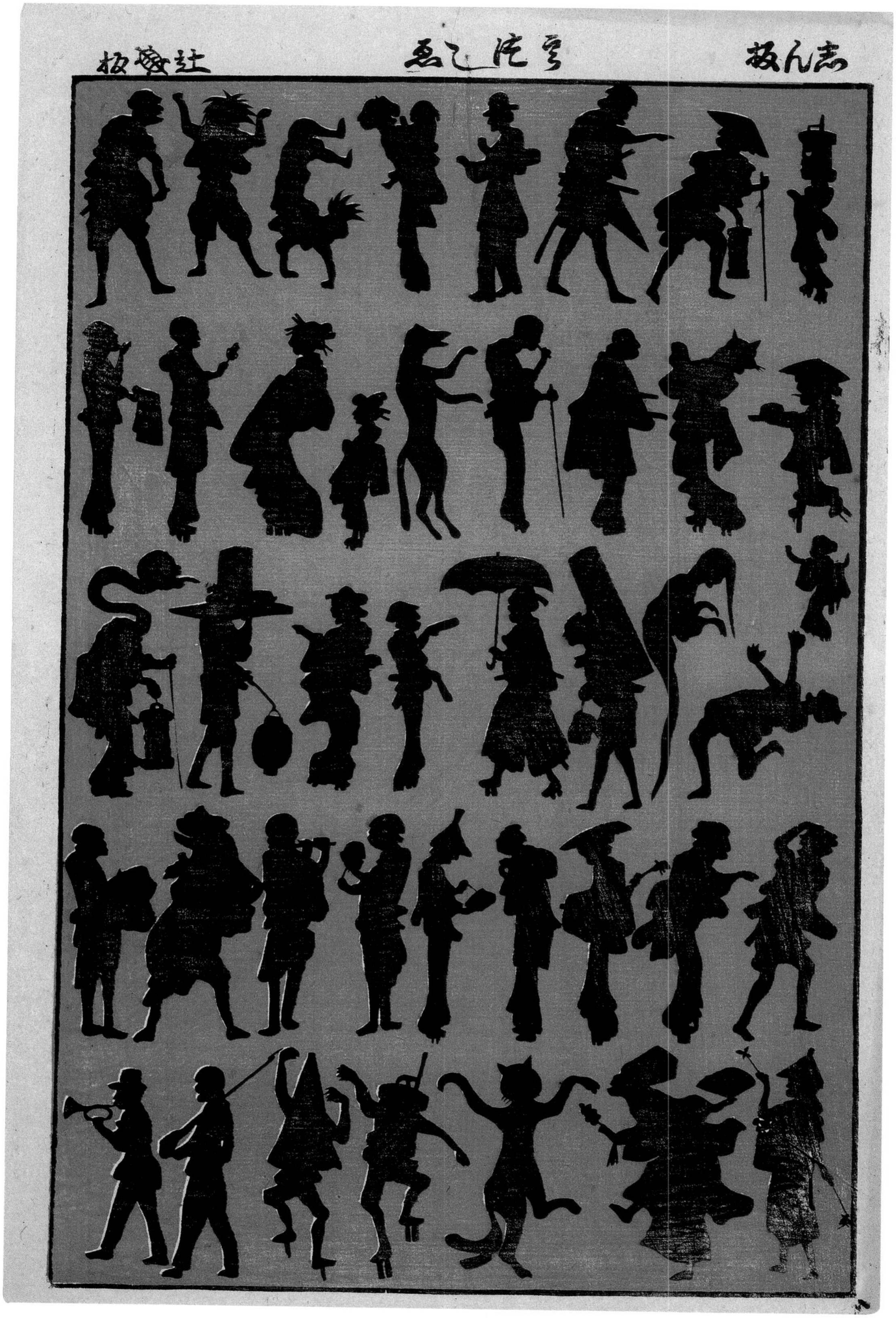

115
Anonymous *nishiki-e* print, Meiji era. © Kumon Institute of Education

This is an example of a print made up of comical shadow-theater silhouettes, which could be brought to life by turning a magic lantern.

116
Anonymous, cartoon film, woodblock print, 1910s. © Kumon Institute of Education

These strips of drawings would come to life when cut out and stuck into a magic lantern.

117
Kobayashi Kiyochika, *The Cats and the Picture*, print, no date. © Ota Memorial Museum of Art

In creating his new technique of *kôsenga** which enabled him to translate light and shade as well as variations in hue, the painter executed a series of prints on animal themes. Here we have two cats, one bristling like a hedgehog and about to leap up, while the other is trying to catch the artfully drawn rooster. The tubes of paint symbolize the artist's attachment to Western techniques.

The expression of movement and speed: from prints to manga

Katsushika Hokusai was a genius at expressing the passage of time and the fugacity of the moment, conveying in his works sensations of speed and dynamism like no other. A source of inspiration for his contemporaries and his successors alike, his techniques remain current in present-day manga. The "manga" that gained such renowm thanks to Hokusai, and that was reused by other painters of *ukiyo-e*, was little by little abandoned by the end of the nineteenth century. Other, older terms such as "*giga**," or "*Tôba-e**" (after the name of the monk Tôba to whom *Frolicking Animals and People* was ascribed) regained favor to refer to caricatures or cartoons, with other words, such as "*ponchi-e**," appearing in the Meiji era to convey the concept covered by manga.

Figs. 130–142
Figs. 143–144

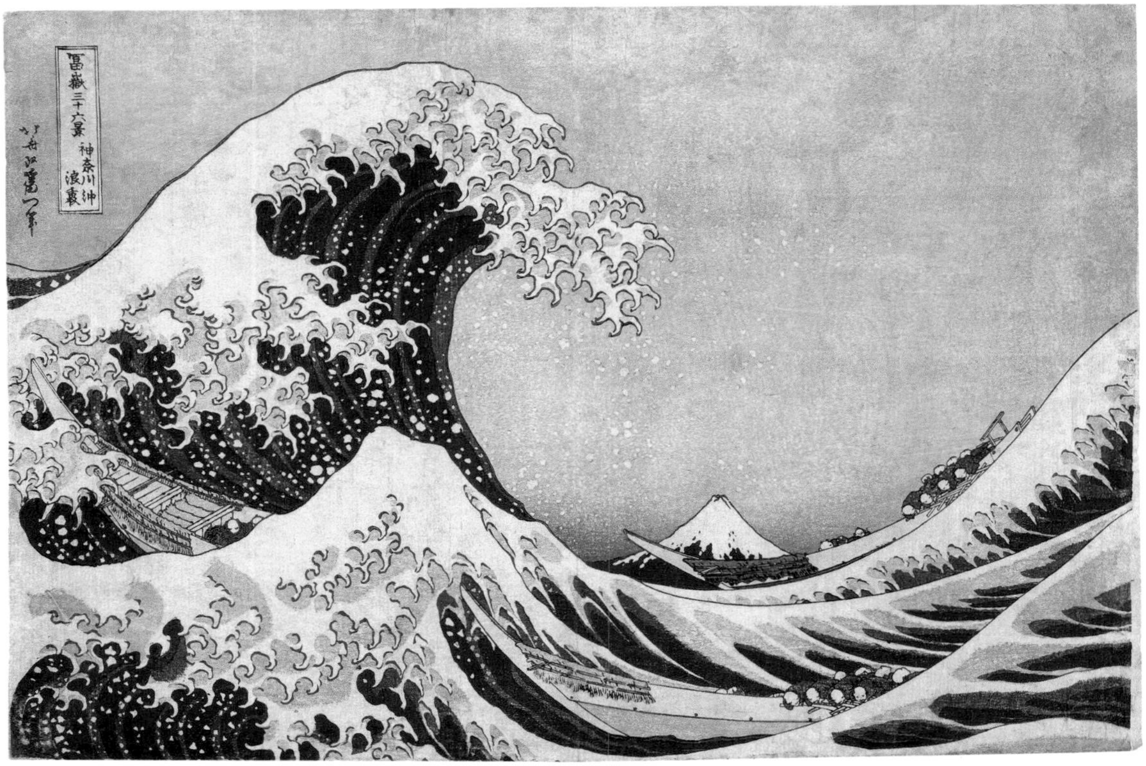
富嶽三十六景
神奈川沖
浪裏

118
Katsushika Hokusai, *Kanagawa oki namiura (The Great Wave off Kanagawa)*, polychrome woodblock print from the series *Fugaku sanjû rokkei (Thirty-Six Views of Mount Fuji)*, c. 1831. © Chiba City Museum of Art

This print—undoubtedly the best known of all Hokusai's and the most frequently reproduced—is, by its beauty, power, and the lines in a range of blues that express the violence of the wave and the spume spouting from the crest of the breaker, an absolute masterpiece of observation. The fruit of thirty years' research, *The Great Wave off Kanagawa* testifies to the artist's perfect grasp of the Western idea of perspective.

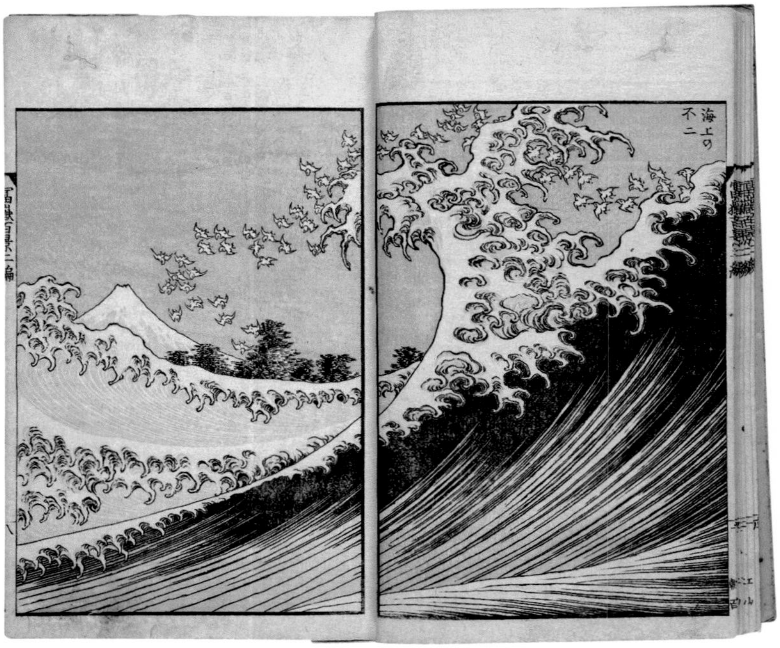

119
Katsushika Hokusai, *Fugaku hyakkei (One Hundred Views of Mount Fuji)*, woodblock print, volume two, 1834. © Chiba City Museum of Art

The lines and the gradations of gray in the spume-topped wave are drawn with fantastic accuracy. By placing himself at the bottom of the scene, the painter exploits visual effects to translate the power of the ocean, with even Mount Fuji seemingly on the point of being engulfed.

120
Katsushika Hokusai, *Hokusai manga (Manga by Hokusai)*, volume ten.
© Chiba City Museum of Art

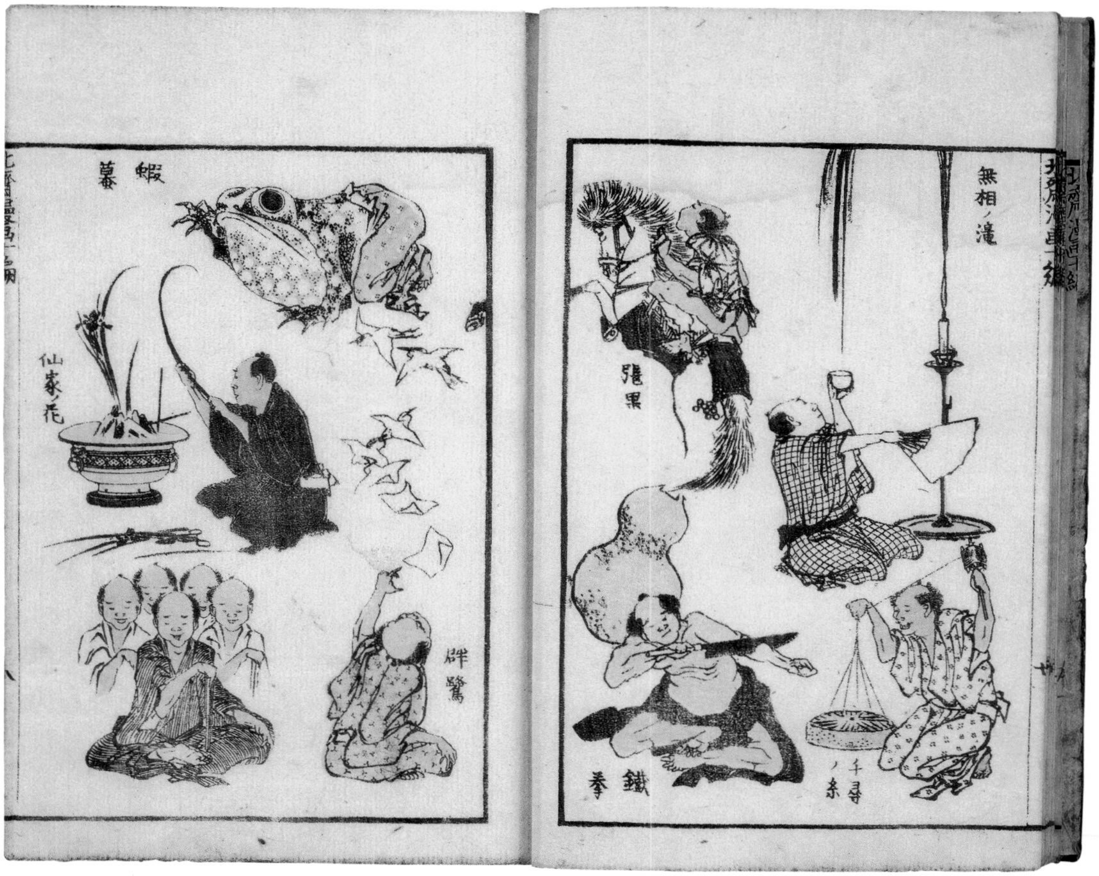

121
Sugiura Hinako, Sarusuberi *(Lagerstroemia)*. *Complete Works of Sugiura Hinako,* vol. 3, Tokyo: Chikuma Shobô, 1995.
© Suzuki Michiko

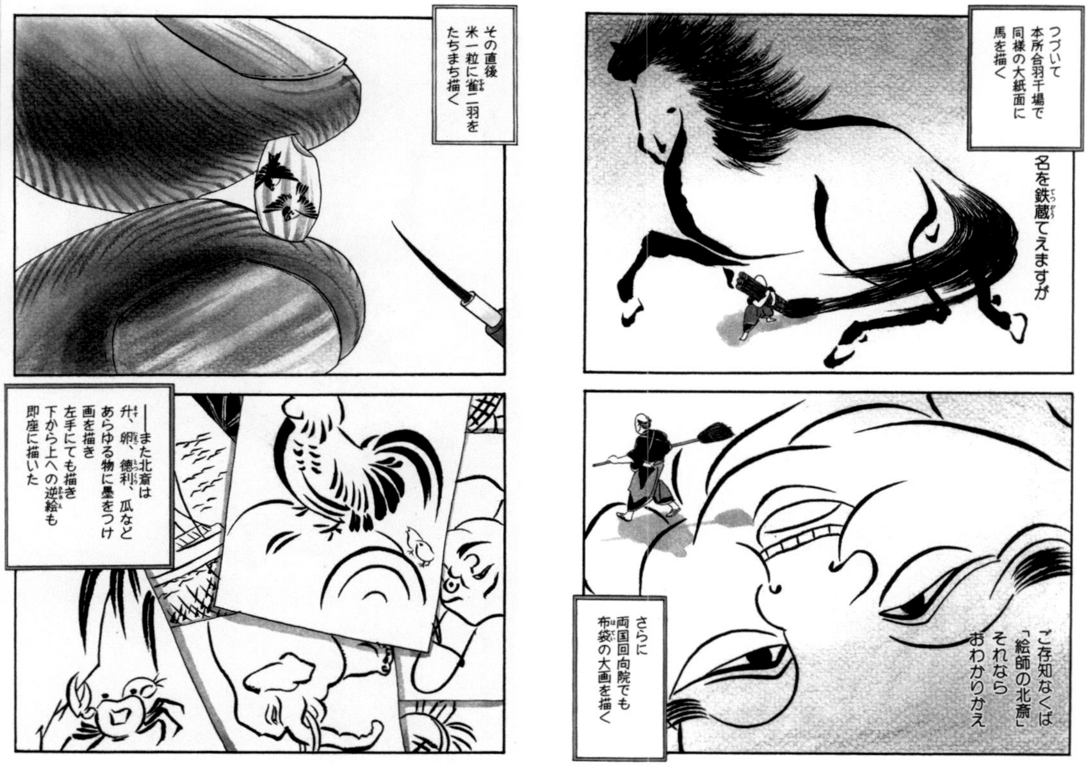
つづいて本所合羽干場で同様の大紙面に馬を描く
名を鉄蔵てえますが
ご存知なくば「絵師の北斎」それならおわかりかえ
さらに両国回向院でも布袋の大画を描く
その直後米一粒に雀二羽をたちまち描く
——また北斎は升、卵、徳利、瓜などあらゆる物に墨をつけ画を描き左手にても描き下から上への逆絵も即座に描いた

HOKUSAI
北斎
石ノ森章太郎
画に生き、画に死した「画狂老人」、葛飾北斎の生き様を見よ！
一挙掲載608ページ!!
定価580円(税込)
角川書店

―北斎!!

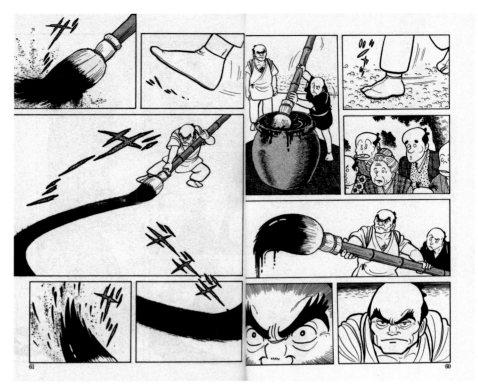

122–124
Ishinomori Shôtarô, *Hokusai,* 1987. © Ishinomori Production

125
Katsushika Hokusai, *The Manga,* 1815, Matsumoto Leiji Collection.
© Katsushika Hokusai

This famous plate from Hokusai's manga is included in the manga
Futatsu Makura (Lacquer Pillows) by Sugiura Hinako (below) as an
illustration for the chapter entitled *Yakusoku (Promise)*.

126
Sugiura Hinako, *Futatsu Makura
(Lacquer Pillows), Complete Works
of Sugiura Hinako,* vol. 1, Tokyo: Chikuma
Shobô, 1995. © Suzuki Michiko

127
Edgar Degas,
Two Dancers at
Rest (or The Blue
Dancers), c. 1898,
pastel on beige
paper,
36 ¼ x 40 ½ in.
(92 x 103 cm)
Musée d'Orsay,
Paris

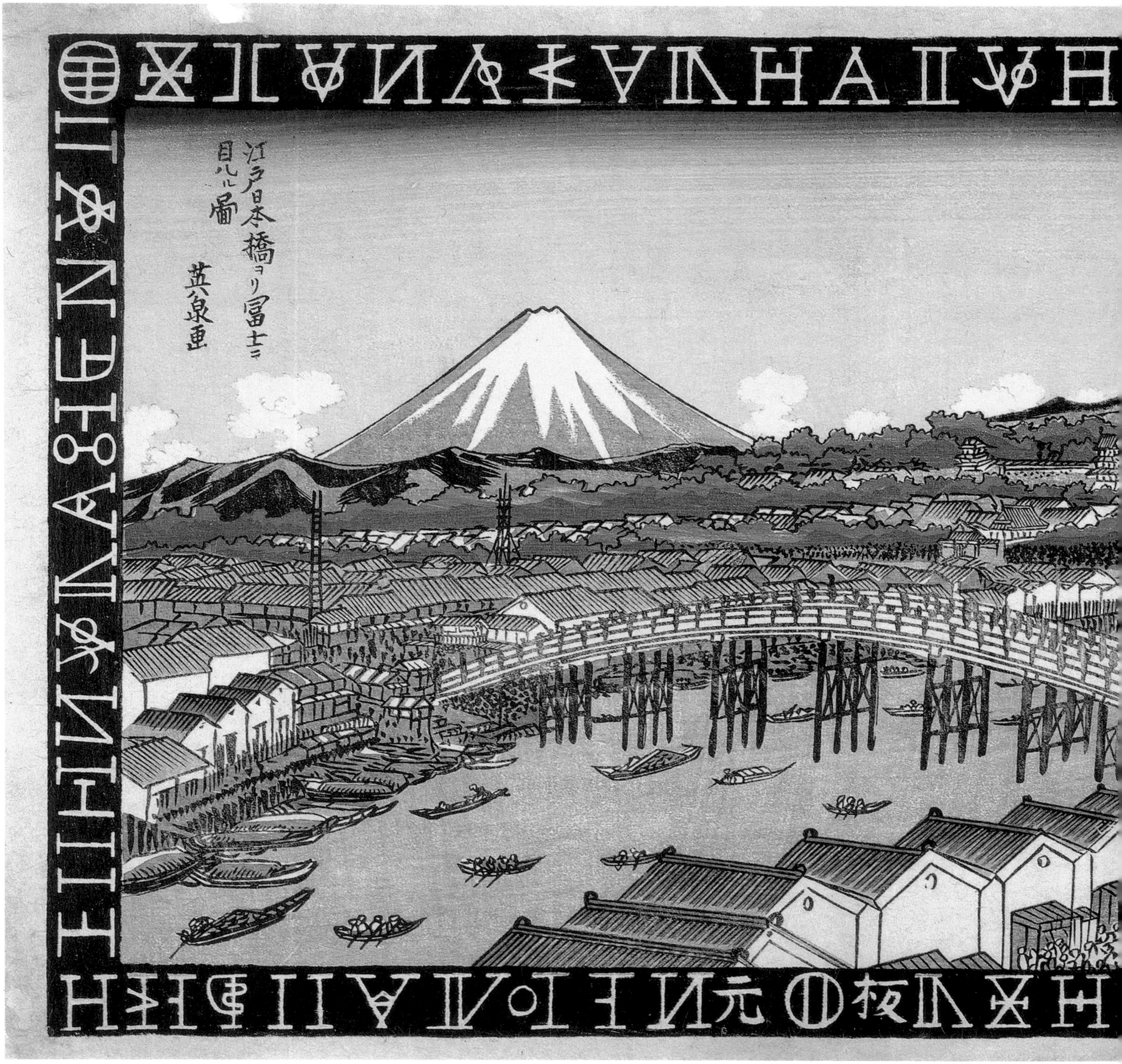
江戸日本橋ヨリ冨士ヲ見ル圖
英泉画

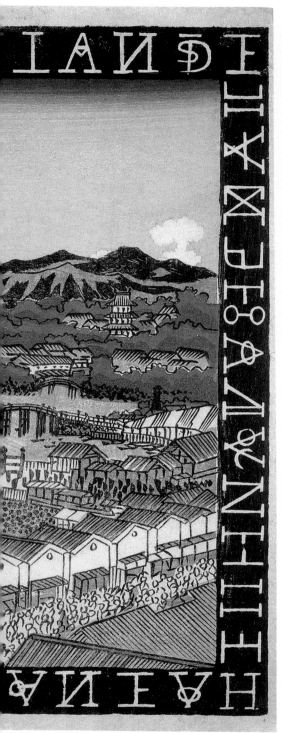

128
Mizuki Shigeru, *Nihon bashi asa no kei (The Bridge at Nihon Bashi in the Morning)* from the series *The fifty-three Stations on the Yôkaidô*.
© Mizuki Productions Co., Ltd. © Yanoman Corporation
© The Adachi Foundation for the Preservation of Woodcut Printings

129
Keisai Eisen, *Mount Fuji Seen from the Nihonbashi Bridge in the City of Edo*, *nishiki*-e print, first half of the nineteenth century. © Edo-Tokyo Museum

As Hokusai had done before him, Keisai Eisen paints a border round his landscape decorated with letters of the alphabet. Numerous masters of the *ukiyo-e* had a keen interest in perspective and in Western techniques, as well as in the frames around such pictures. Many took these as their inspiration, though they kept to their individual painting style. This *nanga**-type ("painting of the South") print attempts to capture light and shade, as well as the movement of the clouds scudding across the sky. On the edge of the frame, and mingling with other decorative notations, one can make out the letters "VOC," designating the Vereenigde Oostindische Compagnie (Dutch East India Company), a major importer of Far Eastern products to the West.

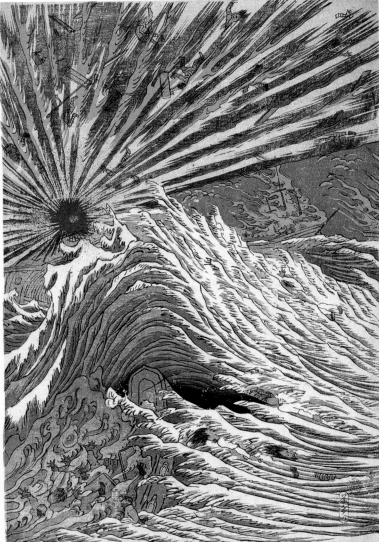

Kawanabe Kyôsai, *The Victory over the Mongol Pirate Boats*,
triptych *nishiki-e* print of *ôban* format, signed Seisei Kyôsai, 1863.
© Kawanabe Kyôsai Memorial Museum

In spite of the title harking back to Japan's victory, thanks
to a divinely sent wind, over eight hundred Mongolian vessels in the fourteenth century, Kyôsai locates the scene in
his own time, showing Western ships capsized by the
Japanese, in a reference to the population's xenophobia.

The movement of the waves, the explosions represented
by multicolored hatching, the ships in flames, and the men
struggling to escape the onrushing waters are rendered with
astonishing dynamism.

131

Katsushika Hokusai, *Strange Tales of the Crescent Moon*, story of Kyokutei Bakin in 28 volumes, 1807–11, Book 1, Part One. © National Research Institute for Cultural Properties, Tokyo

The heroes of this story are attacked by a creature spawned by the thunder that tries to blast them to kingdom come.

132

Katsushika Hokusai, *Strange Tales of the Crescent Moon*, story of Kyokutei Bakin in 28 volumes, 1807–1, Book 6. © National Research Institute for Cultural Properties, Tokyo

The deposed emperor decides to become king over all the forces of darkness and transforms himself into winged demon with a bird's face.

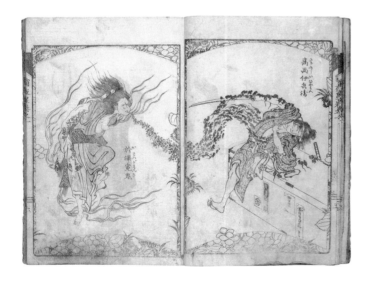

133

Katsushika Hokusai, *Star in a Night of Hoarfrost*, tale of Ryûtei Tanehiko, 1808. © National Research Institute for Farming Properties, Tokyo

The avenging ghost of Osawa, who had died following mistreatment by Ihyôe, spews out a swarm of rats in the latter's direction, which proceed to consume his abscess!

134

Katsushika Hokusai, *Snow in the Garden*, tale of Kyokutei (Takizawa) Bakin (1767–1848). © National Research Institute for Farming Properties, Tokyo

Usuyuki hime, "Princess Fine Snow," holding a lotus, suddenly sees a giant carp appear before her with an image of the bodhisattva Kannon on the top of its head. The dynamism here is reminiscent of Hokusai's wave.

135

Katsushika Hokusai, *Illustrated Life of Sākyamuni*, tale of Yamada Isai, Book 6, 1845. © National Research Institute for Cultural Properties, Tokyo

In this fictionalized account of the life of the Buddha, King Virudhaka, having refused to convert, is hurled into the Buddhist hell.

136

Katsushika Hokusai, *Illustrated Life of Sākyamuni*, tale of Yamada Isai, Book 5, 1845. © National Research Institute for Cultural Properties, Tokyo

Hokusai here illustrates the moment when Devadatta launches an attack on Sākyamuni. But the ground opens and swallows him up as the latter, flanked by his disciples, looks on.

137

Katsushika Hokusai, *Strange Tales of the Crescent Moon*, story of Kyokutei Bakin in 28 volumes, 1807–11, Book 3. © National Research Institute for Cultural Properties, Tokyo

In order to recover a casket, Emperor Shônei has a mound opened up that held captive the powers of evil. The trunk explodes, revealing Mô-un, a malicious monk.

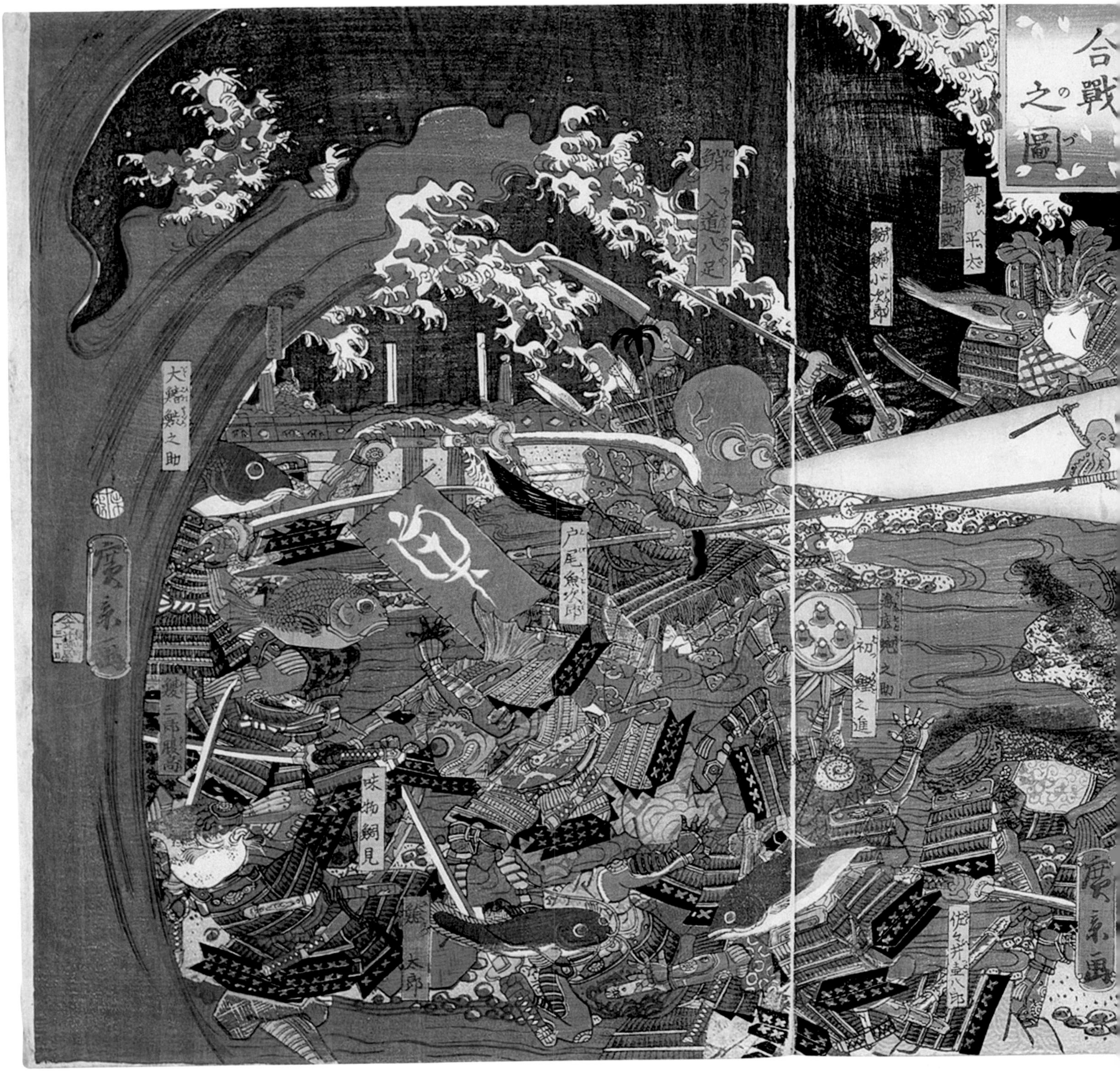

138
Utagawa Hirokage, *Great Battle of the Vegetables and Marine Animals*, triptych *nishiki-e* print, 1859.

Various sea animals—octopuses charging over the beach brandishing swords or savage-looking fish advancing towards the shore braving death—confront some valiant samurai with pumpkin faces. Behind this strange battle lurks the competition between the clans of Kii and Mito, and a critique of the political life of the time. Wriggling out of censorship was

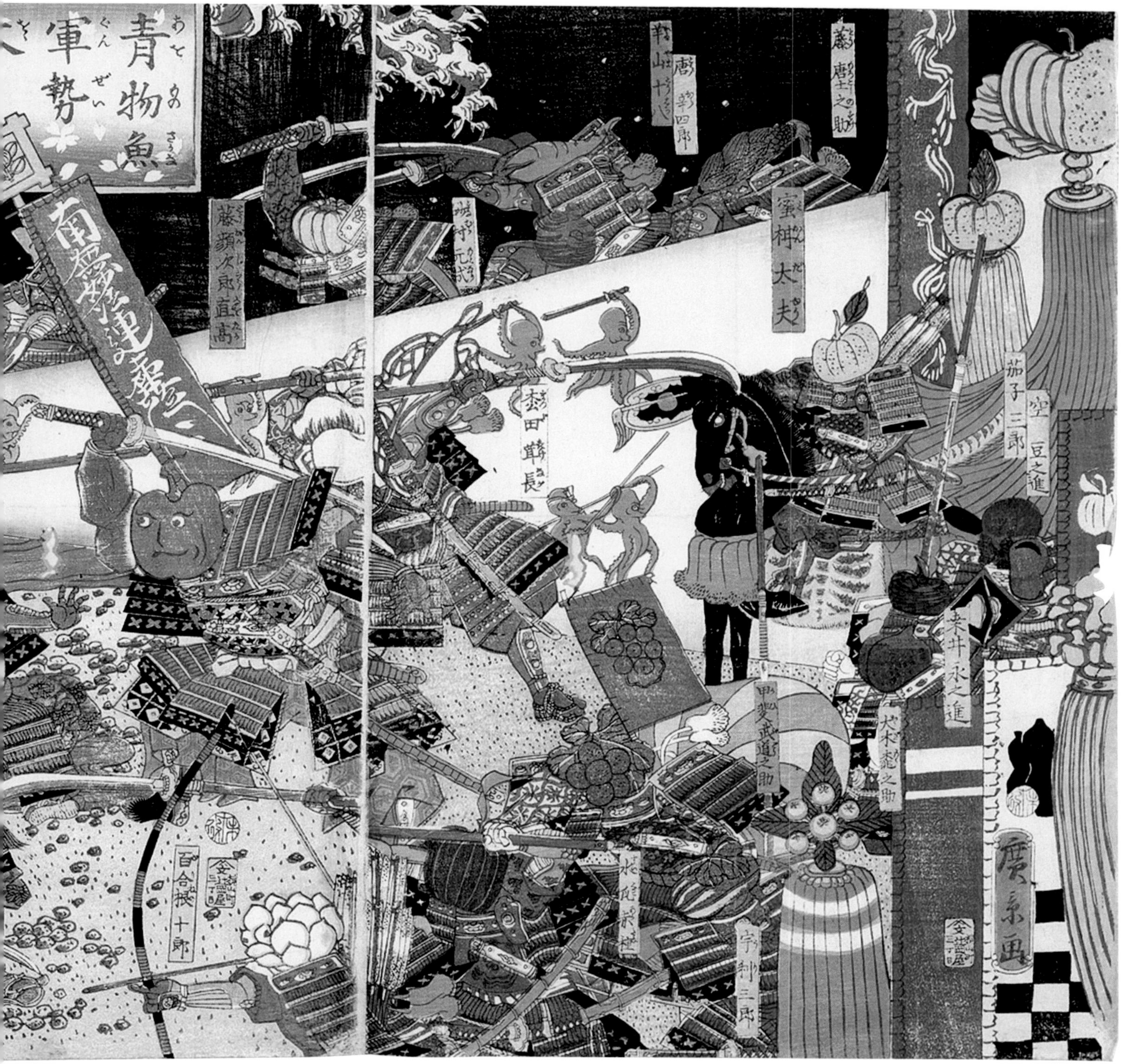
青物魚軍勢
蜜柑大夫
空豆之進
百合根十郎
廣景画

a constant bugbear for graphic artists in the Edo era: the explicit prohibition on representing politicians obliged them to exercise their imagination. On the verso of the print, notes allow the protagonists to be identified.

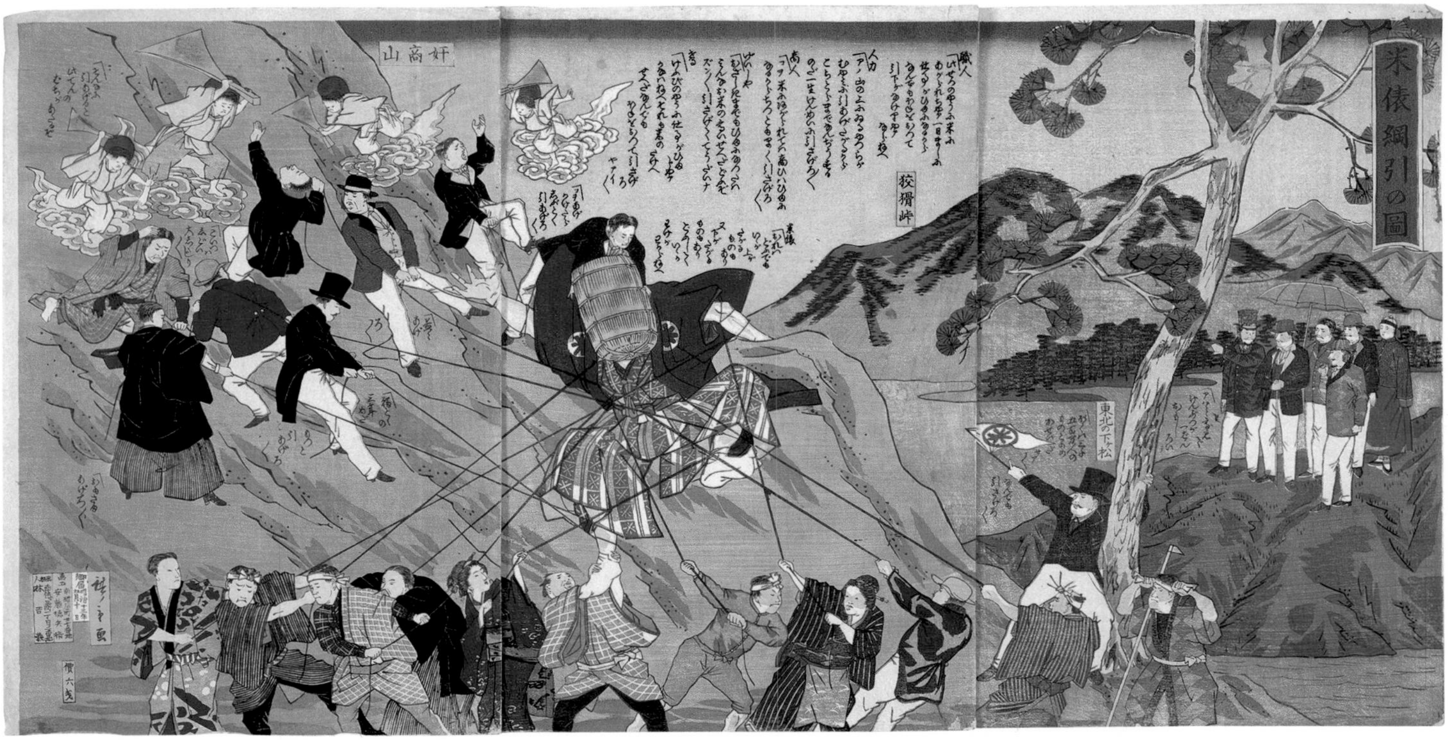
米俵綱引の圖

139
Utagawa Hiroshige II, *Tug-o'-War for a Ball of Rice*, *nishiki-e* print, 1880.

Contemporary political satire.

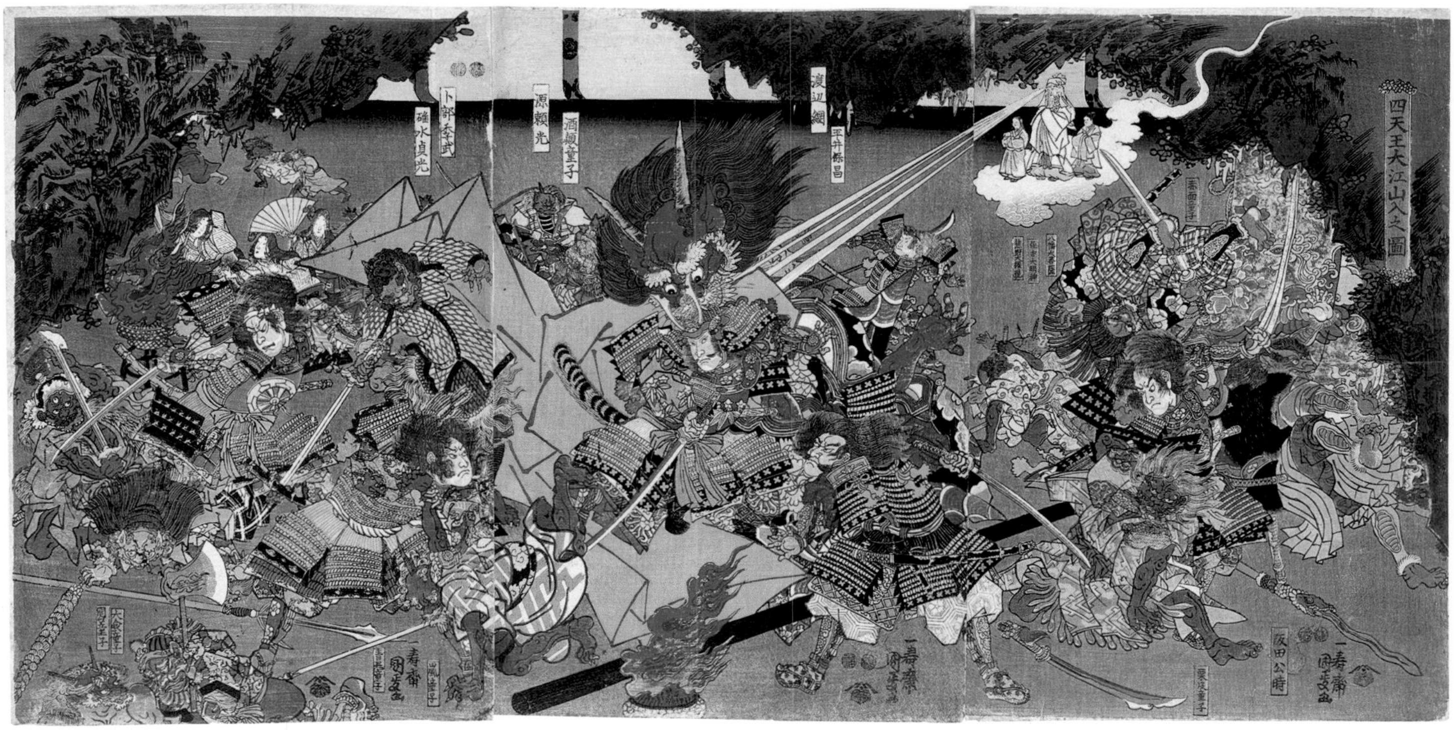
四天王大江山入之圖

140
Ichijusai Kunimasa (Utagawa Kunimasa), *Four Heavenly Kings on Mount Ooe*, triptych *nishiki-e* print, c. 1850.

These four guardians of Buddhist law are shown in full armor, vanquishing various devils.

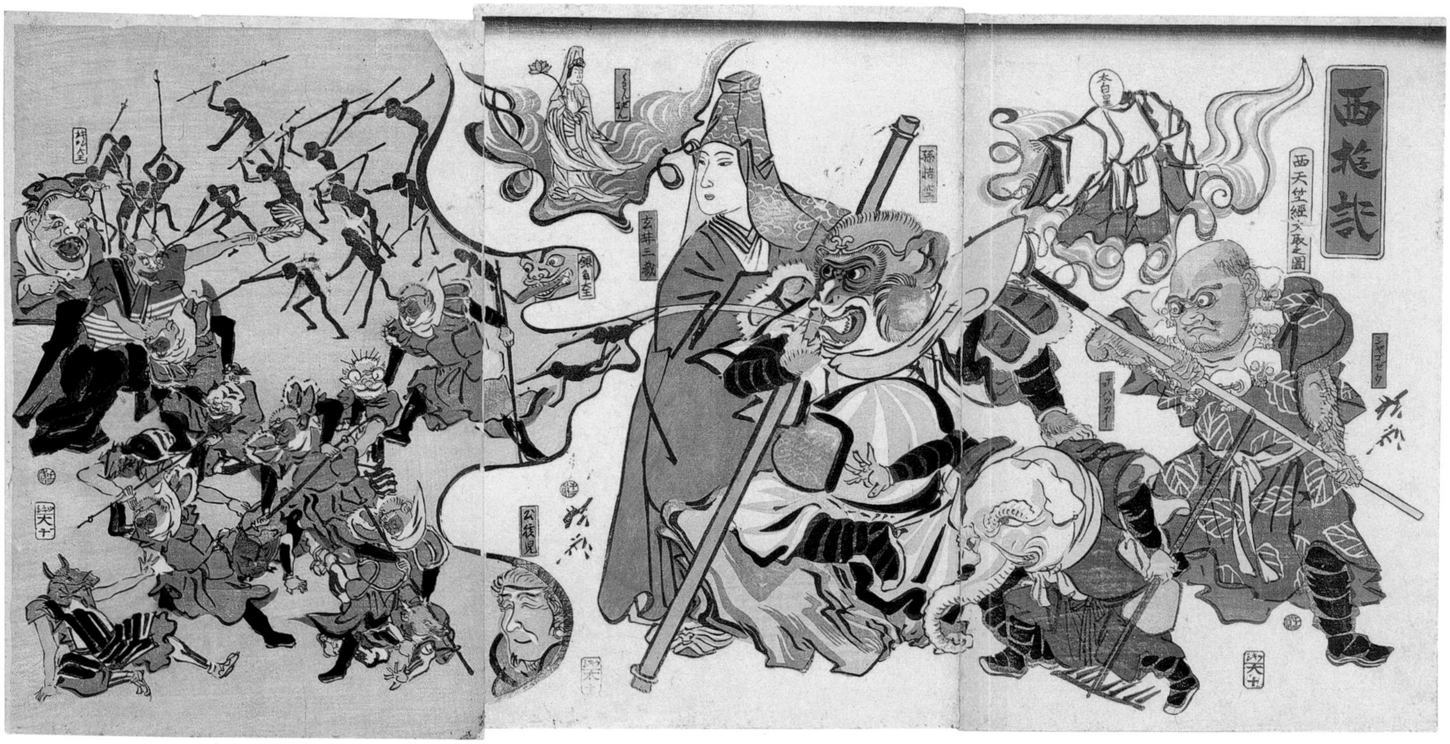
西遊記

141
Kawanabe Kyôsai, *Saiyûki (Nishi tenjiku kyômon tori No zu) (Accounts of a Journey to the West, or Training in the Sutras in India)*, *nishiki-e* print. © Kumon Institute of Education

This work concerns a long Chinese account dating from the sixteenth century and transmitted orally that records the voyage of a Chinese monk, Xuanzang (Japanese, Genjô Sanjô), to India to learn Buddhism. On the way, he bumps into Chohakkai, Sagojô, and the monkey, Songokû, who is able to take on all manner of forms; together, the four manage to dispatch eighty-one demons. In Japan, this story gained popularity in the Edo era.

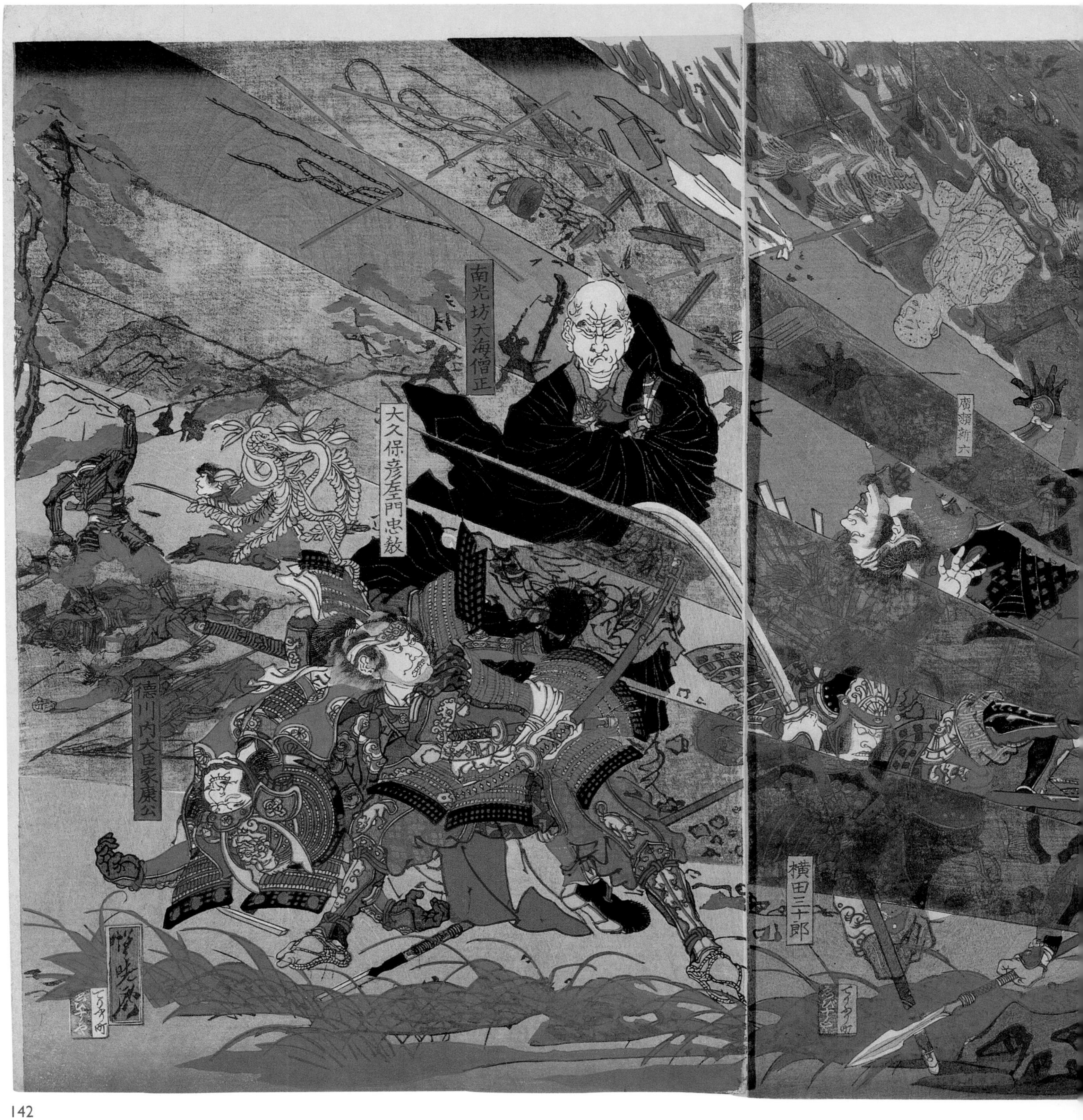
南光坊天海僧正
大久保彦左衛門忠教
徳川内大臣家康公
廣瀬新六
横田三十郎

142

Kawanabe Kyôsai, *The Battle of Nanba*, after 1871. © Kawanabe Kyôsai Memorial Museum

This battle was waged by Tokugawa Ieyasu against the partisans of Toyotomi Hideyori in 1615. In the Edo period it had always been forbidden to depict the Shogun. Four years after the beginning of the Meiji era, the subject was then relatively fresh. Remarkably powerful, the lines from the right convey the terrific violence of the explosion that reduces the Jizô* to smithereens.

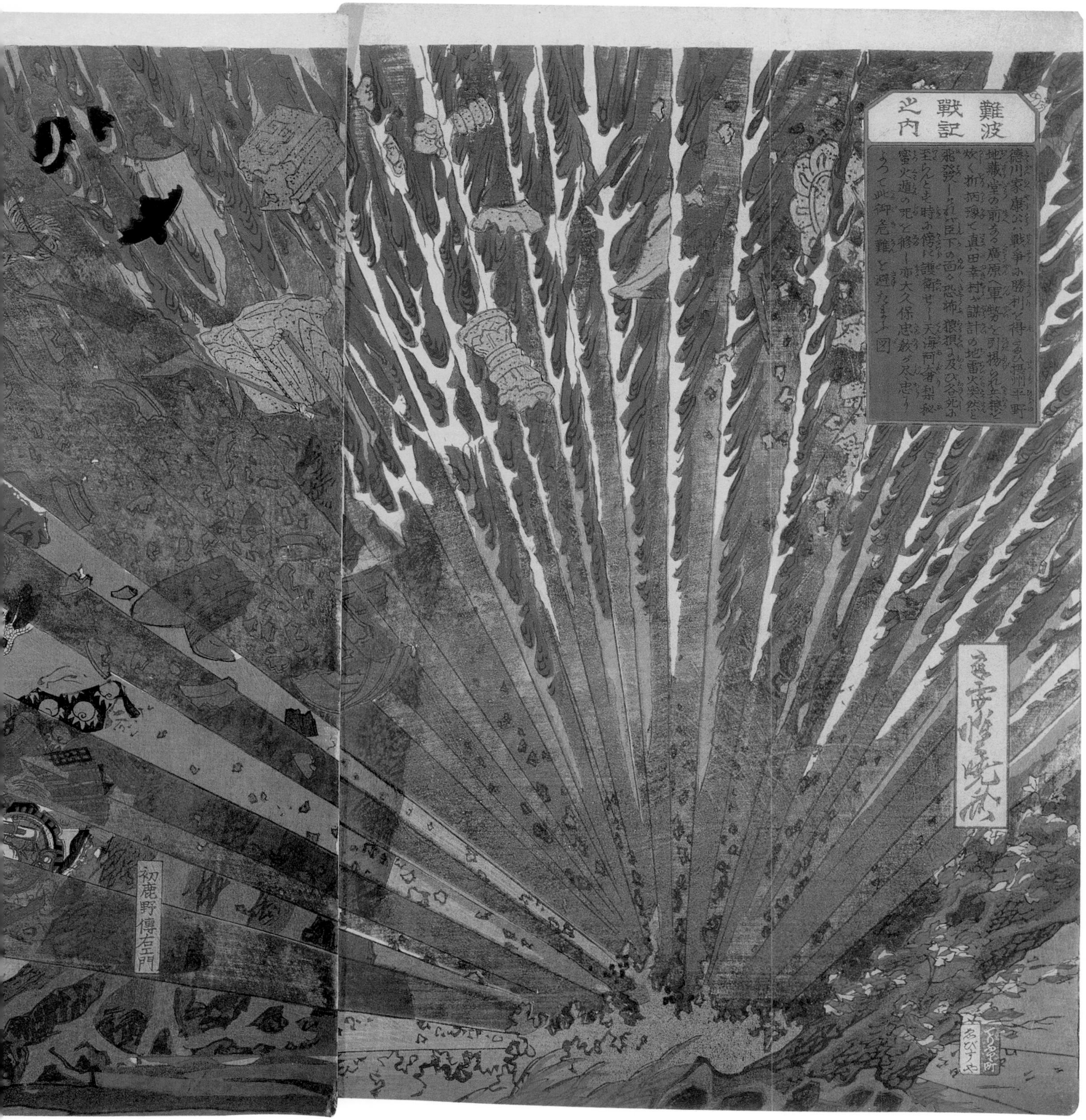
難波戦記之内
初鹿野傳右エ門

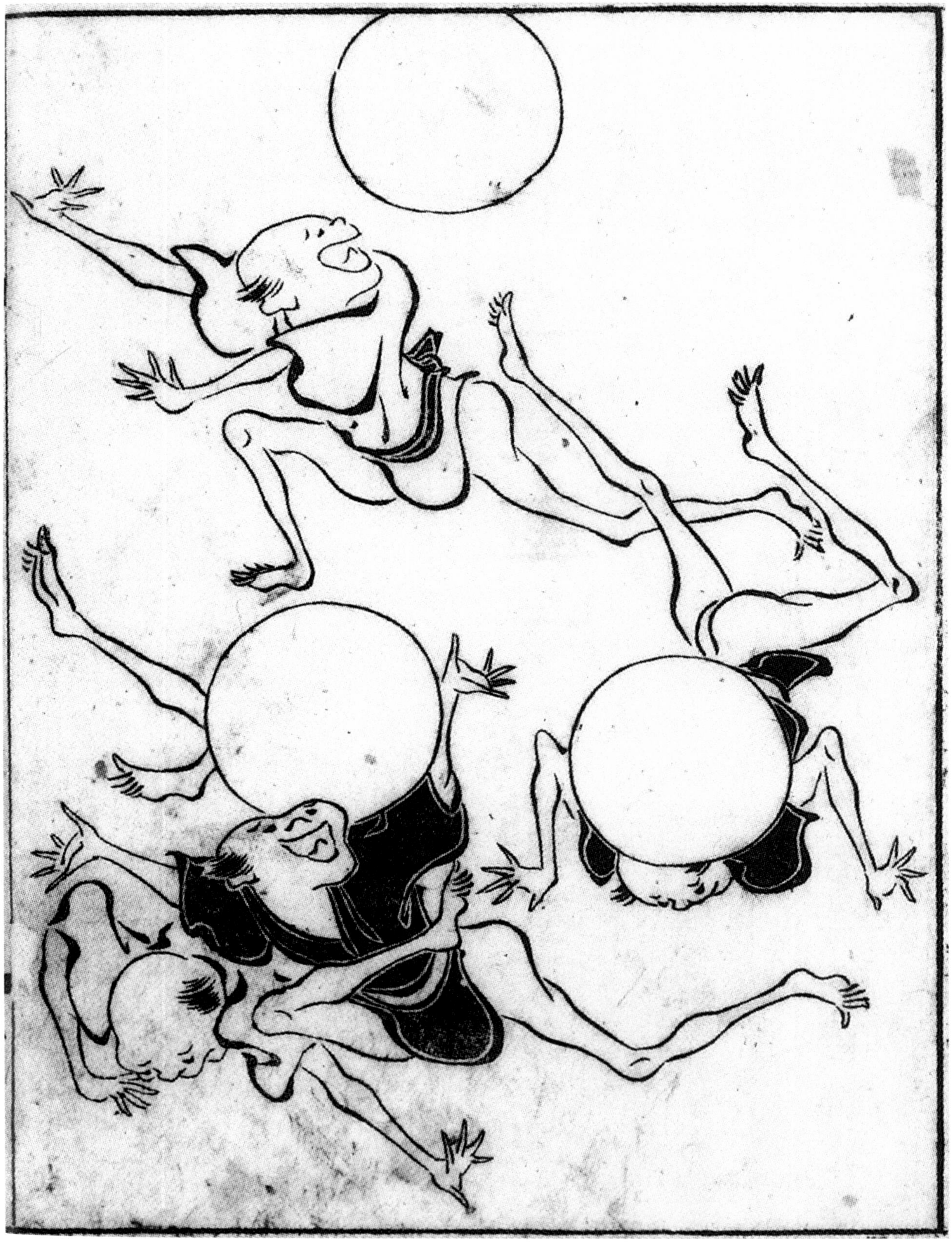

143–144
Takehaha Shunchôsi, typical examples of *tôba-e** from the Edo era. © Matsumoto Leiji Collection

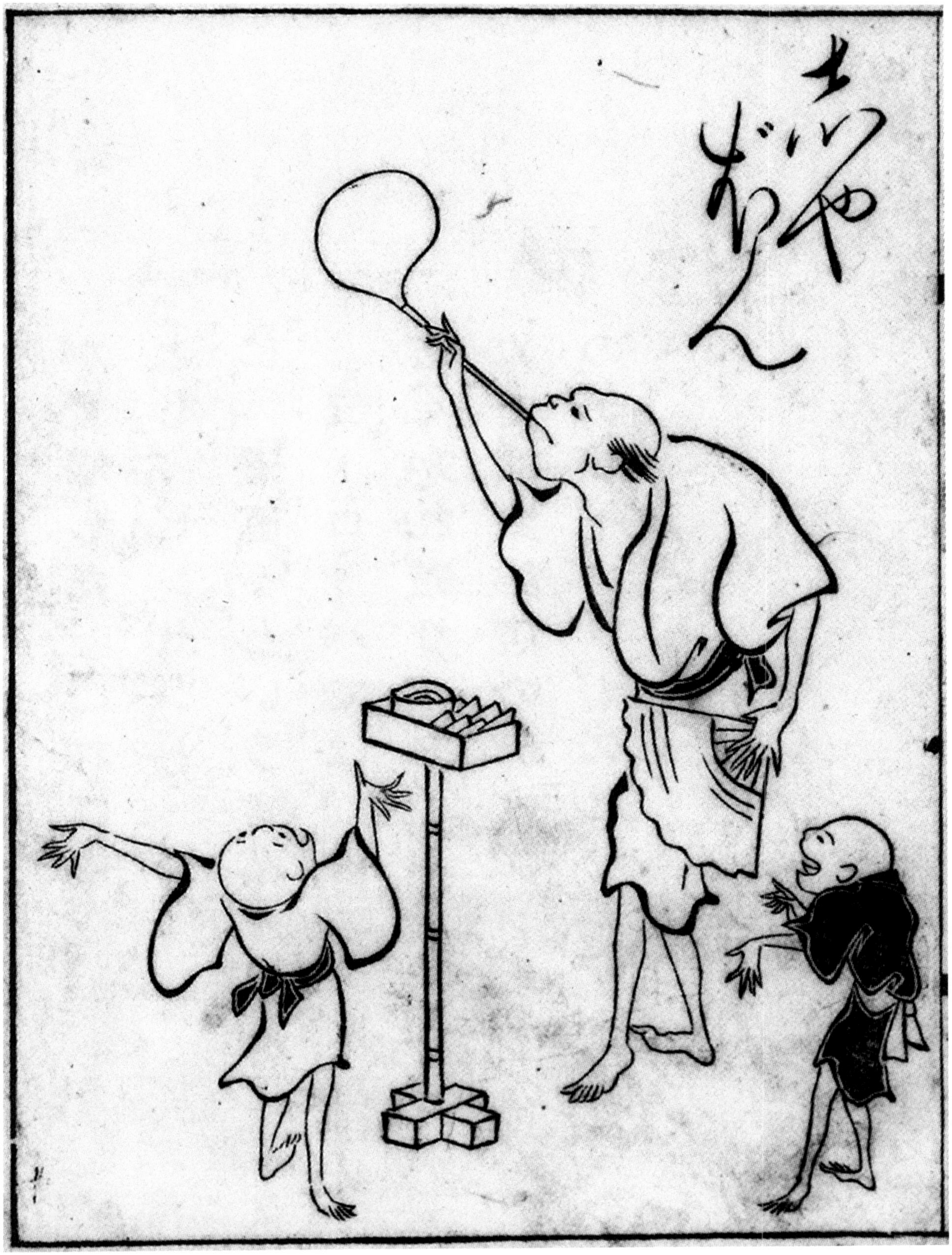

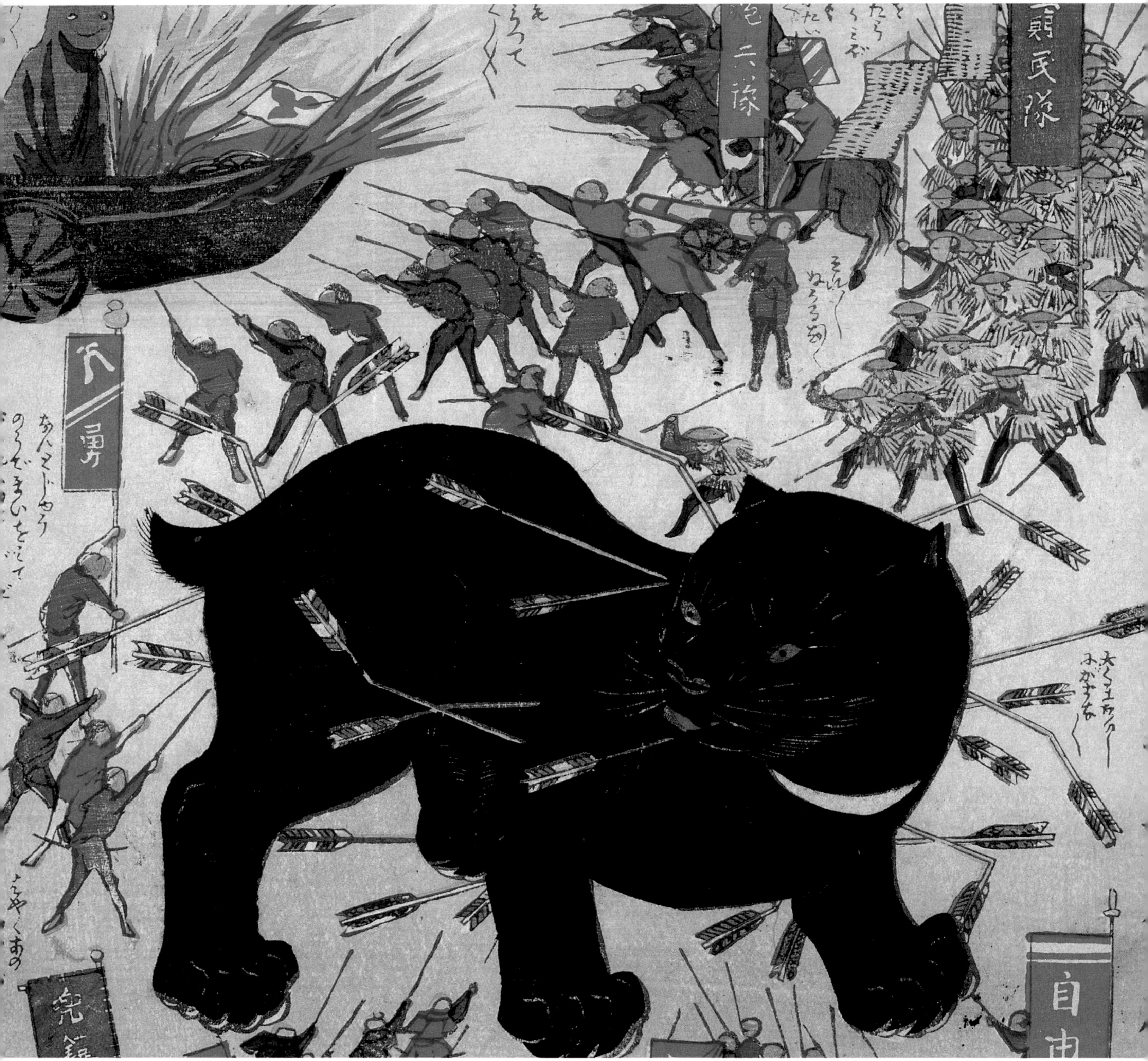
兵隊
民隊
勇

Fig. 156 (detail)

THE DAWN OF A NEW TYPE OF CARICATURE: JAPAN OPENS UP TO THE WEST

From the end of the eighteenth century, Western countries multiplied their attempts to begin trading and forge diplomatic relations with Japan. Though for several decades such efforts proved in vain, by the middle of the nineteenth century they had finally borne fruit. In 1853, Commodore Perry entered the Bay of Uraga and demanded the opening of negotiations in the name of the President of the United States and, by the following year, a treaty had been signed. Europeans, too, soon succeeded in drafting similar agreements.

The *bakufu** (government of Tokugawa), which supported the opening up of the country, was attacked by partisans who demanded further resistance. With the slogan "*sonnô jôi*" ("respect for the emperor, expulsion of the foreigners"), their movement gained broad currency and was seconded by significant clans, such as Satsuma and Chôshû. This led in 1867 to the removal of the Shogun Tokugawa Yoshinobu and to the restoration of the imperial power one year later. This event, known as the "Meiji Restoration," marked the beginning of a new era. The political, legal, territorial, and economic system was entirely recast: the feudal system was permanently abandoned and a modern capitalist state was born.

These radical changes had an upsetting effect on the life of the Japanese. The inhabitants of the capital, renamed Tokyo in 1868, watched with astonishment as their city was transformed almost daily. Tokyo now had little of the charm of Edo* that had made the city into one of the favorite subjects of painters of *ukiyo-e**. At the request of the government, aid from the West was sought to teach technology and science. New buildings were soon springing up in various districts, making Tokyo a modern city lit by streetlighting.

Various means of transport were born that ousted the sedan chair. The rickshaw, a Japanese invention, appeared in Tokyo streets in 1870, followed by imported bicycles and horse-drawn carriages. The following year the first railway line connecting Tokyo's Shinbashi station to the city of Yokohama* was inaugurated. The year 1871 saw the introduction of a new currency: the yen.

The *chonmage** topknot and the wearing of the sword having been banned, men started adopting Western-style costume. Soldiers, police officers, and firemen now had uniforms. The kimono and

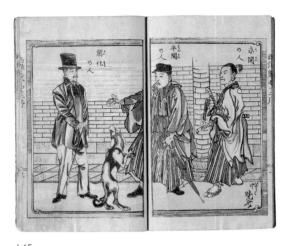

145

Seiyô dochû hizakurige (Shank's Mare to the Western Seas), a novel by Kanagaki Robun, illustrated by Kawanabe Kyôsai, published between 1870 and 1876. © Kawanabe Kyôsai Memorial Museum

On the right we have "a man closed to Westernization"; he wears traditional Japanese costume. In the middle, "a man half-open to civilization," who has adopted the hairstyle, scarf, umbrella, and shoes of the West. On the left is "a man open to civilization," proudly parading in a new suit and topper. Kyôsai pokes fun at his country's excessive Westernization and observes with humor his compatriots' vacillation between two sartorial styles that could spawn some odd hybrids.

*hakama** survived, but those wishing to be in the swing sported hat and umbrella. Fig. 145

Sartorial metamorphosis among women was notable only by the 1880s. The first hybrid hairstyles still owed much to those of previous eras. Then, with the adoption of the dress as against the kimono, they too began to be westernized. Among divers innovations, it was those concerning cooking that must have had the greatest repercussion on everyday life among the Japanese. The government encouraged the population to consume certain products in contravention of Buddhist teaching, such as milk or meat. Even beef dishes began appearing in restaurants. The *anpan**, little round buns filled with kidney-bean paste, attracted consumers in droves, as did beer now that too was brewed in the archipelago. Illustrated books were published to explain newfangled foreign dishes. The use of forks and spoons, however, long remained something of a puzzle to the Japanese.

Even the pleasure quarter of Yoshiwara* seemed to lose much of its attraction at this time, the Japanese being intrigued by more novel distractions. Many parks were created; circuses, acrobats, and fountains sucked in the crowds, as did circular constructions presenting huge panoramic paintings. The Japanese who, since the Edo period, had been fond of animals from distant lands, flooded into recently created zoos.

The school system too was entirely overhauled: a multitude of primary schools and colleges made their appearance. In primary schools, open to all children from six to fourteen, pupils studied seated on chairs before a desk. The ministry in charge of education had schoolbooks from various countries translated and adapted, and wholly new subjects were introduced. Foreign professors taught a whole generation of literati in the newly founded universities.

The Japanese also showed considerable interest in discovering Western music. The army started by adopting the trumpet, and musicians were soon being classically trained to play at balls and receptions thrown by the government. In the 1890s, it became the thing for girls of good family to learn the violin.

The government was determined that a new generation should drink at the wellsprings of Western knowledge. To this end, missions were sent out to Europe and to the United States and students could

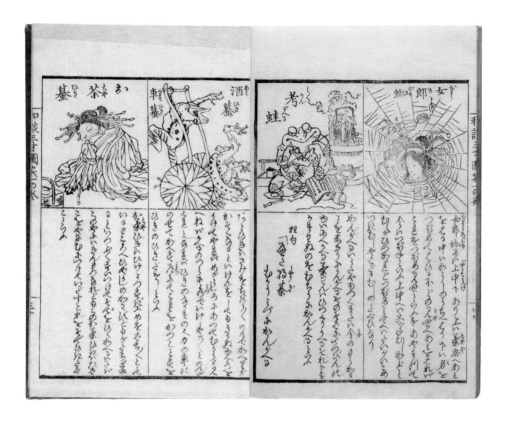

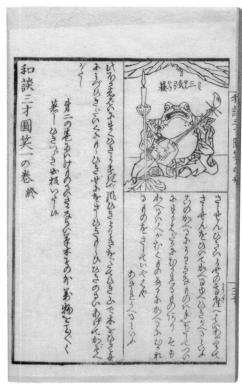

146–147
Wadan sansai zu e (Diverting Encyclopedia of Smiles),
a work by Mantei Ôga, illustrated by Kawanabe Kyôsai,
published in 1873. © Kawanabe Kyôsai Memorial Museum

Animals adopt human form in this humorous encyclopedia.
Playing with words and ideograms, Kyôsai composed drawings with more than one meaning, such as this one entitled
Jôrôgumo. The spider possesses a female face whose hair is
studded with many combs. *Jôrô*, however, can mean both
"big spider" and "spider courtesan"…

148

Sugiura Hinako, *Futatsu Makura (Lacquer Pillows; Wind on the Flowers)*.
© Suzuki Michiko, *Complete Works of Sugiura Hinako*, vol. 1,
Tokyo: Chikuma Shobô, 1995

This spider reappears in the chapter "Conversation in the
Green Houses [i.e. pleasure houses]" of the manga *Futatsu
Makura (Lacquer Pillows)* by Sugiura Hinako.

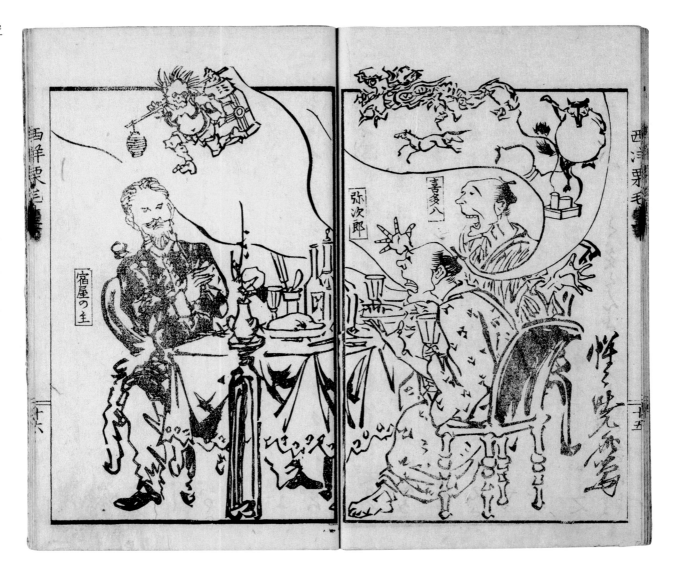

149
Seiyô dochû hizakurabe (Shank's Mare to the Western Seas),
a novel by Kanagaki Robun, illustrated by Kawanabe Kyôsai, published between 1870 and 1876.
© Kawanabe Kyôsai Memorial Museum

The writer here creates a pastiche of another famous novel by Jippensha Ikku (1765–1831), *Tôkaidô dôchû Hizakurige* (Journey on Foot along the Tokaido), which describes in plain but comical language some of the remoter provinces that the Japanese dreamed of discovering.

Here, we follow two characters, Yaji and Kita, just as in the comic stories of the Edo period. On their way to the World's Fair in London, they have to travel across many countries and endure countless adventures. The caricature alludes to a legation sent to London in 1862 by the Edo government, which subsequently stayed in Paris for three weeks. Kyôsai points up various amusing situations, showing in particular how the Japanese would sit at a table with a Westerner; what they really think is shown in the word-bubbles (they seem to compare him to some sort of monster!).

obtain bursaries to continue their studies abroad. The better-off Japanese started traveling beyond their borders. Fig. 149

So it was that Japan was opening up to the world just as the vogue took off in Europe for the traditional art and social mores of the Edo epoch. The Japanese government which, shortly before the Restoration had taken part in the Paris World's Fair of 1867, noted with amazement the Western passion for the prints and decorative arts of the homeland. So as to give a fillip to the export of these objects to pave the way for future World's Fairs, the powers that be organized various events aimed at demonstrating that the expertise of present-day craftsmen was in no way inferior to that of earlier periods.

With a trepidation tinged with enthusiasm, the Japanese watched as their country and way of life underwent a total transformation. Painters and caricaturists deployed all their talent in portraying these wholesale changes in the fledgling Press. Figs. 151–152

荷宝蔵壁のむだ書

150
Utagawa Kuniyoshi, *Amusing Drawings on the Wall of a Storehouse full of Treasure*, *nishiki-e* print, between 1847 and 1852. © Kumon Institute of Education, Ichiyûsai Kuniyoshi

官許
繪新聞
日本地

151–152
Cover (left) and introductory page (right) of the first number of the journal *E Shinbun Nipponchi*, in 1874, illustrated by Kawanabe Kyôsai. On the cover, Kyôsai can be seen in the company of the man of letters and journalist, Kanagaki Robun. © Tokyo University, Meiji Shinbun Zasshi Bunko

This review only lasted a few numbers. Kyôsai, however, found other outlets for his humorous critique of excessive Westernization.

The rise of the media: caricature and comic strip

At the very beginning of the seventeenth century, broadsheets containing news for the population had started to appear in Osaka, before making their way to Edo. These woodblock prints were read by criers, as well as being handed out or sold. Tolerated as long as they did not criticize the ruling powers, it was not long before they added illustrations.

The first genuine newspaper, the twice-weekly and English *Nagasaki Shipping List and Advisor*, saw the light of day in Nagasaki in 1861. The following year, the *bakufu* brought out the first periodical in Japanese, *Kanpan Batavia Shinbun* (Official Publication of the Gazette of Batavia), which diffused news from the Dutch East Indies. Other irregular publications soon followed and, ten years later, the first major national dailies were issued: the *Yokohama Mainichi Shinbun* was launched in 1871, followed by the *Tokyo Nichinichi Shinbun* the following year.

The Japanese print betrayed its close links with the fledgling Press in the birth of the *Shinbun Nishikie* in 1874: this "Prints Journal" presented the events of the last months in picture form accompanied by texts. This type of gazette, which became very popular, was soon replaced by more modern newspapers that abandoned xylography.

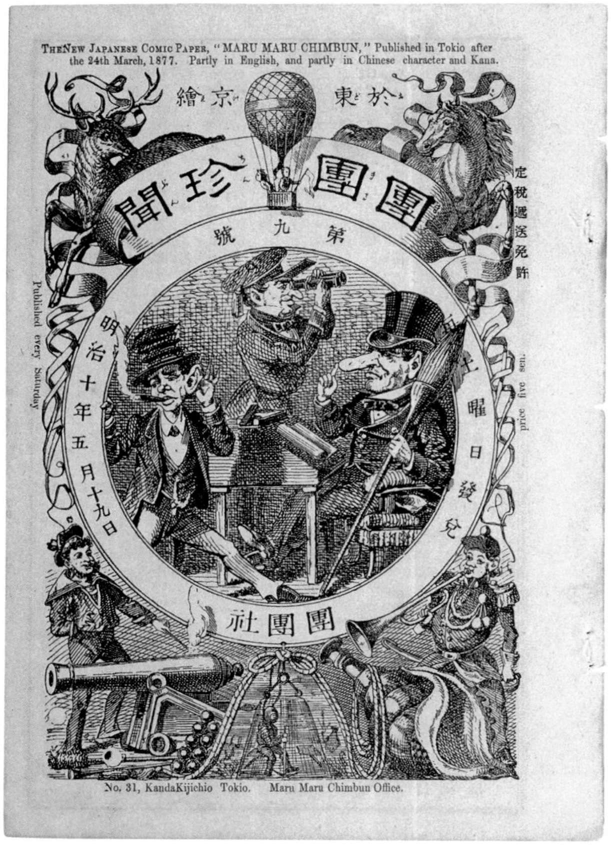
THE NEW JAPANESE COMIC PAPER, "MARU MARU CHIMBUN," Published in Tokio after the 24th March, 1877. Partly in English, and partly in Chinese character and Kana.
團團珍聞
團團社
Published every Saturday
No. 31, KandaKijichio Tokio. Maru Maru Chimbun Office.

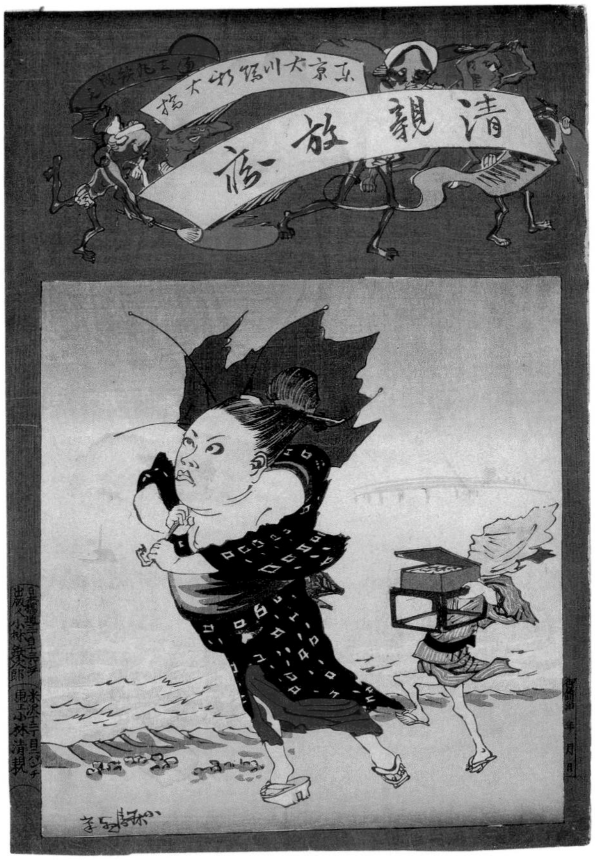

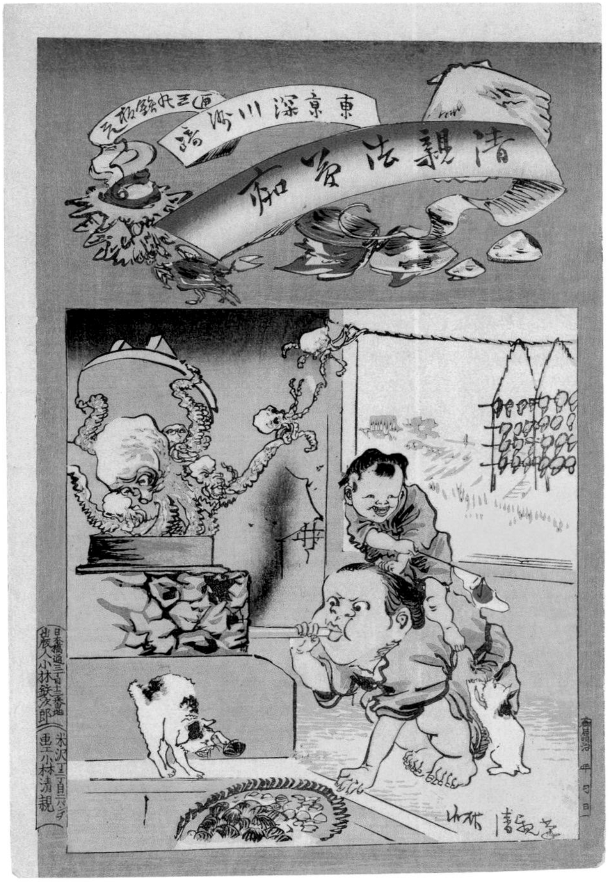

153
Cover of number nine of the caricature review, *Marumaru Shinbun*, which played a pioneering role in the field, May 10, 1877.
© Nihon Manga Shiryô-kan

154
Kobayashi Kiyochika (Kobayashi Tetsujirô), *Kiyochika Ponchi*, woodblock print, 1881. © Edo-Tokyo Museum

Caricature print.

155
Kobayashi Kiyochika (Kobayashi Tetsujirô), *Fukagawa Suzaki in Tokyo*, woodblock print, 1881. © Edo-Tokyo Museum

This drawing features numerous humorous allusions that readers of the time could easily understand, but which are almost impossible to decode today.

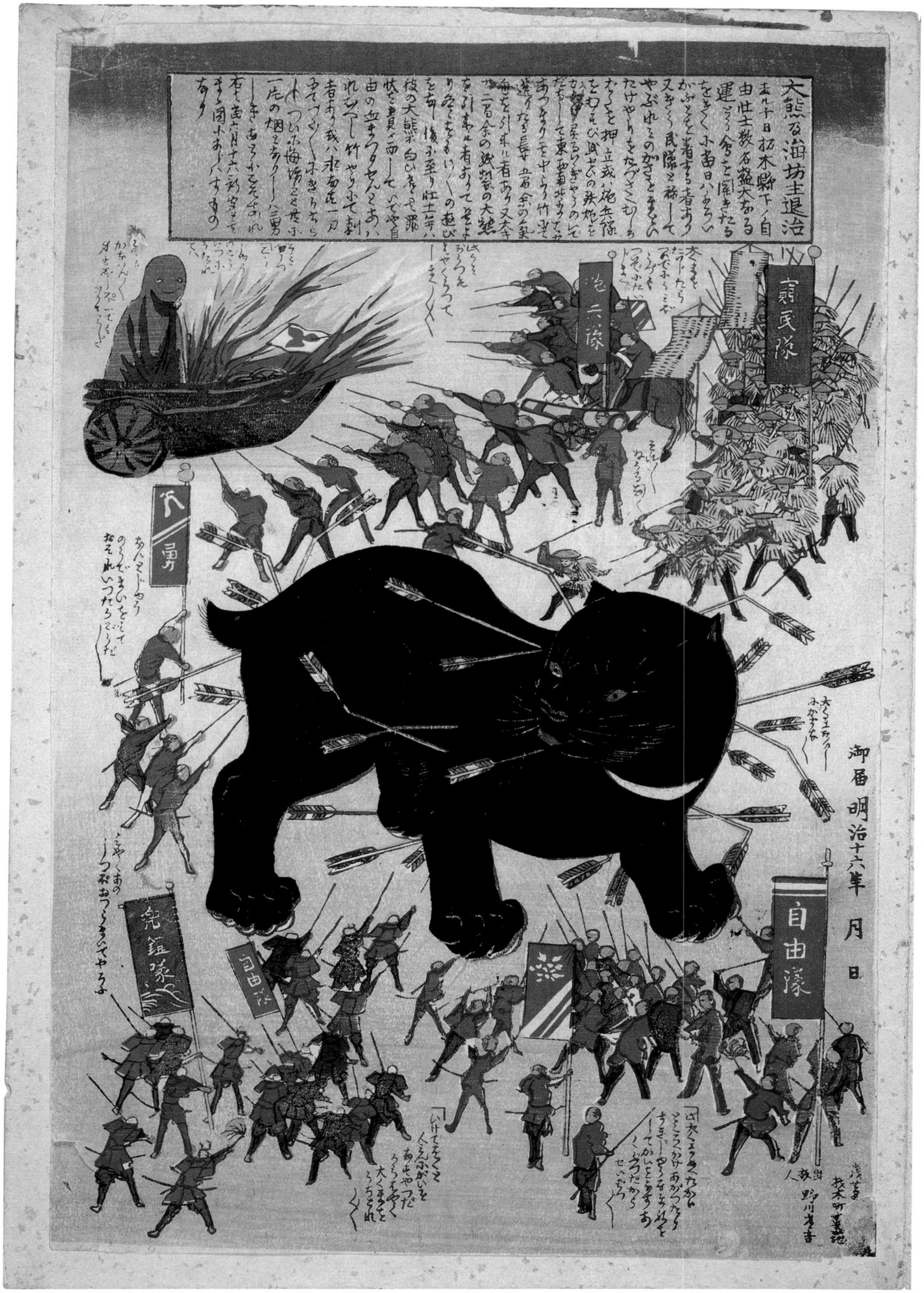
窮民隊
砲兵隊
自由隊
御届明治十六年 月 日

156
Anonymous, *The Extermination of the Bald Ôkuma Shigenobu*, 1883.

This image is not—as might be imagined—an illustration to a folktale, but a virulent political squib.

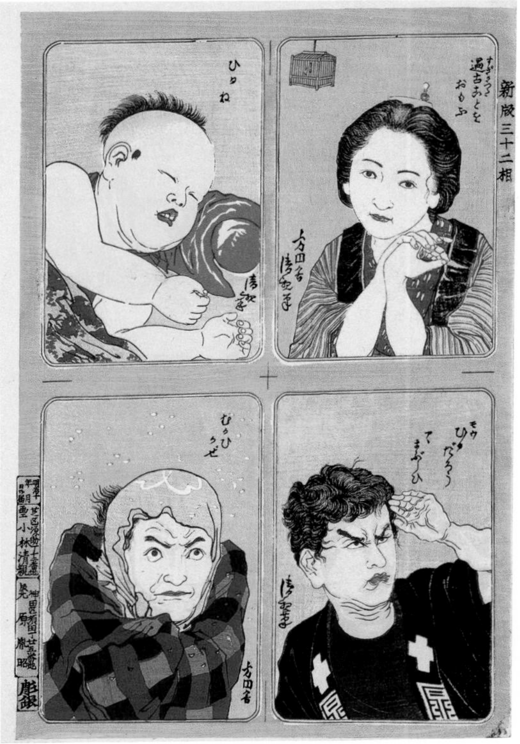
新版三十二相

157
Kobayashi Kiyochika (Kobayashi Tetsujirô), *Thirty-two New Caricatures*, 1877. © Machida City Museum

In this woodblock print taken from a series of eight, Kiyochika depicts various facial expressions with singular humor.

Exactly when the first caricature and satirical drawings against the government appeared in the Edo period is not known. In a convoluted manner, Katsushika Hokusai had already criticized the decadent lifestyle of the nobles and the representatives of the government in one of the last volumes of his *Manga*. The flame was then taken up by other artists, such as Utagawa Hiroshige, Kawanabe Kyôsai, and especially Utagawa Kuniyoshi, one of the most brilliant caricaturists of his Fig. 150 time. During the Meiji era, intellectuals and men of letters, such as Fukuzawa Yukichi, Nakae Chômin, and Kanagaki Robun, who had a thorough knowledge of the Occident, sought to promote the caricature. At this point in time, political satires multiplied: in 1874, there appeared the first review with caricatures, *E Shinbun Nipponchi*. In Figs. 151–152 1877, a new weekly journal, *Marumaru Shinbun*, enjoyed great success with its critical and its satirical drawings. By means of this publication, it was the hope of its founder, Nomura Eumio, who had studied for a time in Britain, to promote the civil rights movement. Around him, he gathered together the best writers and artists, including Kobayashi Kiyochika (1847–1915), celebrated for his many cari- Figs. 153–157 catures. The review continued to appear until 1907.

Two pioneers from the West: the caricaturists Charles Wirgman and Georges Bigot

The world of Japanese caricature was about to be turned on its head by an Englishman and a Frenchman.

The painter and caricaturist Charles Wirgman (1832–1891) arrived in 1861 as a correspondent of *The Illustrated London News*. The following year he founded a review, *The Japan Punch*, aimed at Fig. 158 the expatriate community in Yokohama but also published in Japanese, which continued to appear until 1887. In it, he published many *ponchi-e**, i.e. caricatures (*ponchi* comes from the word "Punch"), the main subject being Japanese society and customs. The followers whom he taught to paint in oils included Takahashi Yûichi and Kobayashi Kiyochika.

Through works that introduced Western humor for the first time, and with a drawing technique that deliberately accentuated facial features, Wirgman left a deep imprint on the caricature and on the beginnings of the Japanese comic strip of the time.

In common with Charles Wirgman, and unknown in his homeland, the French painter and illustrator Georges Bigot (1860–1927) left a host of caricatures of Japanese society. After studying at the Beaux-Arts, he made drawings for Parisian newspapers like *La Vie moderne*, or for novels, such as Zola's *Nana*. In 1881, he met the painter Félix Régamey, who told him about a journey he had undertaken to Japan with Émile Guimet, and about the illustrations Régamey had provided for Louis Gonse's book, *L'Art japonais*. Fired with enthusiasm for the culture of the country, Bigot decided to learn the *ukiyo-e* print technique. He left for Japan, arriving in 1882, and remained there for nearly twenty years. While teaching drawing at the Military Academy in Tokyo, he also Figs. 5–8 begun to publish albums. In 1884, as his contract came to an end, Bigot launched the review *Tôba-e**, named after the monk Tôba to whom the Fig. 160 scroll *Chôjû jinbutsu giga (Frolicking Animals and People)* is ascribed. He hoped through this to earn his keep.

A painter of everyday life, Bigot also tackled political subjects; Fig. 159 although the censors often took a dim view of his satires, he carried on regardless. He was also among the first to divide his drawings into squares or panels. Unlike the foreigners employed by the government, who received a substantial wage, Bigot found it hard to live off his work. Caricature was then regarded as a minor genre and his talent was not as appreciated as it should have been. He wanted to found an art salon in collaboration with other Japanese painters, but this much-cherished project too came to naught. When the Sino-Japanese conflict flared up in 1894, he left for China, having secured a contract with *The Graphic* in London to make drawings of the war. Shortly before his departure, Bigot had married a Japanese woman, with whom he had a little boy, named Maurice, who was born during his absence.

The albums he published subsequently were increasingly satirical, and this critical stance on Japanese life was scarcely tailor-made to please. Embittered and disappointed by the breakneck changes he saw in society and attitudes, he obtained a divorce, and in 1899 left Japan definitively with his son. In France, Bigot continued his career as an illustrator for various Parisian newspapers, before producing popular prints for the Imagerie d'Épinal. Yet, at the bottom of his Figs. 161–162 heart, he continued to cherish the memory of a Japan that had vanished forever.

THE JAPAN PUNCH
YOKO.HAMA
1883 april

158
Charles Wirgman, cover to the April 1883 issue of *The Japan Punch*.
© Archive of Japanese Cartoon History

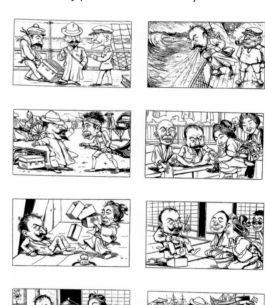

159
Georges Bigot, *Westerners Finding It Hard to Adapt to Japanese Life*, lithograph, no date.
© Kawasaki City Museum

Bigot adds a sentence between each square.

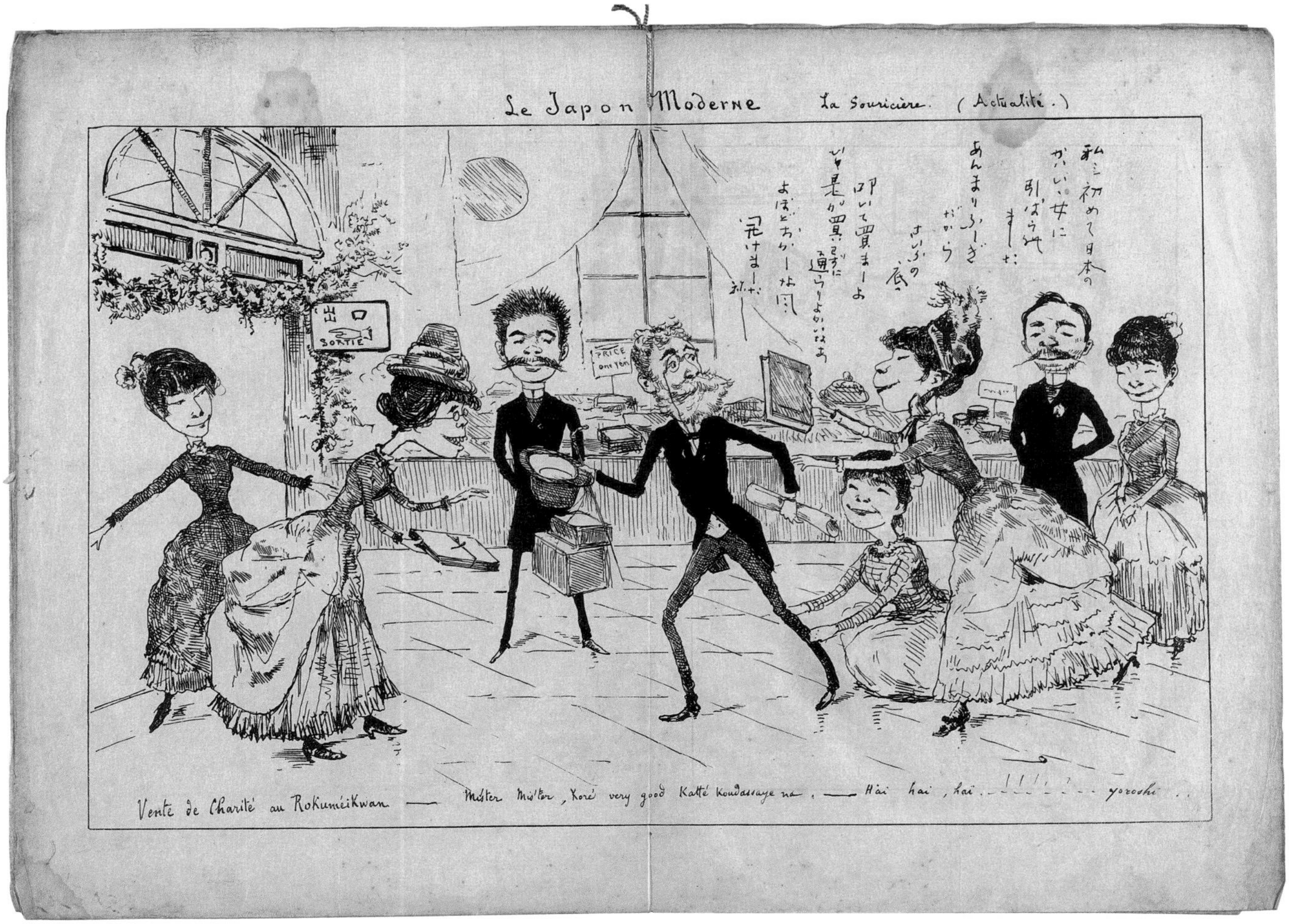
Le Japon Moderne
La Souricière. (Actualité.)
出口
SORTIE
Vente de Charité au Rokumeikwan — Mister Mister, Koré very good Katté Koudassaye na. — Hai hai, hai. ... yoroshi

160
Georges Bigot, *Tôba-e (Satirical Newspaper, Modern Japan)*,
first year, no. 20, bimonthly, drawings, 1887. © Waseda University Library

For each number of this famous journal, Georges Bigot provided cartoons of great quality accompanied by a text in French and Japanese.

In this caricature entitled *Charity Sale in the Rokumeikan*, Bigot has fun mixing the two languages in the French caption: "Mister, mister, *koré* very good, *katté koudassaye na.—Hai hai hai yoroshii*" ("Mister, mister, this is very beautiful, please buy it.—Yes, yes, yes, I get it.").

The Rokumeikan—a building built in 1883 in the Western style by the English architect Josiah Conder (1852–1920)—was a venue for receptions and balls to which were invited both Japanese high society and Western diplomats. It was there that Japanese women, dolled up in the Parisian fashion, vied with each other in elegance and did their utmost to learn Western dances and good manners. Parties and charity fêtes at the Rokumeikan were a favorite subject with artists, and frequently appeared in paintings and caricatures.

Le jeu de volant
La petite guerre
Les poissons volants
La pêche aux crabes
Fête des garçons
(Nobori Koyé)
Le *shamissen*
Les premiers pas de la poupée
Le ballon
Le cerf-volant

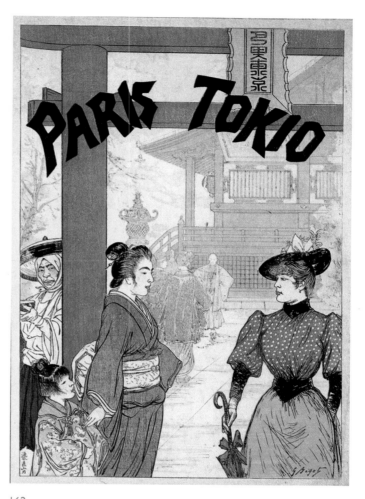

161
Georges Bigot, *Japanese Children's Games*, lithograph, Imagerie d'Épinal, c. 1905. © Archive of Japanese Cartoon History

PARIS TOKIO

162
Georges Bigot, *Paris Tokio*, woodblock print, 1900. © Archive of Japanese Cartoon History

Bigot had acquired mastery of the xylographic technique of the Japanese print, as this poster for the World Fair's of 1900, executed in the Edo tradition, testifies. At a time when the West was so fascinated by Japan, the eyes of two women—from countries so remote and yet with so much in common—meet....

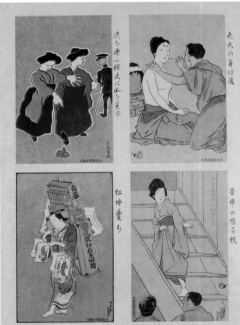

163
World of Postcards of Kokkei Shinbun, weekly
supplement to the *Kokkei Shinbun,* March 5, 1908.
© Photo Takeda Toshihiro
© Communications Tokyo Museum
Below left, a hawker sells his prints to passersby.

The journal *Kokkei Shinbun*

At the beginning of the twentieth century, Miyatake Gaikotsu (his pen name, Gaikotsu, means "skeleton") founded several humorous journals and reviews, including *Kokkei Shinbun*, first in Osaka and then in Tokyo.

If today's school students cannot bear to be without their mobiles and send text messages countless times a day, those of the 1900s were enamored of a new means of communication—the postcard. Young people would pick a nickname and send cards to their friends, inscribed with just the address and pseudonym. The game consisted in discovering the identity of the sender and answering him or her on another postcard. The fashion spread like wildfire through the entire population, reaching a climax after Japan's victory over Russia in 1905. Responding to massive demand from his readers, Miyatake Gaikotsu then decided to create a weekly supplement to *Kokkei Shinbun*: thus was born the *World of Postcards of Kokkei Shinbun*, in which each week he would offer series of postcards printed in color on thin board ready for cutting out. Varied in nature, they sometimes recall Edo-style caricatures, but they might also mimic foreign comics. They enjoyed huge success with his readers, who waited for each new number with bated breath.

Figs. 163–173

料理屋の板場
人形師
郊外の秋
戯作者の画
よく出す女
美術館内の傑作
掌中の珠
第二の日吉丸

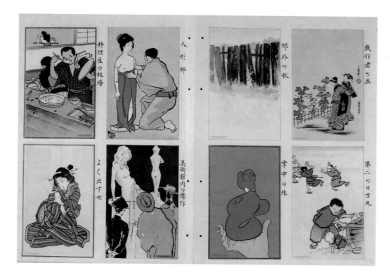

164
World of Postcards of Kokkei Shinbun, weekly supplement of the *Kokkei Shinbun*, November 1, 1908.
© Photo Takeda Toshihiro
© Communications Museum Tokyo

The earliest depictions of nudes by the painter Kuroda Seiki, who had studied in France, shocked the Japanese public. Similar reactions were aroused when sculptors exhibited works in the Western style.

The nude was permitted solely in patently erotic prints; otherwise any parts of the body which might embarrass had to be covered by a piece of cloth (see the two pictures to the right of the facing page).

滑稽新聞定期増刊
繪葉書世界
鯉の飛躍
未來の良妻
一心同體
鋏と糊
切っても切れぬ中
うつとり
子安貝

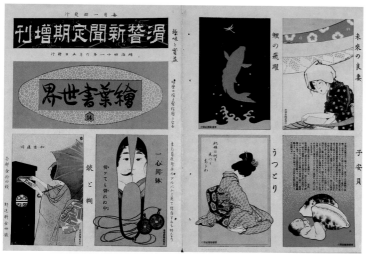

165
World of Postcards of Kokkei Shinbun, weekly supplement of the *Kokkei Shinbun*, cover of the number for June 5, 1908.
© Photo Takeda Toshihiro © Communications Museum Tokyo

A woman posting a letter and the traditional scissors echo the caption: "Bonds one cannot sever"; hence the couple's good relations (see the two pictures below facing page).

尻の衝突
動物園の猿
MとV
河童を釣る法

166
World of Postcards of Kokkei Shinbun, weekly supplement to the *Kokkei Shinbun*, June 5, 1908. © Photo Takeda Toshihiro
© Communications Museum Tokyo

The artist pokes fun at two situations featuring female figures: one group are seated very uncomfortably and showing their toes, while the others are planting rice back to back (the two pictures above). Below, one might wonder who is really in the cage—the monkeys or the men (second picture left)?

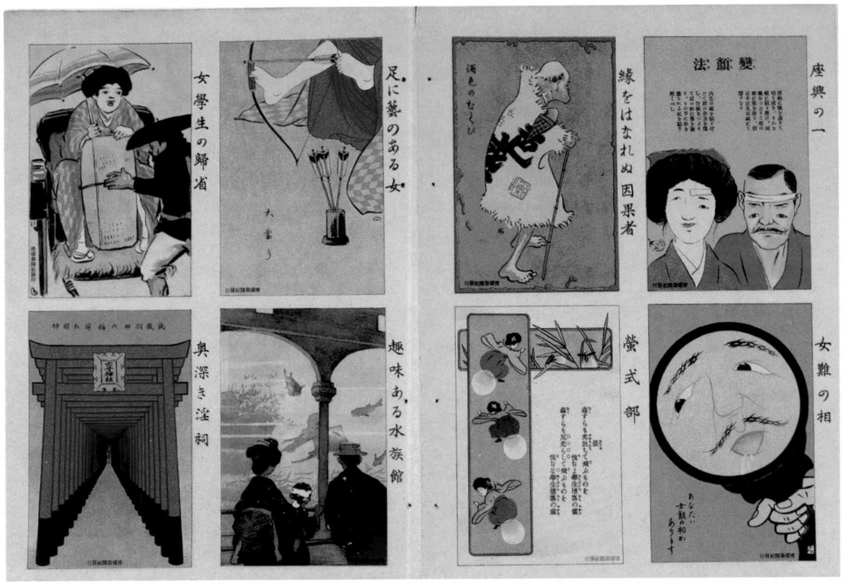
女學生の歸省
足に藝のある女
縁をはなれぬ因果者
座興の一
奥深き淫祠
趣味ある水族館
螢式部
女難の相

Fig. 167

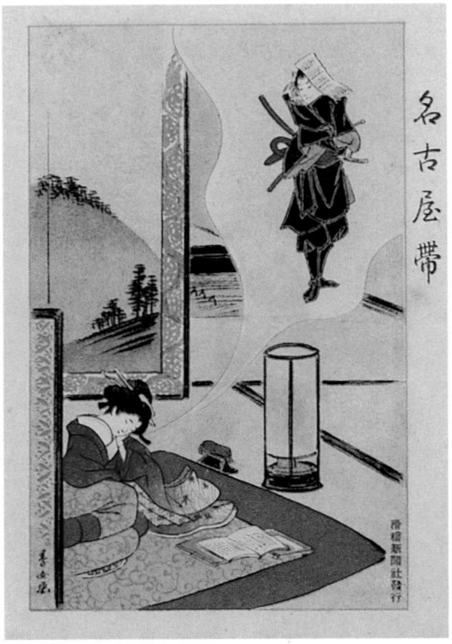
名古屋帯

Fig. 168

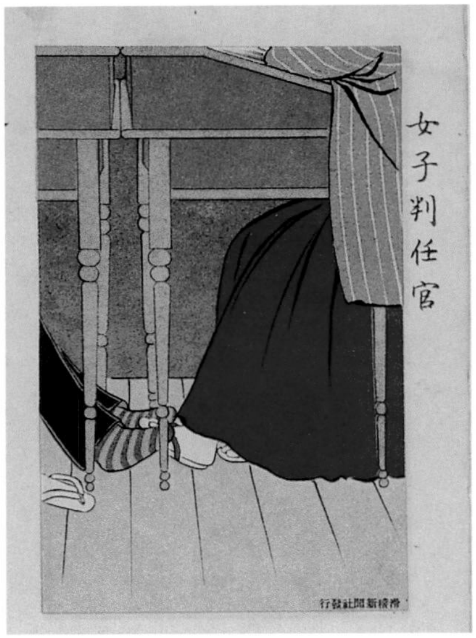
女子判任官

Fig. 169

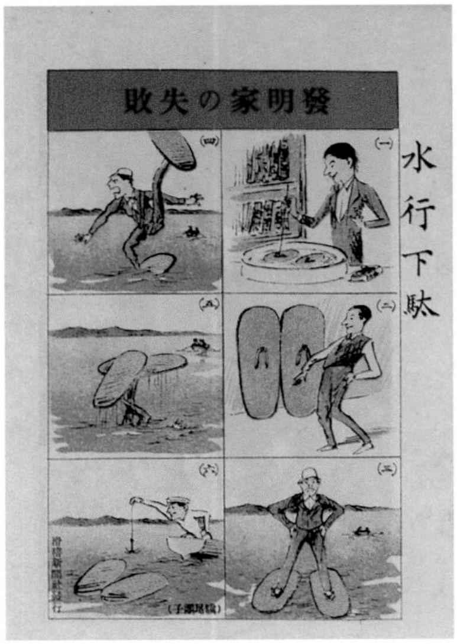
發明家の失敗
水行下駄

Fig. 170

167

World of Postcards of Kokkei Shinbun, weekly supplement to the *Kokkei Shinbun*, June 5, 1908. © Photo Takeda Toshihiro © Communications Museum Tokyo

"You must have woman trouble," the caption reads. The point becomes clearer when one understands that this man's eyebrows and moustache are made of a host of ideograms spelling the word "woman" (bottom right)!

168

World of Postcards of Kokkei Shinbun, weekly supplement to the *Kokkei Shinbun*, December 5, 1907.
© Photo Takeda Toshihiro
© Communications Museum Tokyo

Although this picture dates from the twentieth century, the dream, thought, or desire is expressed in a "bubble," just as in the Edo era. The caption indicates that the young woman wants to buy an *obi** from Nagoya.

169

World of Postcards of Kokkei Shinbun, weekly supplement to the *Kokkei Shinbun*, December 5, 1907.
© Photo Takeda Toshihiro
© Communications Museum Tokyo

The legend explains that this is a meeting between two young people: amusingly, the artist shows us only their feet. But whose then is the woman's shoe in the front?

170

World of Postcards of Kokkei Shinbun, weekly supplement to the *Kokkei Shinbun*, August 5, 1908.
© Photo Takeda Toshihiro
© Communications Museum Tokyo

The title of this page presented in the form of a comic strip is "the inventor's failure: the '*hydrogeta*'" (*geta** are traditional Japanese footwear). As indicated by the ideogram figures, the piece reads vertically from top to bottom, starting from the right-hand column.

身の軽い女
尻の強い男

171
World of Postcards of Kokkei Shinbun, weekly supplement to the *Kokkei Shinbun*, June 1, 1909. © Photo Takeda Toshihiro © Communications Museum Tokyo

These two postcards in fact form a single unit.

親子の愛
女の寒山拾得
娘を驚かす法
九紋龍と魯智深
蜜柑船
昔のカゲマ
禅學研究者
繪草紙屋の店頭

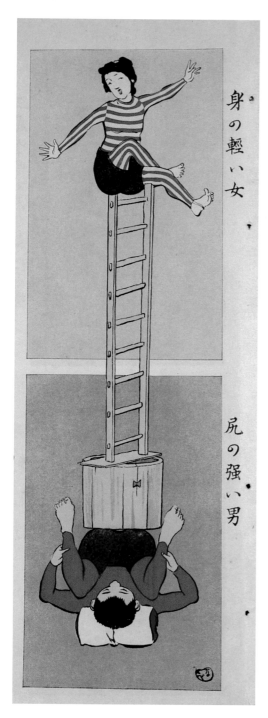

172
World of Postcards of Kokkei Shinbun, weekly supplement to the *Kokkei Shinbun*, September 5, 1908. © Photo Takeda Toshihiro © Communications Museum Tokyo

The scene is an *ezôshiya** (print shop). The character in the foreground is not, despite what one might think, a woman. One only has to look at his kimono to see he's actually a man. But what about the face? A print showing an Edo beauty has been superimposed over his own.

春の猫

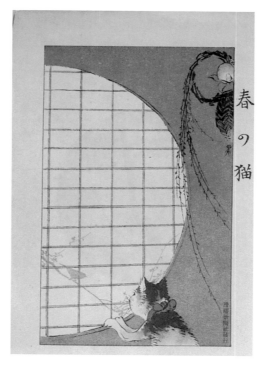

173
World of Postcards of Kokkei Shinbun, weekly supplement to the *Kokkei Shinbun*, January 1, 1909. © Photo Takeda Toshihiro © Communications Museum Tokyo

The kitten would dearly like to get his paws on the bird he can see behind the *shôji** (partition made of light-grade paper).

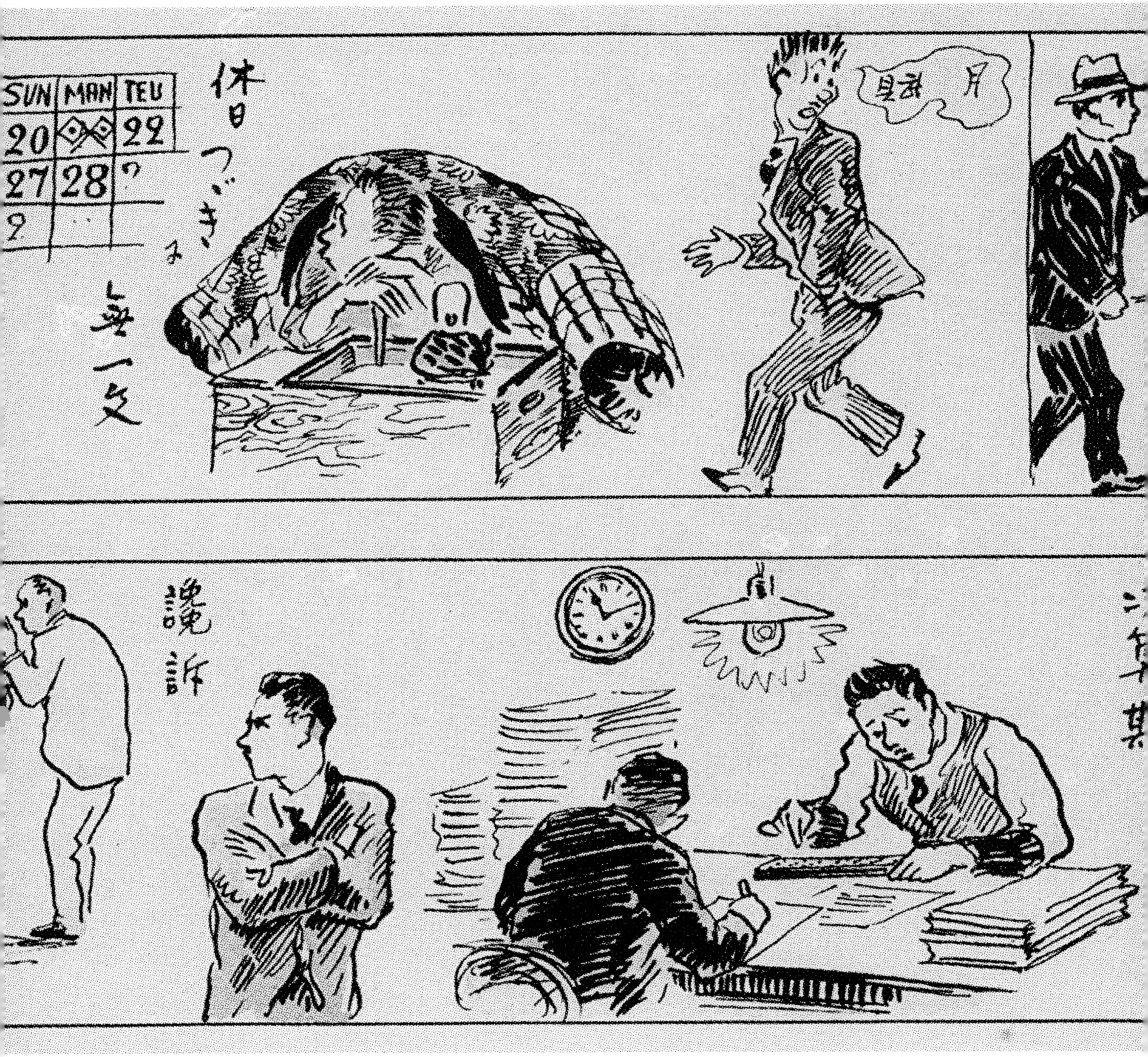
無一文
SUN
MAN
TEU
20
22
27
28
讒訴
Fig. 183 (detail)

Kitazawa Rakuten: pioneer of the Japanese comic strip

Kitazawa Yasuji (1876–1955), later known by the humorous fore-name, "Rakuten," which means "bright sky" or the "optimist," had trained as a traditional painter. In an unlikely transition, he became the precursor of the modern Japanese graphic novel.

Born eight years after the Meiji Restoration, he was profoundly affected by the social and cultural upheavals in his country that he had witnessed in his childhood. His liking for drawing led him to learn traditional Japanese painting—*nihon-ga**—at an early age under direction from Inoue Shunzui, a master of *ukiyo-e**. He then studied Western painting and, in the review *Shokokumin*, discovered the American comic strip, which completely bowled him over. He began by imitating this genre, doing much to make it more widely known in his homeland, before going on to produce original works intended for the Japanese market. He then met the Australian cari-caturist Frank A. Nankivell (1869–1959), who worked for English magazines. Rakuten joined him in *Box of Curios*, a Yokohama weekly published by E. B. Thorne, studying the technique of caricature with him. Although he enjoyed this outlet, Rakuten was intent on acquiring greater freedom of expression. He left *Box of Curios* in 1899, joining the manga* department of the *Jiji Shinpô* founded by Fukuzawa Yukichi, one of the intellectual heavyweights of the time.

The latter, eager to elevate caricature in Japan to the rank it occu-pied in the West, placed great confidence in Rakuten's youth and talent. It was from this moment that the artist started employing the word "manga" to designate his own comics. As much a *mangaka** as a journalist, he became particularly interested in national and inter-national politics and in social problems. An admirer of the success of the review *Kokkei Shinbun*, whose humorous approach had succeeded in attracting a vast readership, Rakuten wanted to go one better. Keen on Western culture and inspired by the French journal *Rire*, and the American *Puck*, *Jiji Shinpô* was not enough to slake his ambi-tion: in 1905, he therefore decided to found a review of his own, *The Tokyo Puck*, which met with meteoric success.

Fig. 174

The first review to be issued in color, it appeared two or three times a month, featuring caricatures with captions in English, Chinese, and Japanese. Following in the wake of Western examples,

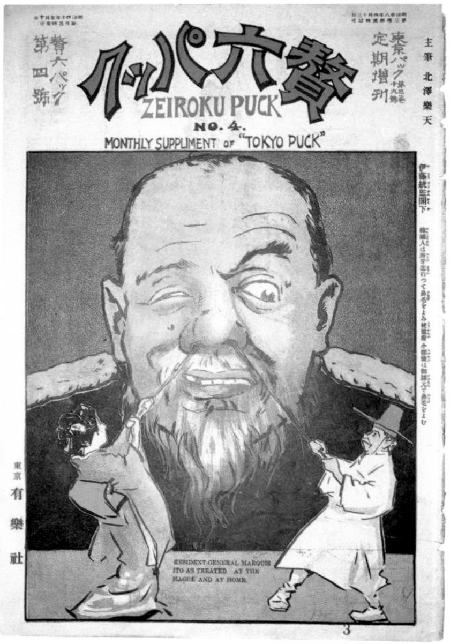
ZEIROKU PUCK
NO. 4.
MONTHLY SUPPLIMENT OF "TOKYO PUCK"

174
Kitazawa Rakuten, cover of *Zeiroku Puck* (supplement to the review *Toby-Puck*) of July 10, 1907.
© Saitama Municipal Cartoon Art Museum

The governor of occupied Korea, Itô Hirobumi, is here held up to ridicule by a Japanese woman and a Korean pulling hairs out of his nose.

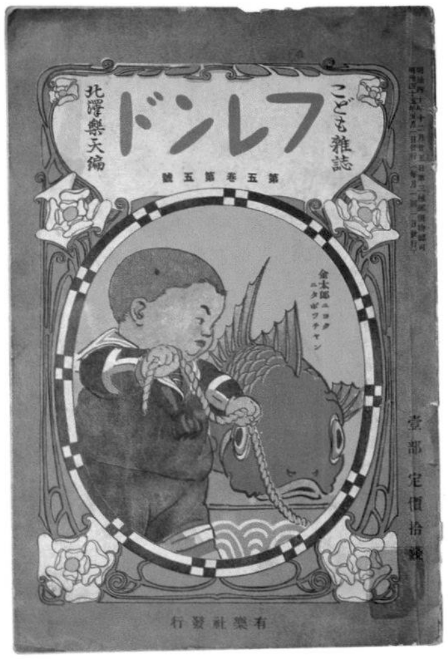
フレンド
こども雑誌

175
Kitazawa Rakuten, cover of the review *Furendo (Friend)*, no. 5 of volume 5, published in May 1912.
© Saitama Municipal Cartoon Art Museum

The magazine for children, *Furendo*, was set up by Rakuten in 1908.

Rakuten started designing comic strips with six panels. He was then the first to launch out in this story-comic line, and today his work is still hailed as being that of a hugely talented pioneer. Fig. 176

Vehemently critical of the political world of his time, Rakuten knew that he was always prone to attack from the government. He never yielded to pressure, though, and *Tokyo Puck* was prevented from publishing on several occasions. The caricaturist always contrived to jokingly announce this fact in the following number, attracting a surge of sympathy from his readers.

In an attempt to reach an ever-wider audience, he went on to launch two further publications in 1912: the *Rakuten Puck* and *Katei Puck*. Fig. 177 Noting that comic strips for children remained thin on the ground, in 1914 he set up the journal *Kodomo no tomo*, in which he unveiled a series entitled "The Childhood of Toyotomi Hideyoshi." He then restarted work on the four-page color supplement to the *Jiji Shinpô*.

Rakuten was very fond of traveling, and his trips constituted a significant source of inspiration for his work. In 1924, he visited Manchuria, and published drawings on subjects from this country in the *Jiji Shinpô*. Fig. 180 A journalist first and foremost, his work was always closely related to topical themes.

In 1929, he undertook a long trip that took him to Europe, Africa, and America, following which he brought out *Memories of My Travels Abroad* and *The Complete Works of Rakuten* in seven volumes. This round-the-world tour was a source of delight to him, providing him with an opportunity to study the expressions, lifestyles, and customs of the many peoples he encountered in various countries. Figs. 178, 180–182

During his stay in Paris, where he produced what are probably his finest drawings, he met a number of Japanese celebrities then living in the capital, including the painter Leonard Fujita. He took the opportunity of showing his work there at an "Exhibition of Works on the Customs and Habits of the Japanese: Pictures by M. Kitazawa Rakuten," which was staged in June 1929 at the Salon d'Art Japonais, held in the Musée du Jeu de Paume. He showed folding-screens and paintings evoking Japanese ceremonies, such as the *Festival of St Nichiren* (celebrated on October 12 in memory of the founder of the Buddhist sect of the same name) or *Dance of the Good* (a ritual in the honor of the dead).

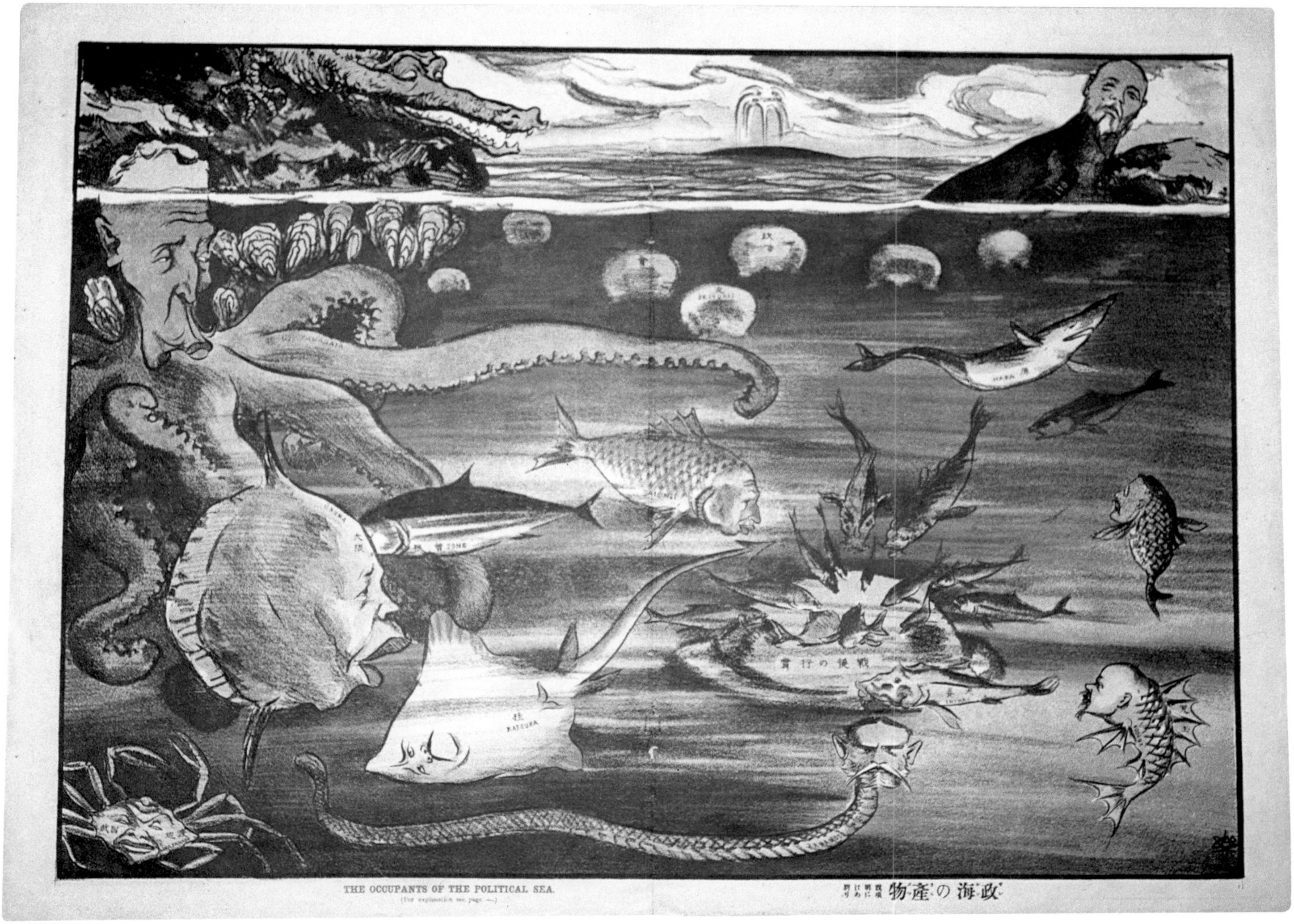
THE OCCUPANTS OF THE POLITICAL SEA.
政海の産物

176

Kitazawa Rakuten, *Produce of the Political Ocean*, July 15, 1906. © Saitama Municipal Cartoon Art Museum

The title itself is a pun in Japanese. The seal, octopus, crab, sea-snake, and even the less remarkable fish each take on the features of a well-known politician whose name is inscribed on a part of its body. They are all the spitting-image of their models. In the center, small fry throw themselves on the booty of war.

Exceptionally here, Rakuten has added captions to each figure. With regard to Itô Hirobumi, drawn as a seal, he writes: "This creature is an amphibian which provides one of the most gorgeous furs. He likes to pop up in places and at times when he is least expected, one day in the United States or Europe, and the next in Korea."

Itô Hirobumi (1841–1909) was a statesman who occupied high positions in the Japanese government after the Meiji Restoration. Prime Minister on several occasions, in 1906 he was named Resident General of Korea.

This caricature is violently critical of the expansionist policy of a Japan which, following its victory over Russia, no longer bothered to mask its ambitions for the future.

177

Kitazawa Rakuten, cover of the review *Rakuten Puck*, dated November 1, 1912.
© Saitama Municipal Cartoon Art Museum

But what are these people all gawping at? The arrival of the first airplane, of course!

178

Kitazawa Rakuten, *The Apprentice Baker*, drawing published in the *Jiji Manga* of September 29, 1929.
© Saitama Municipal Cartoon Art Museum

"They had dirty hands but liked playing with bread," it says at the bottom of the drawing. Rakuten seizes on the smallest events in the street and, with the talent of a reporter who knows the value of the picturesque, drew thumbnail sketches of everyday scenes from Parisian life that a Western eye might have missed. The crisp realism in which their clothing and headgear is treated is equaled by that of the gestures of these two fun-loving Parisian urchins.

He also unveiled pictures representing contemporary life, like *The Two Modern Girls*, in which the protagonists can be seen meeting one another in the street: one, dressed in a kimono and symbolizing traditional Japan, turns round to inspect the other, who is bedecked in the latest European fashions. Rakuten's point here is to describe the period of transition that saw Japan hesitating between modernization on the one side and the traditions of the past on the other. In the background, he adds a gleaming limo that speeds past a rickshaw from which alights another young woman wearing a very simple dress and *geta**. At the end of his show, eager to acknowledge his talent, the French Ministry for Education and the Art Schools named Kitazawa Rakuten *officier d'académie*.

The works Rakuten painted in Paris were then exhibited in London with those he had brought from Japan. The political caricatures were not presented, though, since the organizers did not think that Westerners would be sufficiently *au fait* with the Japanese political situation and would be unable to appreciate them. For the occasion, the poet Komai Gonnosuke, who had long lived in London and who acted as *The Times* correspondent during the Russo-Japanese War, wrote a foreword to the catalog, "Paintings East and West by Kitazawa Rakuten of Tokyo," published by *The Fine Art Society*, February 1930. In it, he compared Rakuten to the most famous masters of the print and affirmed that he was indeed "the foremost painter of the modern *ukiyo-e* school."

The British press lauded his traditional-style paintings to the skies, but lambasted those the artist had created in France. While, on February 27, 1930, *The Times* was praising his work, the *Observer* criticized his Paris pictures, observing unjustly that: "the effect produced was that of a ravishing *gesha* [sic] who has swapped her colorful *kimono* and *obi** for the uniform of a waitress in some London tearoom!" (March 2, 1930). The *Daily Mail* of March 6, 1930, also waxed lyrical over the traditional pieces, but was very severe with regard to the scenes of Parisian life.

Rakuten was not the first to suffer this kind of criticism. Since the end of the nineteenth century, European critics had been questioning why Japanese artists were gradually absorbing Western techniques; many would have preferred them to confine themselves

Fig. 180

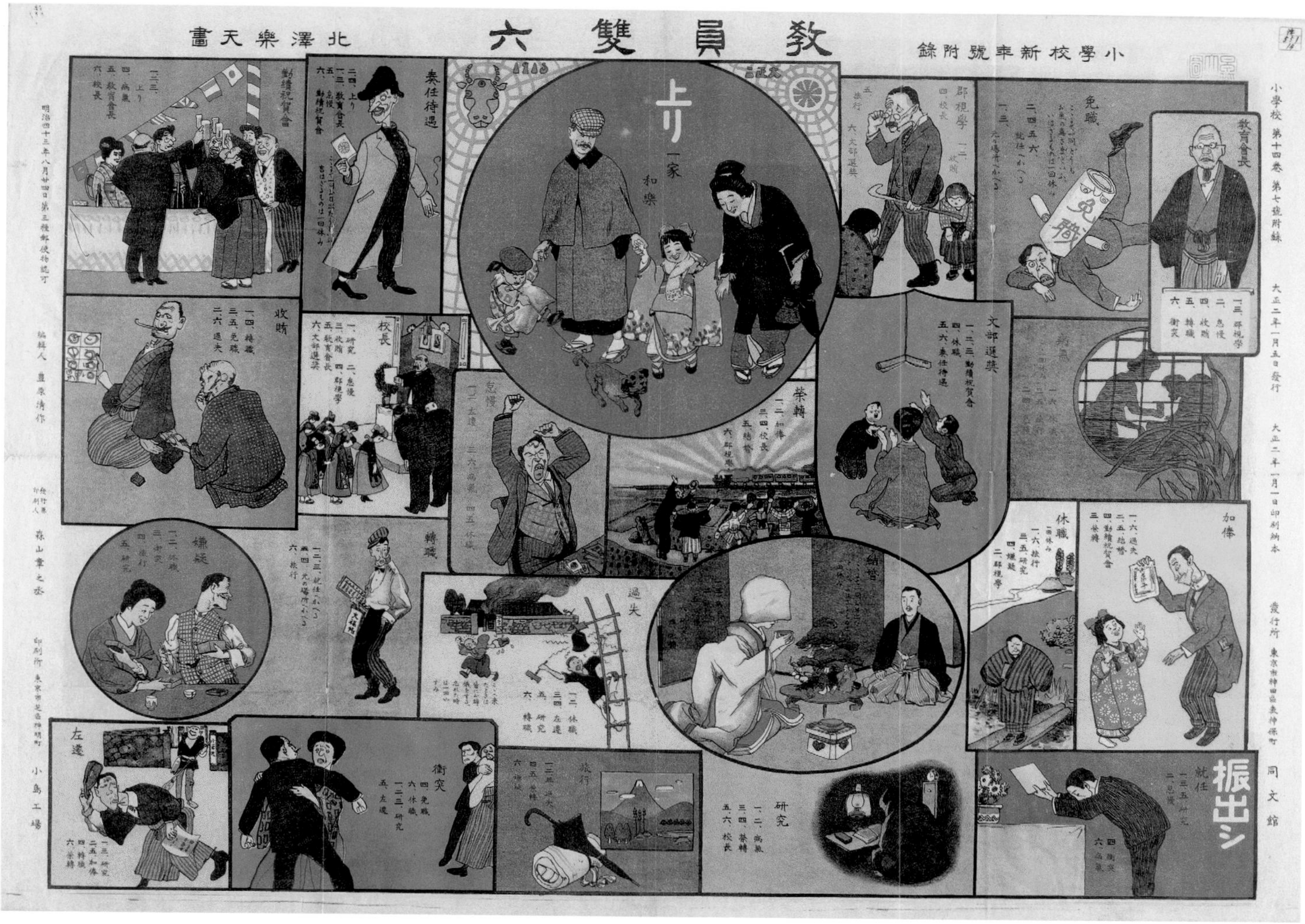
教員雙六
北澤樂天畫
小學校新年號附錄
上リ
一家和樂
振出シ

179

Kitazawa Rakuten, *The Primary School*, board game, supplement to no. 7 of volume 14 of the review *Shôgakkô (Primary School)*, 1913. © Waseda University Library

Like many print-masters and manga artists, Rakuten also drew board games. This one provides a humorous description of the lives of teachers.

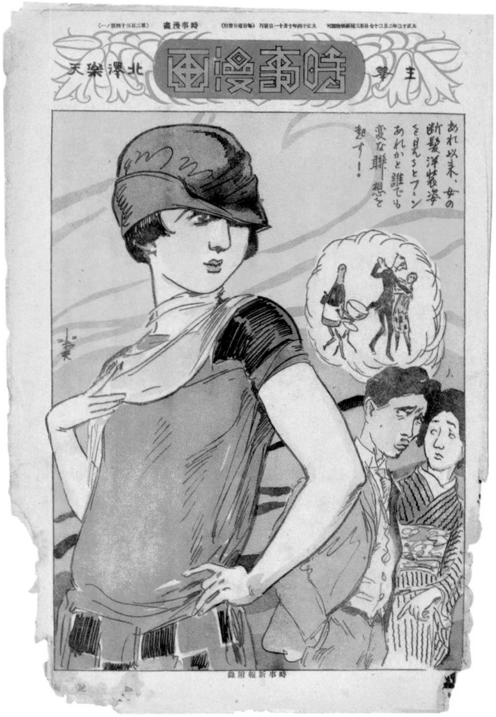
時事漫畫
時事漫画
主筆 北澤樂天
あれ以来、女の断髪洋装姿を見るとフーンあれかと誰でも変な聯想を起す！

180

Kitazawa Rakuten, *Modern Girl*, drawing published in the *Jiji Manga (Manga on Current Topics)* of October 11, 1925. © Saitama Municipal Cartoon Art Museum

Rakuten here immortalizes a news item of the time: a dissolute seventeen-year-old girl had taken a revolver and shot and killed a foreigner who had refused to pay her. The public were dumbfounded by her ice-cold attitude during the trial. The journalist has written at the top of the picture: "If you meet a Japanese woman dressed Western style, you won't be able to prevent yourselves thinking of this one!"

181
Kitazawa Rakuten, *Young Woman Selling on the Island of Marken. Impression of Holland,* drawing published in *Jiji Manga,* June 8, 1930.
© Saitama Municipal Cartoon Art Museum

Throughout his European trip, Rakuten liked to take pictorial notes and write about his encounters. He was particularly enchanted by The Netherlands. "Here the ground lies below sea level. During the summer holidays, the restaurants and souvenir shops close to the port in Rotterdam are jam-packed. There was a young woman wearing clogs and selling things who was particularly pretty." Although the handling might seem eminently Western, it is nonetheless obvious that the drawing is by a Japanese artist. The low-angle view and the boats in the foreground arranged diagonally—only one end of which can be seen—are both redolent of traditional print compositions.

to producing the time-honored illustrated scrolls and folding-screens. In their eyes, Kitazawa Rakuten could pass for an excellent traditional painter, but he would never be recognized as a key figure in modern Japan, or as the pioneer of caricature and manga that he actually was.

On his return to Japan, Rakuten continued collaborating with the Press. Fig. 183

In 1932, the artist left the *Jiji Shinpô* and opened, in his own house, the Rakuten Manga Studio for his many disciples. At the approach of the Second World War, the Japanese Press was stifled and caricaturists had to bend to governmental demands, something that was unlikely to please Rakuten. In 1942 the Manga Association of Japan, the Nihon Manga Hôkôkai, was created and he became its first president. Evacuated during the war to the prefecture of Akita, he remained there until 1948 when he could at last return home.

Rakuten continued to draw and paint until the very end of his life. Although admittedly his manga and caricatures betray Western influences, the artist never disavowed his traditional training, and it Fig. 184 is this that gives his drawings their undoubted charm. After his death in 1955, his wife donated their house to the city of Ômiya; in 1966 a Municipal Museum of Manga was opened there.

A new profession: manga journalist

The Taishô era (1912–26) heralded the birth of the movement of the "New Progressive Representatives of Manga," whose ranks numbered some prestigious names, including Okamoto Ippei (1886–1948). He had studied at the Fine Art School in Tokyo, in the Western painting section, before turning to manga and, from 1912, working for the major national daily, *Asahi*. His political caricatures were much appreciated, but he also strove to make better known early American comic strips, such as *Bringing up Father,* in the weekly *Asahi Gurafu*. In conjunction with Rakuten, he is regarded as Fig. 187 one of the fathers of the modern Japanese comic. With some *mangaka* friends, he coined the term *manga kisha* ("manga journalist") before, in 1915, going on to set up the group, Tokyo manga kai, the Association of Tokyo Manga.

The founders were soon joined by many artists. In 1921, intent on further publicizing their profession, eighteen *mangaka* traveled

182

Kitazawa Rakuten, *Knocking at the Door.*
© Saitama Municipal Cartoon Art Museum

This work was the last Rakuten was to draw during his journey to Europe in 1929–30. One may suppose that he had spotted a chambermaid using her foot to knock on a guest's door in some hotel. Struck by the gesture, he transformed it, with his customary humor, into a caricature of Parisian mores.

サラリーマンの地獄
ラッシュアワー
サラリーマンの地獄
洋服屋の姿を見た時
SUN MAN TEU
サラリーマンの地獄
決算期
讒訴
サラリーマンの地獄
重役の自動車とタクシーの悲哀
首の心配

183

Kitazawa Rakuten, *The Office Worker's Hell*, the seventh volume of *The Complete Works of Kitazawa Rakuten*, 1930, Atorie-sha Publishers.
© Saitama Municipal Cartoon Art Museum

Packed trains, wearisome work, overtime, and a journey back home through the snow, dogged by the terror of losing his position—such is the everyday life of this wretched employee. In the final panel at the bottom, two headless bodies are feeling the strain: the allusion is to the Japanese expression, *kubi*, "to lose one's neck"—here synonymous with "getting the sack." As in a print, Rakuten uses bubbles in which he places drawings, and not text.

184

Kitazawa Rakuten, *Tôba-e*, no date. © Saitama Municipal Cartoon Art Museum

Training as a traditional painter, Rakuten created folding-screens and *kakemono** of great quality. He amuses himself by giving a new interpretation of the famous scroll *Frolicking Animals and People*.

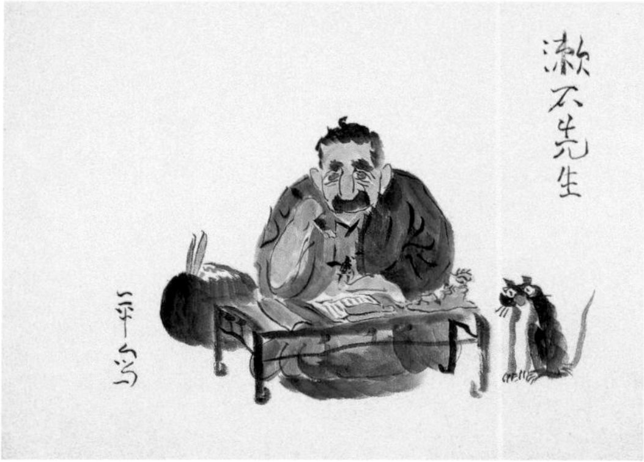
漱石先生

185
Okamoto Ippei, *Natsume Sôseki*, painting, 1927.
© Machida City Museum

This is a caricature of the great writer Natsume Sôseki (Taniguchi Jirô based his book, *The Times of Botchan*, on Sôseki's famous *Botchan*, see figs. 298–299). Sôseki had written one of the most famous novels in all Japanese literature, *I Am a Cat*, in which the eponymous animal records its impressions of contemporary society. Okamoto Ippei has not forgotten to include his erstwhile familiar.

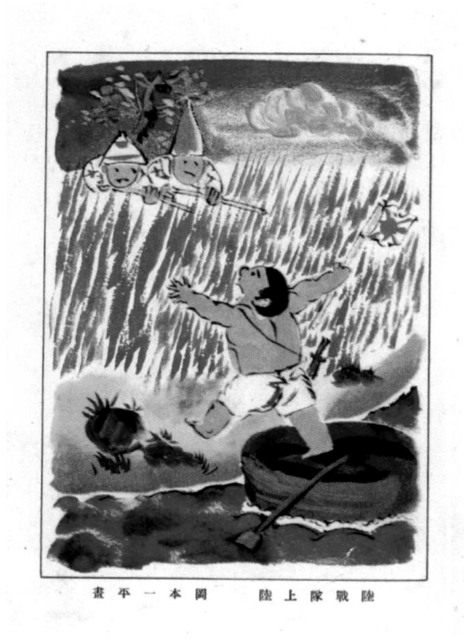
陸戰隊上陸 岡本一平畫

186
Okamoto Ippei, *The Arrival of the Marines on the Continent*, *Chûôbijutsusha*, 1928.
© Matsumoto Leiji Collection

in six cars along the fifty-three stopping-places on the Tokaido, thus journeying, as in the past, from Tokyo to Kyoto. They composed a scroll based on their pilgrimage entitled *Tôkaidô gojûsan tsugi manga emaki* (*Manga Painting-Scroll of the Fifty-three Stations of the Tokaido*). In 1923, the group was dissolved, giving rise to the Nihon Manga-kai, the Japanese Manga Association.

Okamoto Ippei proved an immense success with Japanese high-school girls who enjoyed his works enormously, but he acquired faithful readers among male readers too. In a style different from but just as varied as Rakuten's, Okamoto Ippei gave a new twist to manga. Unlike those of Rakuten, which always portrayed faces realistically, even when presenting his characters in animal form, Okamoto Ippei's caricatures were characterized by exaggerated and simplified features. Fig. 185

During the 1920s, the law "safeguarding peace," promulgated in 1925, was marshaled to stifle Press freedoms. At the beginning of the 1920s, there existed many Marxist-leaning publications, but this relaxation proved short-lived and, by this new law, the government once again attempted to exercise absolute control and gag the Press. Transgressors of the law were severely punished. By this time, all the main national dailies had their manga magazine, which henceforth had to stick to "politically correct" stories. It was also at this juncture that the first reviews for children started appearing, the most significant being *Shônen Kurubu* ("Boys' Club"), in 1914, *Shôjo Kurubu* ("Girls' Club"), in 1923, and *Yônen Kurubu* ("Younger Children's Club") in 1926. These publications offered primarily literature, illustrated stories, and a number of didactic articles, in addition to manga.

Cornering the youth market

Many manga for children were included as supplements (from sixteen to twenty-four pages) in the women's press, such as *Shufu no tomo (The Housewife's Friend)* or *Fujin kurabu (The Club for Women)*. Others appeared in the form of independent volumes that were printed on very heavy, tough paper and were not more than eight to ten pages long. These extremely colorful comic strips were intended to be read by mothers with their young children. Today they are impossible to find. Figs. 186, 188–190, 194 Figs. 195–212

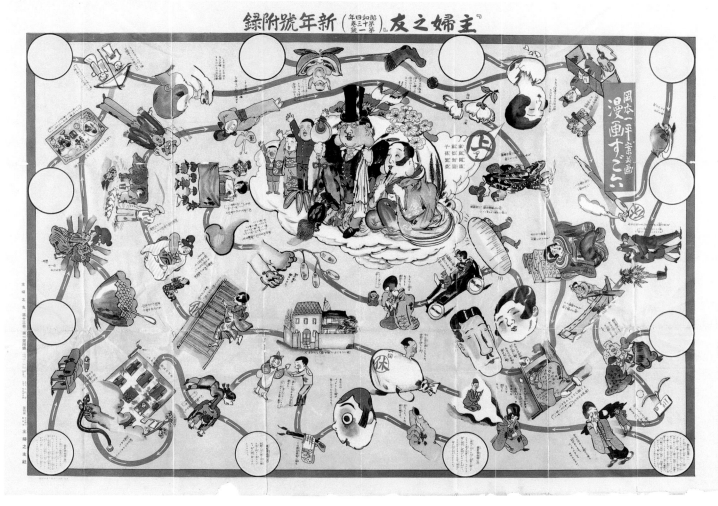

録附號年新（昭和四年）主婦之友

岡本一平漫画すごろく

Okamoto Ippei, Supplement to the review, *Shufu no tomo*, 1929
© Waseda University Library

When the artist drew this game of "snakes-and-ladders,"
he was at the zenith of his career. Each image is a rebus
that the players are challenged to work out.

188

Covers for the manga supplements from the review,
Yônen Kurabu, together with a reprint of *Koguma Korosuke
(Korosuke the Little Bear)*, Yoshimoto Sanpei, *Dainihon Yûbenkai
Kôdansha*, 1936. © Matsumoto Leiji Collection

The bear Korosuke proved a runaway success and for
six years appeared in the magazine *Yônen Kurabu* before
being issued in volume form. The author represents the
bears clothed and playing sports, as well as confronting
various dangers and having human feelings.

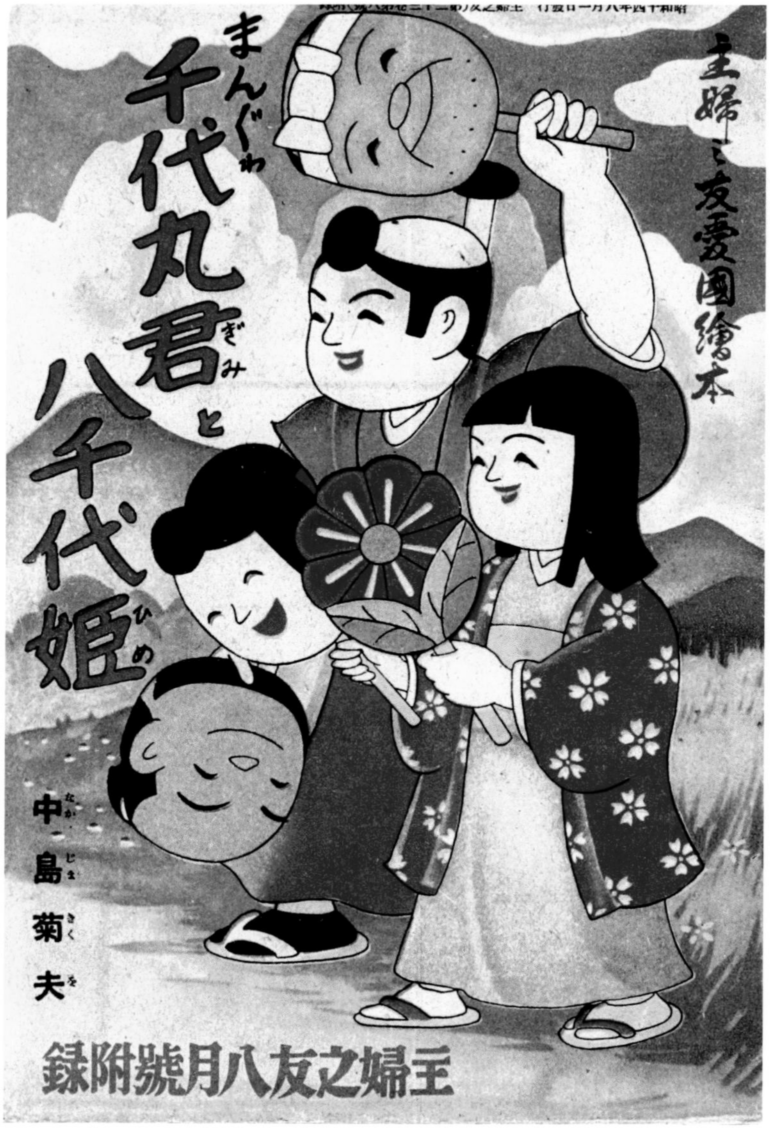
まんぐゎ
千代丸君と八千代姫
主婦之友愛國絵本
中島菊夫
主婦之友八月號附録

189
Nakajima Kikuo, *Manga: Chiyomaru and Princess Yachio* (supplement to *Shufu no Tomo*), 1939. © Matsumoto Leiji Collection

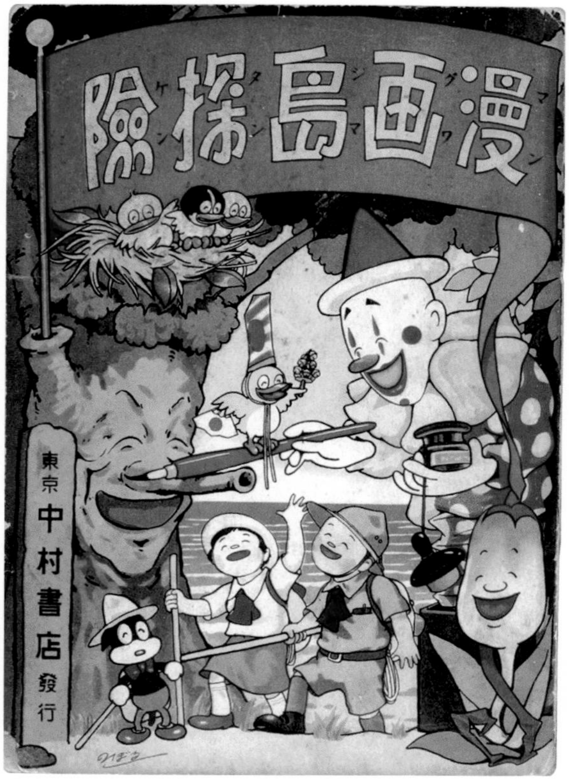
漫画島探険
東京
中村書店
發行

190
Various authors, *Exploration of the Island of Manga*, Nakamura Shoten, 1939.
© Matsumoto Leiji Collection

Manga collection aimed at very young children.

漫画スタジオ風景
42
43

あの汽車は
國府津から山北を
まはつて來た
沼津行き列車
今富士のすそ野を
廻つてゐる所よ
太郎！ ごらん 富士山だ
いやあ富士山!! 素敵だなあ
バンザーイ
いいお山ねーエ
62
63

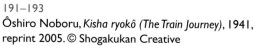

191–193
Ôshiro Noboru, *Kisha ryokô (The Train Journey)*, 1941, reprint 2005. © Shogakukan Creative

This story tells of Tarô's train journey in the company of his father to join his mother, his brother Jirô, and his sister Michiko in Kyoto. During the journey, Tarô takes the opportunity of visiting a cartoon studio. Originally the book was to run to 160 pages, but publishing constraints meant it consisted only of 128 pages, ending the journey in Nagoya instead of Kyoto! This manga, which greatly impressed Tezuka Osamu and taught him a great deal in terms of content and in the use of color, still retains much of its charm today.

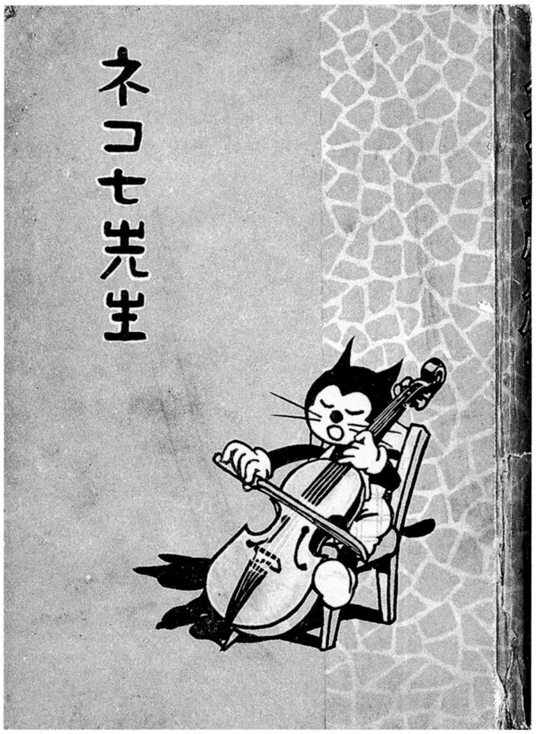
ネコ七先生

194
Shimada Keizô, *Neko Shichi sensei, Dainihon yôbenkai Kôdansha*, 1940. © Matsumoto Leiji Collection

The nameless cat offers a humorous critique of the society of its time.

The spirit of adventure

Some of the most famous adventure manga titles are *Norakuro* by Tagawa Suihô, which tells the story of a lazy black dog who enlists in the imperial army, and *Supîdo Tarô (Speed Tarô)* by Shishido Sakô, whose hero has to foil international conspiracies. But the one that made the most impact was *Shôchan no bôken (The Adventures of Shôchan)*, drawn by Kabashima Katsuichi, published in 1923 in the first number of *Asahi Gurafu*. In the United States, *Yellow Kid* is regarded as the earliest comic strip to use speech bubbles; in Japan, it was *Shôchan no bôken*. This work reuses the principle of the caption as employed in earlier manga. The artist relates the adventures with great imagination and humor, in a tone halfway between the past and the modern era, using a new graphic style which anticipates that of the following decades, and accompanied by word-bubbles. The starting point for this manga was a cartoon in the *Daily Mirror* of London whose central character was a penguin; here, it is a squirrel who befriends a little boy. In its turn, *Shôchan no bôken* was a springboard for many subsequent manga.

Figs. 214–2
221

Figs. 216–2

A taste for travel

Travel manga were already popular before the Second World War. The most interesting on the graphic level is undoubtedly *Kisha ryokô (Train Journey)*. Beginning their exploration in the Edo* era, as transport developed, the Japanese could begin traveling far and wide throughout the archipelago. Such journeys not only fulfilled a desire to get away, but also allowed the population to discover the famous places they had admired first in prints and then postcards.

Figs. 191–1

A far cry from being a tourist guide, manga on this subject were targeted at children. Fun yet educational, with a wealth of illustration, they would tell stories, accompanied by a smattering of geography.

The postwar renaissance

As war approached, there was an upswing in Japanese nationalism, and manga were diverted from their primary goal of amusing children. Under government pressure, the heroes of manga started preaching national defense and were soon being used as a propaganda tool. After the conflict, many unemployed,

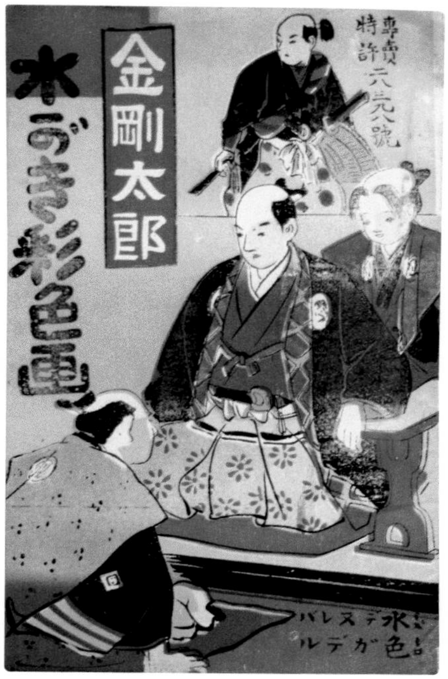
金剛太郎
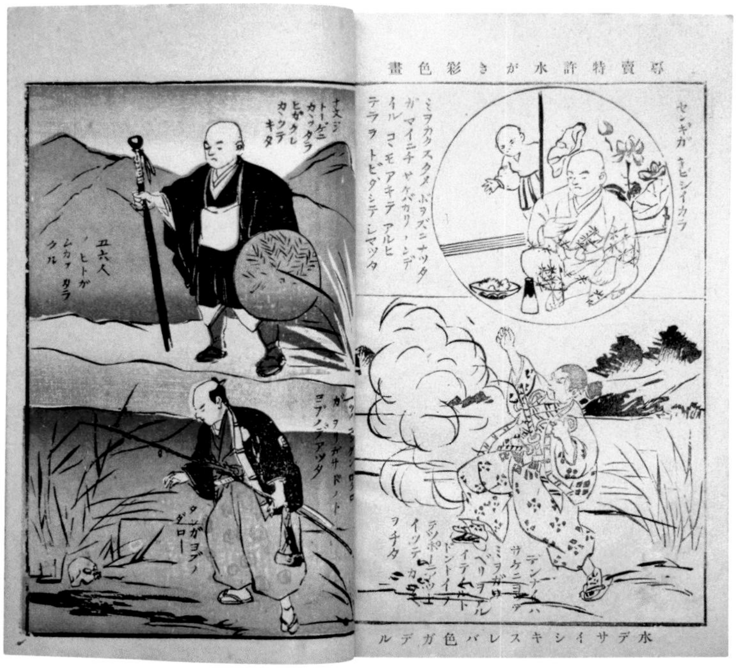
専賣特許水ぎき彩色畫
水デサイシキスレバ色ガデル

195–196
Anonymous, *Kongotarô*, tale for children, lithograph, c. 1912–26.
© Kumon Institute of Education

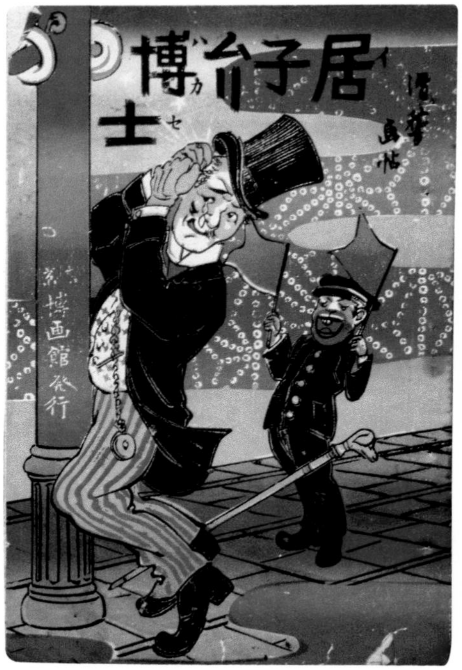
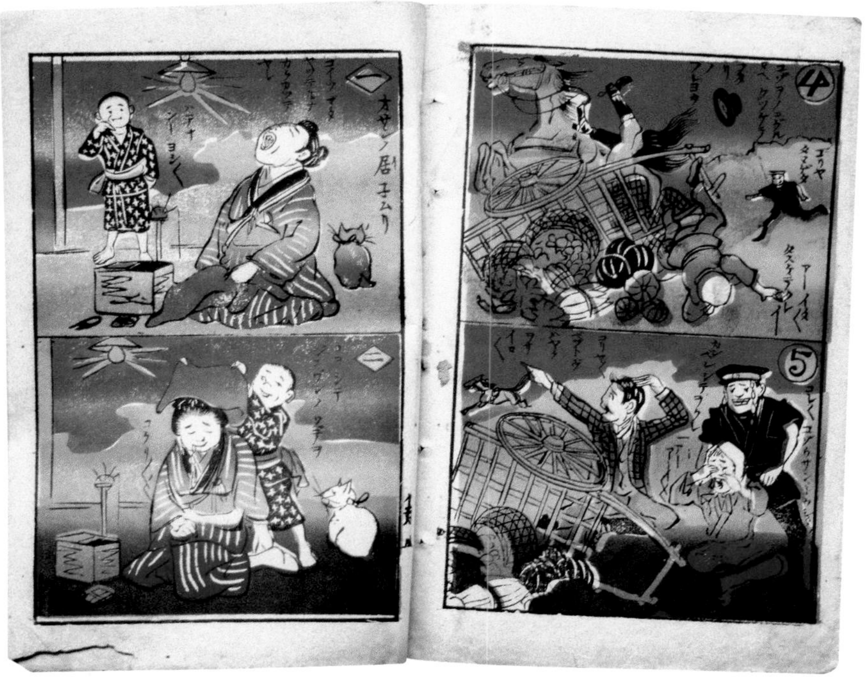

197–198
Anonymous, *The Snoozing Doctor*, comic book, lithograph, c. 1912–26.
© Kumon Institute of Education

和漢準源氏
蓬生
桃太郎
一勇斎國芳画

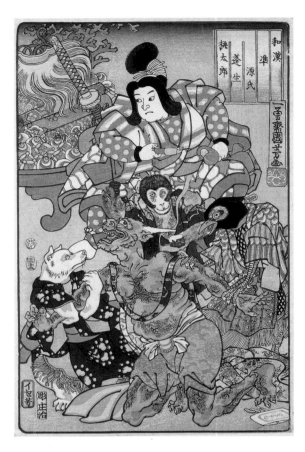

199

Ichiyûsai Kuniyoshi, *Momotarô, the Child Born from a Peach*, *nishiki-e* print, 1855.

© Kumon Institute of Education

Momotarô is accompanied by the three friends who help him overcome ogres.

教育画話
桃太郎とポンチ

モモタロウハマイニチオウマニノルケイコヲシテマス
オヤ〱
モモノナカカラアカンボカテマシタ
モモタロウトナヲツケマシタ
カハユイコドモダ
日本一
ニツポンイチノキビダンゴヲコサヘテアゲマス

200–201

Anonymous, *Momotarô and Ponchi*, lithograph, c. 1912–26.

© Kumon Institute of Education

This book of *Ponchi-e* (manga) contains a number of short stories.

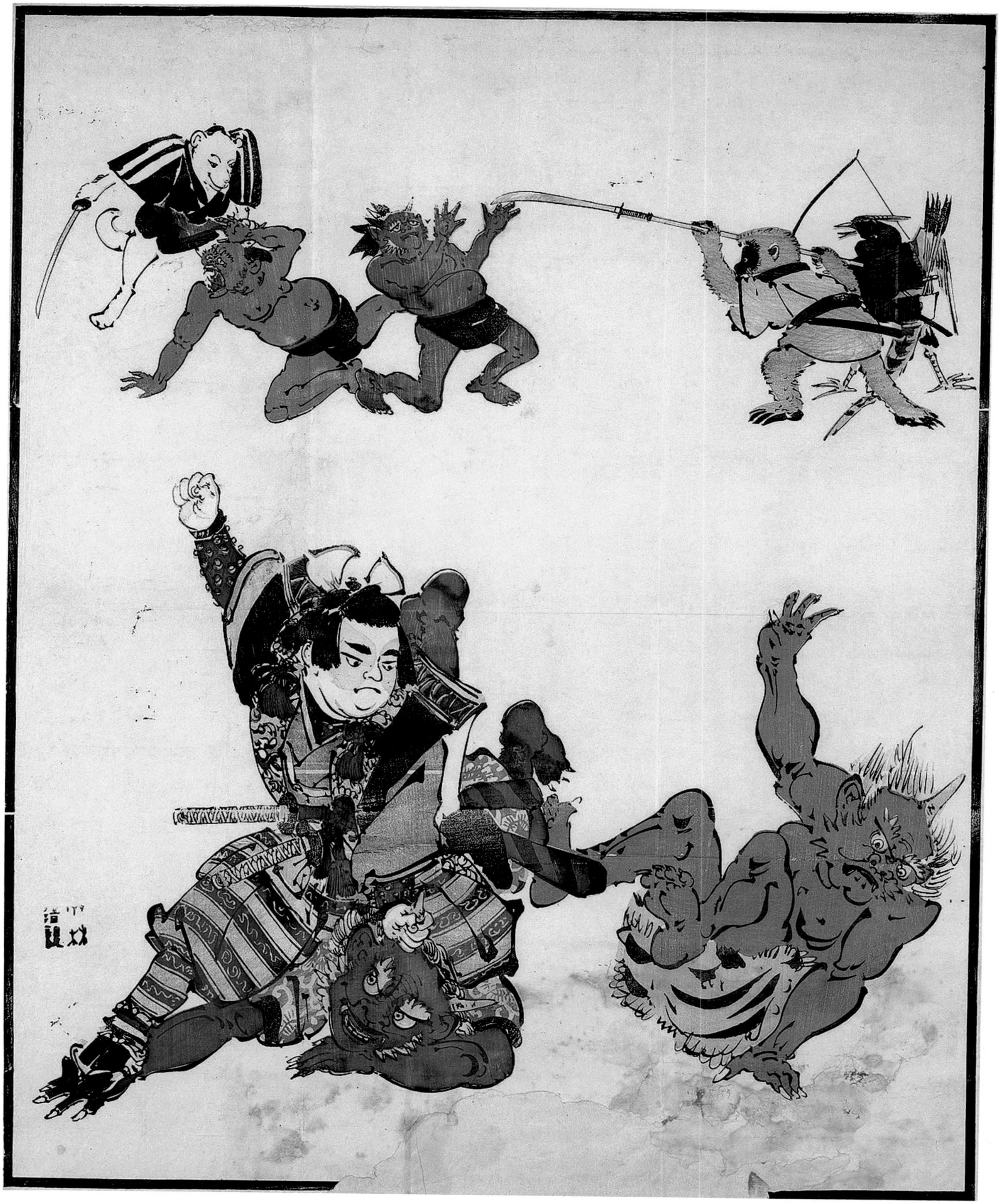

202
Kobayashi Kiyochika, *Momotarô Exterminates the Demons, nishiki-e* print, beginning of the 1870s. © Kumon Institute of Education

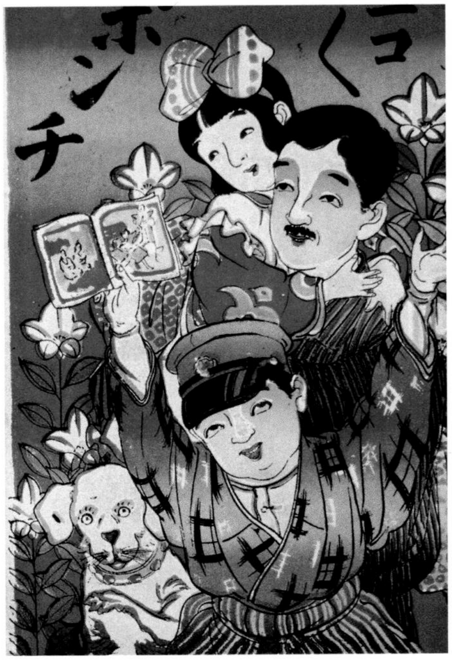
ニコく
ポンチ

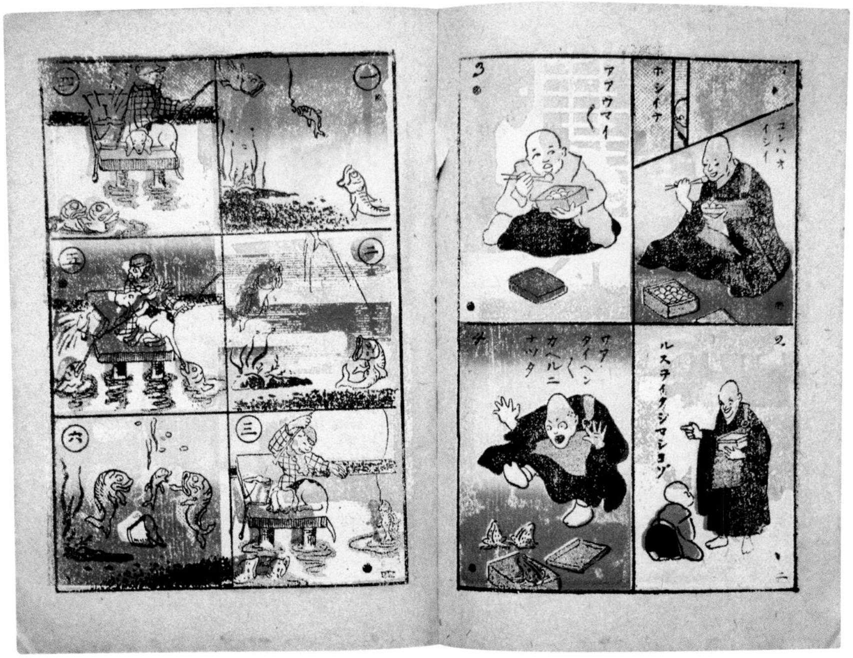

203–204
Anonymous, *Nikoku Ponchi*, lithograph, c. 1912–26. © Kumon Institute of Education

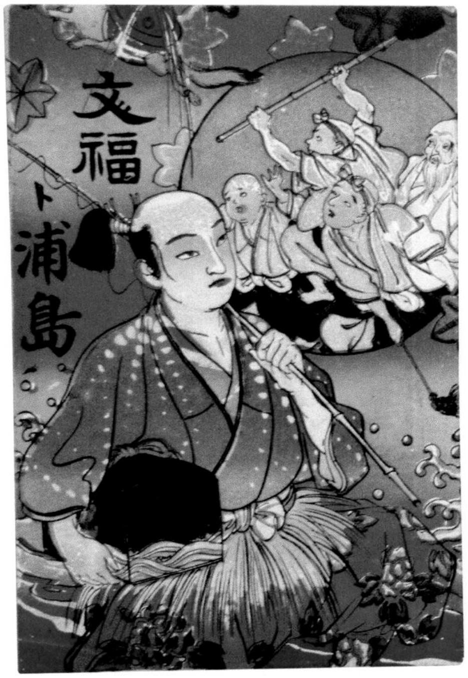
文福ト浦島

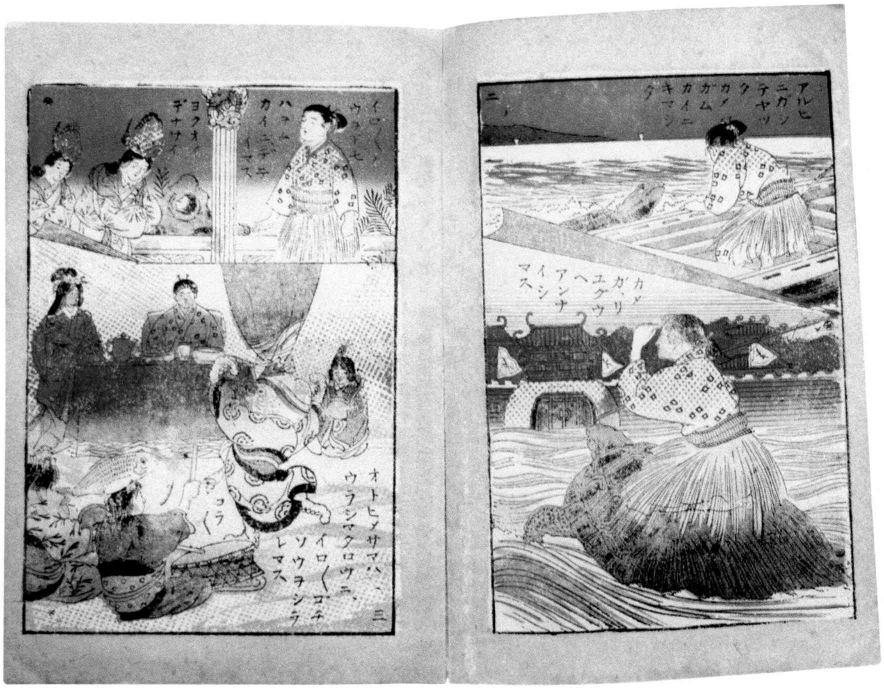

205–206
Anonymous, *Urashima Tarô and Bunpuku*, lithograph, Taishô period. © Kumon Institute of Education
Both these famous tales are presented in this work.

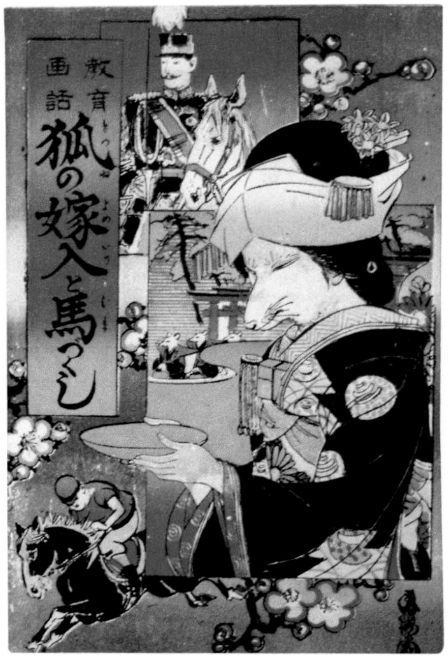
教育画話
狐の嫁入と馬づくし

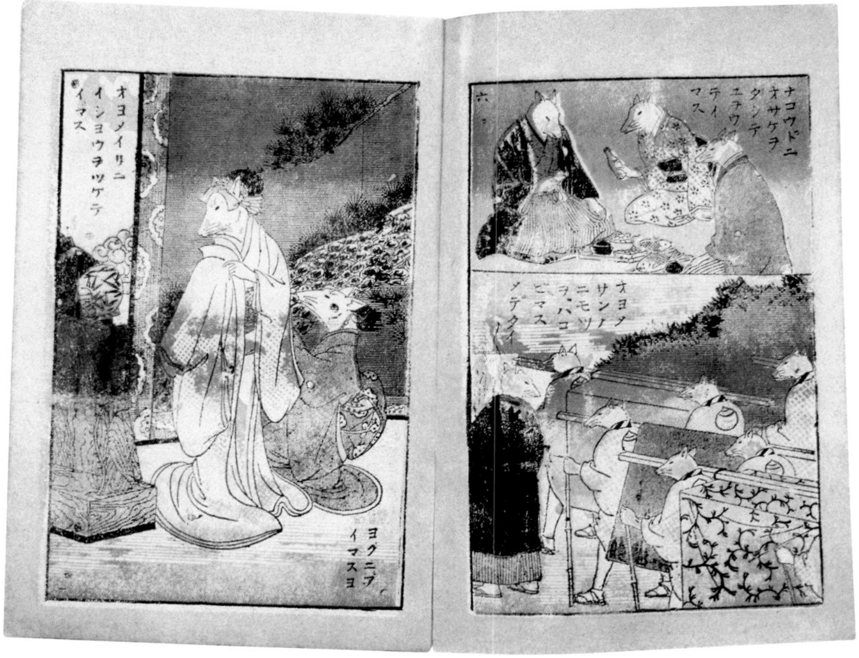
六
ナコウドニオサケヲダシテユヲウテイマス
オヨメサンノニモツヲハコビマスメデタイ
オヨメイリニイショウヲツケテイマス
ヨクニアイマスヨ

207–208
Anonymous, *The Fox's Wedding*, lithograph, Shunyô School, c. 1920. © Kumon Institute of Education

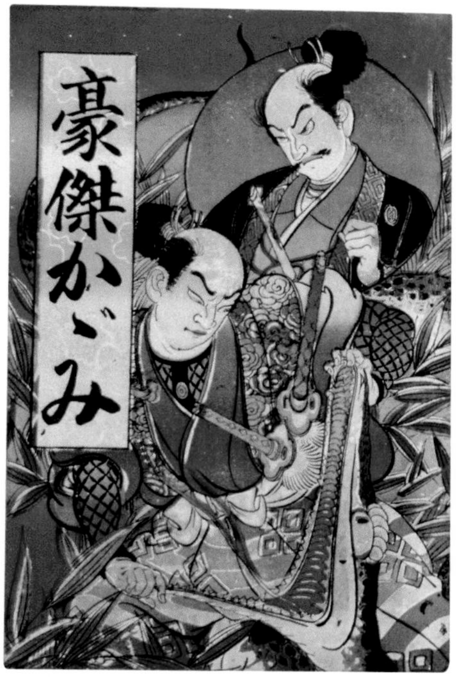
豪傑かゞみ

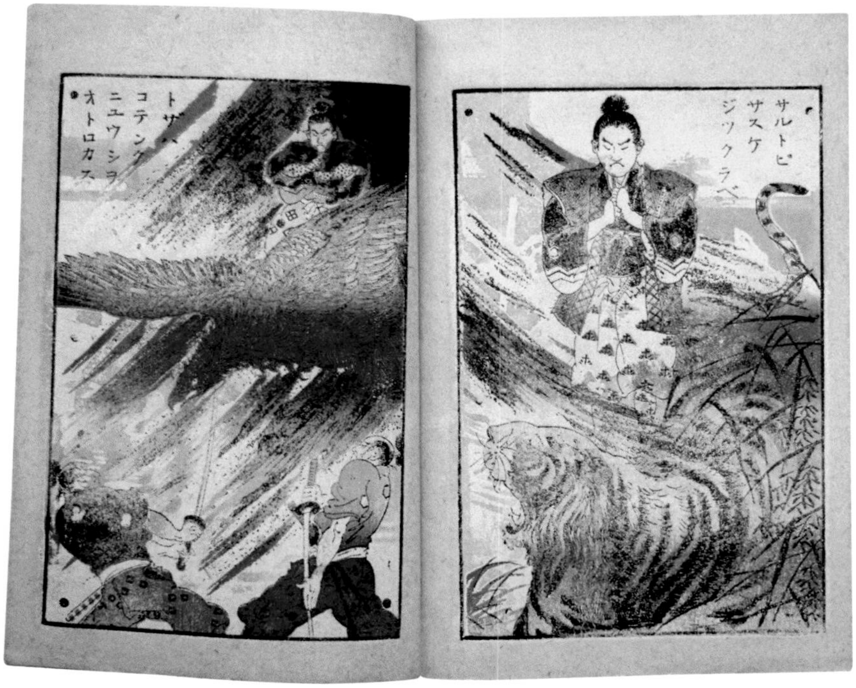
サルトビサスケジツクラベ
トザハコテングニユウシヲオトロカス

209–210
Anonymous, *A Strange Mirror*, lithograph, c. 1912–20. © Kumon Institute of Education

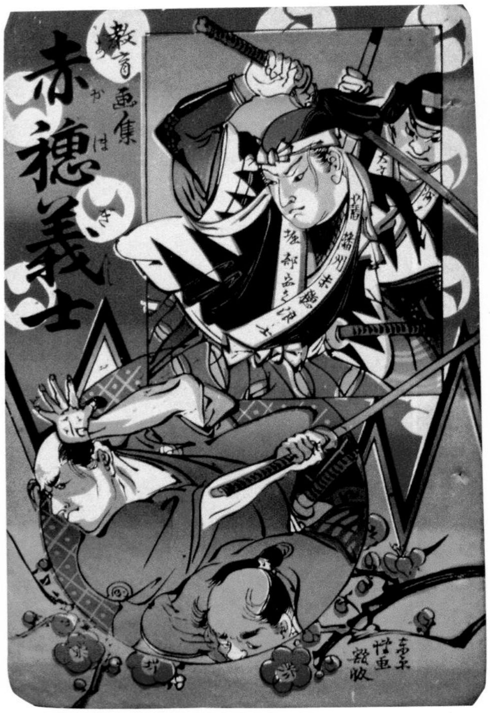
教育画集
赤穂義士

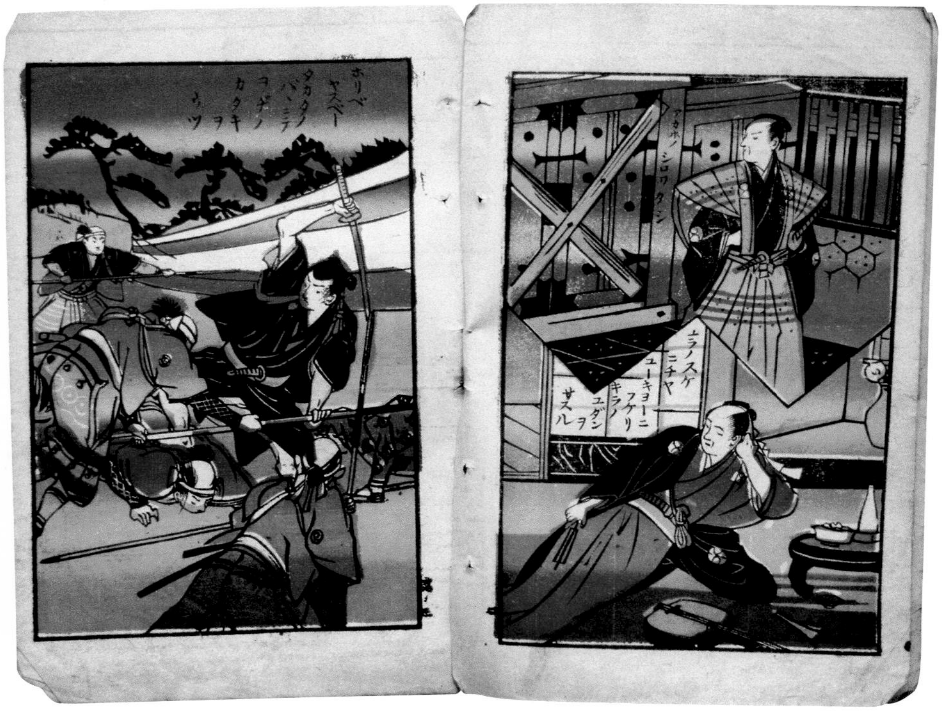

211–212
Anonymous, *The Story of the Brave Samurai of Akô*, lithograph, c. 1912–20. © Kumon Institute of Education

This is one of the most famous history stories in all Japan, known under the title *The Forty-Seven Rônins**. The drama, represented in *kabuki** theater and with many screen and TV adaptations, takes place at the beginning of the eighteenth century. The emperor sent ambassadors to the Shogun* to present him with his good wishes. The latter appointed two lords to oversee the formalities. One of them, Asano Nagamori, the *daimyô** of the domain of Akô, sought advice from the master of ceremonies, Kira Yoshinaka, who refused assistance. A furious Asano Nagamori wounded him with his sword in the Shogun's palace. He was then condemned to ritual suicide so the three hundred samurai under his command lost all means of subsistence and became *rônins*. One of them, Ôishi Kuranosuke, resolved to avenge his master and joined with forty-six men of the same clan. They beheaded Kira and offered his head to their onetime master by depositing it on his tomb and then gave themselves up to the authorities. Acclaimed by the people of Edo, they were nonetheless condemned to commit *seppuku**, doing so on February 4, 1703. Only the one ordered to announce the death of his comrades to Akô escaped death; on his return, he was granted an amnesty by the Shogun.

demobilized soldiers crisscrossed the country performing picture plays in the street, *kami shibai**, greatly appreciated by children for whom any entertainment was a rare treat. Many *mangaka*, such as Shirato Sanpei and Mizuki Shigeru, started out producing drawings for these traveling troupes. The latter recounts how to survive he had to turn out up to ten sheets a day.

The comic strip got back on its feet after the war. Satirical newspapers reappeared, as did weekly cartoons, such as the one in the *Sazae san* in 1946. Its creator, Hasegawa Machiko, was the first woman *mangaka* whose talent was recognized. Her famous manga continued for some years and are still broadcast on television in anime* form. In spite of the conflict, *The Shônen Club* and *The Yôji Club* had continued to appear. In 1946 the review, *Shônen*, first appeared, followed by many others. Gradually their format evolved and they began to tackle a wider range of subjects.

The immediate postwar period belonged to the "red books," *akahon**, published primarily in Osaka, which carried all before them. So-called because of their gaudy, mainly red cover, they were sold in toy and candy stores with, in general, neither the name of their author nor their extremely reasonable price appearing on the cover. Up to 1950, the American occupying forces, which were wary of the combative spirit of the Japanese and their values of obedience and sacrifice drawn from the *bushidô**, banned certain manga subjects. *Jidai geki**, historical subjects whose action was set before the Meiji Restoration, judo, kendo, karate, and all Japanese combat sports were prohibited, and replaced by themes such as baseball and science fiction.

As "red books" became increasingly expensive during the 1950s, the young turned to borrowing their fare from *kashihon manga**, outlets that began opening all over the country. By lending out manga to children for a very small sum, these stores fostered the blossoming of much new talent. This was also the time when the "story manga*," generally issued as serials, made an appearance under the influence of Tezuka Osamu. After 1950, manga for boys were permitted to choose their inspiration from the past, present, or future of Japan or elsewhere, and they began featuring stories of robots, battles, adventures, samurai*, and cowboys. Those for girls preferred to revel in the Japan of earlier epochs or chose settings in foreign

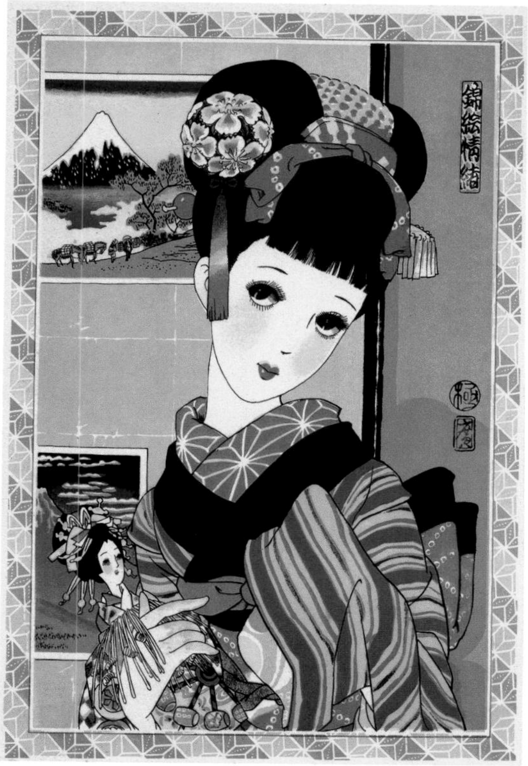
錦絵情緒

213
Nakahara Junichi, *The Charm of Nishiki-e Prints*, *nishiki-e* print, 1930s © Kumon Institute of Education

This girl with such big eyes seems rather reminiscent of today's manga characters. Her doll, which is dressed like an *oiran** (courtesan), and the landscapes on the prints one can see behind her, such as Hokusai's famous *Red Mount Fuji*, nostalgically evoke an age long gone.

正チャンの冒険
画／樺島勝一 作／織田小星
発行 小学館クリエイティブ 発売 小学館

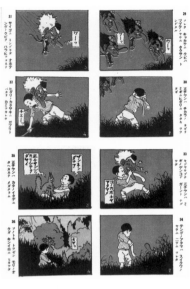

214–215
Oda Shôsei Kabashima Kaksuichi *The Adventures of Shôchan*, 1925, Matsumoto Leiji Collection, reissued 2003. © Shogakukan Creative

As evening falls, Shôchan is walking through the mountains with his squirrel friend when they are set upon by *tengus** (demons), but Shôchan gets the upper hand.

タンクタンクロー
阪本牙城著

216–218
Sakamoto Gajô, *Tanku Tankuro*, 1935, Matsumoto Leiji Collection, republished 2005. © Shogakukan Creative

Having studied painting for five years, Sakamoto Gajô (1895–1973) turned to manga on the advice of Okamoto Ippei. In 1934, the character Tanku Tankuro appeared in the magazine *Yônen Club* and did much to increase its readership. Tanku Tankuro is the ancestor of Tezuka Osamu's Astro Boy and of Doraemon. He is regarded as the originator of science-fiction manga.

Tanku Tankuro is a kind of eight-holed bowling-ball possessed of a human head. Readers can never guess in advance what he hides in his eight holes: sometimes it's weapons, other times propellers, enabling him to soar into the air like a helicopter. He takes on all manner of guises in his fight against evil.

そこの丸窓からのぞいてごらん
あら！看護婦さんが見送つてゐるわ
看護婦さーん
さらば火星よ！
もうどの位飛んだかしら
出發してから一分五秒！
早さはどの位？
おゝものすごい！一時間七千キロメートルの早さだ!!
あれえ？變だぞ早く舵をさがしてくれ
どうしたの？
舵はどれかしら
どうも見當がちがつた地球ぢゃない月に向つて走つてゐるらしいんだ!!
えッ！月に向つて？
大變だわどうしやう

火星探險

219–220
Kasei Tanken (The Exploration of Mars): drawings by Ôshiro Noboru (1905–1998), texts by Asahi Tarô (1901–1940), 1940, republished 2005.
© Shogakukan Creative

Kasei Tanken, published in 1940, was one of the earliest of the science-fiction manga. The hero, Tentarô, is the son of a scientist who works in an observatory. He falls asleep and wakes up on Mars surrounded by pinhead men. Accompanied by his cat Nyanko and his dog Pichi-kun, he sallies forth on his adventures. This work proved a considerable influence on younger artists, in particular Tezuka Osamu.

8

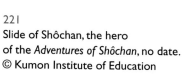

221
Slide of Shôchan, the hero of the *Adventures of Shôchan*, no date.
© Kumon Institute of Education

The story is shown to children through a succession of slides.

愉快な鐵工所
ゆかいなてっこうしょ

222–223
Kazutaka Kurimoto, Ôshiro Noboru, *Yukai na tetsu kôjo (An Odd Metal Factory)*, 1941, republished 2005. © Shogakukan Creative

Well before Astro Boy, this manga featured robot characters: the story shows a *mangaka* who, in a dream, meets a scientist and his son, travels with them in an air-balloon and then visits metal factory where the workmen are all androids. Having worked in a metal factory himself, the author, Ôshiro Noboru, made use of his personal experiences. Appearing in 1941, this manga was very popular at the time, and anticipates many cartoons starring robots that appeared after the Second World War.

こがらし剣士

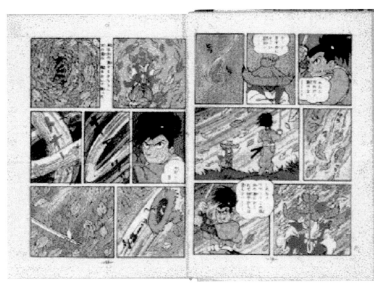

224
Shirato Sanpei, *Kogarashi Kenshi (The Samurai of the Winter Wind)*, Toroe Shuppan, 1957. © Matsumoto Leiji Collection

225
Nakamura Haruyuki, *The Famous Detective Shinchan*, Hoikusha, 1947. © Matsumoto Leiji Collection

Crime stories in which the evildoers are always caught by a clever detective flourished after the Second World War. Today, *The Detective Conan*, which replaced *Shinchan*, is one of the highest-selling manga. Here, Shinchan leaps on his bicycle and rushes to the help of a young girl who is being abducted.

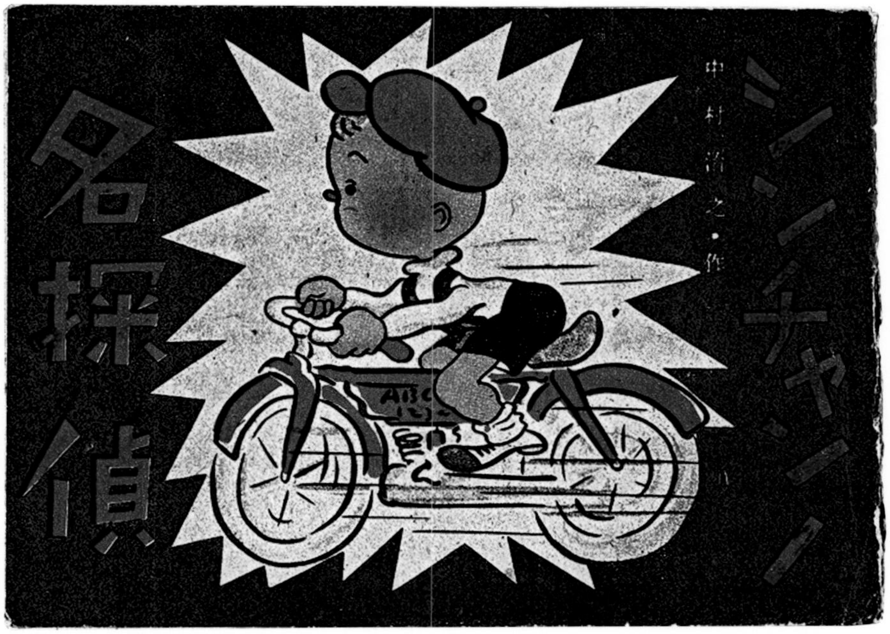
シンチャン
名探偵

226
Yamakawa Sôji, *Ginsei (The Silver Star)*, Gakudôsha, 1952.
© Matsumoto Leiji Collection

This tale, set in 1912 in the United States, tells the adventures of a wonder horse which people try to kidnap to make money. This story, like the following, is one of a type of illustrated narrative known as *emonogatari**. By its graphic style and themes, it is clearly inspired by the work of American artists.

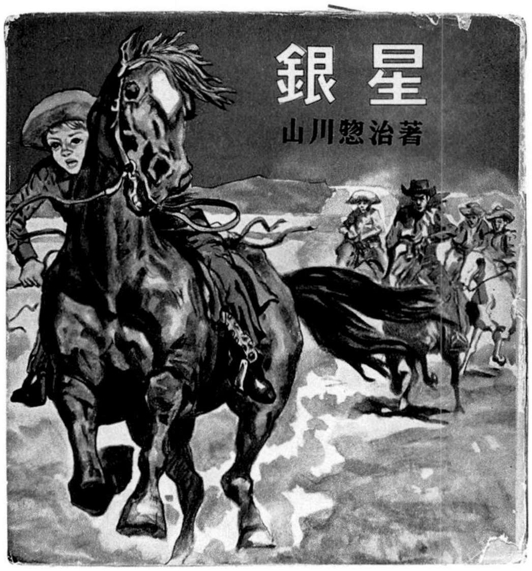
銀星
山川惣治著

227
Fukushima Tetsuji, Akita Shoten, *Sabaku no Maô (The Devil of the Desert)*, 1953.
© Matsumoto Leiji Collection

The author of this adventure story, Fukushima Tetsuji, admits the influence of American comic strips. He chose an imaginary setting which, he says, resembles Africa and is inhabited by lions. The action is located during the Second World War, with the hero performing exploits worthy of *Superman*, a comic Fujishima Tetsuji had greatly enjoyed looking through rather than actually reading in the original version. The story proved a huge success, and for six years from 1949 to 1954 it appeared in the magazine *Bôken ô (The King of Adventure)*.

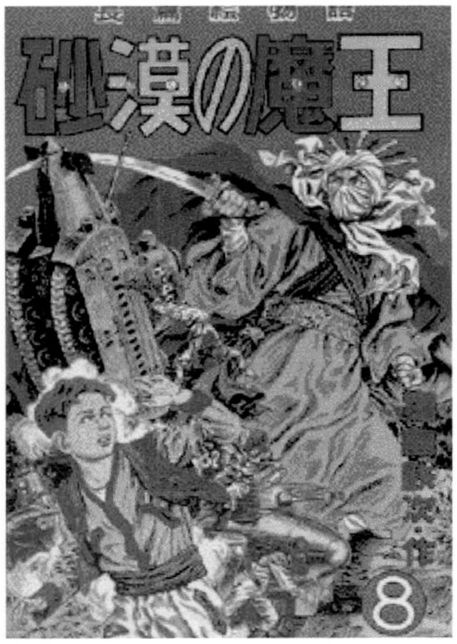
砂漠の魔王
8

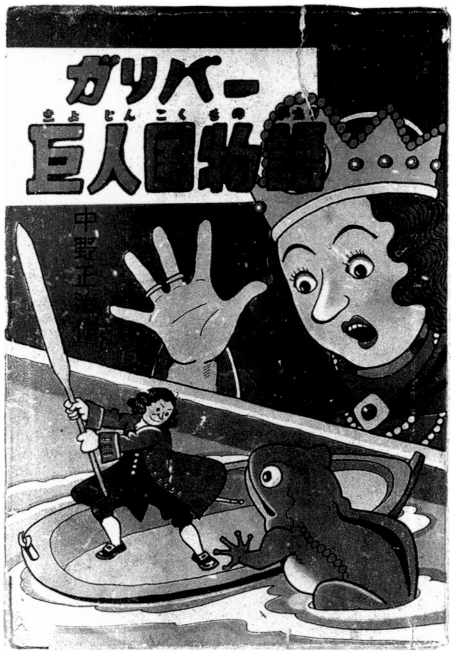
ガリバー

228
Nakano Masaharu, *Gulliver in the Land of the Giants,* Seibundô, 1948. © Matsumoto Leiji Collection

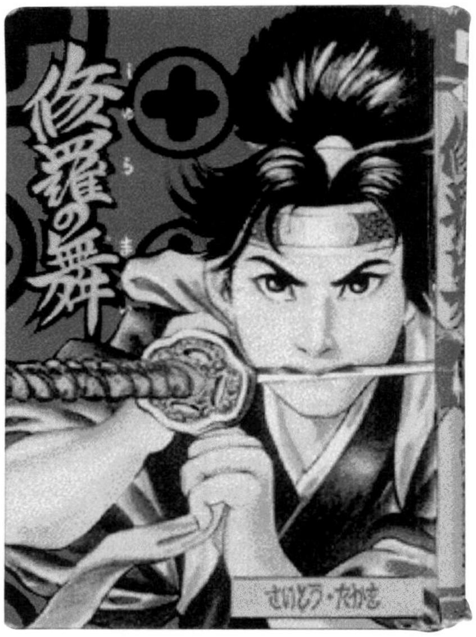
修羅の舞
さいとう・たかを

229
Saitô Takao, *Shura no Mai (The Dance of War)*, 1956. © Matsumoto Leiji Collection

lands. Children's manga often told romantic stories or took their inspiration from Western novels. Very colorful and attractive, they were extremely varied.

New heroes

Following the defeat of Japan, manga was reborn from its ashes and was able to offer new hope for young lives. Boys in particular were enthralled by American heroes such as Tarzan, which were repackaged Japanese-style by the *mangaka*, and countless stories set in the United States invaded the market. Figs. 226–22 230

Making initial strides before the war in *Tanku Tankuro*, the robot made serious inroads into the world of postwar manga and, following the success of Tezuka Osamu's *Astro Boy*, invaded the entire market. Coming in all sizes, sometimes kindly, at others more threatening, these heroes, gifted with all sorts of powers, demonstrated the interdependence between man and machine. Figs. 231–23

Manga adventures intended for boys concentrated on surpassing limits and achieving personal goals. This drive to make light of every obstacle surfaces even in collections intended for the very young. Figs. 235–23 Sometimes magic intervenes, allowing the hero, after many adventures, to discover a treasure or to achieve his goal. Fig. 234 It is a theme that features in many present-day manga. Figs. 224, 22 Stories of samurai, banned during the war, once again became popular in the 1950s. Japan found new energy by going back to its roots and traditional culture, and many *mangaka* composed stories starring samurai who avenged their lord or killed for a good cause.

As early as the Meiji period, the Japanese had begun translating, Figs. 228, 23 239, 241 often rather approximately, the great classics of European literature, but complete versions only became available at the beginning of the twentieth century. Filled with enthusiasm for these Western novels, *mangaka* were not long in offering their own interpretations.

Manga intended for girls were often inspired by tales illustrated for the most part by men. Matsumoto Leiji, Ishinomori Shôtarô, and Chiba Tetsuya, inter alia, drew for magazines such as *Shôjô Friend*, *Ribon* and *Margaret*, but gradually they abandoned the field to women illustrators such as Mizuno Hideko and Maki Miyako. Figs. 237–25

From the end of the Second World War, the numbers of manga reviews for the young, satirical magazines, and humorous comic strips swelled ceaselessly. The advent of manga that were modern in subject matter or graphics, in particular in the drawing of futuristic machines or figures, already prefigures contemporary manga, but the real revolution was sparked by Tezuka Osamu. It was thanks to his countless innovations, in the areas of graphics and framing in particular, that manga became the worldwide success it is today.

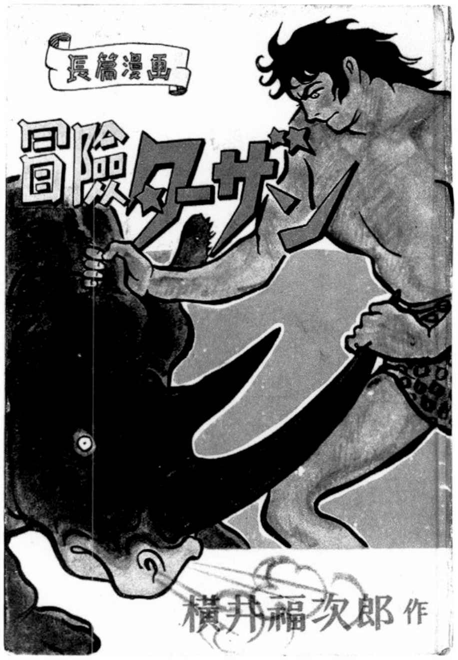

長篇漫画
冒険ターザン
横井福次郎 作

230
Yokoi Fukujirô, *The Adventures of Tarzan*, Kôbunsha, 1948. © Matsumoto Leiji Collection
In this tale, a young American detective goes to Africa to meet Tarzan who is looking for his mother. He takes him off to New York to continue his quest.

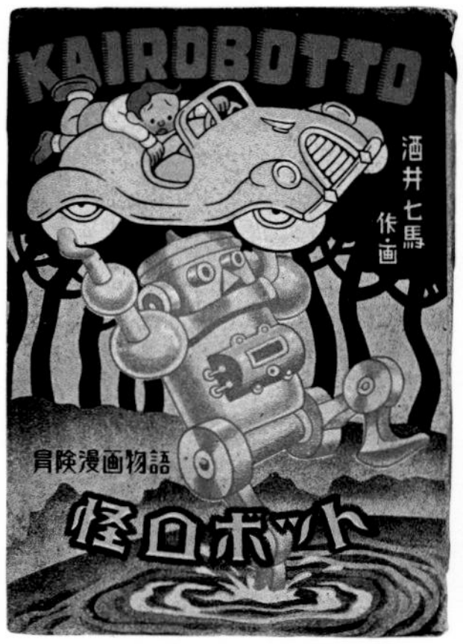
KAIROBOTTO
酒井七馬作画
冒険漫画物語
怪ロボット

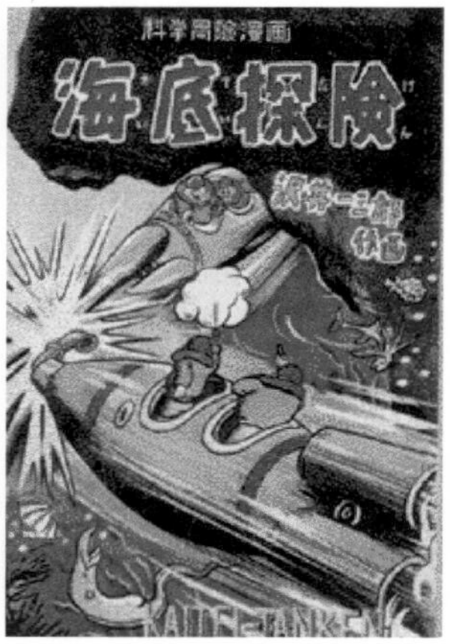
科学冒険漫画
海底探険

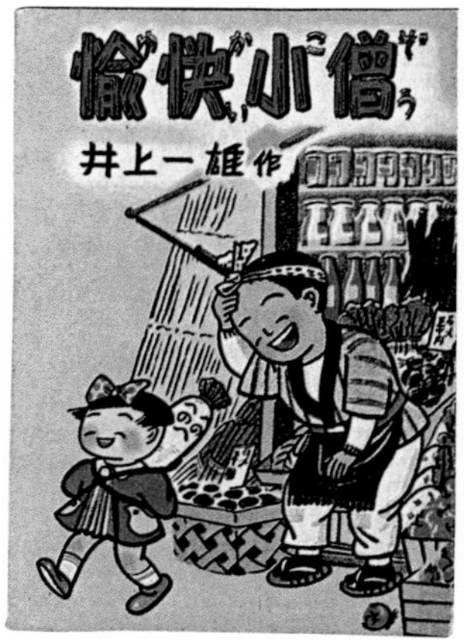
愉快小僧
井上一雄作

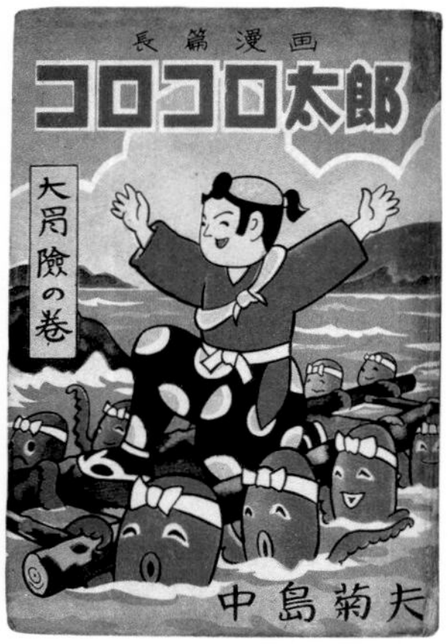
長編漫画
コロコロ太郎
大冒険の巻
中島菊夫

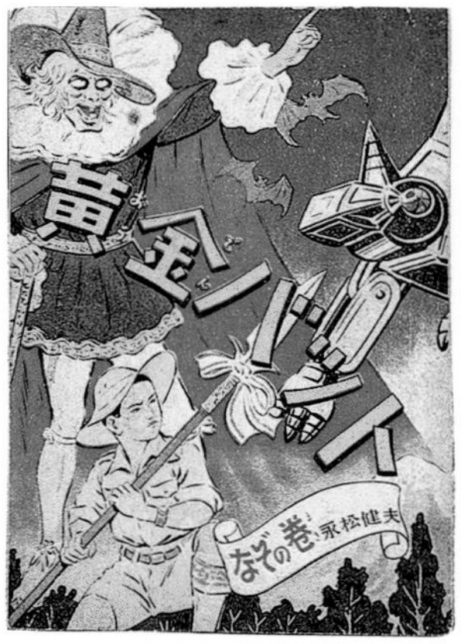
黄金バット
なぞの巻

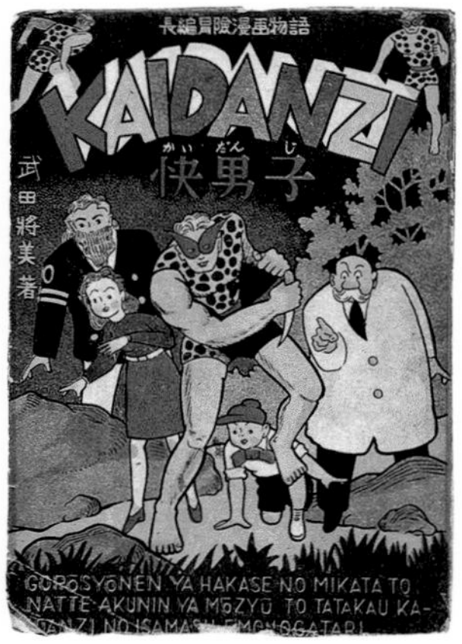
長編冒険漫画物語
KAIDANZI
快男子
武田将美著

231
Sakai Shichima, *A Strange Robot*, Jikunsha, 1947. © Matsumoto Leiji Collection

The evil scientist Zebra uses a remote-controlled robot to kidnap Dr. Peeble and his medicine bag with its special drugs. The robot, able to move at high speeds and having the strength of two hundred men, manages to abduct the wretched Peeble with ease. His youthful assistant, however, calls the police, who find him. Peeble restarts the robot, Zebra is arrested, and everything returns to normal.

232
Sawai Ichisaburô, Bunrinsha, *Kaitei-Tanken (Deep-sea Exploration)*, 1948. © Matsumoto Leiji Collection

Marui is a scientist convinced that the depths of the ocean are inhabited. Determined to elucidate the mystery, he starts exploring the abyss with a rather surprising machine: a rocket. His hypothesis proves correct: there are indeed beings living on the ocean floor. After a lengthy series of adventures, he manages to return to dry land, overjoyed to have been the first man to meet such extraordinary creatures.

233
Inoue Kazuo, Tsuru Shobô, *A Nice Kid*, 1949. © Matsumoto Leiji Collection

This young boy leaves his mountain home to go and work in a Tokyo greengrocer's. Invariably in an excellent mood, he is the epitome of a positive character and was much liked by children.

234
Nakajima Kikuo, *The Great Adventures of Korokorotarô*, Kin no hoshisha, 1949 © Matsumoto Leiji Collection

The hero of this manga, Korokorotarô, discovers a bottle containing a map of a treasure island on a beach. A white-haired old man gives him a magic ball that allows him three wishes, thanks to which he attains his goals.

235
Nagamatsu Takeo, *Ôgon Batto*, Meimeisha, 1947. © Matsumoto Leiji Collection

The character of Ôgon Batto, a superhero fighting baddies, had been created by Suzuki Ichirô (script) and Nagamatsu Takeo (graphics) for the *kami shibai** (paper theater), which became massively popular after the war. He was then taken up by Nagamatsu Takeo alone.

236
Takeda Masami, *Kaidanji (A Fine Fellow)*, Kôyô Shuppan, 1947. © Matsumoto Leiji Collection

In this adventure manga, recounting the struggle between good and evil, the courageous and extremely young Kaidanji ends up getting the better of the culprits.

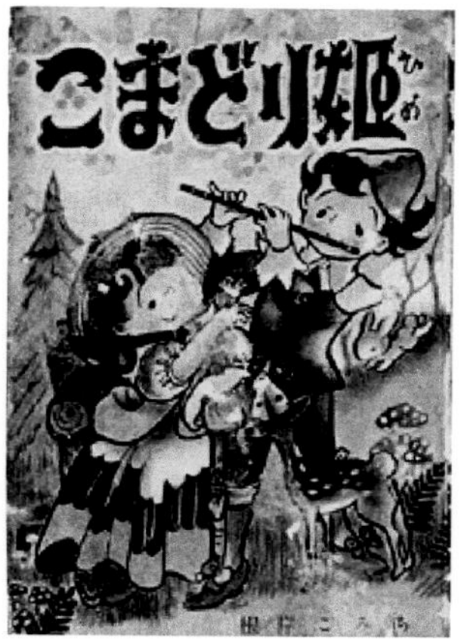
こまどり姫

237
Negishi Komichi, *The Robin Princess*, Akebono Shuppan, 1951. © Matsumoto Leiji Collection

A collection of tales reinterpreted as manga.

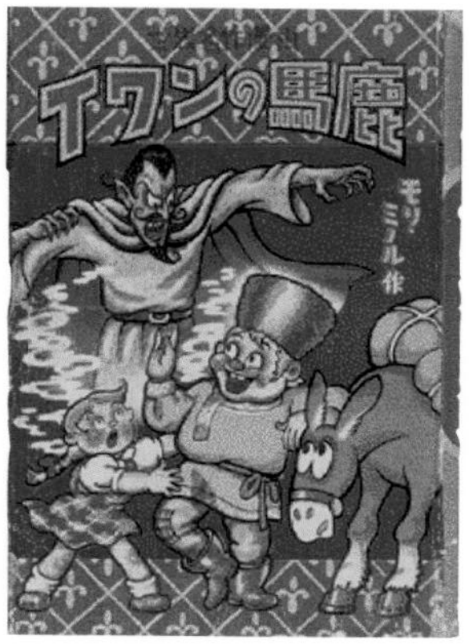
イワンの馬鹿

239
Mori Minoru, *The Death of Ivan Ilich*, Nihon Komikkusha, 1952. © Matsumoto Leiji Collection

A free interpretation of Tolstoy's famous tale.

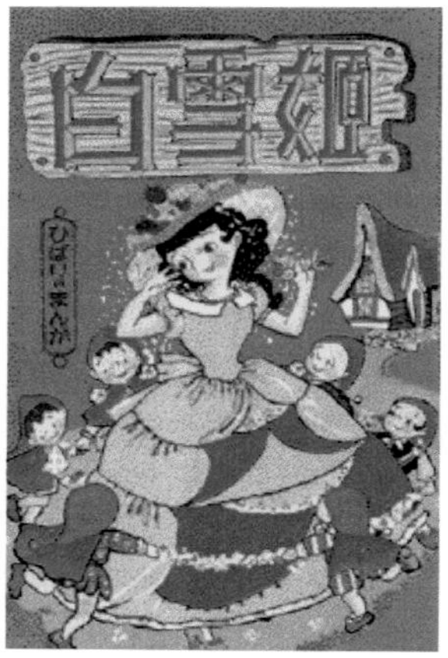
白雪姫

241
Negishi Komichi, *Snow White*, Hibari Shobô, 1951. © Matsumoto Leiji Collection

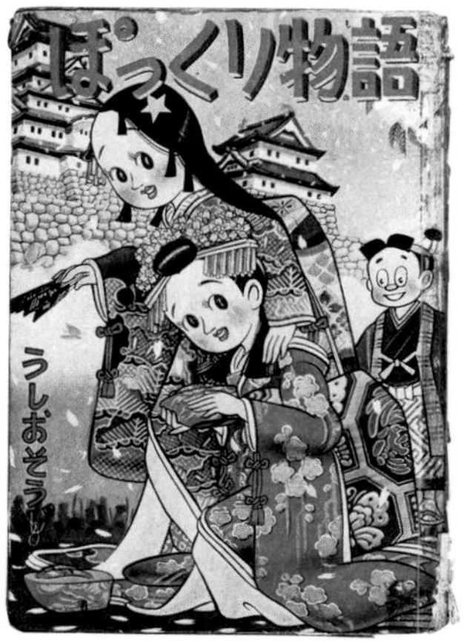
ぽっくり物語

238
Ushio Sôji, Nakamura Shoten, *The Story of the Princess in Geta*, 1952. © Matsumoto Leiji Collection

A young orphan girl, Hiyori, comes to Edo to sell clams to earn a living. She meets Komakichi with whom, when she learns of his true origin, she decides to live. Born of noble family, little Hiyori is in fact a princess of high rank. She then resides in her ancestors' castle, but this idle if luxurious existence does not satisfy the two youngsters, and they soon opt to go back on the road.

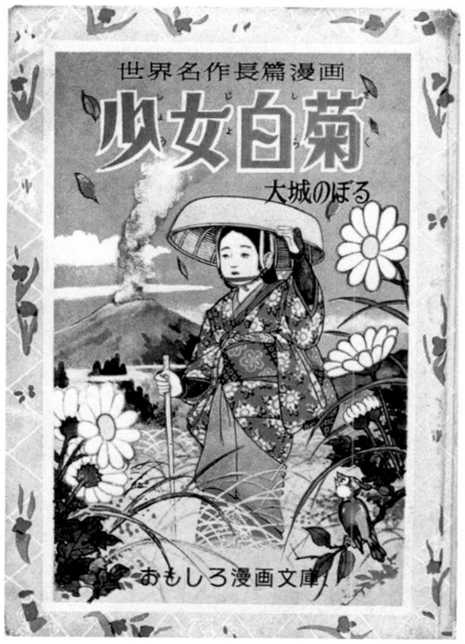
世界名作長篇漫画
少女白菊
大城のぼる
おもしろ漫画文庫

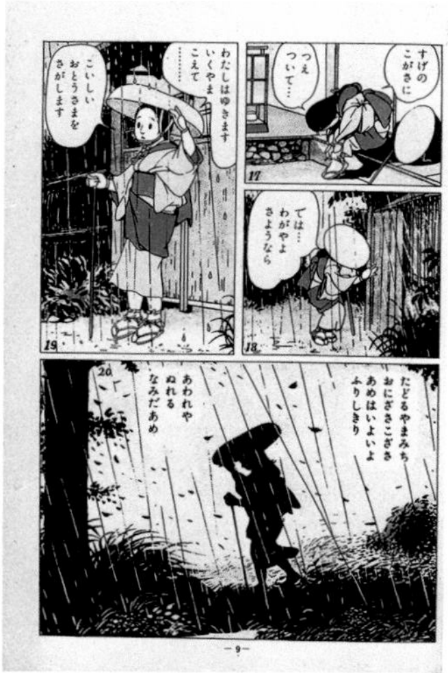

240
Ôshiro Noboru, *Little Shiragiku*, Shûeisha, 1954. © Matsumoto Leiji Collection.

The drama takes place in the Edo period. The little Shiragiku ("White Chrysanthemum") is worried that her father is late back from the hunt. Actually he has gone to the defense of the Satsuma clan in the Civil War of 1877 that preceded the Meiji Restoration. Deciding to go off and search for him, the little girl will have to overcome countless obstacles.

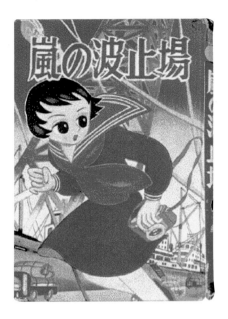

242
Akatsuka Fujio, *The Landing-stage in the Storm,*
Akebono Shuppansha, 1956. Matsumoto Leiji Collection

Adventure manga especially for girls were also issued.
The young Midori and her friend have to find the
stolen plans for a rocket. Displaying great ingenuity,
they manage to get hold of them and so foil the spies.

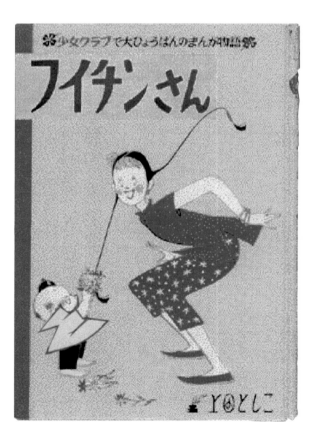

243
Ueda Toshiko, *Fuichin-san,* **Kôdansha, 1958.**
© Matsumoto Leiji Collection

Miss Fuichin is the Chinese heroine of this exceptionally successful manga.

A young member of the staff in the service of a wealthy
family, she shows undaunted courage. Always looking on the
bright side and never losing her cheerfulness in the face of
adversity, her story refers to the difficult situation in
Manchuria and China during the Second World War. The
author of this very popular series, Ueda Toshiko, spent her
childhood in Manchuria, where she took drawing lessons and
decided to become a *mangaka*.

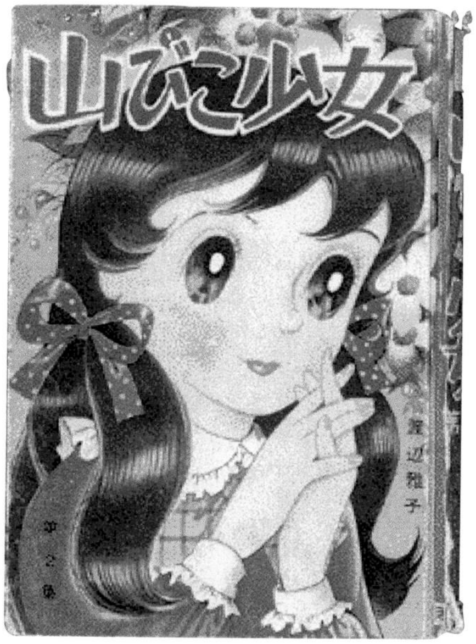
山びこ少女
渡辺雅子

244
Watanabe Masako, *The Little Girl of the Mountain Echo*, Wakagi Shobô, 1958. © Matsumoto Leiji Collection

There was a time when twins were thought unlucky. Shortly after the birth of twin daughters, a man sees his house consumed by flames and decides to split them up, keeping one at home and sending the other to live in the mountains. The one who stays with him in Tokyo contracts polio, but the story unfolds beautifully when the two sisters meet once again.

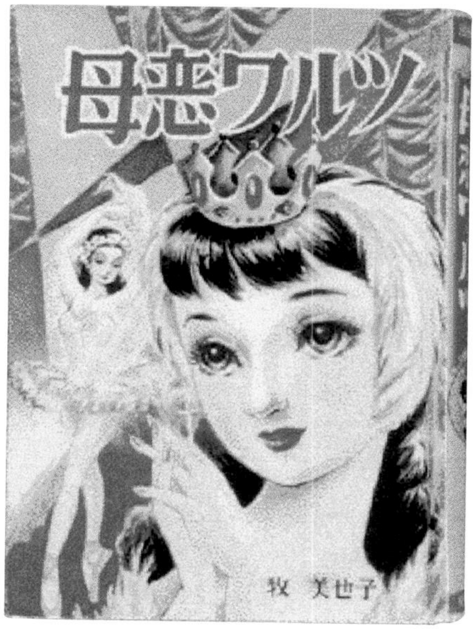
母恋ワルツ

245
Maki Miyako, *Waltz for my Mother*, Tôkôdô, 1957. © Matsumoto Leiji Collection

The first manga dedicated to ballet dancing, this was followed by many on the same subject. After ten years in France, a ballerina returns to Japan and decides to concentrate her efforts on her daughter, who also shows a precocious gift for dance.

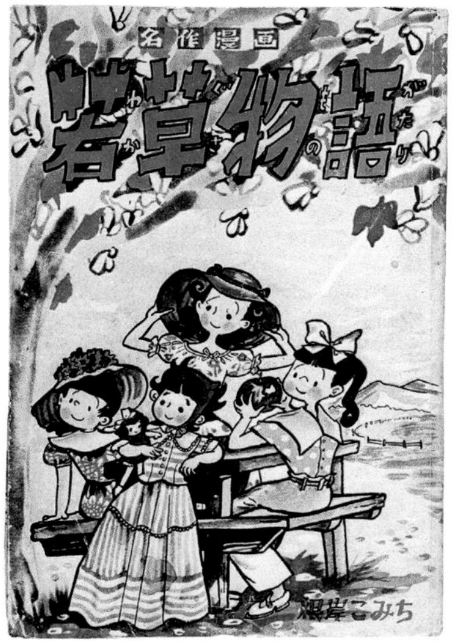
名作漫画
若草物語

246
Negishi Komichi, *Wakakusa Monogatari (Little Women)*, after the novel by Louisa May Alcott, Akebono Shuppan, 1951. © Matsumoto Leiji Collection

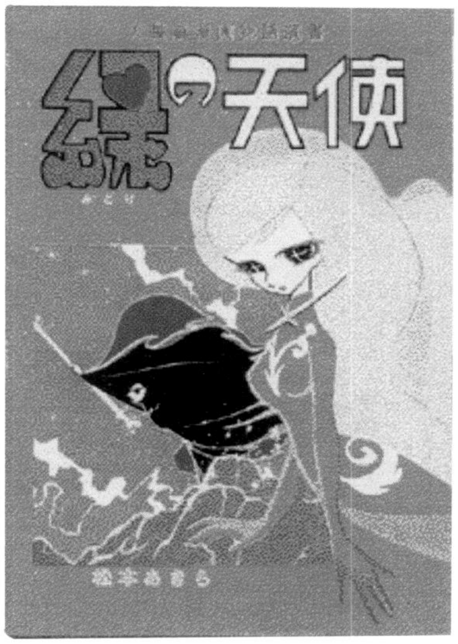
緑の天使

247
Matsumoto Akira (Leiji), *Midori no Tenshi (The Green Angel)*, Wakaba Shobô, 1959. © Matsumoto Leiji Collection

For this youthful work, Matsumoto Akira set the story in Antiquity. A power struggle between two fictitious European peoples involves the reader in the adventures of a merciless queen.

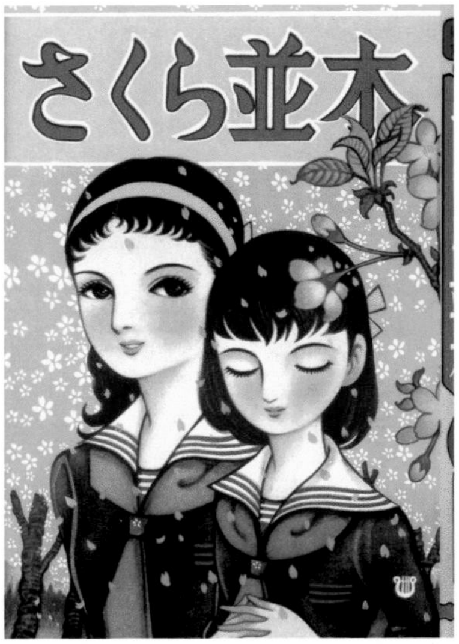
さくら並木

248
Takahashi Makoto, *Sakura Namiki (Cherry-tree Lane)*, 1961, republished 2006. © Shogakukan Creative

A story of female students in a high-flown style.

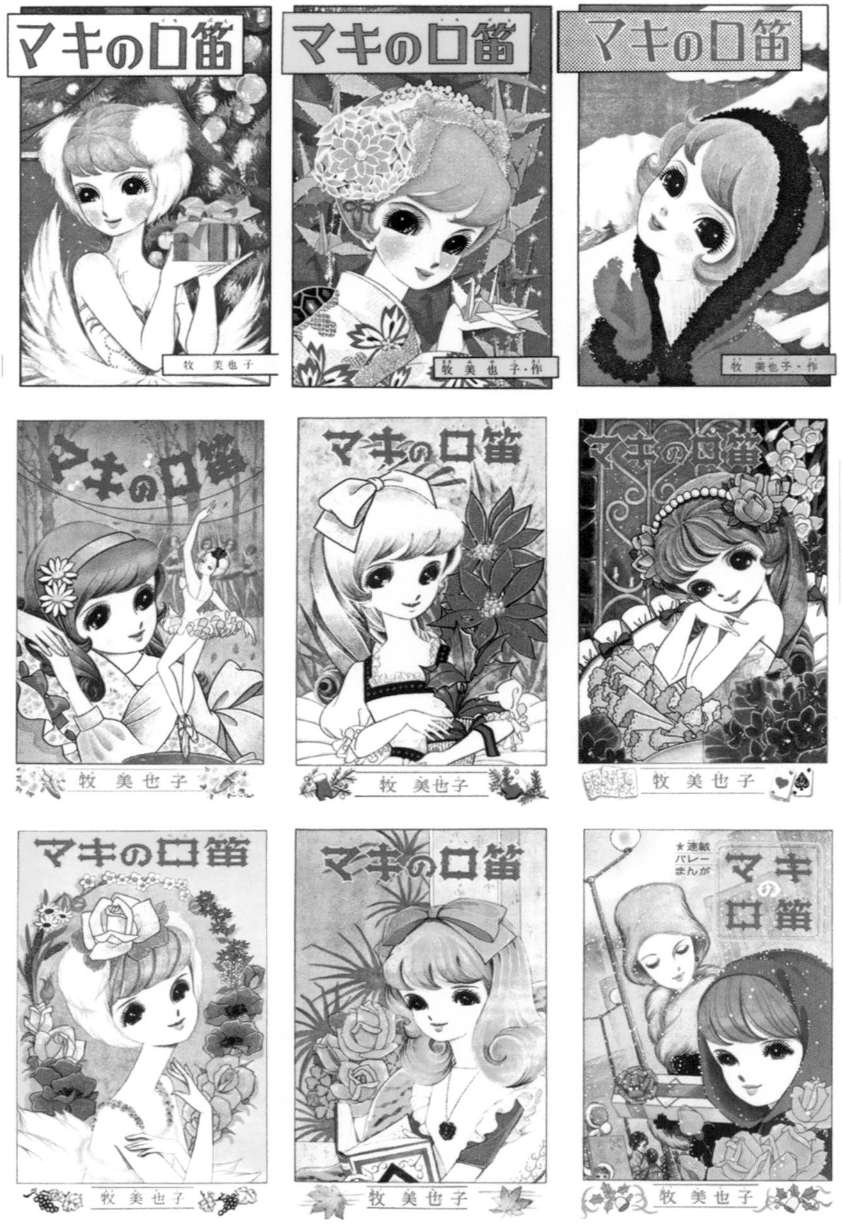
マキの口笛
牧美也子

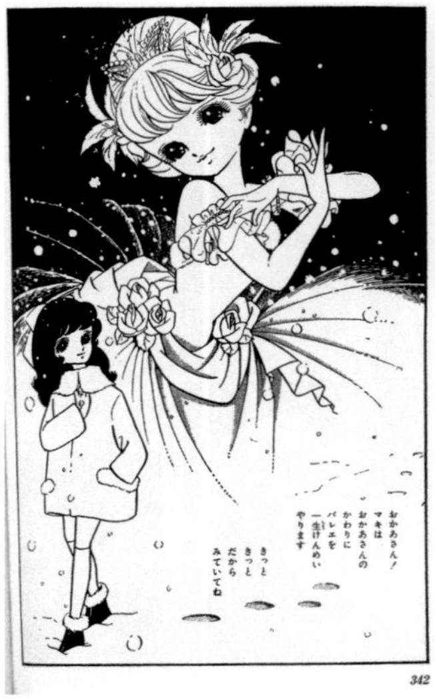

249–250
Maki Miyako, *Maki no kuchibue (Maki's Whistle)*, reprint Tokyo, 2006. © Shogakukan Creative

With *Maki's Whistle* (published from 1960 to 1963 in the review *Ribon* and reissued by Shogakukan Creative), Maki Miyako also chose the world of the ballet as a backdrop. The young heroine, Maki, has a passion for dance, and learns as she grows up that she is the daughter of an actress who was once a famous ballerina, rediscovering her mother only a few months before her death. The delicious drawings and the romantic story make this into a manga that little girls followed with bated breath. The cover of each number of *Ribon* showed the heroine in different attire.

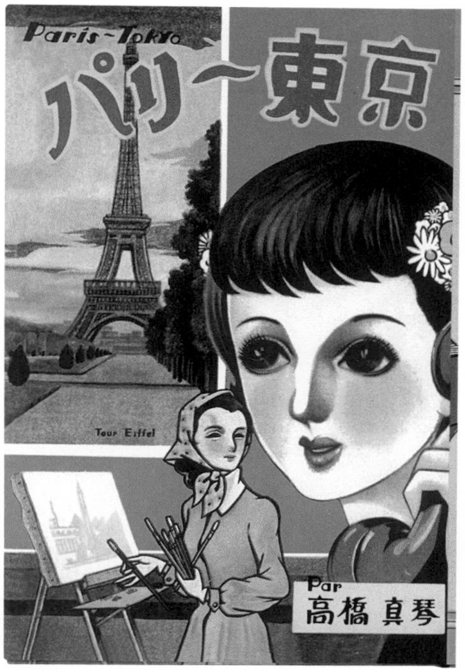
Paris~Tokyo
パリ〜東京
Tour Eiffel
Par
高橋真琴

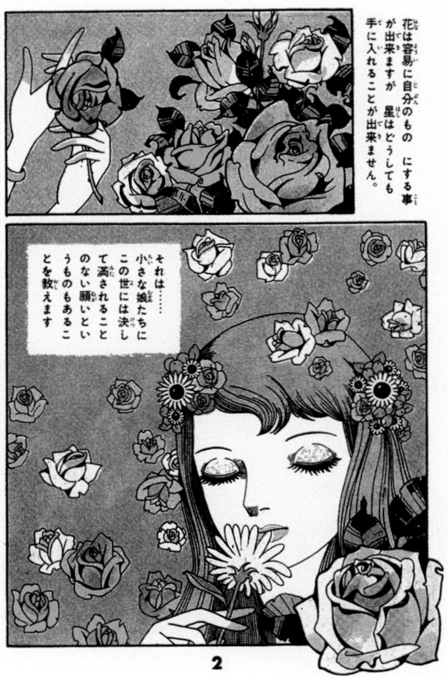
花は容易に自分のもの にする事が出来ますが 星はどうしても手に入れることが出来ません。
それは……小さな娘たちにこの世には決して満されることのない願いというものもあることを教えます
2

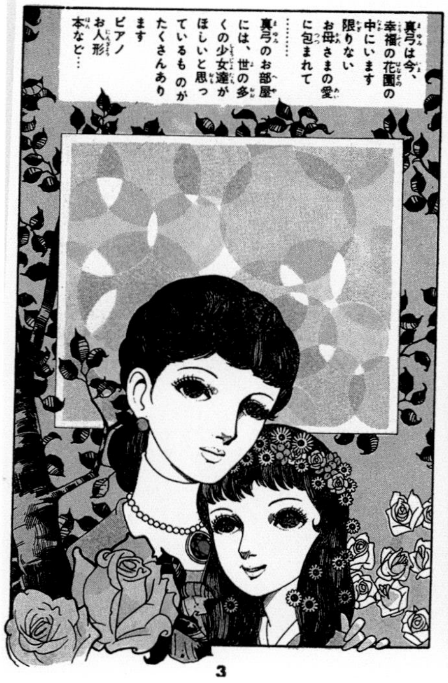
真弓は今、幸福の花園の中にいます 限りない お母さまの愛に包まれて……
真弓のお部屋には、世の多くの少女達がほしいと思っているもの がたくさんあります
ピアノ
お人形
本など…
3

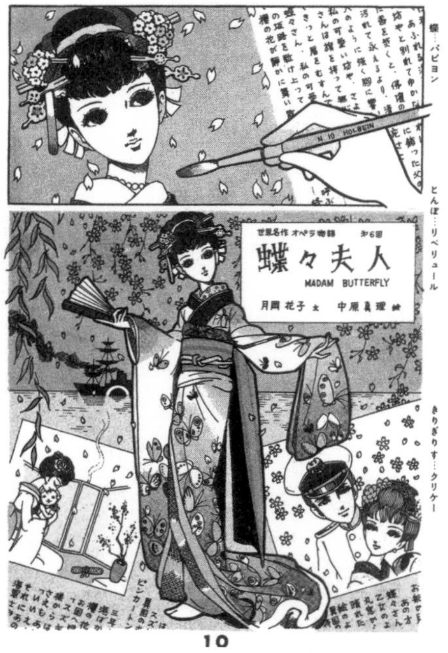
蝶…パピヨン
とんぼ…リベリュール
きりぎりす…クリケー
HOLBEIN
世界名作オペラ物語 第6回
蝶々夫人
MADAM BUTTERFLY
月岡花子 文 中原真理 絵
10

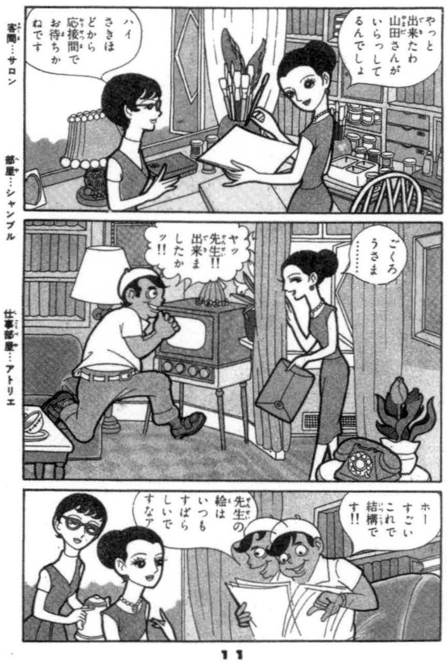
客間…サロン
部屋…シャンブル
仕事部屋…アトリエ
やっと出来たわ 山田さんがいらっしてるんでしょ
ハイ さきほどから応接間でお待ちかねです
ごくろうさま……
ヤッ先生!! 出来ましたかッ!!
ホー すごい これで結構です!!
先生の絵はいつもすばらしいですなア
11

251–253

Takahashi Makoto, *Paris Tokyo*, 1961, republished 2006. © Shogakukan Creative

A fourteen-year-old lives with her mother, a painter. She discovers the identity of her father who resides in France and sets off to meet him. In an interview, the author noted that this was the first time that French words appeared in a Japanese text. He studied Parisian fashions in reviews to make his heroines more elegant, gave them fair hair, and, in drawing the Japanese girls, took inspiration from a number of famous actresses.

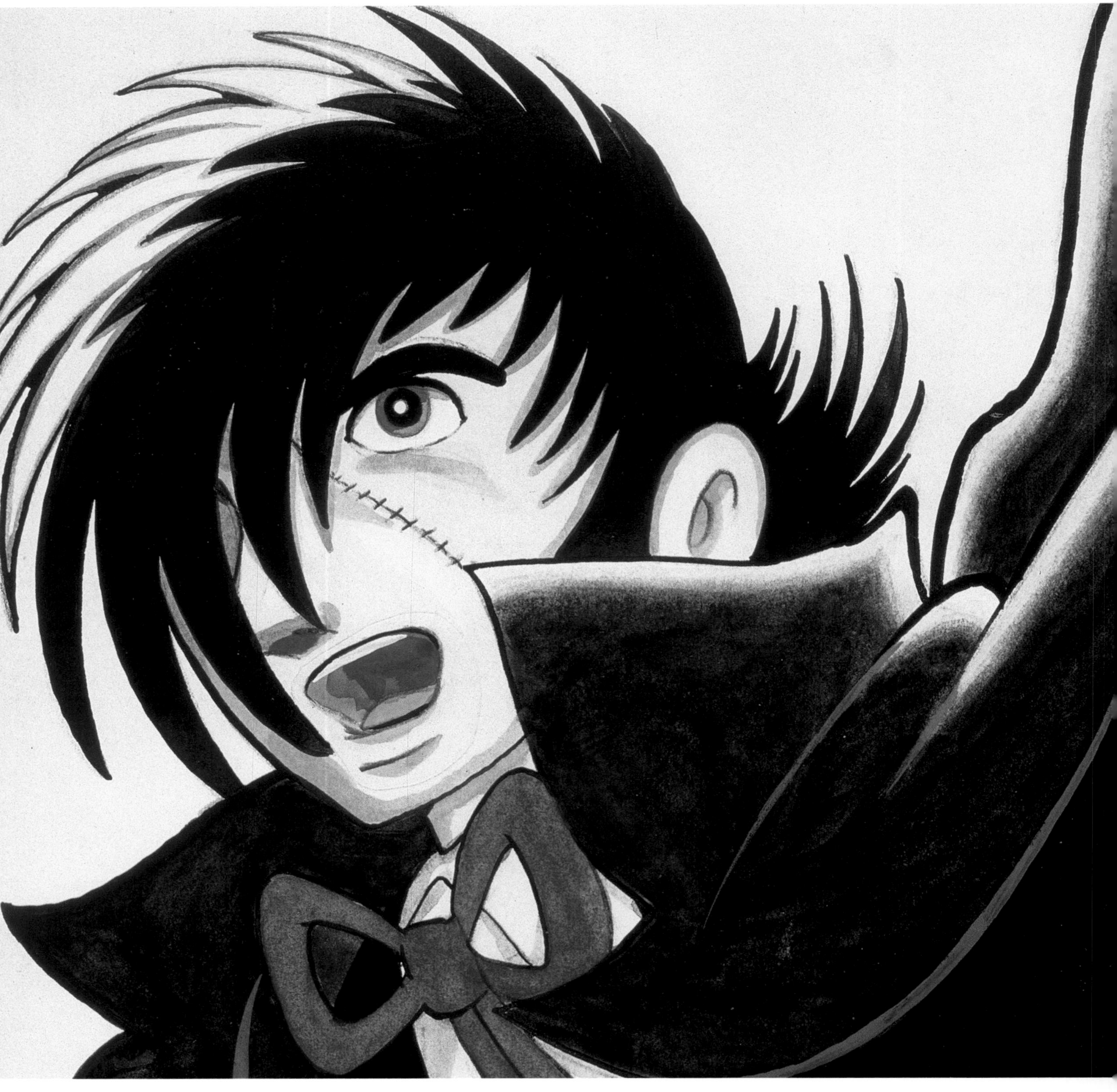

Fig. 266 (detail)

The man and his work

Manga* could never have become what they are today without the remarkable oeuvre of Tezuka Osamu (1928–1989). Physician, excellent musician, an expert on insects, in Japan this artistic genius remains the best-known *mangaka** of all.

The articles, monographs, and reportages devoted to him are countless, while Tezuka himself has published an invaluable testimony of his life, *My Life in Manga* ("Boku no manga no jinsei," *Iwanami shinsho*, no. 509, Tokyo, 1997, 2nd edition, 2006). In this he tells of his childhood and youth, as well as of his work and the events that most influenced him and made him become a *mangaka*.

The image that contemporaries had of him was of a brilliant yet very respectful man; untiring, sleeping little, who produced an endless stream of work. When a child, however, young Osamu, timid and of a fragile constitution, was bullied by a gang in his class at school because he wore glasses. He got used to keeping out of the way and, to avoid his classmates, he would change his route back from school each day. Later on, at high school, he again had to bend to the law of the strongest. The family home was a haven of peace he could hardly wait to get back to.

His mother taught him to be patient and to persevere, giving him an early taste for reading through the many books and manga she read to him. Initiated into astronomy by one of his friends, the young Osamu was soon filled with an enthusiasm for the sciences. He acquired a passion for insects, observing and drawing them for hours. He even changed the spelling of his first name, adding the ideogram meaning "insect" (the pronunciation remains unaltered), and from then on used this new name on all his homework, in spite of complaints from his teachers. This was to become his lifelong *mangaka* name.

Every month, his father would give him some pocket-money to buy manga. "At that time, manga were not regarded as real books at all but as entertainment," he explained, "and nobody asked what their influence on young people could be. My mother bought me them instead of toys. I read them again and again unceasingly and I knew the stories and drawings off by heart." He owned some two hundred volumes; on Sundays the local kids would rush over to his

冒険漫画物語
新寶島
原作・構成 酒井七馬
作 画・手塚治虫

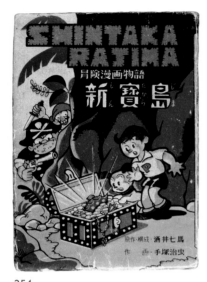

254
Tezuka Osamu (drawings) and Sakai Shichima (script), *Shin-Takarajima (The New Treasure Island)*, 1947, Ikuei Shuppan. © Tezuka Production

Tezuka here offers a free interpretation of Robert Louis Stevenson's novel *Treasure Island*. Later on, Tezuka drew other adaptations of famous works of Western literature, including Goethe's *Faust* in 1950, Dostoyevsky's *Crime and Punishment* in 1953 (see fig. 255).

Resolutely new on the formal level, *Shin-Takarajima* is a manga that stresses an analytical division of the action with a dynamic and novel "staging" that influences both the pace of reading and the length of the narrative. With more than 400,000 copies sold, the piece made a considerable impact, not only on readers, but also on the young *mangaka* of the time. *Shin-Takarajima* represents the first demonstration of a graphic style of storytelling that Tezuka was to continue developing, finally imposing it on the manga industry much later in the mid-1950s. Gradually, Tezuka was to graft elements on his manga, "inspired" by the language of cinema, which had hitherto rarely been exploited by his predecessors. Over the years, the increasing use of such processes (variations in scale, changes in angle and point of view, etc.) added considerably to the attractiveness of his drawing style, turning it into a template that was to be much copied by his colleagues.

home where his mother offered them various tidbits. It was thanks to a shared taste for manga that Osamu managed to overcome his wariness of other children.

His father, a keen moviegoer, had bought a small camera and started filming his family. Little by little this passion was transmitted to his son, constituting an unconscious influence on his way of seeing things. Tezuka too would often go to the cinema, afterward reproducing what had struck him in the movie. He spent a substantial amount of time drawing, and was copying and imitating his favorite manga when he was only about nine. Two years later, after encouragement from his schoolmates, he produced his own first manga, followed by drawings for *kami shibai** (paper theater), which he also hugely enjoyed. In every Japanese city, these small traveling theaters were an immense success: a man would arrive banging a pair of wooden sticks together like a clapper to call out the children; he would then sell them candy and tell them stories with the aid of drawings representing the main scenes, which he would slide into a wooden frame.

In spite of a pronounced taste for drawing, in 1945 Tezuka enrolled to study medicine; a number of members of his family had exercised this profession in the Edo* era and, much later, he was to devote a manga to the theme, *Hidamari no ki* (*The Tree in the Sun*, 1981–86). However, he never stopped drawing, even depriving himself of sleep, and during this time he published his first manga. With a degree in his pocket, he hesitated over his future, but chose to become a *mangaka*, all the while preparing his doctorate in medicine. Tezuka maintained that his studies had been an immense advantage to him, encouraging him to reflect on the meaning of life and death.

His graphic idiom evolved profoundly, growing in refinement as his career progressed. In the beginning unquestionably influenced by Walt Disney and the Fleischer Brothers, he lost no time in forging a style of his own. Following a debut manga that appeared in a magazine for children in 1946, *Mâ-chan no nikkichô (The Intimate Diary of Mâ-chan)*, he laid the foundations of modern manga with *Shintakarajima* (*The New Treasure Island*, 1947). Fig. 254

罪と罰
手塚治虫

255
Tezuka Osamu, *Tsumi to Batsu (Crime and Punishment)*, Tôkôdô, 1953. © Tezuka Osamu, Tezuka Production

長篇科学冒険漫画
THE GREAT CITY IN 20TH CENTURY
METROPOLIS
手塚治虫著
大都会

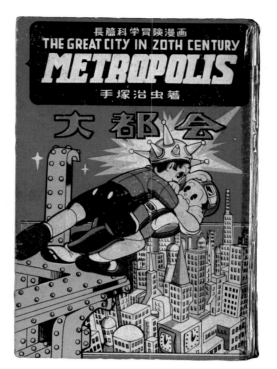

256
Tezuka Osamu, *Metropolis*, Ikuei Shuppan, 1949. © Tezuka Osamu, Tezuka Production

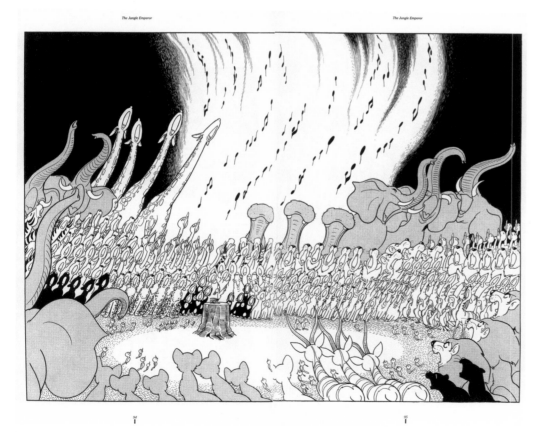

257
Tezuka Osamu, *Janguru Taitei (Kimba the White Lion)*, Gakudôska, 1950. © Tezuka Osamu, Tezuka Production
A jungle symphony is performed by the animals in honor of Kimba's birth.

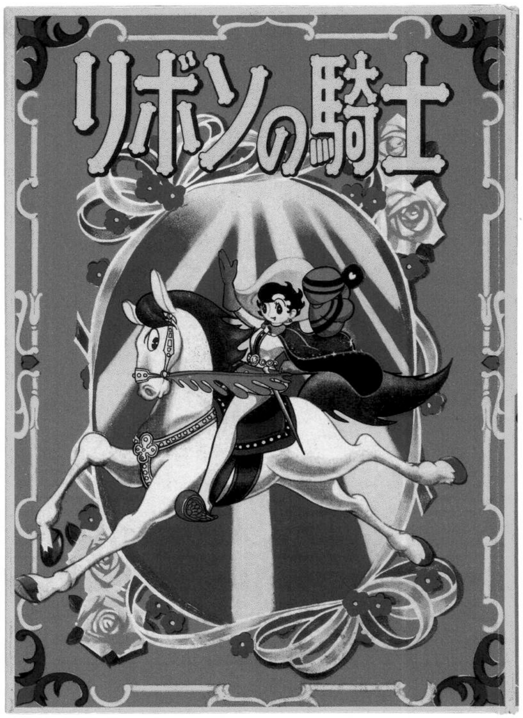
リボンの騎士

258
Tezuka Osamu, *Ribon no kidi (Princess Knight)*, Kôdasha, 1963–64. © Tezuka Osamu, Tezuka Production

Initially aimed specifically at girls and constructed like a film, the story of Princess Sapphire (who is also known as Princess Knight) garnered a much larger audience. Up in heaven, an angel mistakenly apportions the heart of a boy to a little girl. God sends the angel to earth to make good his blunder. The child is the Princess Sapphire, brought up as a prince in a country where only a boy can ascend the throne. One evening the princess puts on a dress and meets a prince. It's love at first sight on both sides, but Duke Duralumin discovers Sapphire's secret and makes a bid to usurp the throne....

However, it was from the 1950s that Tezuka Osamu's talent truly came into its own. *Kimba the White Lion* (also known as *The Jungle* Fig. 257 *Emperor*), with its touching animal character, brought him an international reputation. But the work that made him a household name, and which remained, in the eyes of his public, his masterpiece, is Fig. 259 *Astro (Tetsuwan Atomu)*, 1952–68.

When the manga of Astro Boy first came out, it received a hostile reception, with some of Tezuka's works even being burnt in the street. Accused of exerting a harmful influence on youth, he was roundly condemned. Soon the media got involved—it was widely thought ridiculous to make animals speak or robots fly. But children sensed that Tezuka was sincere and, when *Astro Boy* was adapted for television, the ratings were incredible. Tezuka never sought to hide his admiration for Disney, from whom he took inspiration on several occasions, in particular for *Astro Boy*: "I was unconsciously influenced by Mickey Mouse. Astro Boy resembles him. Mickey has two ears. Astro always has two horns. In fact, they are not 'horns' at all, but licks of hair. Oddly, Mickey Mouse can turn any way he likes, but one still sees two ears. From certain angles, they should by rights overlap, but this never happens. It is in such trickery that the magic of animation resides."

He goes on to add that it is the same for Astro Boy, who always presents two "horns" and is always bare-chested. Long ago, Mickey Mouse did not wear trousers, but shorts, like his own hero. Both have overlarge shoes. Tezuka explains that he made a hole in Astro Boy's glove following Mickey's lead. Tezuka Osamu really wanted to create animated drawings like those of Walt Disney, but the process proved far too expensive. In order to reduce costs, after many hours of research, he managed to attain first-rate result with fewer images and occasionally reutilizing earlier ones. Fully convinced that animation knows no borders and could be more easily understood than manga, he did much to develop the technique in Japan.

A precursor in all fields, Tezuka wrote the first true *shôjo manga** (manga for girls), *Princess Knight* (a.k.a. *Princess Sapphire*) in 1953. A Figs. 258, 260–262 few years previously, other artists had already made sporadic attempts at producing work for this market, but such manga, even if specifically written for girls and based on their ways of thinking or

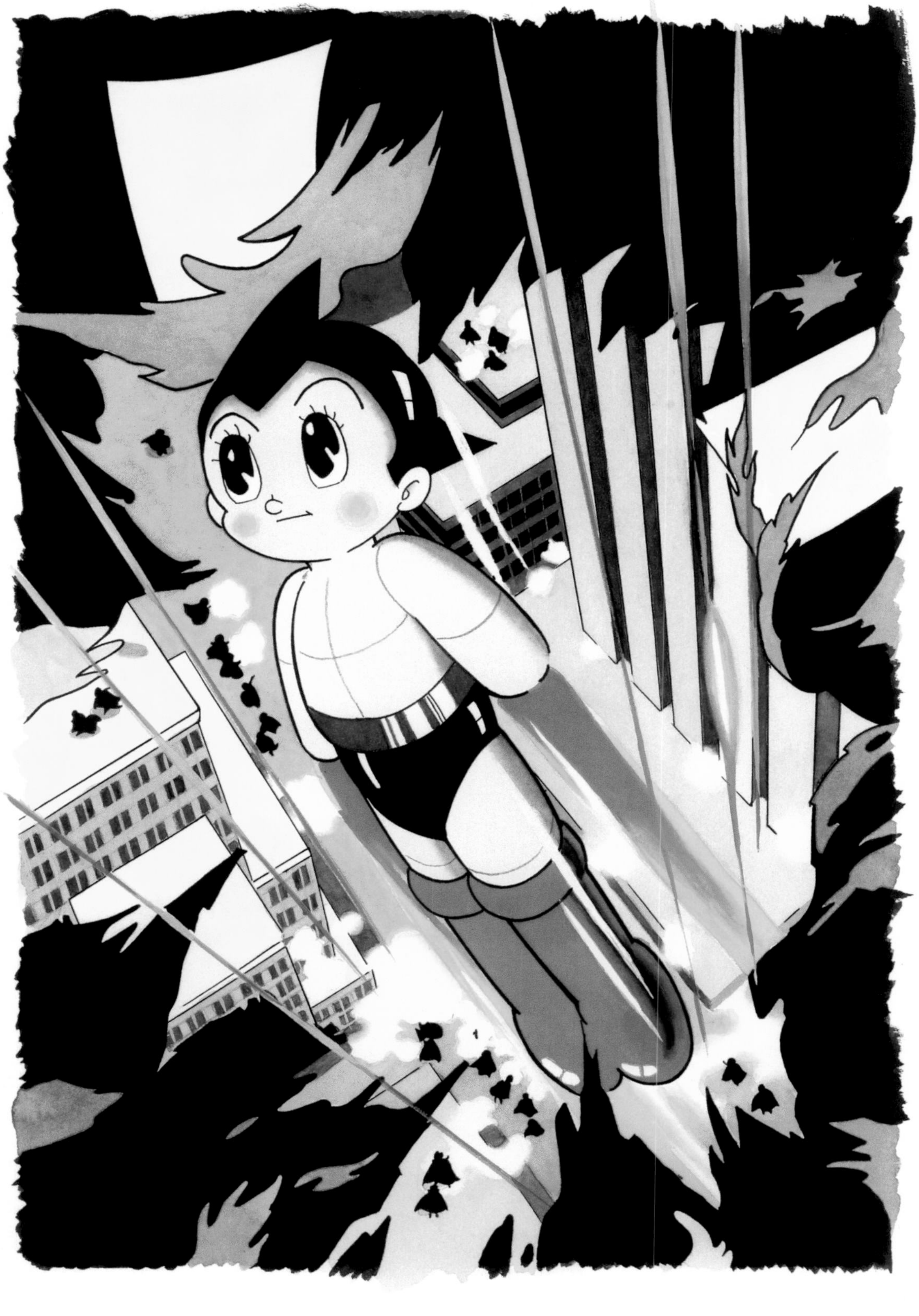

259
Tezuka Osamu, *Astro Boy*, 1960 © Tezuka Production

260
Tezuka Osamu, *Ribon no Kishi*
(*Princess Saphire*), 1963-1964, Kôdansha
© Tezuka Production

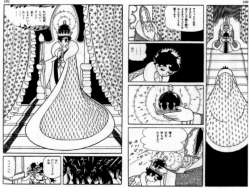

261–262
Tezuka Osamu, *Ribon no Kishi*
(*Princess Sapphire*), 1963–1964, Kôdansha
© Tezuka Production

expressing themselves, as well as on their tastes, never attained the quality of Tezuka's.

Tezuka came originally from the town of Takarazuka, home to one of the most famous theaters in Japan, whose troupe was entirely female, with all roles being played exclusively by actresses. His mother would often take him to performances there. Once he had become an artist, he regularly wrote manga for the theater's journal. His famous heroine, Princess Sapphire, complete with the characteristic shining stars in her huge eyes, resembles those of the Takarazuka Theater as much she does Disney animation.

The success of this manga led Tezuka to turn it into a film. He was surprised to learn that foreign audiences failed to understand why he drew faces with such large eyes. He explained that these features were meant to be idealized, but not even this seemed to convince them, though a few years later he noted that American and French artists started drawing precisely this type of *shôjo manga*.

The stories Tezuka Osamu favors are tinged with deeply humanist and spiritualistic convictions. His favorite, and the one regarded today as the quintessence of all his manga and anime*, is *Phoenix (Hi no tori*, also known as *The Firebird)*, begun in 1954. Tezuka Osamu's output was immense and deserves to be better known. In Japan, various manga recall his life, and TV programs are regularly devoted to him, including one magnificent reportage broadcast on the national TV station, NHK, in autumn 2006. Fig. 263

Figs. 264–26

From his many interviews, and in the light of the precious moments he spent in schools speaking to children about life and war, and about the need to protect life on earth, it is clear that he was a man of acute sensitivity. After being the butt of so much criticism, he was subsequently lauded as "the god of manga"—a moniker he found rather embarrassing. Like all great artists, he went through a difficult period in which his drawings were regarded as soppy compared to *gekiga**, realistic manga which did not shrink from scenes of violence. But "Doctor Tezuka," the man who more than anything else desired that children keep their love of life, always refused to cede to the demands of fashion. His manga *Black Jack* instilled renewed confidence in him and gained him new readers, with *Phoenix*, *Buddha*, and *Tell Adolf* (a.k.a. *The Three Adolfs*) confirming his place as a major artist. Fig. 266

263
Tezuka Osamu, *Hi no tori (Phoenix* a.k.a. *Firebird)*, 1976.
© Tezuka Osamu, Tezuka Production

"I wanted to write a work on the continuity of life. The bird is a symbol of life. The characters one meets with around him are afraid of death. They reject it. They want to live forever, to be rejuvenated, and they suffer from their inability to do so. All humans are like this and have to find meaning in their lives. […] As the phoenix often tells them: 'Human life lasts fifty years. You are lucky to live so long and yet, despite this, you crave eternal life! Behold the dragonfly! She molts, and yet she doesn't even possess a stomach. She can't even eat before dying. Her life expectancy is extremely short, but she copulates, procreates, and expends all her strength before dying.' Insects find it enough to live for just a few days."

手塚治虫物語
漫画の夢、アニメの夢
伴俊男+手塚プロダクション
1960—1989
Dream of Creating New Comics and Animated Films
朝日文庫
A STORY OF OSAMU TEZUKA

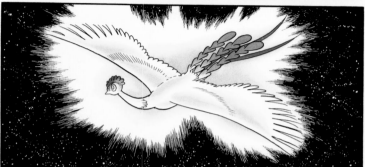

264
Ban Toshio et Tezuka Production, *Tezuka Osamu Monogatari (The Story of Tezuka Osamu)*, 1992, Asahi Shinbunsha
© Tezuka Production

265
Ban Toskio and Tezuka Production, *Tezuka Osamu Monogatari (The Story of Tezuka Osamu)*, Asaki Shinbunsha, 1992. © Tezuka Production

After his death, Tezuka rejoins the phoenix, but men will cherish him in their hearts forever.

A tireless worker, Tezuka regretted not being able to devote more time to his family and children. His lasting image is that of a talented, eminently humane man who, to the end, fought for the respect of life.

Birth of the *gekiga*

The work of Tezuka Osamu deeply influenced the universe of manga. Some *mangaka*, however, reacted to what they considered childish drawings and puerile stories with realistic manga, more closely reflecting the society in which they lived, producing work in which there could be both violence and gore.

Arising in the Kansai region in the late 1950s, this movement is represented by artists such as Saitô Takao, Satô Masaaki, Tatsumi Yoshihiro, and Matsumoto Masahiko. All had cut their teeth postwar composing manga intended for the hire market. Their drawings took the name *gekiga*, "dramatic pictures." Bereft of humor, their stories offer a bleak reflection of everyday life and social problems.

While the media was fueling public disaffection for manga, this group deployed topical themes to pose fundamental social questions. In his now mythical manga *Ninja Bugeichô (Chronicles of a Ninja's Military Accomplishments)*, produced 1959–62, Shirato Sanpei presents an historical fresco in which a group of *ninja** defends the poor and outcasts, or *burakumin*, against a cruel overlord.

Little by little, the *gekiga* gained a status as a genre in its own right, attracting the interest of certain intellectuals who were becoming aware of the strength and ideas behind some of them. Soon, *mangaka* such as Tsuge Yoshiharu, Nagashima Shinji, and Kojima Gôseki joined the ranks of the creators of *gekiga*. After the Second World War, Japan was one of several countries to experience a baby boom, and it was the children of this generation who built contemporary manga or became its most faithful readership.

The economic boom and social advancement, progress in technology, and the appearance of television in every home transformed Japanese life wholesale. The young were no longer satisfied with manga magazines coming out monthly. It was to answer their expectations that the publishers Shogakukan and Kôdansha launched weekly reviews, respectively, *Shûkan shônen Sunday* and *Shûkan*

266
Tezuka Osamu, *Black Jack,* 1976. © Tezuka Osamu, Tezuka Production

All forms of life are precious and must be respected. In another major work, *Black Jack,* Tezuka, inspired by his own experiences when a medical student, openly raises questions of life and death.

A source of envy for a number of his colleagues, Black Jack is struck off the register and thus has to practice medicine unofficially. An excellent surgeon, he demands huge fees from his patients, but sometimes wonders whether it's worth saving them. He worries about man's ever-increasing longevity, which will lead to insoluble problems of overpopulation, of the destruction of nature, and of food supply.

shônen Magazine, on March 17, 1959. These two magazines fomented a revolution in the comic strip. *Mangaka* worked at breakneck speed to satisfy their young customers, whose income enabled them to buy this kind of review, without recourse to the hire stores which began to feel the pinch. Their success encouraged other publishing houses to chance their arm, resulting in a plethora of weekly magazines.

Whereas the *Shônen Sunday* found room in its pages for manga by Terada Hiroo and Eujiko Eujio (whose little ghost, *Obahe no Kyûtarô*, delighted an entire generation of children) *Shûkan shônen Magazine* had acquired the participation of such *mangaka* talents as Tezuka Osamu and Yokoyama Mitsuteru, who brought out many successful works. Offering a mix of story manga* and *gekiga*, this review attracted an increasingly wide public, with attractive works such as the celebrated *Ashita no Joe (Tomorrow's Joe*, 1968–73) by Chiba Tetsuya and Kajiwara Ikki, which became legendary.

The milieu of boxing and prizefighters is here described with such realism that, when one of the two heroes died, readers wanted to stage a funeral for him; they traveled en masse carrying flowers to Kôdansha, where a ceremony was held by a Buddhist monk in a boxing-ring built by the publishers for the occasion.

From the 1960s onward, *shôjo manga* also proliferated. In 1963, Kôdansha launched the weekly *Shûkan Shôjô Friend* (Friend for Girls) and Shûeisha the weekly *Shûkan Margaret*. Until this juncture, this type of manga had been created primarily by men and peddled an idealized image of woman as well-brought-up paragon, model wife, or devoted mother. In their turn, female *mangaka* started sharpening their pencils, giving a new twist to this image of womanhood, making her less perfect, more accessible, and less remote from reality.

From the Tokyo Olympic Games in 1964, sport too acquired pride of place in manga, a tendency that continues to this day. This same year saw the launch of a very important monthly review, *GARO*. Shirato Sanpei offered *GARO*'s founder, Nagai Katsuichi, the opportunity to bring out his famous manga, *Kamui Den (The Legend of* Fig. 267 *Kamui)*, which has continued to be published in other magazines for forty years.

Then Tsuge Yoshiharu joined the review, adding further luster to the *GARO* stable, which went on to acquire fresh impetus from an upcoming generation of *mangaka*.

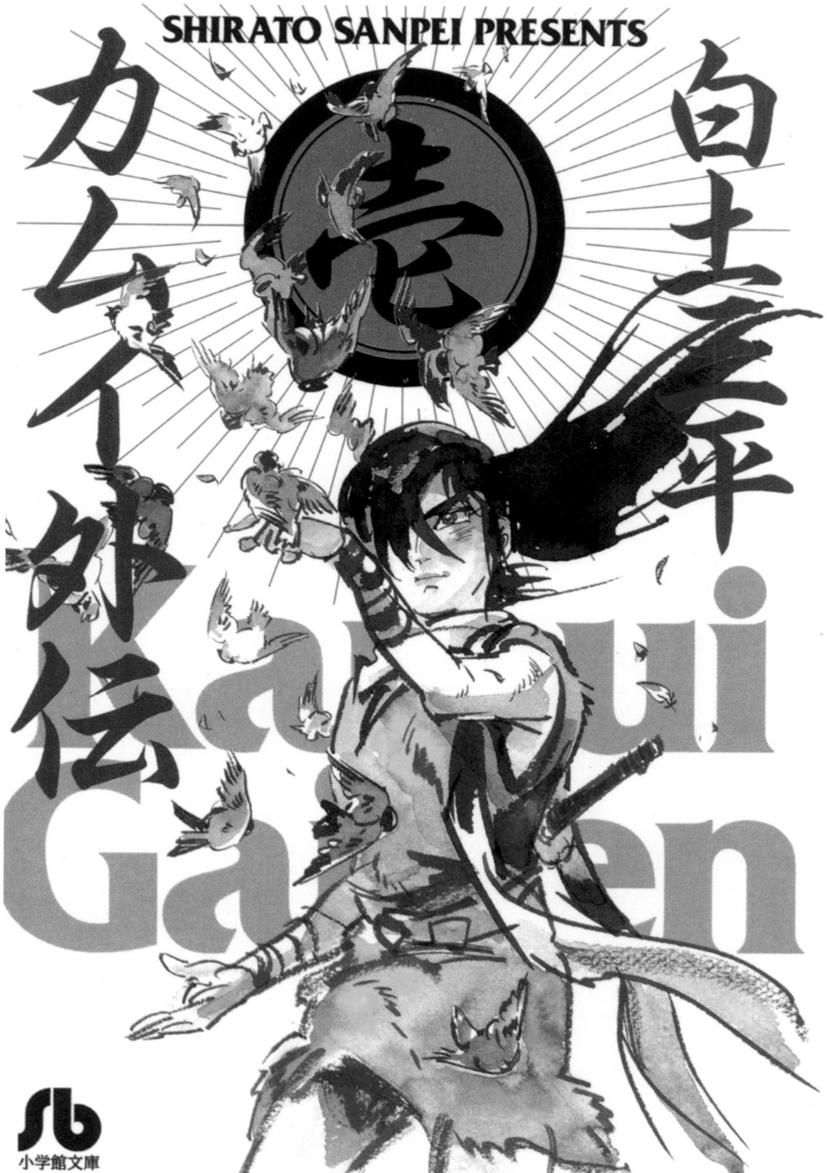
SHIRATO SANPEI PRESENTS
白土三平
壱
カムイ外伝
小学館文庫

267
Shirato Sanpei, *Kamui Den (The Legend of Kamui)*.
© reprint, Shogakukan, Tokyo, 2002
The hero, a ninja fighting social injustice in the late 1960s, became an emblem of student protest.

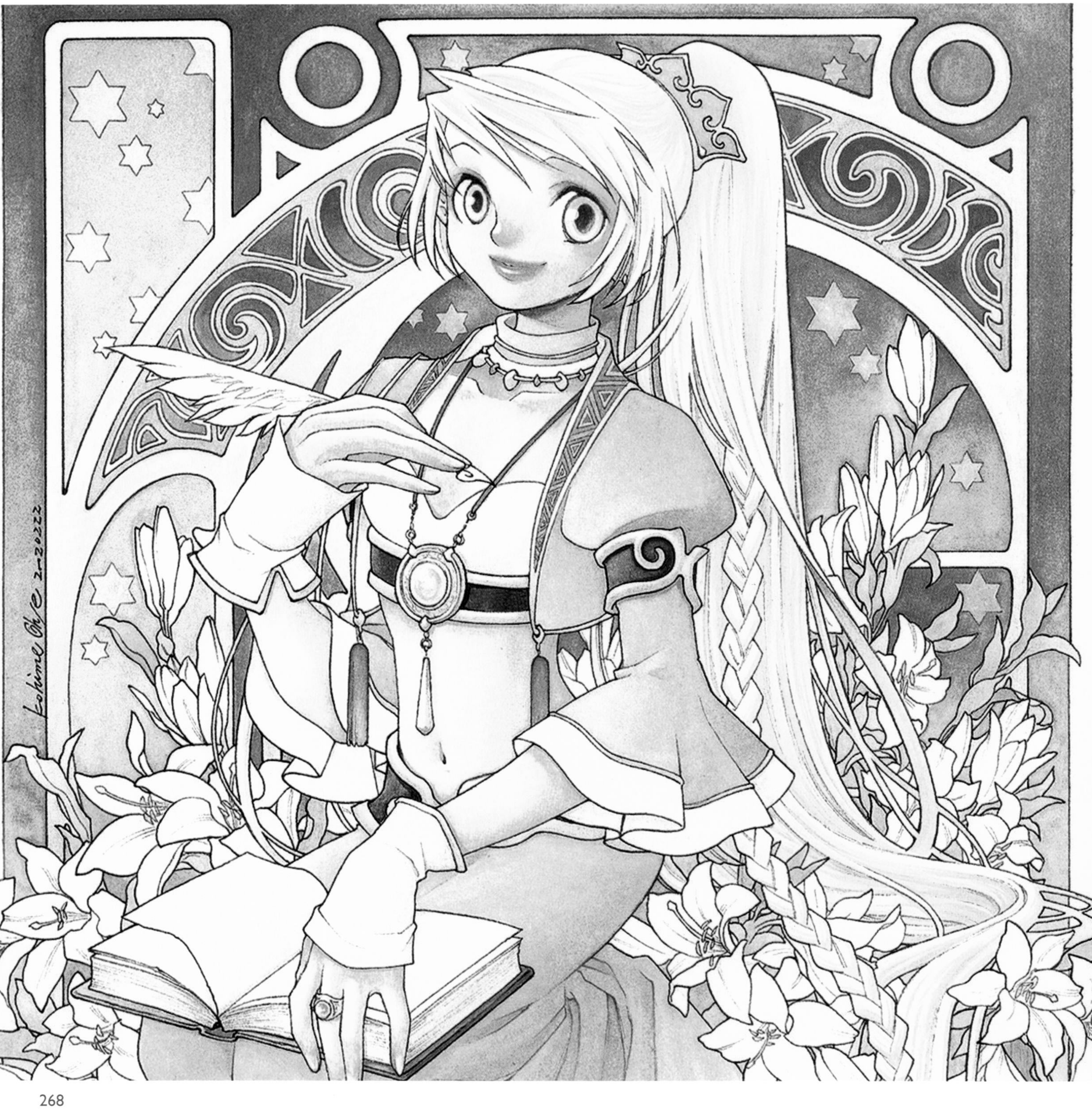

268
Detail, Ôse Kohime, *Tiru na nogu*, © Ôse Kohime, Bijutsu shuppan-sha, 2003

The manga industry

By the beginning of the 1970s, the enormously expanding market for manga* had acquired the profile it enjoys today. Since that time, 75 percent of the market has been dominated by just three publishers: Shogakukan, Kôdansha, and Shûeisha. Their sales turnover would put to shame any Western publishing house.

After reaching an apogee in the 1990s, however, manga sales in the archipelago have slumped, chiefly due to a growth in second-hand bookshops and hire stores, to the appearance of "manga cafés," and a growth in titles that subscribers to certain networks can read on their mobiles.

Paradoxically, while manga publishing has suffered a downturn, the readership is exploiting new technologies; these are undergoing dramatic progress, with the number of people reading manga on mobiles increasing massively. It is tempting to wonder whether these new distribution networks might in a few years oust hardcopy reviews completely. The rise of video games has also influenced consumers, some of whom have abandoned the manga for amusements of this type. The situation is alarming for manga publishers, who are struggling to ride out the storm by developing Asian and Western markets in tandem.

A revolution: the birth of the first free manga

One young publisher has reacted to the problem in a new way. On January 16, 2007, *Gumbo*, the first free manga magazine, published by Dijima, was launched. This revolution in the world of manga is sure to spark other experiments of the same kind; many free reviews in various fields are already regularly distributed throughout the archipelago. The birth of *Gumbo* was much commented on in major national dailies and on the TV news. One hundred thousand copies are distributed free at the entrance to the main stations in the capital and in the outskirts every week, on Tuesdays and Wednesdays.

Fig. 269

The magazine is aimed at male readers aged between twenty and forty. So as to be less cumbersome than *shônen manga**, the number of pages has been cut by half; it is 130 pages long, with 26 of those devoted to advertising material to cover the publication expenses. In the future, Dijima also hopes to bring out the series in book form.

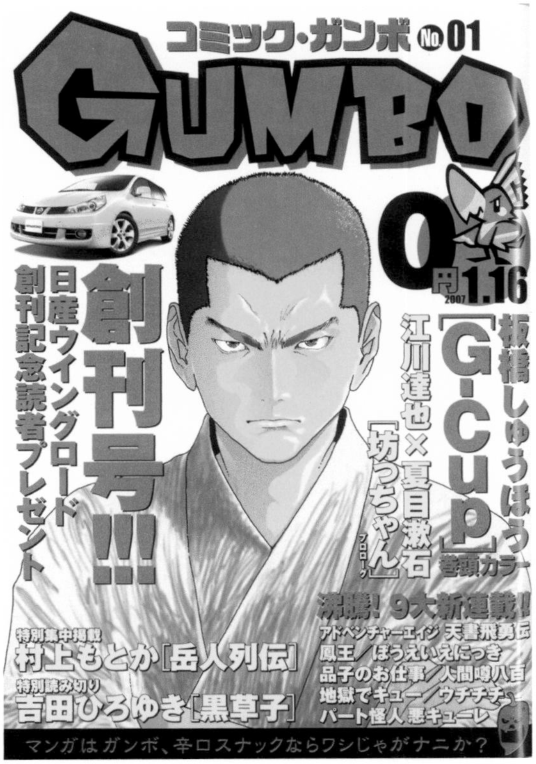
コミック・ガンボ No.01
GUMBO
0円
2007 1.16
板橋しゅうほう
「G-Cup」
巻頭カラー
江川達也×夏目漱石
「坊っちゃん」
プロローグ
創刊号!!!
日産ウイングロード
創刊記念読者プレゼント
9大新連載!!
アドベンチャーエイジ 天書飛勇伝
鳳王/ほうえいえにっき
品子のお仕事/人間噂八百
地獄でキュー/ウチチチ
パート怪人 悪キューレ
特別集中掲載
村上もとか『岳人列伝』
特別読み切り
吉田ひろゆき『黒草子』
マンガはガンボ、辛ロスナックならワシじゃがナニか?

269
First number of *Gumbo*, January 16, 2007, illustration by Egawa Tatsuya. © Tokyo: Dijima, 2007

Manga in the daily life of the Japanese

Someone unacquainted with Japan cannot hope to appreciate the role that manga plays in the everyday life of its inhabitants. Even if not all Japanese are regular consumers, they all read at least some in their childhood. Intellectuals unblushingly chat about their favorite manga. It is the new culture par excellence—a popular culture, of course—manga are everywhere. There is no need even to cross the threshold of a bookshop to find them; they are on sale in kiosks in stations and the subway, in *conbini*, small 24/7 retail outlets; they rub shoulders with other reviews at the dentist's, hairdresser's, in certain cafés, and in particular *manga kissa**, establishments where, for a small fee, one can read as many as one likes. Adults read them in trains and leave them on the luggage rack for the next commuter. These manga will be then collected and sold off on street corners for a few yen before being recycled.

*Mangaka** might take inspiration from the street, but manga in their turn influence fashion, hairstyles, make-up, etc. Far from being looked down on, the manga is seen as a medium in its own right that can convey information of any kind. Even the Ministry for Education utilizes the genre in special sections of its textbooks.

Initially published in a magazine, if it sells well, the manga then appears in a special volume called a *bunko* (4 ¼ x 6 in. [10.5 x 15 cm]), of approximately 200 pages, with only the cover in color, or in pocketbook format (4 ½ x 7 in. [11.5 x 17.5 cm]). One volume contains ten chapters.

Readers of manga reviews are an assiduous lot. In exchange for a tiny gift they will readily reply to questionnaires on their favorite series. If after a few reprints, it so happens a manga comes out in a deluxe edition under hardcover (6 x 8 ¼ in. [15 x 21 cm]) with color pages, readers will collect and preserve them jealously.

Sometimes a manga can be spawned by a fiction bestseller. *Densha Otoko* (The Man on the Train), a novel that became a bestseller in 2005, was turned into a film *(Train Man)*, a TV series, and into three manga versions brought out by different publishers. The novel takes as its starting point a true story, that of a young *otaku** from the district of Akihabara*, who comes to the aid of a girl attacked on a train by a drunk, falling in love with her. Not knowing how to declare his affection, he asks surfers on the Web to give him hints on how to win her over and confess his attraction.

Maison Ikkoku is a famous manga which was turned into a cartoon film for children in the 1980s. It is a realistic look at Japanese society through the love affair between a student and a young widow, and was created by Takahashi Rumiko (author of *Ranma 1/2* and *Inu Yasha* among many other works). Japanese television shot a new adaptation that was broadcast in May 2007.

Competition is fierce: if a manga series is thought a failure, it stops dead in its tracks and its publication is halted. A handful of *mangaka* earn a good living, but the majority finds it tough to make ends meet. Some of those who started out as assistants of established *mangaka* end up creating their own titles, but in general they remain in the shadow of their master throughout their careers.

In the eyes of many Westerners, manga are above all a vehicle for sex, violence, and gore. Though not new, this tendency represents only a fraction of production, however. Such manga are tributary of a pictorial tradition from the Edo* period when the greatest print-masters drew *shunga** (erotic prints). Hokusai, to quote but one example, made some magnificent series of prints of this kind, including *Kinoe no Komatsu*, in which the "diving girl ravished by octopuses," described so eloquently by Edmond de Goncourt, appears. At the end of the Edo and the beginning of the Meiji era, illustrated journals like *Shinbun Nishikie* presented woodblock prints showing morbid and bloody events that even today's manga would be hard-pressed to outdo.

Sentimental manga—often closely related to the erotic and to stories of *bishônen** or *shônen ai* that describe young men's romantic longings—are too numerous to mention, as are the female equivalent, *bishôjo** or *shôjo ai*. All these manga are grouped into the category, *etchi**, the pornographic ones being dubbed *hentai**. Though it's true that erotic prints revealing the most intimate parts of the anatomy are on show at major international events, it seems rather unjust to condemn by the same token manga that leave rather more up to the imagination. As for the violence expressed in some manga that is so decried in the West, it is not a reflection of everyday life: Japan remains one of the safest countries in the world. Acting as a sort of safety valve, manga seem to allow readers to give

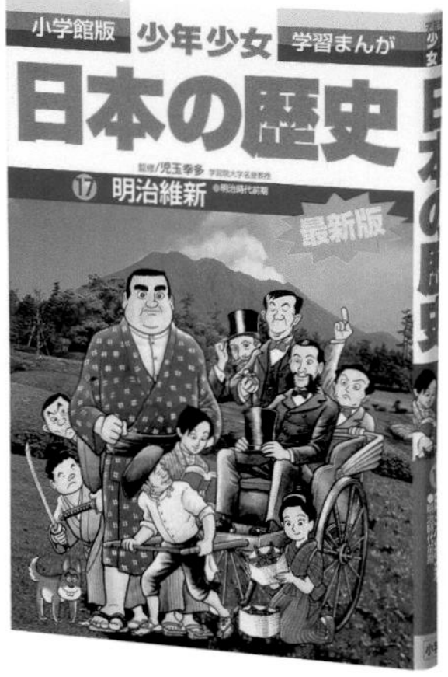
小学館版
少年少女
学習まんが
日本の歴史
⑰ 明治維新
最新版

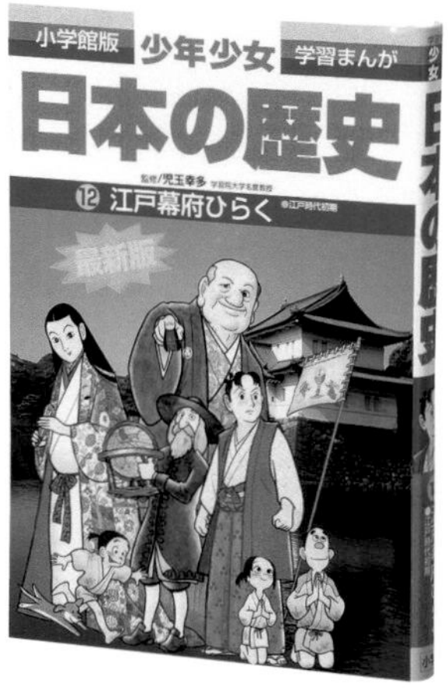
小学館版
少年少女
学習まんが
日本の歴史
⑫ 江戸幕府ひらく
最新版

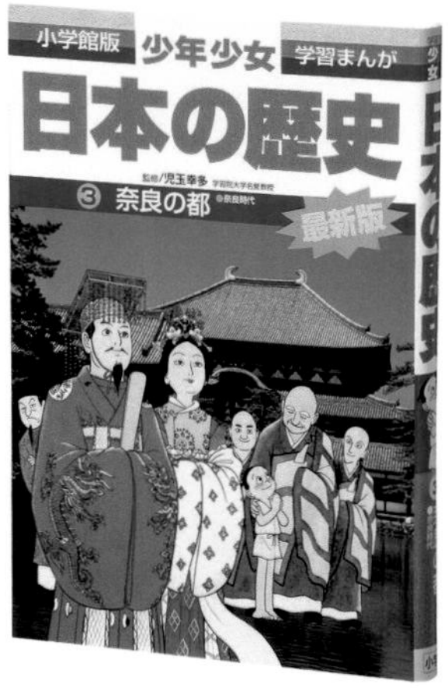
小学館版
少年少女
学習まんが
日本の歴史
③ 奈良の都
最新版

270–272
Aomura Jun, *History of Japan.* © Shogakukan, 1981–83
If Japanese children want to add to their knowledge about their country's history, they can always read this playful and instructive manga.

vent to their stress and satisfy their fantasies. Countless other categories of manga aimed at an increasingly diverse demographic have invaded the market and deserve to be better known.

Pedagogical manga

Educational manga are among the least known in the West, but they rank among the most interesting. Whether featuring literature, history, science, art history, or biographies of famous people, manga offer children amusement and education simultaneously. Horrified voices are raised to say that textbooks would do the job better than any manga; nonetheless their teaching effectiveness has been indisputable. The drawings are attractive, the simple texts are placed in word-bubbles, and, at the end of each volume, basic explanations illustrated with color photographs and a rigorous and detailed chronology complement a more thorough approach. Designed for both children and teenagers, these titles have also proved their worth with adult readers. Figs. 270–30

Cult series

Dozens of new manga pour from the presses each month but the majority are short-lived. What, one might then wonder, makes a manga take off? Even major publishers themselves acknowledge the unpredictability of the phenomenon. At the same time, readers seek continuity—as in the works of Matsumoto Leiji, where key characters return series after series—*and* unexpected innovations. The story must be original and the drawing style crafted to engage with the readership to which it is addressed.

The themes of contemporary bestsellers are those that gave earlier manga their success, and the values young readers seek in them have hardly altered since the Edo period, when the literary tradition inculcated steadfastness in the face of adversity. The Japanese place great store by tenacity, and this remains the case in everyday life today: at school, in the workplace, even in love when it comes to attaining one's heart's desire. One still very frequently hears the expression "*ganbarimashô*" ("let's just do our best"). Figs. 303–30

Manga heroes—particularly those intended for boys, but more and more some written for girls—must always exceed their limits.

273–275
Minamoto Tarô, *Fuunjitachi (Great Destinies)*.
© Minamoto Tarô, Leed, 2002

This series turns a very special spotlight on history. The manga tells extraordinary life stories in great detail, such as the terrific destiny of Daikokuya Kôdayû, the captain of the *Shinshômaru*, who, at the end of the eighteenth century, set off with his crew to Edo. A terrifying storm threw the ship off course to the north and all were shipwrecked on the shore of an island close to the Bering Strait. Inspired by Kôdayû, an individual of singular moral fiber, the companions picked up the local language from the natives and then learnt Russian from fur trappers.

Eager to return to his homeland, Kôdayû proceeds to lead his men through Russia. He ends up having an audience with Empress Catherine II, who helps him return to Japan after ten years packed with adventure. Kôdayû had lost half his men, while others had converted to Orthodoxy and thus stayed in Russia. His return was no less dramatic. As Japan's borders were then closed to outsiders, he met with incomprehension on the part of the authorities and his family.

The narrative of the loneliness of a courageous man, this manga offers the young a picture of a long-lost epoch and of a larger-than-life historical character.

On the manga's cover, against a background showing church domes, Kôdayû, dressed in Western style, is preparing to meet Catherine of Russia. The author of the manga has even gone so far as to furnish a few sentences in Cyrillic. In this spread, Russians and Japanese watch on helplessly as a ship coming to their rescue is overturned by the raging waves and is smashed to smithereens on the reef.

ワイド版
風雲児たち
みなもと太郎
FUUNJITACHI 9
PRESENTED BY MINAMOTO TARO
SPコミックス

とにかくおびただしい侠客 博徒が上州はじめ関八州から群がり出たのは
あの天明の浅間焼けが大きな原因の一つになっているのであった!!
ついでながら戦国時代上州の武士はなぜか二本差しを嫌い
一本刀で戦場を駆け城下をねり歩いた
その伝統がヤクザに受けつがれ
「長脇差」は上州ヤクザの代名詞になったという
(刃わたり 60~75センチ)
222

Спасибо ありがとう!!
Благодарю вас за доброту 親切は忘れないよ~~~!!
До свидания さようなら!!
Прощайте さようなら!!
スパシーボ!!
ダ スヴィダーニャ!!
わからん 奴等だ……
うむ……
何で帆をたたまねえんじゃろかい
わからん! 初めて見るロシア船じゃものなァ
あんなにでかくて帆や柱が多いと急にはいじくれんのかな
そんなはずあ あるまい
嵐を知らんだけじゃ……
な なんだ あれ!!
ボートをおろしてやがるぞ
船を見捨てやがった!
78

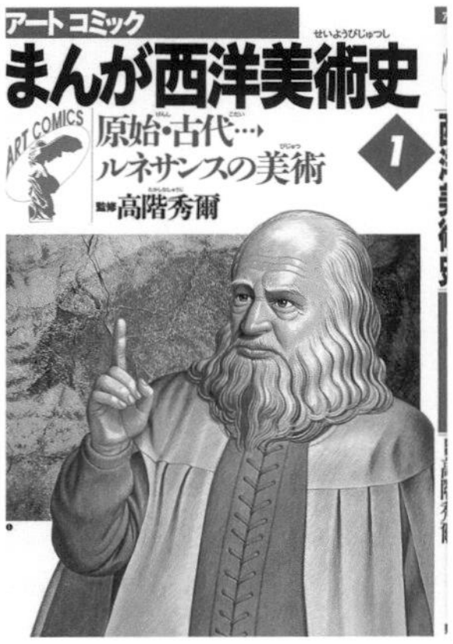
アートコミック
まんが西洋美術史
ART COMICS
原始・古代…→
ルネサンスの美術
1
監修 高階秀爾

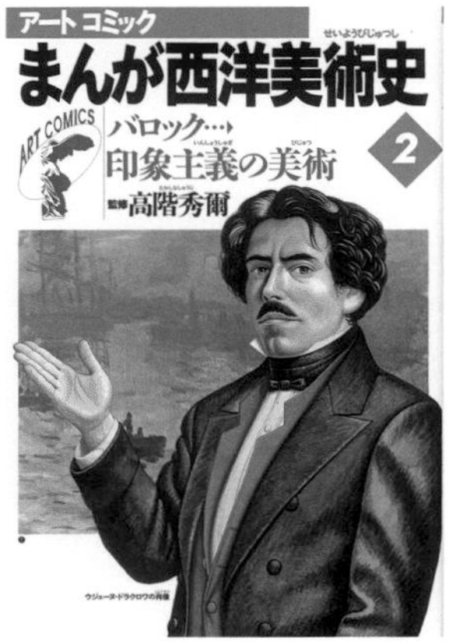
アートコミック
まんが西洋美術史
ART COMICS
バロック…→
印象主義の美術
2
監修 高階秀爾

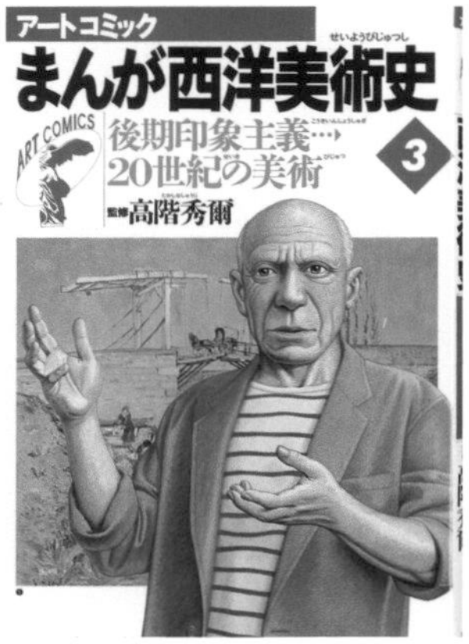
アートコミック
まんが西洋美術史
ART COMICS
後期印象主義…→
20世紀の美術
3
監修 高階秀爾

276–278
Manga seiyô bijutsushi (History of Western Art in Manga I), general editors Takashina Shôji, Komori Tetsuro.
© Tokyo: Bijutsu shuppan-sha, 1994

The history of Western art is also featured in this series of manga, in which Leonardo da Vinci, Delacroix, and Picasso invite children to discover their work.

Going beyond oneself so one's team can win, or overcoming one's enemies so as to survive or save the lives of others, are leitmotifs in practically every manga, whether the subject is sport, adventure, or armageddon. Feelings of the vanity of man and of the fleetingness of time are also very strong. The fear of earthquakes and epidemics is clearly betrayed in Edo period prints that were believed to be prophylactic. In present-day manga, such subjects, like the dangers of nuclear technology and natural disasters, often reflect this sense of transience blended with youthful angst.

Teamwork

Quite apart from the talent of the *mangaka* and his or her assistants and the subject chosen, what makes a manga successful is the publisher. In the Edo era, a print was a joint endeavor between the painter, the engraver, the printer, and the publisher (see the chapter on Mizuki Shigeru). It is a situation that has hardly changed. A manga cannot become a bestseller in isolation; an experienced publisher is needed to set authors on the right course and then allow them their freedom.

Mangaka choose the subject in conjunction with the publishers or, alternatively, if they feel particularly strongly about it, try to pitch it to them. Starting by drawing the characters so as to fix a style, a *mangaka* will show the outline to the commissioning editor; then, if the project is taken on, pass instructions on to his or her assistants, who do the breakdown and graphics with pencilers and inkers, while the *mangaka* continues working on the script and corrects what comes in from the assistants. Tezuka Osamu revolutionized manga in both form and expression and his successors took up much of his technique, modernizing it in their turn and adding further graphic innovations.

If *mangaka* keep to the storyboard, they have on the other hand total freedom of expression for the drawing and layout, and it is here that they display their talent, trying out every kind of placement in the panels of every conceivable shape and size chosen so as to intensify the action or increase the feeling of speed or the esthetic impact.

Sophisticated manga that lay the stress on the beauty and elegance of design are a million miles away from the simplified lines of

279–280
Cover by Tôju Kichiko, drawings by Akiyama Kôki, with texts by Honda Satoshi, *Manga inshôha no gakatachi (Manga: The Impressionist Painters I).*

The Japanese possess unbounded admiration for the painters of Impressionism. The life and work of these artists, who were themselves much influenced by Japanese prints, are universally known. Manga for children provide accurate outlines of the beginnings of this famous art movement.

Here we have Claude Monet and Edmond Renoir (Auguste's brother) in the studio of the photographer Nadar on Rue des Capucines where the first Impressionist exhibition was held. Even a photograph of the catalog cover appears.

In the second volume, the painters start working in the open air, in a quest for the light effects and the fleeting moment that will enable them to convey a sense of color to their canvases.

まんが
アートコミック
印象派の画家たち
ART COMICS
監修 島田紀夫
画 あきやま耕輝
作 本田 諭
I

12
第1回グループ展～印象派の誕生～
EXPOSITION
CATALOGUE

281–282
Cover by Tôju Kichiko, drawings by Akiyama Kôki, with text by Honda Satoshi, *Manga inshôha no gakatachi (Manga: the Impressionist Painters I).* © Bijutsu shuppan-sha, 1999

Monet welcomes the Japanese collectors Mr and Mrs Kuroki into his home and shows them round his garden with the famous pond full of flowering waterlilies and the little bridge. Monet was an ardent champion of Japanese prints, and decorated his house with them; their compositions were a key inspiration in his oeuvre. He also drew on the example of *fusuma** and the Japanese folding-screen for *Les Nénuphars*, which is now in the Musée de l'Orangerie in Paris.

まんが
アートコミック
印象派の画家たち
ART COMICS
監修 島田紀夫
画 あきやま耕輝
作 本田 諭
II

those that depict their characters in a cartoony manner, with huge eyes to communicate their feelings and a personalized hairdo to aid identification. In both "schools," however, *mangaka* vie with each other with ingenious layouts in an effort to impose a characteristic stamp on their works.

Sequential slicing of the action and changes in framing increase the impact of a narrative, which is accompanied by speech bubbles containing, in addition to dialog, onomatopoeias and punctuation marks.

The publisher will regularly come to inspect how work is progressing and the story is unfolding, to encourage the troops, and to collect any print-ready episodes. Just as in the Edo period, a publisher must sell vast quantities of a series or be prepared to shut down production. Meanwhile the *mangaka* take catnaps and live on the edge, terrified lest their success evaporate overnight. Ever vigilant, it is the publisher's job to look over the shoulders of *mangaka* and keep their spirits up.

A diversity of themes

Sport has pride of place in manga: baseball, tennis, football, judo, etc. are favorite themes with children. Many young champions freely admit to having taken up a sport after seeing it in a manga series or anime*. The spirit of the samurai* too is ever-present, especially for male readers, young and adult alike. One of the best-known series Figs. 308–309 in this field is *Lone Wolf and Cub*.

Children too like to identify with characters that resemble them, as with Shinchan, a five-year-old whose inventive and silly antics Fig. 303 have captured the imagination of countless young readers.

A subject linked to a fad can also catch on in a big way, as seems Fig. 304 to be the case with *Yakitate Ja-Pan*. In this manga, a young boy has been obsessed with bread from infancy and dreams of becoming a baker. As luck would have it, he knows how to knead dough better than anyone else. He goes to Tokyo in the hope of getting a job in the prestigious Pantasia bakery chain. Full of beans but a bit naïve, he has many adventures before attaining his goal. Such a weird subject surprises European readers, who might wonder whether bread is a common sight in Japan. In point of fact, over the last few years

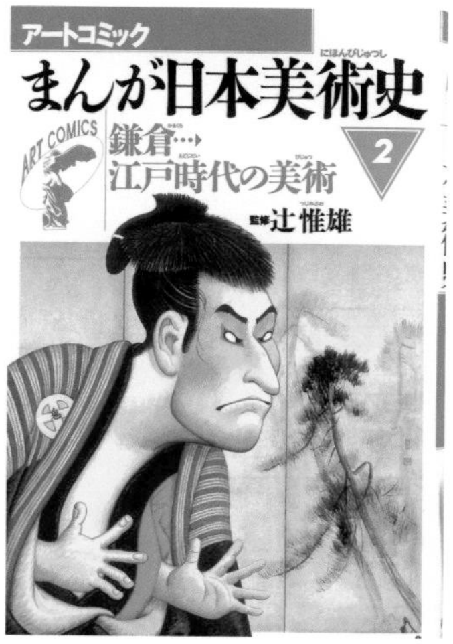
アートコミック
まんが日本美術史
にほんびじゅつし
ART COMICS
鎌倉…→江戸時代の美術
2
監修 辻惟雄

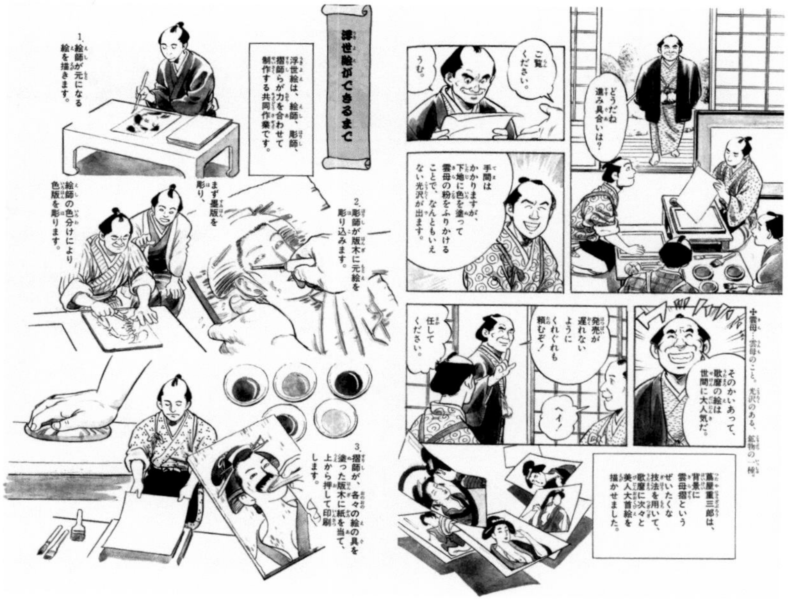
どうだね 進み具合いは？
ご覧ください。
うむ。
手間はかかりますが、下地に色を塗って雲母の粉をふりかけることで、なんともいえない光沢が出ます。
そのかいあって、歌麿の絵は世間に大人気だ。
✣雲母…雲母のこと。光沢のある、鉱物の一種。
発売が遅れないようにくれぐれも頼むぞ！
ヘイ！
任してください。
蔦屋重三郎は、背景に雲母摺というぜいたくな技法を用いて、歌麿に次々と美人大首絵を描かせました。
浮世絵ができるまで
浮世絵は、絵師、彫師、摺師らが力を合わせて制作する共同作業です。
1. 絵師が元になる絵を描きます。
2. 彫師が版木に元絵を彫り込みます。
まず墨版を彫り、
絵師の色分けにより色版を彫ります。
3. 摺師が、各々の絵の具を塗った版木に紙を当て、上から押して印刷します。

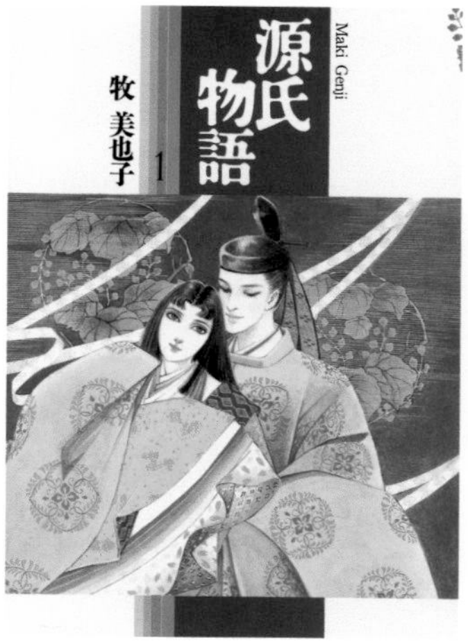
源氏物語
Maki Genji
牧美也子
1

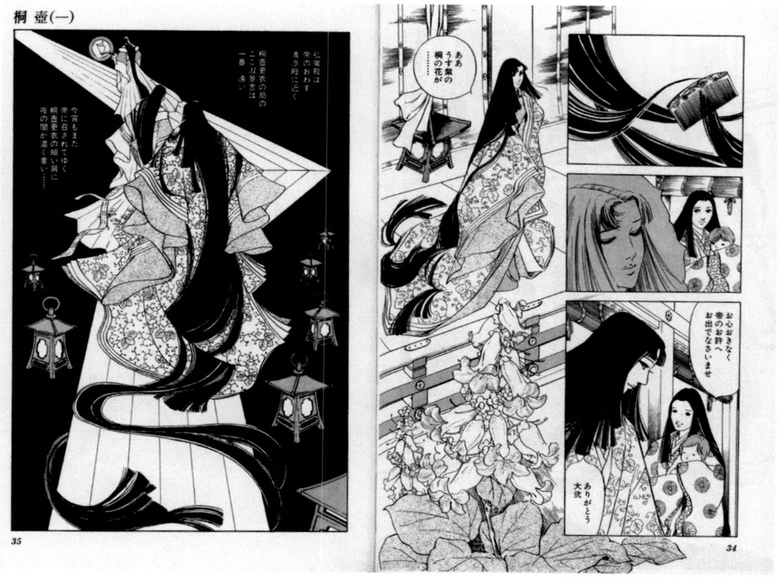
お心おきなく帝のお許へお出でなさいませ
ありがとう大弐
ああうす紫の桐の花が……
34
桐壺(一)
弘徽殿は帝のおわす清涼殿に近く
桐壺更衣の局のここ淑景舎は一番遠い
今宵もまた帝に召されてゆく桐壺更衣の細い肩に夜の闇が濃く重い……
35

283–284

Cover by Komori Tetsurô, drawings by Wada Junichi, *Manga (The History of Art of Japan, 2)*. © Tokyo: Bijutsu Shuppan-sha, 1996

The history of Japanese painting is the subject of another series. The cover features a celebrated portrait of a *kabuki** actor by the *ukiyo-e** painter Sharaku. Many hypotheses have been advanced as to his true identity. Readers are also shown how a print is created: using a disk-shaped pad called a *baren**, the printer rubs the sheet of paper over the engraved board to print off each color.

285–286

Maki Miyako, *Genji monogatari (The Tale of Genji)*. © Maki Miyako, Shogakukan, Tokyo, 1988

The *Genji monogatari* offers a fresco of the court society in the Fujiwara era and was written around the year 1000. Its author, the lady-in-waiting and woman of letters Murasaki Shikibu (978?–1014), relates the life of Prince Genji and his son. Various love stories, and the pictures it affords of court life, make this monumental novel into the supreme masterpiece of classic Japanese literature. Maki Miyako depicts the characters and costumes of this time with grace and flair.

くもんのまんが
古典文学館
竹取物語

かぐや姫と帝との
手紙のやりとりが
はじまってから、
三年ほどたった
春のある日のことです。
どうしました?
かぐや姫
なにか
心配ごとでも
あるのですか?
いいえ
なにも……
近ごろの
かぐや姫のようすは
ただごとでは
ありません
なにかを
ひどく
心配している
ようです
かぐや姫や
どうして
そんなに
悲しそうな顔で
月を見るのじゃ?
114
115

オズの魔法使い
THE KUMON MANGA LIBRARY
L・F・バウム
いがらしゆみこ

東のわるい
魔女を
あなたのおうちが
たいじして
くれたのよ
長い間
わるい魔女に
くるしめられていた
東の国の人たちは
とてもよろこんで
いるわ
ここはどこ?
あなたは
いったい
だれなの?
わたしは
北の国の
よい魔女です
そして
ここは
オズの国
オズの国の
北と南には
よい魔女が
そして
東と西には
わるい魔女が
すんでいるのよ
わたしは
カンザスに
もどりたいわ
おじさんと
おばさんの
ところに
帰りたい
クスン
では
エメラルドの
みやこにすむ
オズさまに
おねがい
しなさい
北の魔女は　ドロシーに
しんでしまった
東のわるい魔女の
くつをはくように
いいました
エメラルドの
みやこは
遠いけれど
気をつけて
いくのですよ
わたしは
エメラルドの
みやこにいって
オズさまに
会うわ!
そして
カンザスに
帰る方法を
教えてもらうの

287–288

General editor Hirata Yoshinobu, drawings by Kishina Satsuki, *Taketori monogatari (The Tale of the Bamboo Cutter*, known as *The Princess from the Moon).* © Kumon Publishing, Co., Ltd., 1991, 2003

The author of this famous Japanese tale, written around the tenth century, remains anonymous. One day a poor logger comes across a princess from the moon and raises her as his own daughter. Her peerless beauty attracts various princes, and even the emperor himself, but her demands are such that the suitors give up. The girl then dons a gown made of feathers and returns to her homeland.

289–290

Igarashi Yumiko, *The Wizard of Oz* (after the novel by Lyman Frank Baum, 1856–1919). © Kumon Publishing Co., Ltd., 1998

Graphic artist Igarashi Yumiko is renowned for her character, Candy, and her style reappears in the features of the heroine in *The Wizard of Oz*. Her drawings, in which no detail is left to chance, lead her young readers through the story by the hand. Here, the frightened Dorothy realizes that she has entered the wizard's realm and, with tears in her eyes, pleads to be let back to her family.

怪盗ルパン1
THE KUMON MANGA LIBRARY
ルパンの逮捕
ARSÈNE LUPIN
モーリス・ルブラン 原作
一峰大二 画

これを見てください
あっ
ん!!
Arsène Lupin à votre bord, première classe, cheveux blonds, blessure avant-bras droit, voyage seul, sous le nom de R
船中にアルセーヌ・ルパン潜入、一等船室、金髪、右腕に傷、ひとり、名前R……
だめです 電波が中断されました
この先は?
ルパンがこの船に……
Lupin Encore Trompe La Police
怪盗紳士ルパン またまた警察をあざむく
LE FIGARO

シャーロック・ホームズ 1
THE KUMON MANGA LIBRARY
A Study in Scarlet
緋色の研究

ロンドン……
ストランド街……
わたしの名前はジョン・H・ワトスン 第二次アフガニスタン戦争に軍医として参戦し イギリスにもどってきたのは 一八八一年のことだった……
あっ
どうも失礼!

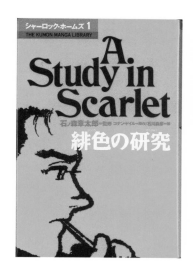

291–292
Kazumine Daiji, *Arsène Lupin, Gentleman Cambrioleur* (after the novel by Maurice Leblanc, 1907).
© Kumon Publishing Co., Ltd., 1997

The gentleman thief, Arsène Lupin, is a very popular character in Japan. Interestingly, French is used in the text.

293–294
Storyboard by Takahashi Miyuki, drawings by Ishikawa Morihiko, supervised by Ishinmori Shâtarô, *Sherlock Holmes, a Study in Scarlet* (after the novel by Sir Arthur Conan Doyle, 1859–1930, published in 1887). © Kumon Publishing Co., Ltd.

The action is set in London in 1878. Dr Watson and Sherlock Holmes meet and decide to share a house. They will soon have a murder to solve.

小学館版 学習まんが人物館
Marie Antoinette
監修
石井美樹子
まんが
市川能里
革命の犠牲になったフランス最後の王妃
マリー・アントワネット
小学館

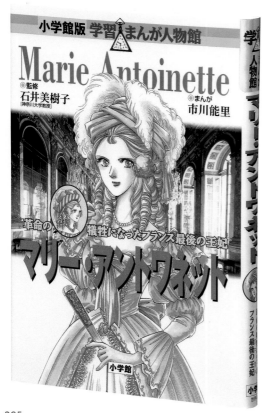

295
Ichikawa Nori, *Marie-Antoinette*.
© Ichikawa Nori, Shogakukan, 2005

Marie-Antoinette is one of the best-known historical figures in Japan and numerous biographies in the form of manga and books have been devoted to her. The pomp and circumstance of Versailles, the destiny of the young queen, and her feelings for the Comte de Fersen enjoy universal appeal.

home bread-making has really taken off and beginners' courses in baking and confectionery have become very popular. And that's just as a hobby; in fact there are many bakeries and competition is ruthless. They sell bread from all countries; timetables for the various batches are even posted up so that customers can always buy bread at its freshest. But Japanese consumers soon tire of a product, so that new rolls and loaves have to be concocted every season: thus last spring, one of the best-known bakers in Japan changed the flavor of the traditional *Kugelhopf* (Alsatian in origin) from chocolate to tomato. So the situations in this manga are far from unlikely in the eyes of readers who are used to consuming such products, and it is scarcely astonishing that a *mangaka* came up with the bright idea of tackling the theme.

The fantastic

Jules Verne captivated thousands of readers both in France and abroad, and postwar *mangaka* were prone to taking his novels as a starting point. Adventures at the bottom of the sea or on some remote planet remain one of the favorite subjects among every strata of the readership. The supernatural powers of manga heroes, which all children dream of possessing, also afford a rich vein. Heirs to the stories of the Edo period, fantastic manga in which demons take an active part in human life, are just as frequent. More disconcerting in that it imbues the action with a morbid atmosphere, *Death Note*, for example, presents the young with questions of a positively existential nature.

Figs. 310–31
Figs. 305–30
312–315
Fig. 306

Humor

The Japanese—like everyone else—are very fond of comedies. Nineteenth-century travelers, such as Émile Guimet or Felix Régamey, had already noted their gaiety, and today humor occupies a key place in TV programs with the *owarai bangumi*, literally "laughter shows." Manga too are consistently designed to raise a smile, one of the funniest being *One Piece*.

Figs. 300, 316–317

Cops and criminals

Crime and detective stories have always attracted a wide audience, and there are plenty of manga on the subject, with the most famous series starring Detective Conan.

Fig. 318

小学館版 学習まんが人物館
L·v·Beethoven
監修 黒田恭一
生きる喜びと情熱を作曲した大音楽家
ベートーベン
小学館

＊「月光」一五二ページを見よう。
美しい月の光の中で、ベートーベンがジュリエッタに愛を語った曲、
それがのちに「月光」と呼ばれるようになったピアノソナタでした。
幸せのベールに包まれていたベートーベンでしたが、
その背後に不幸の影が、そっと忍びよってきていたのでした。
56
第四章 苦しみをのりこえて
一八〇一年。ベートーベン三〇歳。
お客さま、ご注文はお決まりですか。
お客さま？
うわっ。
57

アクションコミックス
『坊っちゃん』の時代
凛冽たり近代 なお生彩あり明治人
関川夏央
谷口ジロー
双葉社

そんな事はいらないと云っても中々承知しない。
ピチャピチャ
ペロペロ
プラットフォームの上へ出た時、車へ乗り込んだおれの顔を昵と見て「もう御別れになるかも知れません。随分御機嫌よう」と小さな声で云った。目に涙が一杯たまっている。
おれは泣かなかった。然しもう少しで泣くところであった。
ふわっ
漱石はそれぞれ「清」と「マドンナ」という名を与えることにした
出立の日には朝から来て色々世話をやいた。
来る途中小間物屋で買って来た歯磨と楊子と手拭をズックの革鞄に入れてくれた。

296–297

Ichikawa Nori, *L.V. Beethoven.* © Ichikawa Nori, Shogakukan, 1997

The many biographies of famous characters from history tackled in manga for children include the lives of the greatest musicians. School students often later have an opportunity to hear some of their works.

298–299

Taniguchi Jirô and Sekigawa Natsuo, *In the Time of Botchan.*
© Taniguchi Jirô, Sekigawa Natsuo, Futabasha, 1987

In this manga, Taniguchi Jirô turns to Natsume Sôseki (1867–1916), author of the novel *Botchan* (1906), one of the most gifted intellectuals and writers of his generation. He is shown where he lived and worked, writing a manuscript, with his cat—the hero of his debut novel, *I Am a Cat*, in which, endowed with the power of speech, he observes Meiji society. Here, the writer, exhausted after hours of work, has fallen asleep on his *tatami.*

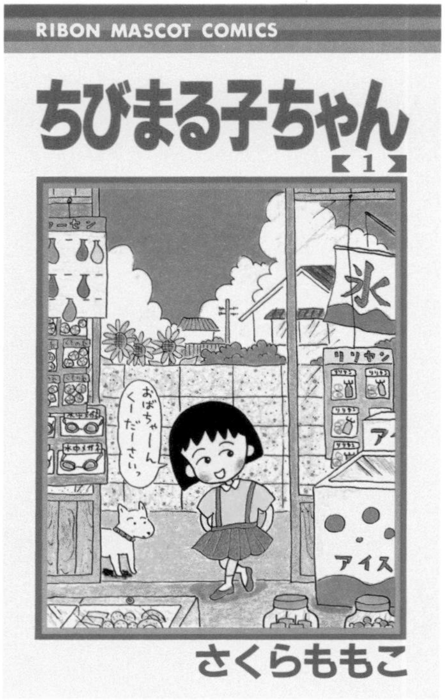
RIBON MASCOT COMICS
ちびまる子ちゃん
1
おばちゃーん くーだーさいっ
氷
アイス
さくらももこ

300
Sakura Momoko, *Chibi Marukochan (Little Maruko).*
© Sakura Momoko, Shûeisha, 1987

When Maruko was eight she was still so tiny that people nicknamed her "Little Maruko." Her everyday life is described with humor, and her candidness and blunders make readers and viewers laugh out loud. The anime taken from this manga is still broadcast on TV.

The world of dance

Ballet dancing, a hugely popular activity in Japan since the end of the Second World War, exerts an enormous fascination on children, especially girls. Maki Miyako was the first to devote a number of manga to classical dance, making it better known and serving as a spur to many a fledgling ballet dancer.

Daily life in manga

Manga are aimed at every type of audience and adults show a no less vibrant interest in them. If pedagogical manga for children offer an ever-expanding market, the same is true of works of a practical nature, concerning sport or cooking, for instance. Subjects such as cuisine and wine tasting have a particular attraction for the Japanese, who pride themselves on their gourmet tastes. Culinary specialties from round the globe are served in many restaurants along with world-famous wines; these establishments vie with each other to satisfy ever more demanding customers. It is a phenomenon the manga was unlikely to ignore. Figs. 328–32

The medical world, too, is the subject also of many a TV show, and manga are never far behind, one of the most interesting to appear recently being *Iryû Team Medical Dragon*. Fig. 326

The vogue for Art Nouveau

If manga, nourished by styles and stories from earlier times, has been evolving continuously since the beginning of the century, one other aspect hard to overlook might be described as the "return of *japonisme* to Japan." Various manga signed by talented artists now take inspiration from Art Nouveau. In the nineteenth century, when the vogue for things Japanese gripped Europe, plenty of artists became interested in the composition and graphic style of Japanese prints. Initiators of a new movement in the visual arts, these artists imitated their sources, particularly in theater and advertising posters. Art Nouveau borrowed various elements from Japan, and the Czech painter Alfons Mucha (1860–1939) had a marvelous flair for integrating them into his incredibly successful stage posters, in particular using the vertical *kakejiku* format. Figs. 333, 336–339

Today, some *mangaka* remain much influenced by the Art Nouveau style, and by Mucha in particular, one of Japan's favorite

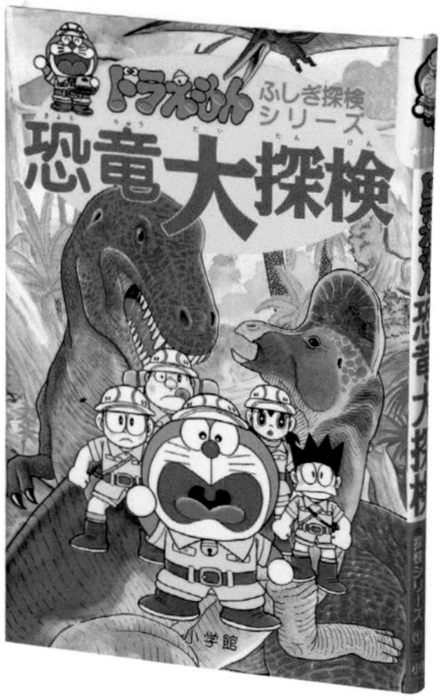
ドラえもん
ふしぎ探検シリーズ
恐竜大探検
小学館

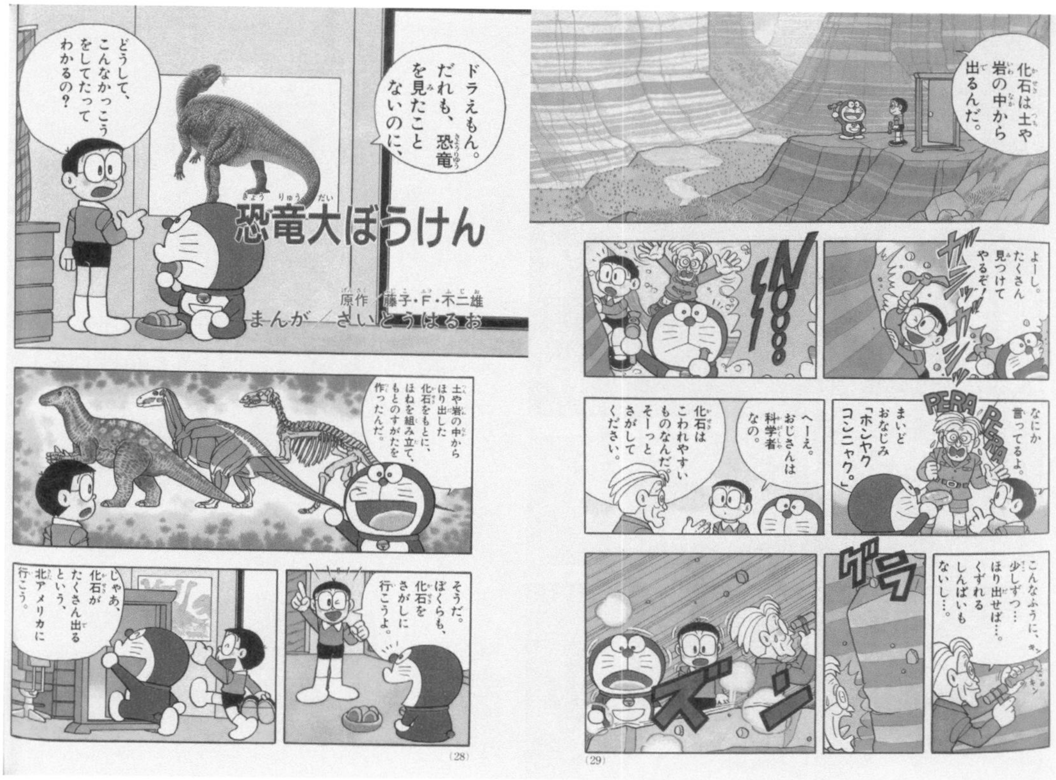
ドラえもん。だれも、恐竜を見たことないのに、
どうして、こんなかっこうをしてたってわかるの?
恐竜大ぼうけん
原作/藤子・F・不二雄
まんが/さいとうはるお
土や岩の中からほり出した化石をもとに、ほねを組み立て、もとのすがたを作ったんだ。
そうだ。ぼくらも、化石をさがしに行こうよ。
じゃあ、化石がたくさん出るという、北アメリカに行こう。
(28)
化石は土や岩の中から出るんだ。
よーし。たくさん見つけてやるぞ!
ガシッ ガシッ
NOOOO
なにか言ってるよ。
まいどおなじみ「ホンヤクコンニャク。」
PERA PERA
へーえ。おじさんは科学者なの。
化石はこわれやすいものなんだ。そーっとさがしてください。
こんなふうに、少しずつ…ほり出せば…。くずれるしんぱいもないし…。
グラ
ズン
(29)

301–302
Fujiko F. Fujio, *Discovering Dinosaurs*. © Fujiko F. Fujio, Shogakukan, 1992

All aspects of physics, chemistry, natural history, and science are covered by manga. The dinosaurs in this strip are tracked by the sympathetic Doraemon, one of most famous comic heroes, who is adored by Japanese children. The historical and scientific information at the end of the book provides a fun way of learning more.

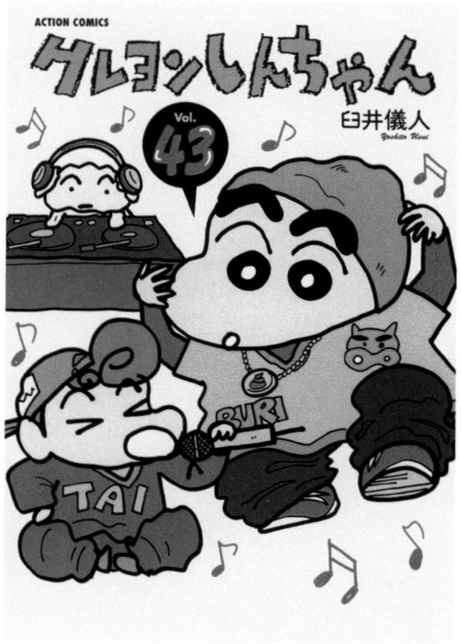
ACTION COMICS
クレヨンしんちゃん
Vol. 43
臼井儀人
BURI
TAI

303
Usui Yoshito, *Crayon Shinchan*. © Usui Yoshito, Futabasha, 2006

Shinchan spends his time playing silly pranks and getting his parents into embarrassing fixes. A bestseller since 1992, the author wins readers over with a critique of the defects of Japanese society and of adults in general, seen through the eyes of the young hero.

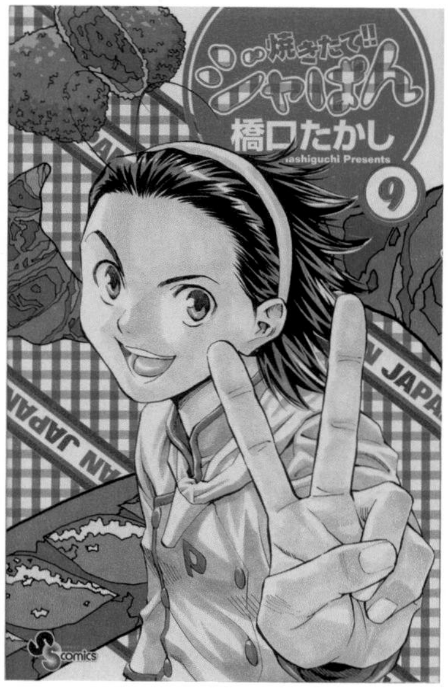
橋口たかし
9

304
Hashiguchi Takashi, *Yakitate! Ja-Pan*. © Hashiguchi Takashi, Shogakukan, 2003

JUMP COMICS
DRAGON BALL
ドラゴンボール
鳥山 明
巻一
孫悟空と仲間たち

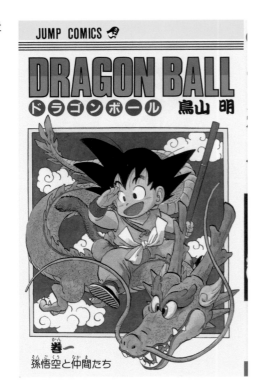

305
Toriyama Akira, *Dragon Ball Songokû and Friends.*
© Toriyama Akira, Shûeisha, 2006

Since launching in 1984, the success of this manga has been phenomenal and has been further strengthened by spin-off TV and movie anime. Inspired by a great classic of Chinese literature, the story relates a quest for seven crystal balls that, if reunited, will make it possible to invoke a sacred dragon—the dragon can make any wish come true.

artists. The tendrils, sophisticated attire, and long, flowing hair of his models, dissolving into curls against a floral backdrop, provide a storehouse of possibilities for many artists.

CLAMP is the name chosen by a group of women *mangaka*. Figs. 330–33 Numbering seven at the outset, they continued their brilliant career with a reduced team of four. Their works, initially aimed at a female demographic, now attract a more varied readership. Immensely popular throughout the archipelago, they do every stage of the work: script, drawing, spin-offs, and merchandise. The attractiveness of their characters, which live in a dramatic and dazzling world, is undeniable. The Art Nouveau-style frames they place in the background, like the robes and jewels with which their heroines are adorned, are not without similarities to posters of Sarah Bernhardt and other Belle Époque beauties painted by Mucha. Their sophisticated hairstyles, the scrollwork, and plants are drawn with immense care and refinement and inevitably recall the European artist, while the format is redolent of the *kakemomo** and the folding-screens that connoisseurs of *japonisme* were so fond of. Another young *mangaka*, Ôse Kohime, draws in the Figs. 335–33 *kawaii** ("cute") style, reworking in her own way a manner derived from Mucha. Her heroines, with their great green eyes, their pose, profile or full face, their long, flyaway hair catching on the floral decor, and the luxuriant backdrop are nothing short of ravishing.

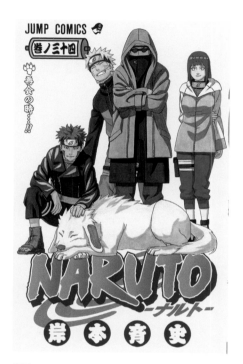

306
Ôba Tsugumi, Olata Takeshi, *Death Note*.
© Ôba Tsugumi, Digitalogue, Shûeisha, 2006

307
Kishimoto Masashi, *Naruto*.
© Kishimoto Masashi, Shûeisha, 2006

This manga and its film adaptation are one of the greatest successes of recent times. The second film came out in Japan at the end of December 2006 and confirmed the popularity of a thrilling story that keeps readers and audiences on the edge of their seats from beginning to end.

A young man discovers a book with malevolent powers that the god of the dead has placed in his path. All he has to do is write the name of a person down in it for them to die in a matter of minutes. At first the hero uses the book to eliminate wrongdoers and then for self-protection. But the burning question the manga asks its readers is: Does one ever have the right to kill?

Extremely popular in Japan, this adventure-packed manga features a hero whose very name, Uzumaki Naruto, is a pun. Naruto is a city where a unique natural phenomenon occurs: the *uzumaki* (eddies, whirlpools), which were drawn by Hiroshige in some remarkable prints. Naruto is a young boy who at the outset seems pretty normal. He dreams of becoming a hero, but hardly shines at the school of martial arts. But appearances can be misleading, as he later discovers he possesses special powers. This action manga describes the unhappy childhood of a young *ninja** and his struggle with destiny as he fights evil with his pals.

子連れ狼 2
LONE WOLF CUB
Story 小池一夫
Art 小島剛夕
KING SERIES

新世紀エヴァンゲリオン
Volume 10
漫画／貞本義行
原作／GAINAX

もしもし
はい……
え!?
あ…… ミサトさん……
綾波が……
生きてる？
107

308–309

Kojima Kôseki to an outline by Koike Kazuo, *Kozure Ôkami (Lone Wolf and Cub)*. © Koike Shoin Publishing, Co., Ltd, 2001

A major classic, *Kozure Ôkami* appeared in 1970 and is the story of a *rônin** (a samurai without a master). A victim of a conspiracy that has lost him his status, he crisscrosses Japan in the company of his little boy, Daigorô, hiring himself out as an assassin.

Kojima's oeuvre is characterized by energetic, realist handling that emerged from the *gekiga** style. It is composed with great spontaneity of line in pen and/or brush and ink. He possesses a keen and intuitive sense of the resources of the panel, combined with an analytic rigor in poses and movements, which are rendered with great assurance. A specialist in earlier period manga, Kojima shows elegance and subtlety in amplifying his battle set-pieces, as well as what makes them flare up. Everything derives from his feeling for esthetics and choreography. Each "shot" is framed for its narrative impact, to capture the beauty of a gesture, or to demonstrate the techniques of the art of war in the purest samurai tradition.

310–311

Sadamoto Yoshiyuki, *Shinseiki Evangelion (Neon Genesis Evangelion)*. © Sadamoto Yoshiyuki, Gainax, Kadokawa Shoten, 2006

Evangelion has pride of place among adventure and science-fiction manga. The reader is thrown into a world in which half the population has been eradicated following a cataclysm and now has to confront belligerent giant anthropoids of unknown origin.

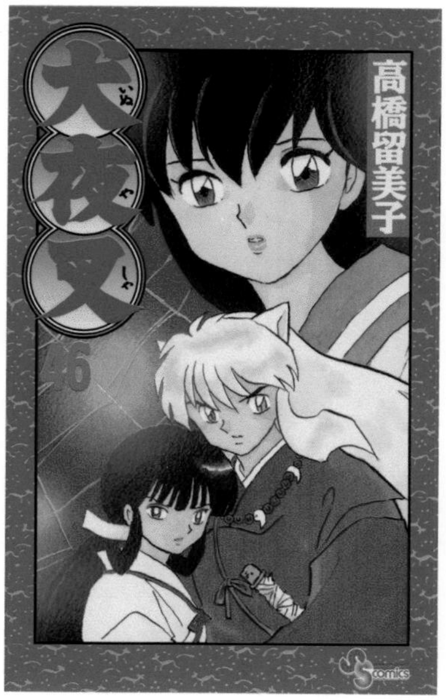
犬夜叉
26
高橋留美子

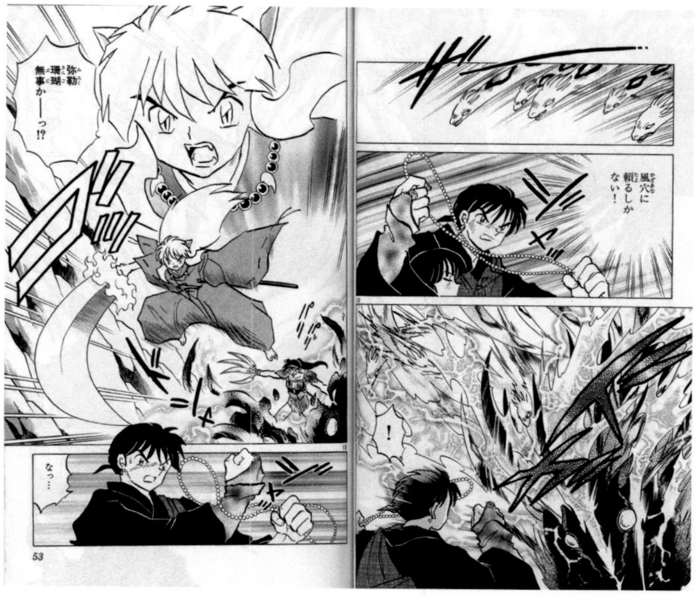
風穴に頼るしかない！
!
弥勒 珊瑚 無事か——っ!?
なっ…
53

312–313
Takahashi Rumiko, *Inu Yasha.*
© Takahashi Rumiko,
Shogakukan, 2006

Many fans of anime still fondly remember the thrilling series *Ranma 1/2.* In *Inu Yasha*, its author, Takahashi Rumiko, tells the story of a fifteen-year-old girl living in Tokyo. One day, she tumbles down a well and is whisked back to the time of Sengoku (fifteenth to sixteenth centuries), where she meets an extraordinary being: man, dog, and demon all rolled into one. In his quest for the pearl of Shikon, this hybrid creature will involve her in breathtaking adventures.

Takahashi Rumiko's drawings are action-packed, and his unique and highly imaginative monsters are no longer inspired by traditional forms. From series to series, he manages to renew his style, and has captivated a whole new generation of readers.

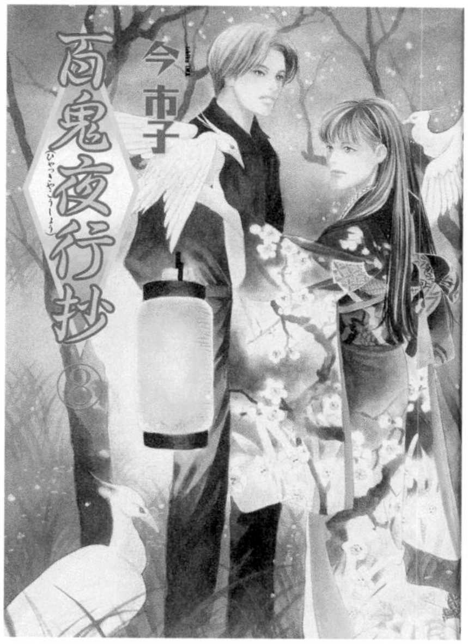
百鬼夜行抄
3
今市子

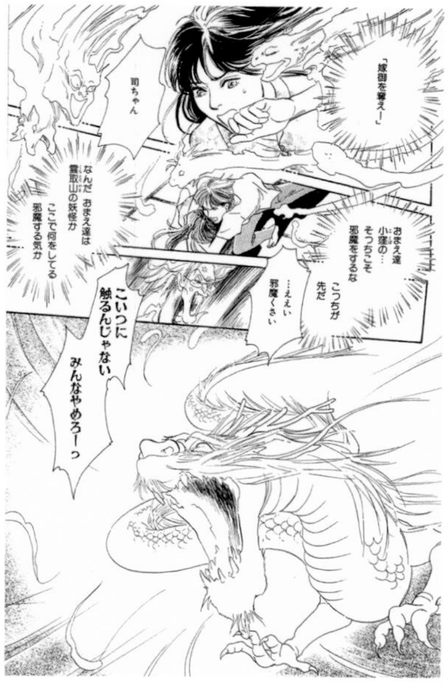
「嫁御を奪え！」
司ちゃん
おまえ達 小鬼の…そっちこそ邪魔をするな
こっちが先だ
…ええい 邪魔くさい
なんだ おまえ達は 霊取山の妖怪か ここで何をしてる 邪魔する気か
こいつに触るんじゃない
みんなやめろーっ

314–315
Ima Ichiko, *Hyakki Yakôshô (Story of the Parade of the Hundred Demons).* © Ima Ichiko,
Asahi Sonorama, Tokyo, 2005

The title of this manga is a throwback to the past: *The Parade of the Hundred Demons* was a favorite theme in painted scrolls. The action here is updated to our modern times and is the fantastical story of a high-school student with the ability to perceive souls and demons. Because of this supernatural power, which makes the unhappy boy seem strange to his schoolfellows, he fails to make any friends. He does all he can to lead a normal life and to escape from his powers, but bizarre happenings dog his every step.

Appearing for the first time in 1995, this manga's covers are esthetically very sophisticated, printed on a mica paper seldom employed for this kind of title. Such refinements are probably explained by the fact that the author used to be an illustrator before becoming a *mangaka*.

Le Cirque de Karakuri
からくりサーカス
43
comics
藤田和日郎
KAZUHIRO FUJITA PRESENTS

316
Fujita Kazuhirô, *Karakuri sa-kasu (Karakuri Circus).*
© Fujita Kazuhirô, Shogakukan, 2006

A martial arts master, Katô Narumi is afflicted with a serious disease. If he wants to survive, he has to make people laugh—but only one of his audience is ever amused at his antics. One day, he is kidnapped, and Katô promptly leaves to find him. The reader, unsure whether to laugh or cry, is caught up in the action and just has to follow each episode of this enthralling thriller to the end.

巻四十三 "英雄伝説"
JUMP COMICS
ワンピース
ONE PIECE
尾田栄一郎
EIICHIRO ODA

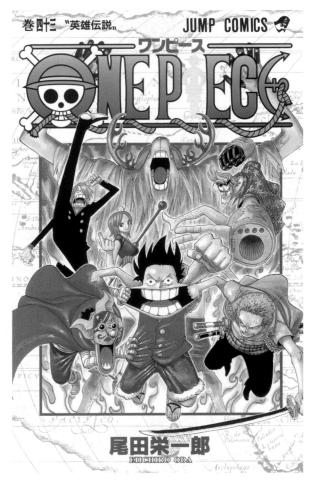

317
Oda Eiichirô, *One Piece.*
© Oda Eiichirô, Shûeisha, 2006

The continuous stream of jokes, mishaps, and gags carries readers away on a surge of adventures. The exaggerated features of the characters combined with their energy makes them very engaging. The hero, Luffy, is gifted with an incredible flexible body and plies the seven seas with his pals, intent on finding the treasure that will make him king of the ocean. The story has a moral undertone as well: wherever he comes ashore, Luffy always tries to help the inhabitants.

To date this manga holds the absolute record for sales from its first edition; as soon as a number comes out, it goes straight into the best-seller list.

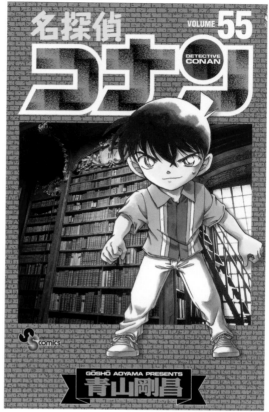

名探偵コナン
VOLUME 55
DETECTIVE CONAN
comics
GÔSHÔ AOYAMA PRESENTS
青山剛昌

Fig. 318

松本大洋 2
ナンバーファイブ
吾
Matsumoto Taiyou
IKKI COMIX

Fig. 319

318
Aoyama Gôshô, *Meitantei Conan (Detective Conan)*. © Aoyama Gôshô, volume 55, Shogakukan, 2006

This series of manga, which have been made into movie and television films, is a favorite of old and young alike. In it, the investigations undertaken by the perspicacious hero always result in the culprits being apprehended. Conan, a high-school pupil, has been a victim of a plot: someone has made him drink a potion that has made him younger, and now he looks like a primary schoolkid. Hiding his true identity, he calls himself Edogawa Conan and helps the father of his friend Ran to get to the bottom of some puzzling events.

319
Matsumoto Taiyô, *Number Five*, 2006.
© Matsumoto Taiyô, Shogakukan

A great hit with teenagers, this manga mixes adventure and science fiction. In a futuristic world, the marksman Number Five has suddenly disappeared, fleeing with a young woman, Matriochka. The members of Rainbow, an armed peacekeeping organization, are hot on their trail.

321
Toriyama Akira, *Dr. Slump*.
© Toriyama Akira, Shûeisha, 2005
(first published in 1980)

Doctor Norimaki thinks that in Arale, who looks like a little girl, he's manufactured the perfect robot. But he hasn't realized that he has also made her unbelievably strong and she proves quite a headache.

Unlike any other, Arale's language is mimicked by countless little Japanese girls. Its author, Toriyama Akira, is now a household name; the series *Dragon Ball* is world famous, while *Dr. Slump*, *Sandland*, and *Cowa* offer confirmation of an exceptional talent.

KEKKAISHI
結界師
13
comics
田辺イエロウ

Fig. 320

320
Tanabe Yellow, *Kekkaishi*
© Tanabe Yellow, Shogakukan, 2006

This manga, shown every week on TV as an anime, is a great hit with youngsters.

JUMP COMICS
Dr.
ドクター
スランプ
第11巻
♡ガッちゃん
ガッちゃんの巻
鳥山明

Fig. 321

白鳥
SWAN
13
有吉京子
Kyoko Ariyoshi
PRINCESS COMICS DELUXE

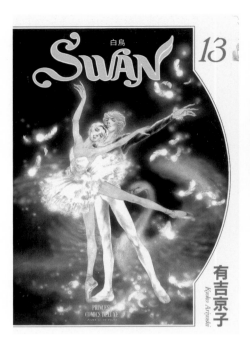

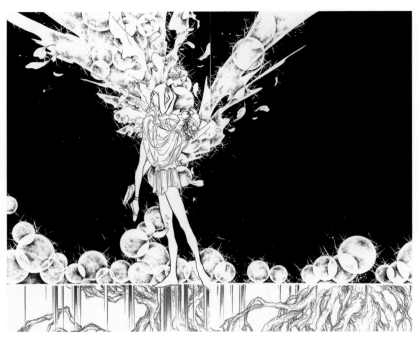

322–323

Kyoko Ariyoshi, *Swan*. © Kyoko Ariyoshi, Akita Shoten, 1992

Audiences normally only see the brilliance and beauty of the world of dance. Here we have something far closer to reality. Backstage amours and jealousies are captured by a line of singular finesse, in irregularly shaped panels. For this manga, the author has adopted an original layout, which makes for a novel of exceptional graphic quality.

その夜の お山は ごきげん だった
ふたりを 祝って 笑い続けた
お山の 笑い声は 風に乗り 海を渡って ふたりの 眠る窪地に 流れこみ……
ふたりの まわりに 咲き乱れる 赤い花々を
静かに白く 変えていった……
259
258

324

Maki Miyako, *Kôshoku gonin onna (Five Exceptionally Beautiful Women)*.
© Maki Miyako, Chuokoron-Shinsha, 2006

Already well known for remarkable adaptations of literary works, such as the *Tale of Genji*, Maki Miyako also excels in stories from the Edo era.

Kôshoku gonin onna contains love scenes of marvelous refinement. The artist uses asymmetrical panels and gradations of gray to juxtapose the roar of the volcano with the serenity of the young couple.

RIBON MASCOT COMICS Cookie
NANA
16
矢沢あい

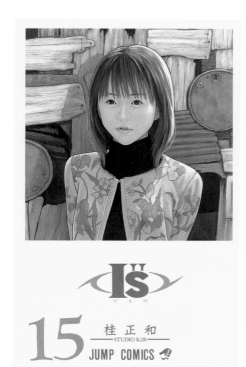

325
Yazawa Ai, *Nana.* © Yazawa Ai, Shûeisha, 2006

This manga has been an enormous success and, after inspiring a first film shot two years ago, *Nana 2* hit Japanese screens in December 2006.

It is the story of two girls with the same first name, Nana, who are opposites in every way and who have no earthly reason to meet. One day, however, they sit next to each other in a train to the capital. By chance, they then both view the same apartment and decide to live there as joint tenants. Komatsu Nana, romantic and decked out in the latest fashions, has made the journey to the city to join the one she loves. The second Nana, whose style is more punk, wants to get a rock group going. In spite of appearances, they actually complement one another and they forge a deep friendship that transports readers to a world in which the young are always looking for love.

医
[いりゅう]
Team Medical Dragon
龍
University hospitals,
Japan Medical Association,
and the Administration.........
Serious distrust of medical treatment
finally obliges you to speak
the necessity of reforms.
Your real intention is,
however, to protect your own field.
Patients still have been victims
behind superficial reforms today.
Nogizaka Taro
乃木坂太郎
Nagai Akira
[原案]永井 明
9
BIG COMIC SUPERIOR

326
Nogisawa Tarô, Nagai Akira, *Iryû Team Medical Dragon.* © Nogisawa Tarô, Nagai Akira, Shogakukan, 2006

This manga, since adapted for television, is set in today's world of medicine, with its intrigues, many imperfections, and inconsistencies: the top jobs don't invariably go the best-qualified doctors, and the decisions taken by the consultants are often plain wrong. Emotionally charged cases are described that have readers holding their breath. The well-crafted plot and the thought-provoking subject make this series a telling reflection of contemporary society.

I''s
15
桂正和
STUDIO K2R
JUMP COMICS

327
Katsura Masakazu, *I's (Aizu).* © Katsura Masakazu, Shûeisha, 2000

The majority of this artist's works are devoted to love stories, always featuring seductive yet understanding girls. All the covers are drawn with great finesse. Two young people working in show business fall in love. The girl prefers to throw in her artistic career so as to be with the one she loves.

美味しんぼ
94 医食同源対決!!
作・雁屋 哲
画・花咲アキラ

328–329

Kariya Tetsu, Hanasaki Akira, *Oishinbô (Gourmet)*.

This manga on cooking presents various dishes drawn with such realism and delicacy that the reader soon works up an appetite. First issued in 1983, it was one of the first manga on the subject.

The hero is a lover of fine cuisine who agrees to prepare sophisticated menus for the staff on the newspaper where he works. He pushes himself to his limit so as to prove to his father, with whom he is in conflict, that he is capable of the heights of culinary refinement. In the competitive atmosphere of the kitchen, the author focuses on the intricate or simple recipes that make haute cuisine a lifestyle choice.

昔、お母さんが作ってくれた蒸しご飯。
私の流儀で作ってみたわ。
餅米七分うるち米三分のお米に、
ニンジン、シイタケ、ゴボウ、レンコンを刻んで甘辛く煮たもの、
ちりめん山椒を混ぜて、
56
美味しんぼ94
蒸籠で蒸して…
仕上げに錦糸卵、
鯛のでんぶ、
焼き海苔の細切りを乗せたのよ。
57

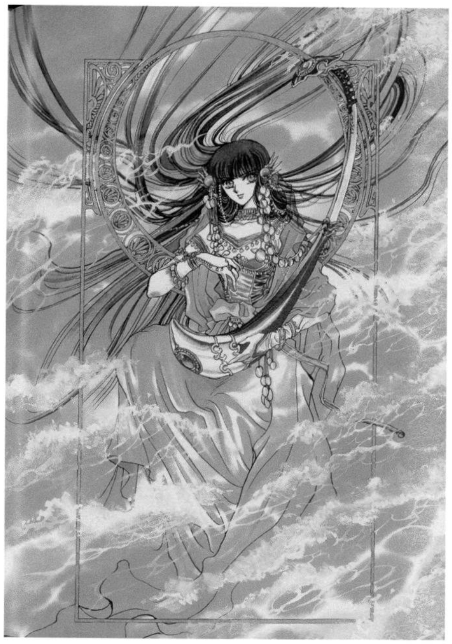

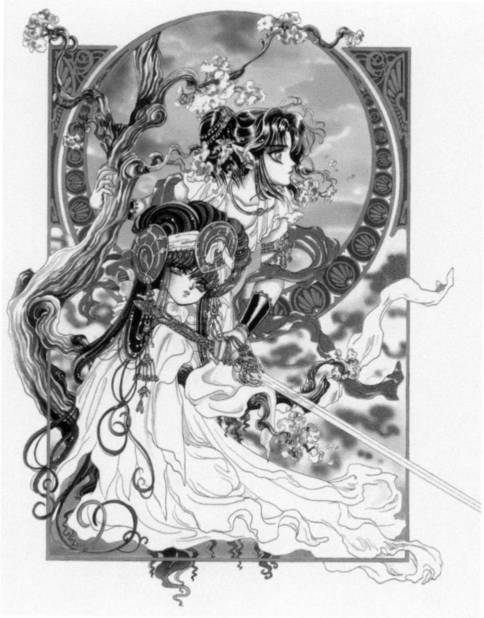

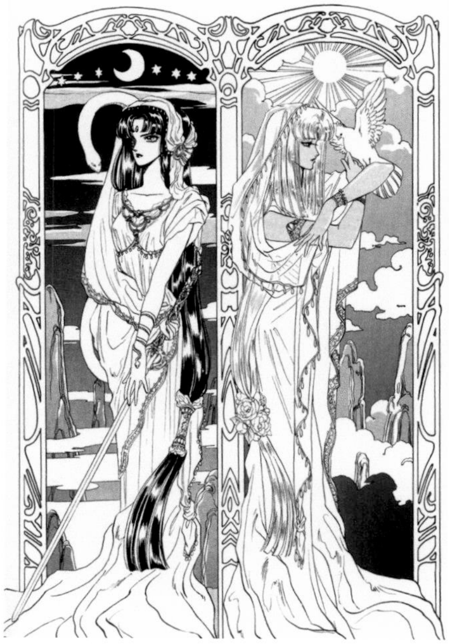

330–332
CLAMP, *Tenmagouka, "RG Veda" (Illustrations Collections)*. © CLAMP, Shinshokan, 2001

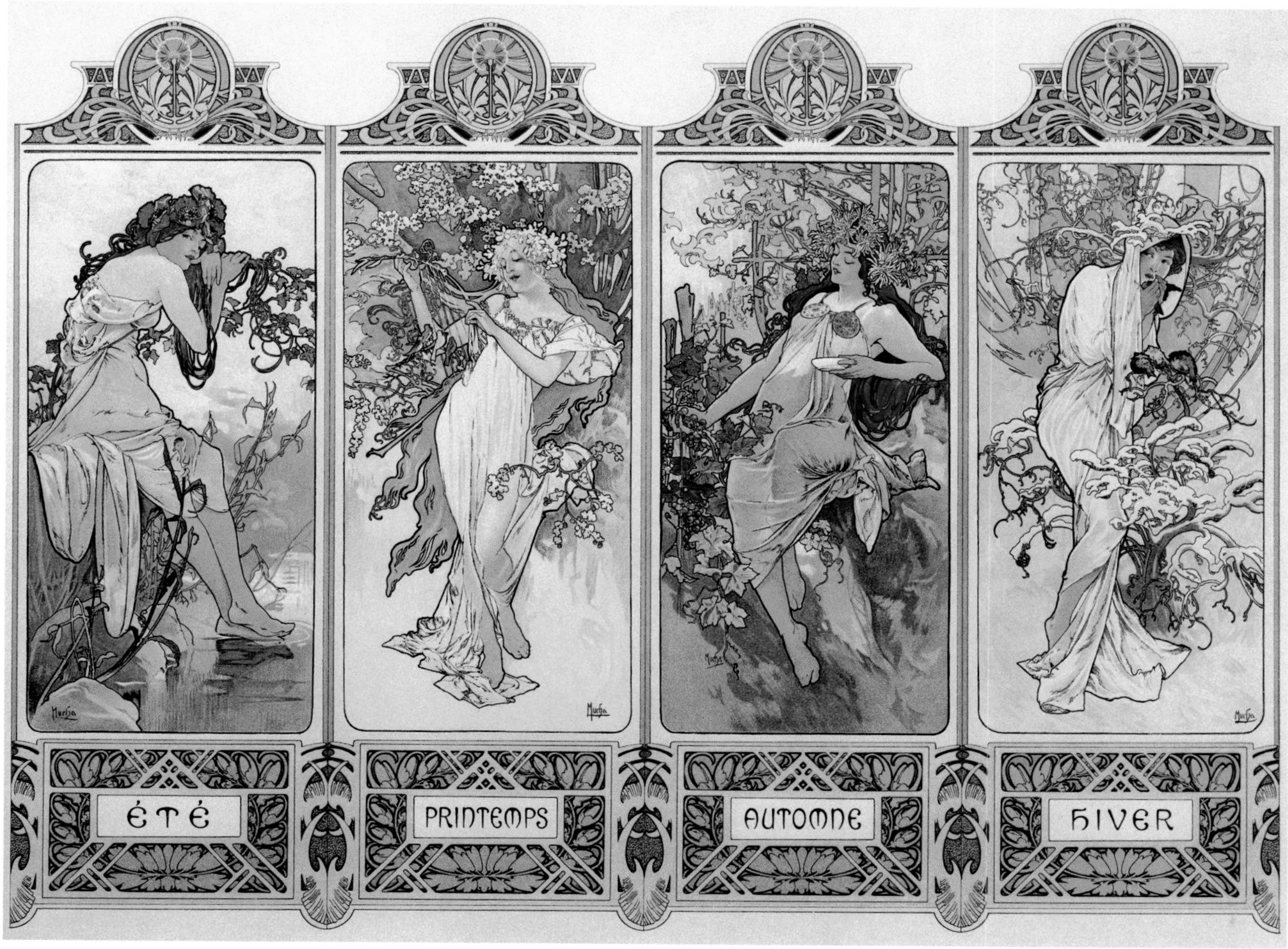
ÉTÉ
PRINTEMPS
AUTOMNE
HIVER

333
Alphonse Mucha, *Les Quatre Saisons (The Four Seasons)*, 1896, lithograph. © Sotheby's/akg-images/Mucha Trust/ADAGP, Paris, 2007

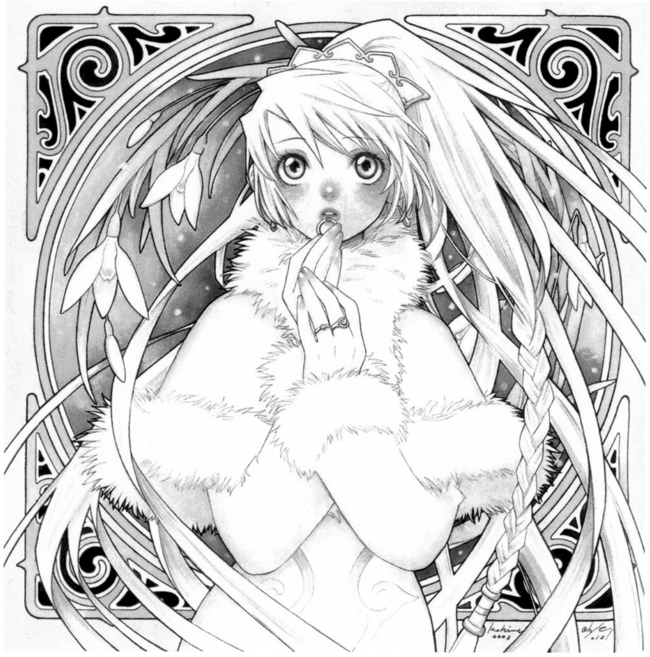

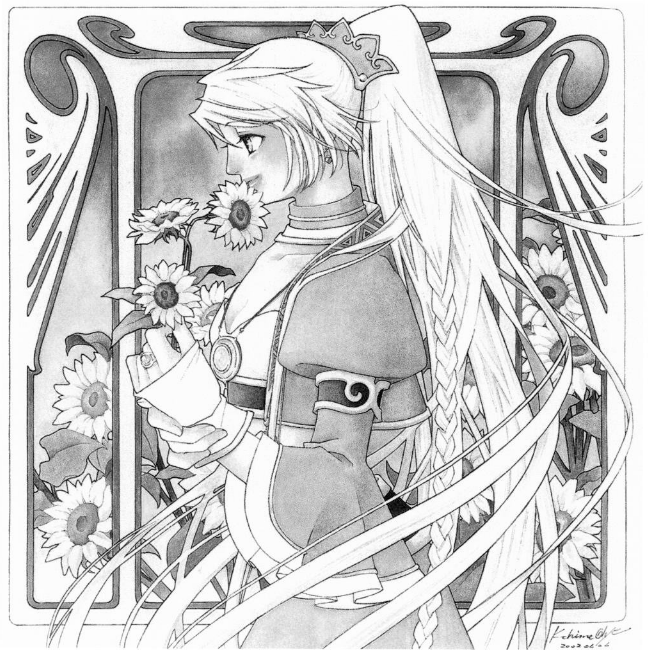

334–335
Ôse Kohime, *Tiru na nogu*.
© Ôse Kohime (Rig. Marge), Bijutsu Shuppansha, 2003

The treatment in this wonderfully poetical manga—in which a doll that seems to have stepped out of a nineteenth-century fairy tale takes on human form in an effort to reunite a father and his daughter—is alive with tenderness.

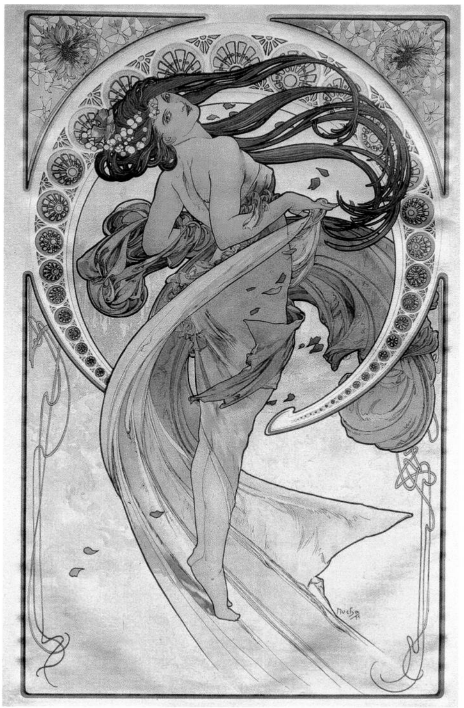

336
Alphonse Mucha, *Danse (Dance)*, 1898, lithograph.
© Sotheby's/akg-images/Mucha Trust/ADAGP, Paris, 2007

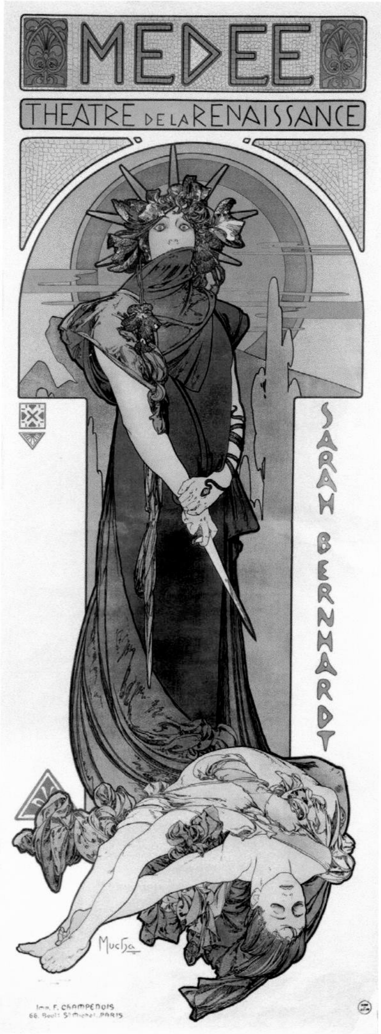
MEDEE
THEATRE DE LA RENAISSANCE
SARAH BERNHARDT
Mucha

337
Alphonse Mucha, *Médée (Medea)*, 1898, lithograph.
© Sotheby's/akg-images/Mucha Trust/ADAGP, Paris, 2007

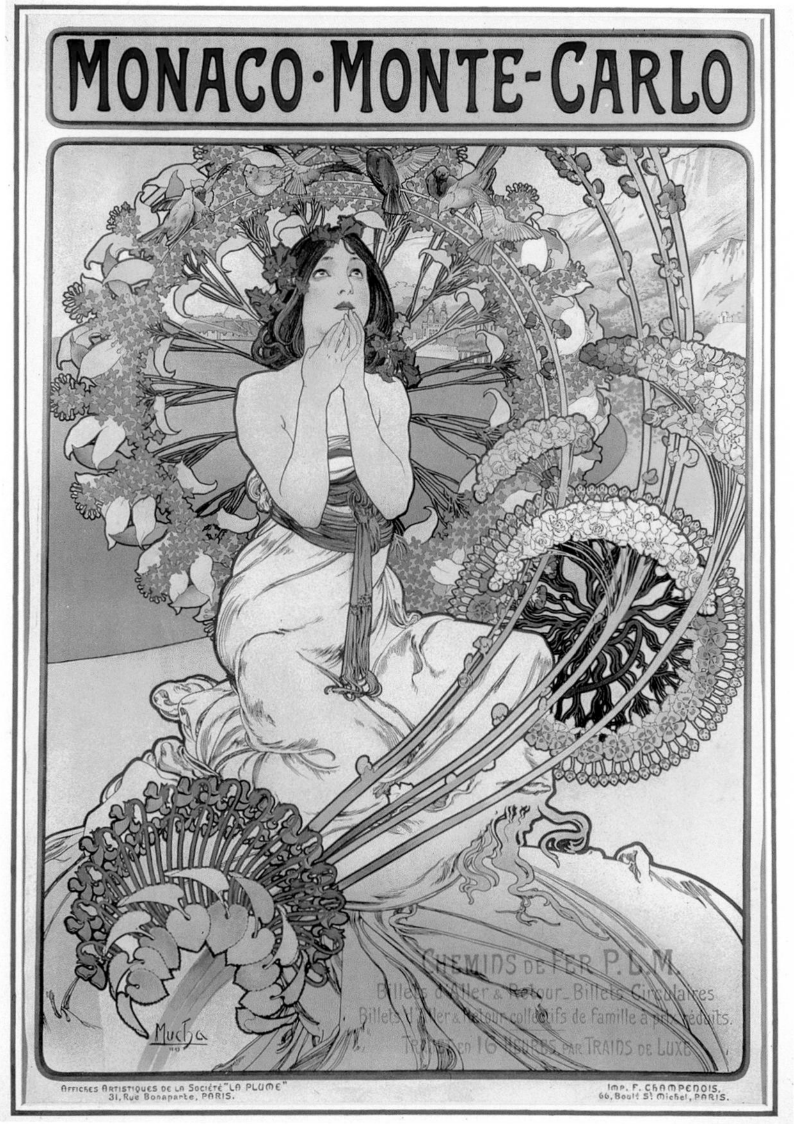
MONACO·MONTE-CARLO
CHEMINS DE FER P.L.M.
Mucha
AFFICHES ARTISTIQUES DE LA SOCIÉTÉ "LA PLUME"
31, Rue Bonaparte, PARIS.
Imp. F. CHAMPENOIS,
66, Boulᵈ Sᵗ Michel, PARIS.

338
Alphonse Mucha, *Monaco, Monte-Carlo*, 1897, lithograph.
© Sotheby's/akg-images/Mucha Trust/ADAGP, Paris, 2007

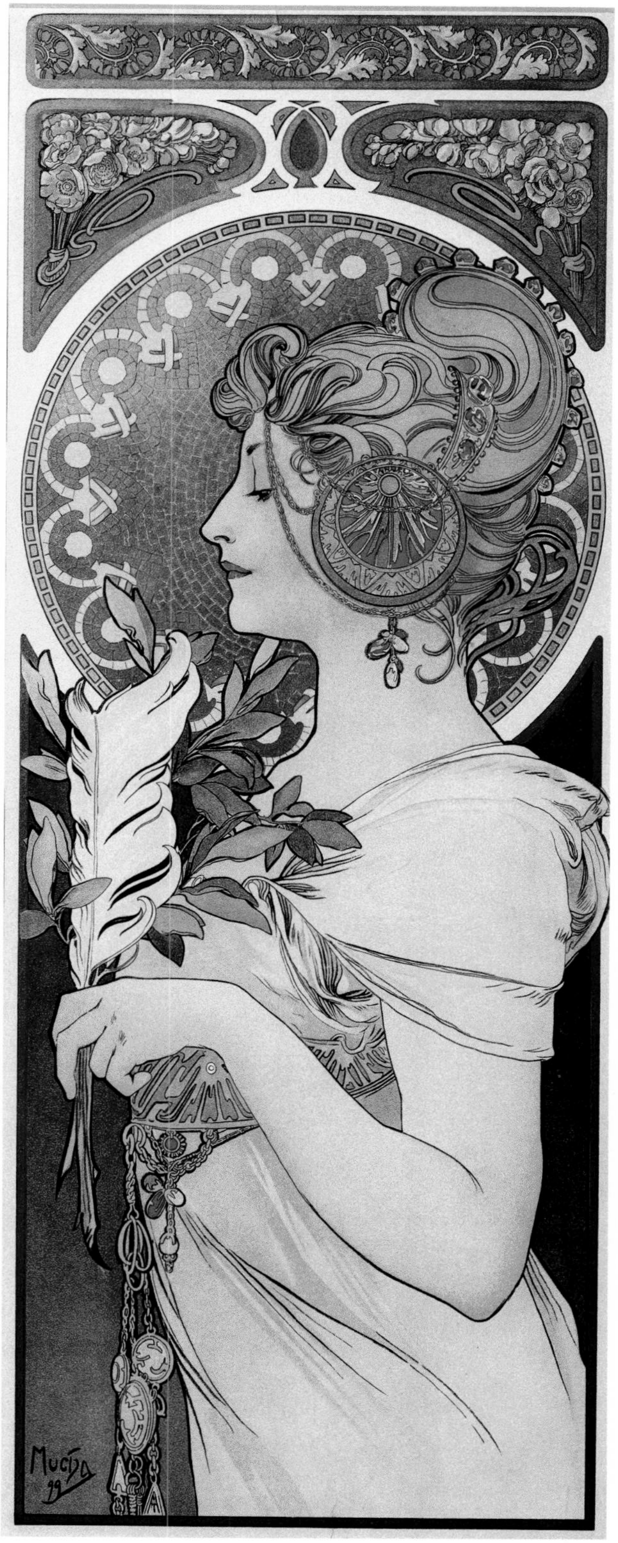
Mucha
99

339
Alphonse Mucha, *Plume (Feather)* 1899, lithograph.
© Sotheby's/akg-images/Mucha Trust/ADAGP, Paris, 2007

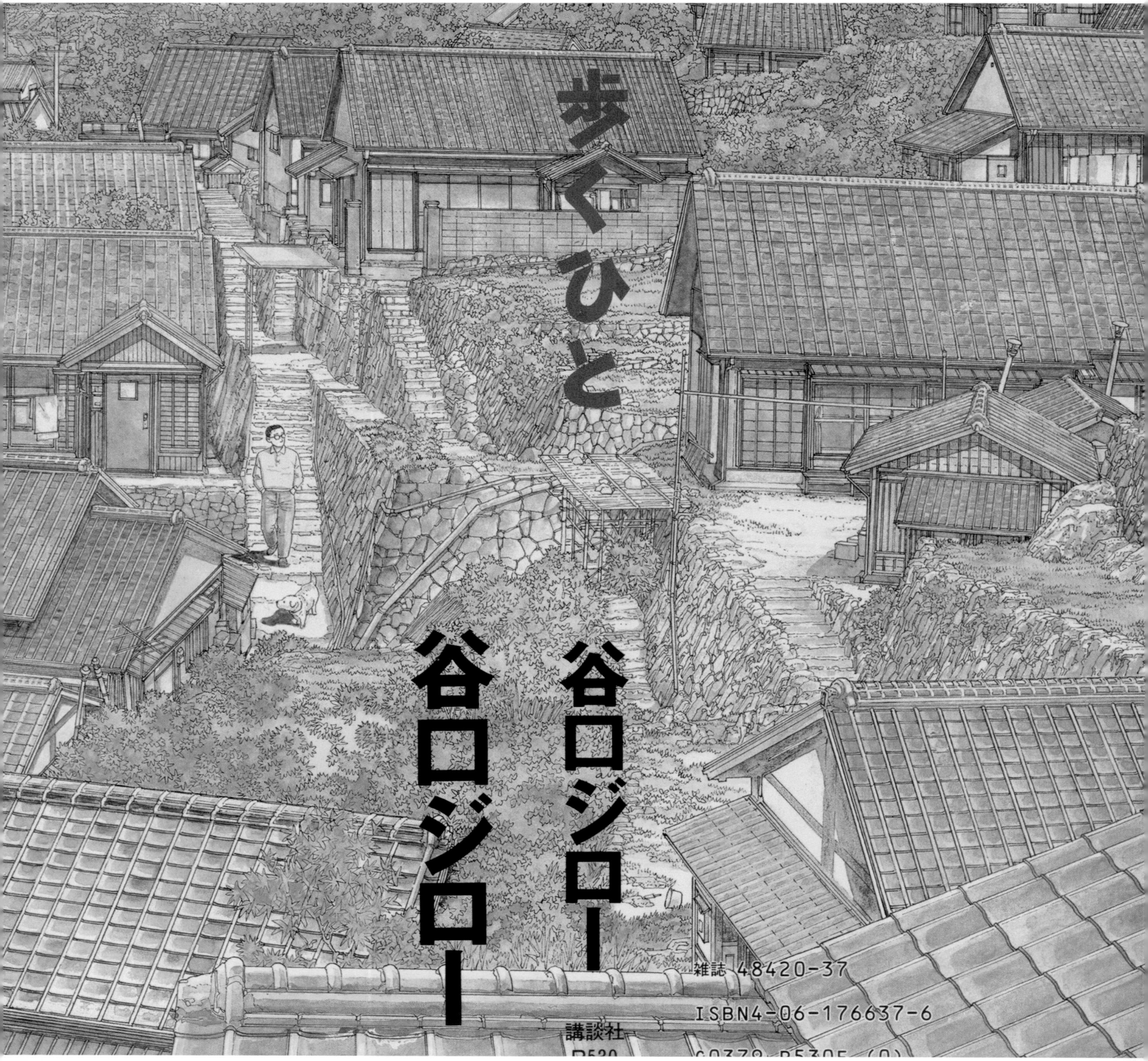
歩くひと
谷口ジロー
谷口ジロー
雑誌 48420-37
ISBN4-06-176637-6
講談社

Fig. 375 (detail)

Ikeda Riyoko: birth of the new *shôjo manga*

*Shôjo manga** reflects the evolution of women in Japanese society. A teenager's life as described in the first *shôjo manga* from before the Second World War has—of course—little in common with that of the emancipated females of today, such as the heroines of *Nana*.

Unquestionably, the author who most fomented this revolution in *shôjo manga* was Ikeda Riyoko. Her masterpiece is *Versailles no bara (The Rose of Versailles*, 1972–73; a French film Figs. 347–351 was taken from it and released under the title of *Lady Oscar)*, a fictionalized life of Marie-Antoinette, thanks to which many Japanese women have been induced to learn French and become interested in French history. Drawing on the biography of Marie-Antoinette by Stefan Zweig, the manga* retraces the life of the young French queen, but it is the character of Oscar that really fascinates readers. His androgynous nature, probably inspired by the Chevalier d'Éon, combined with the star-crossed love affairs that pepper the narrative, have charmed an essentially female market. Having studied literature, Ikeda Riyoko is no less keen on music and song. She has published many historical manga, including *Empress Catherine* (based on the life of Catherine II of Russia) and *The Ring of the Nibelung* after Richard Wagner, com- Figs. 340–346 bining great delicacy of line with a good deal of research, in details of dress in particular.

Sugiura Hinako: a passion for the Edo period

This talented *mangaka**, who passed away prematurely in 2005 at the age of forty-six, left an extremely rich oeuvre devoted entirely to the Edo* era. Her sister-in-law Suzuki Hiroko kindly agreed to tell us something of what Sugiura Hinako was like, describing her as a merry, spontaneous person.

Sugiura Hinako acquired her love of drawing very early on. While still a child, she reused the paper replaced in the sliding partitions at home and covered it in drawings. This habit she never lost, and Suzuki Hiroko tells us that, when she redid the walls in her apartment, Sugiura Hinako, using a spray gun, painted a splendid landscape of Mount Fuji. When drawing, she would concentrate for hours, ignoring everything around her.

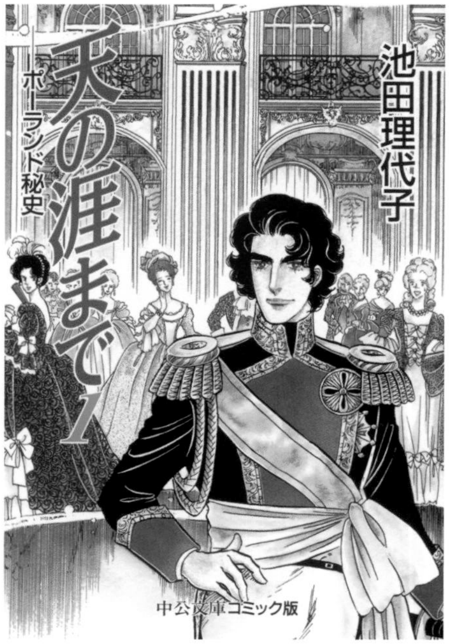
池田理代子
天の涯まで 1
ポーランド秘史
中公文庫コミック版

340
Ikeda Riyoko, *To the End of the Sky, The Secret History of Poland*, Chûôkoron-shinsha, 1999.
© Ikeda Riyoko Production

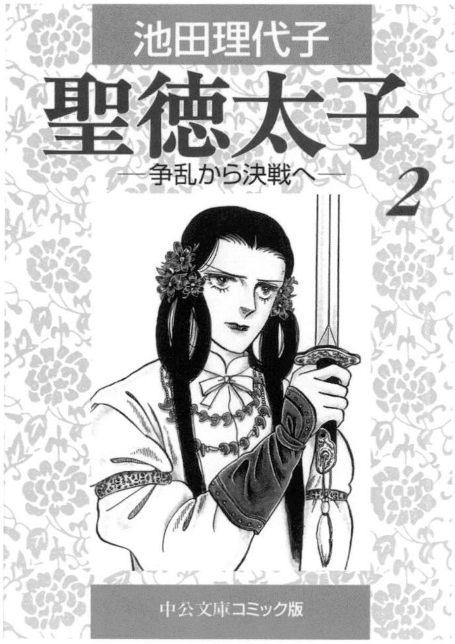
池田理代子
聖徳太子
争乱から決戦へ
2
中公文庫コミック版

341
Ikeda Riyoko, *The Story of Shôtokutaishi from the Beginning to the End of the War*, Chûôkoron-shinsha, 1999. © Ikeda Riyoko Production

Sugiura Hinako gave up studying design to follow courses given by Inagaki Shisei, a specialist in the Edo period. It was an epoch that entirely won her over, and she strove to recreate its atmosphere in manga, reading widely so as to understand its manners and mores. It seemed to her that the Japanese were then happier and felt less stress than in the Meiji period. Sugiura Hinako published many manga, all set in the Edo epoch: *Tsugen Muro kore Ume* (her first manga, 1980), *Edo e yôkoso* (*Welcome to Edo*, 1986), *Futatsu Makura (Lacquer Pillows)*, *Edo Suzume* (*The Sparrows of Edo*, 1987), *Hyaku Monogatari* (*The One Hundred Tales*, 1986–93), *Sarusuberi* (*Lagerstroemia*, 1996). Figs. 108, 1 352–357

Having carried off several prizes, she gave up manga to devote herself to researching the Edo era and became an adviser for historical films, writing several works and taking part in TV programs on the subject. While they have a hint of the erotic, Sugiura Hinako's manga, in which the art of suggestion is subtly handled, never degenerate into vulgarity.

As one of the few *mangaka* to draw in the style of the *ukiyo-e** painters, she liked to return to the oeuvres of great masters such as Utamaro and Hokusai, working them seamlessly into her stories. Only someone with a true passion for history like her could reproduce with such accuracy the tiniest detail of a comb or kimono, or the décor of the "green houses" of the pleasure district of Yoshiwara*; she derived much of the background from the biography of Utamaro originally published by Edmond de Goncourt in 1891. This is how he attempts to describe their atmosphere. "These houses are almost all set back from the pavement, and this little gap is planted with shrubs to provide greenery, together with flowers on the façade. The entrance lies in general to the right. Behind a sliding door in artistically crafted trellis-work, there is an anteroom with a beaten earth floor, at the back of which there is a stone stair [...]. In the middle a staircase rises to rooms on the upper floors: this staircase is always shown in pictures of the 'green houses,' with courtesans leaning over the banister saying a tender farewell to their customers [...]. Except for a few rooms allotted to the house's special clients who want an apartment leading straight out to the garden, all the women's apartments are located on the first and

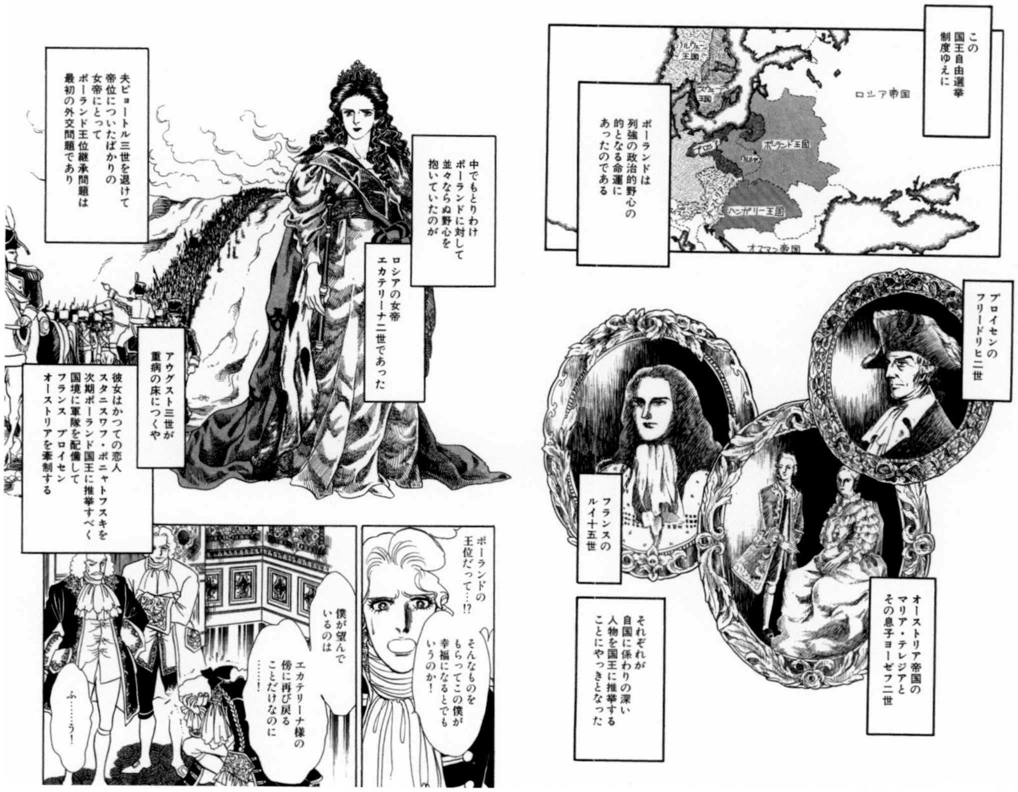
この
国王自由選挙
制度ゆえに
ロシア帝国
ポーランド王国
ハンガリー王国
オスマン帝国
ポーランドは
列強の政治的野心の
的となる命運に
あったのである
プロイセンの
フリードリヒ二世
オーストリア帝国の
マリア・テレジアと
その息子ヨーゼフ二世
フランスの
ルイ十五世
それぞれが
自国に係わりの深い
人物を国王に推挙する
ことにやっきとなった
中でもとりわけ
ポーランドに対して
並々ならぬ野心を
抱いていたのが
ロシアの女帝
エカテリーナ二世であった
夫ピョートル三世を退けて
帝位についたばかりの
女帝にとって
ポーランド王位継承問題は
最初の外交問題であり
アウグスト三世が
重病の床につくや
彼女はかつての恋人
スタニスワフ・ポニャトフスキを
次期ポーランド国王に推挙すべく
国境に軍隊を配備して
フランス プロイセン
オーストリアを牽制する
ポーランドの王位だって…!?
そんなものをもらってこの僕が幸福になるとでもいうのか!
僕が望んでいるのは
エカテリーナ様の傍に再び戻ることだけなのに……!
ふ……う!

342
Ikeda Riyoko, *To the End of the Sky, The Secret History of Poland*, Chûôkoron-shinsha, 1999.
© Ikeda Riyoko Production

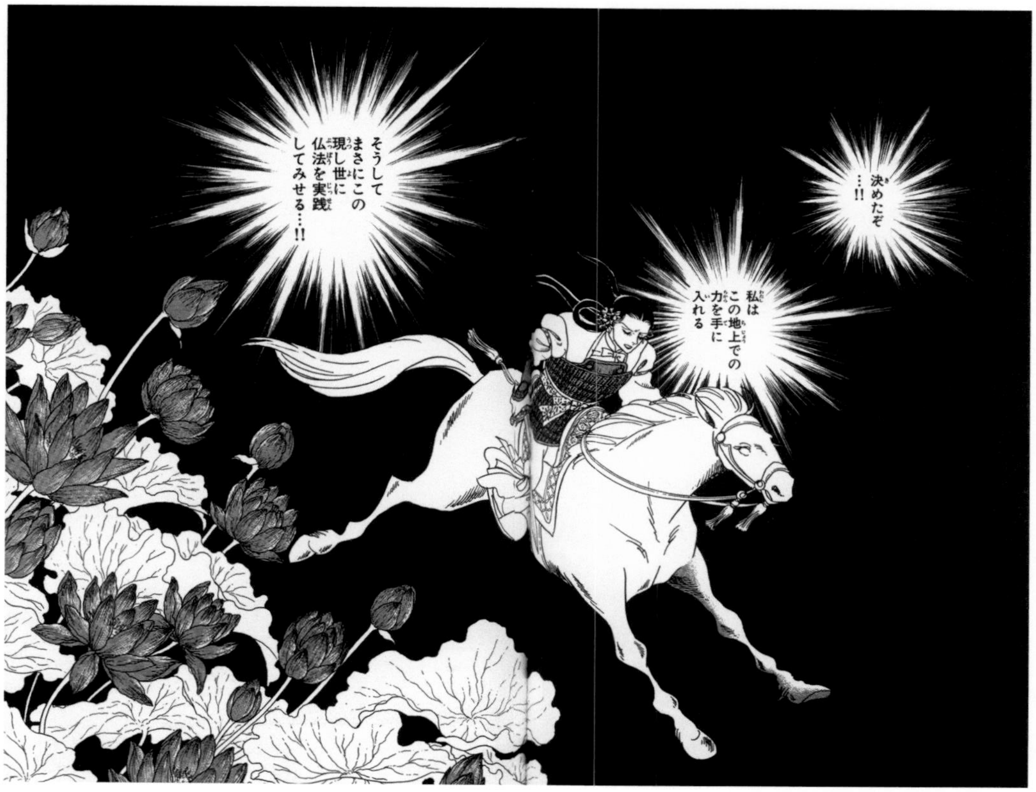
決めたぞ…!!
私はこの地上での力を手に入れる
そうしてまさにこの現し世に仏法を実践してみせる…!!

343
Ikeda Riyoko, *The Story of Shôtokutaishi from the Beginning to the End of the War*, Chûôkoron-shinsha, 1999.
© Ikeda Riyoko Production

Prince Shôtokutaishi (574–622) was the son of Emperor Yômei. An ardent opponent of Shinto, he strove to spread Buddhism among the nobility, enshrining it as the State religion.

In this scene, he appears on his galloping horse, proclaiming his firm determination to establish Buddhism in Japan.

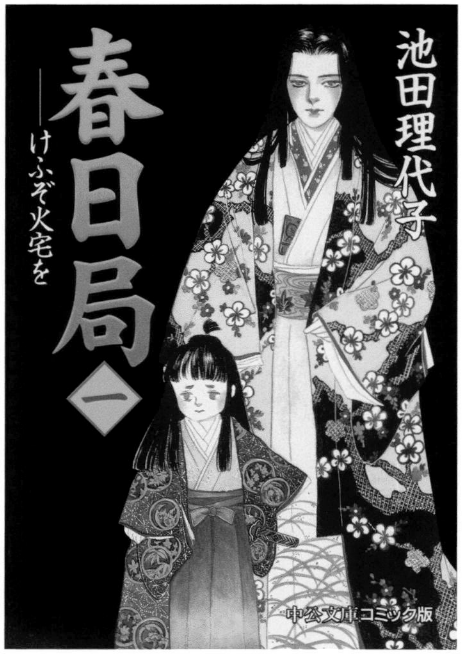
池田理代子
春日局
——けふぞ火宅を
一
中公文庫コミック版

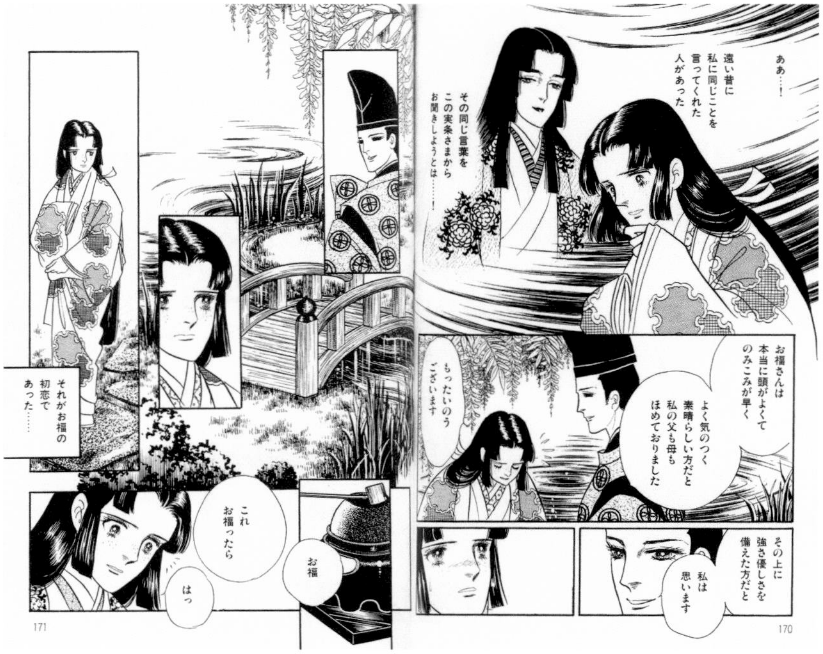
ああ……！
遠い昔に私に同じことを言ってくれた人があった
その同じ言葉をこの実条さまからお聞きしようとは……！
お福さんは本当に頭がよくてのみこみが早く
よく気のつく素晴らしい方だと私の父も母もほめておりました
もったいのうございます
その上に強さ優しさを備えた方だと
私は思います
170
それがお福の初恋であった……
お福
これお福ったら
はっ
171

344–345
Ikeda Riyoko, *Kasuga no Tsubone*, Chûôkoron-shinsha, 2000.
© Ikeda Riyoko Production

Kasuga No Tsubone (1579–1643) served as nurse to the Shogun* Tokugawa Iemitsu (1604–1651). Scion of a great family, she went on to occupy the post of director of the women's quarters in the Shogun palace.

Here, on the cover, she is shown as a little girl, before becoming a young woman and marrying Inaba Masanari with whom she had four sons.

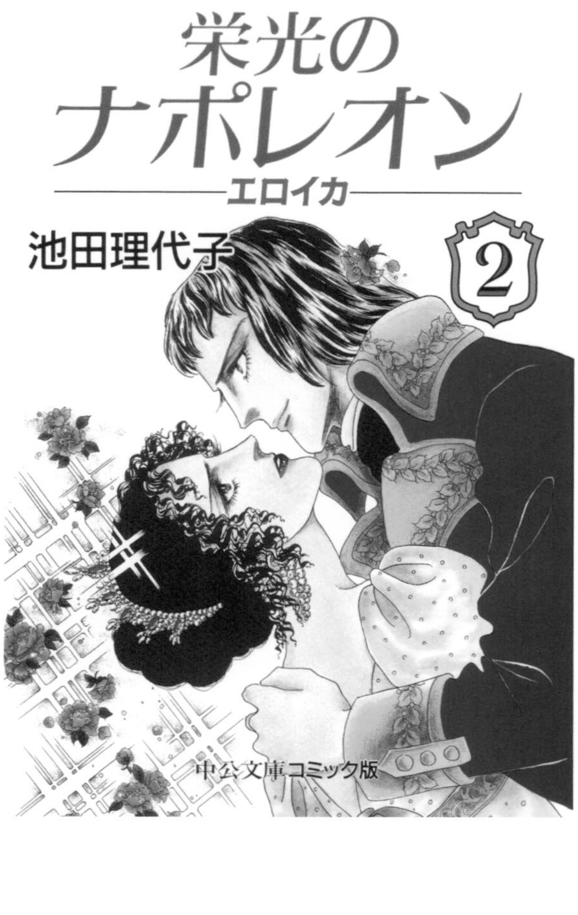
栄光のナポレオン
エロイカ
池田理代子
2
中公文庫コミック版

346
Ikeda Riyoko, *The Glorious Napoleon*, Chûôkoron-shinsha, 1997. © Ikeda Riyoko Production

Napoleon I is one of the historical characters to whom the largest number of works have been dedicated in Japan: it is hard to keep up with all the exhibits devoted to him. The version of his life given by Ikeda Riyoko is necessarily simplified but the illustrations are wonderful.

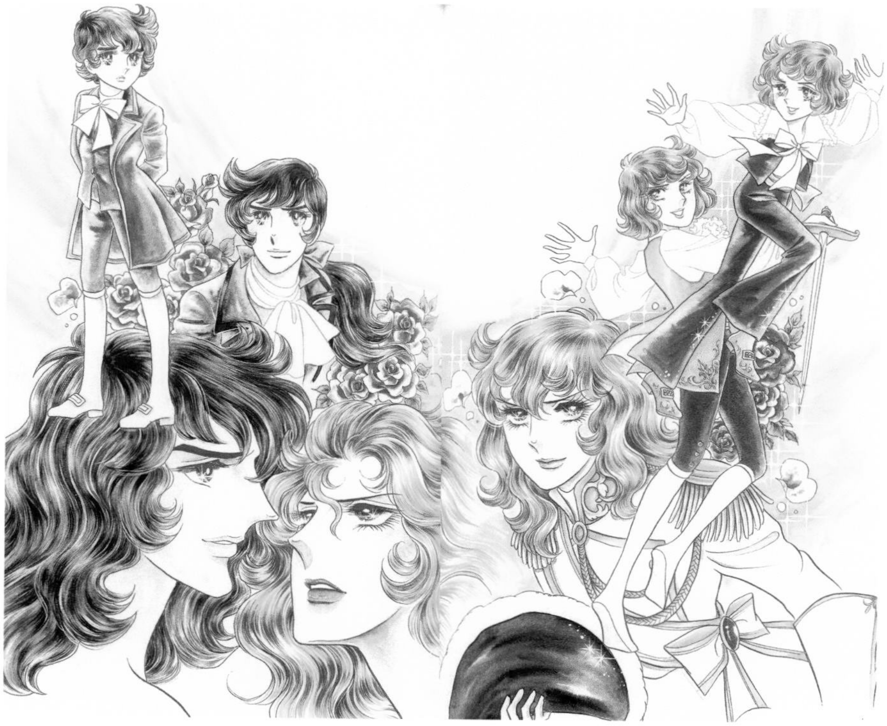

Fig. 347

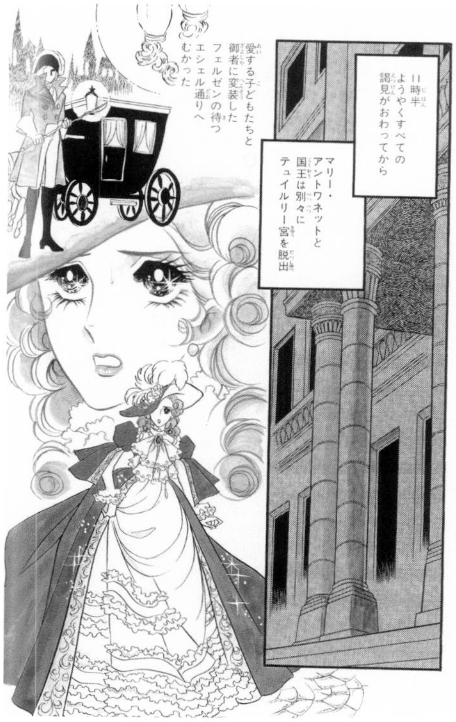
11時半 ようやくすべての謁見がおわってから
マリー・アントワネットと国王は別々にテュイルリー宮を脱出
愛する子どもたちと御者に変装したフェルゼンの待つエシェル通りへむかった

Fig. 348

Marie-Antoinette and Louis XVI leaving the Tuileries separately

347–351

Ikeda Riyoko, *Versailles no bara* (*The Rose of Versailles*), Shueisha, 2006. © Ikeda Riyoko Production

Versailles no bara was first published in serial form in the review *Margaret* in 1972. Through this manga, Japanese women readers became hooked on Marie-Antoinette. It was later turned into an anime* that became famous throughout the world, while in Japan the Takarazuka theater troupe staged it as a musical.

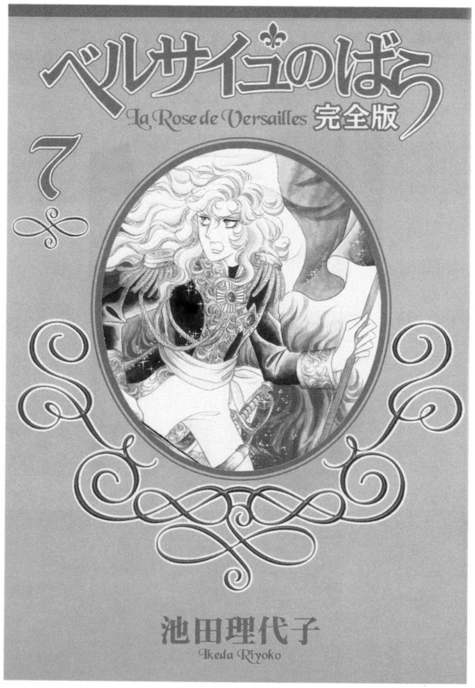
ベルサイユのばら
La Rose de Versailles 完全版
7
池田理代子
Ikeda Riyoko

Fig. 349

The cover to volume 7

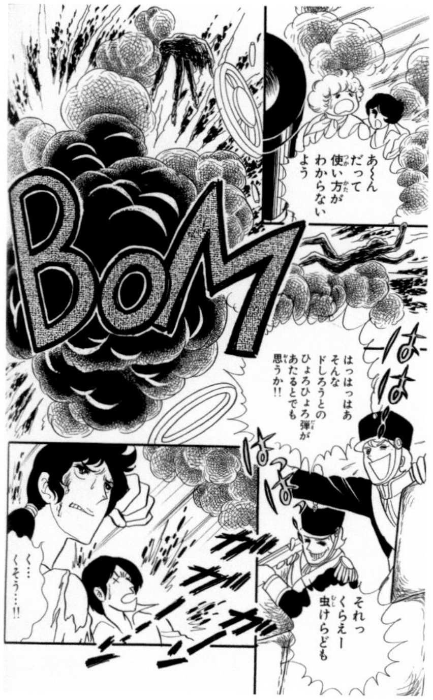
あ〜ん だって使い方がわからないよう
BOM
ははは
はっはっはあ そんなドしろうとのひょろひょろ弾があたるとでも思うか!!
それっ くらえー 虫けらども
く… くそう…!!

Fig. 350

The Storming of the Bastille

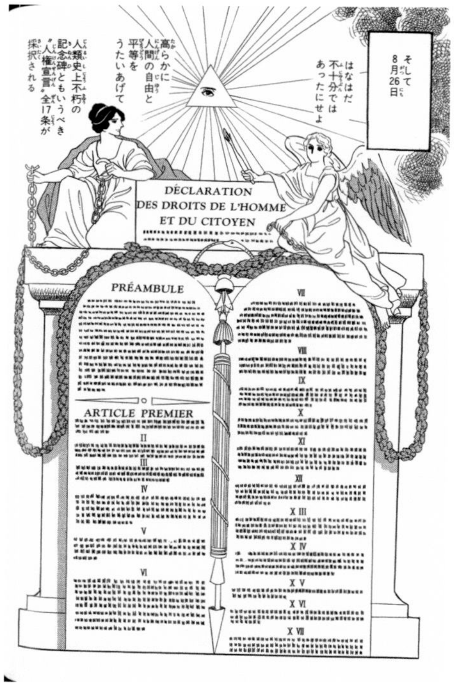
そして8月26日
はなはだ不十分ではあったにせよ
高らかに人間の自由と平等をうたいあげて
人類史上不朽の記念碑ともいうべき〝人権宣言〟全17条が採択される
DÉCLARATION DES DROITS DE L'HOMME ET DU CITOYEN
PRÉAMBULE
ARTICLE PREMIER

Fig. 351

The Declaration of the Rights of Man and of the Citizen

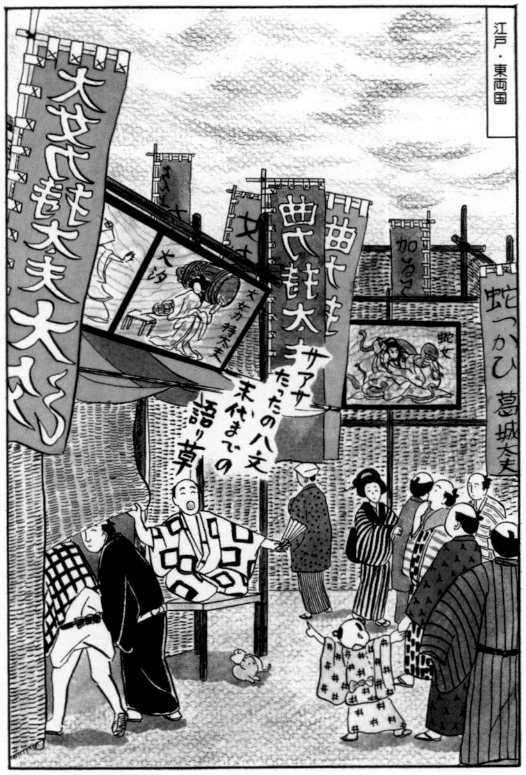
江戸・東両国
サアサ たったの八文 末代までの語り草
蛇つかひ 葛城太夫
蛇女

352
Sugiura Hinako, *Sarusuberi* (*Lagerstrœmia*).
© Suzuki Michiko, *Complete Works of Sugiura Hinako*, volume 3, Tokyo: Chikuma Shobô, 1995

In addition to the pleasure quarters of Yoshiwara, in their search for amusement people would visit the Ryôgoku* district to watch theater shows or acrobatic performances.

second floors. Beyond the openwork galleries behind the house extend the spacious gardens represented in prints, all pink and full of flowers, and adorning airy structures drenched in the sunlight that pours in through the immense bay windows and glazed walls" (*Outamaro, le peintre des maisons vertes*, p. 61, Paris: UGE 10/18, 1986).

Sugiura Hinako left more than seventy-five works on the theme of the culture of Edo, with manga accounting for only a third of her vast oeuvre. Beginning to be translated abroad, they afford an open invitation to discover the opulence and refinement of an extraordinary period in the history of Japan.

Matsumoto Leiji: to the frontiers of the galaxy

His characters, in particular Captain Harlock (or Albator in French-speaking countries) and the delectable Maetel, have earned Matsumoto Leiji world fame and confirm his place as one of the great *mangaka* of his time. Figs. 365–36

He began his career with *shôjo manga* under his real name, Matsumoto Akira, before taking the pseudonym of Leiji in 1965. Married to Maki Miyako, who has pursued her own career as a *mangaka*, his prolific output has been adapted as animations for both television and cinema. His first science-fiction manga, *Sexaroid*, proved an immense success and got him interested in producing action manga for boys.

His admiration for the great artists of the past has led him to the creation of several series. Thus, in *Nibelungu no yubiwa* (*The Ring of the Nibelungen*), he pays homage to Richard Wagner in adapting his work, which he locates on the planet Rhine. Leonardo da Vinci inspired another enthralling narrative: *The Vessel of Space-time of the Angel: the Legend of Leonardo da Vinci* (see figs. 370–79). Figs. 369–3

Matsumoto Leiji is one of the first *mangaka* to have his film work released abroad. Such fame might have been enough for him, but the artist has the more elevated ambition of seeing manga—from its origins to the present day—occupy its rightful place in international culture.

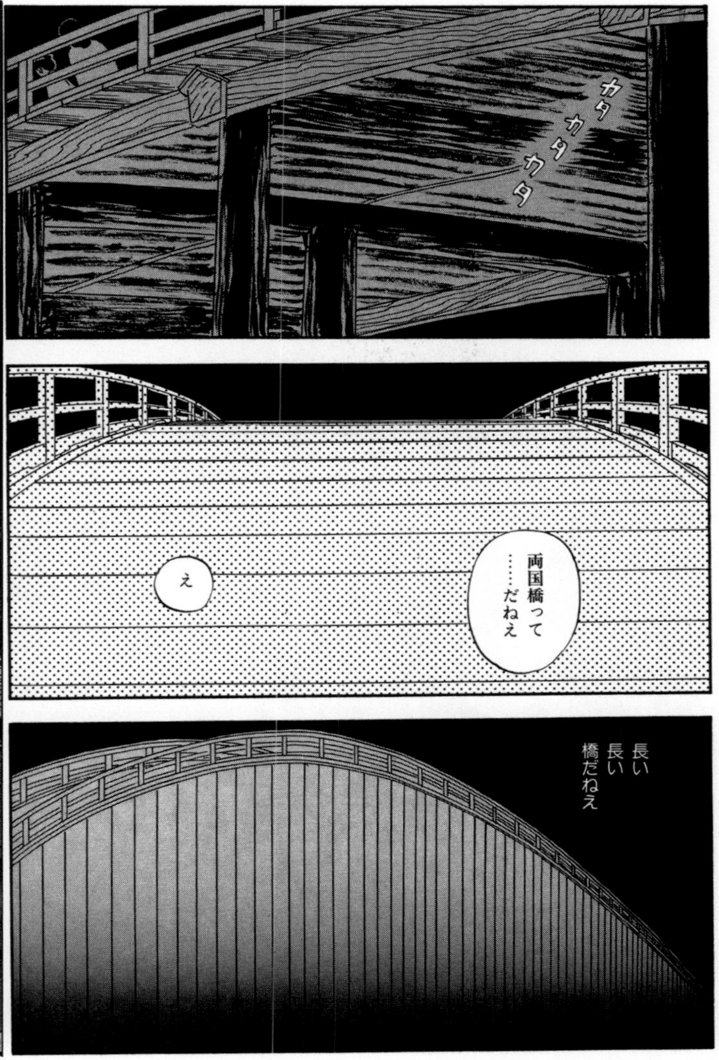
カタカタカタ
両国橋って……だねえ
え
長い長い橋だねえ

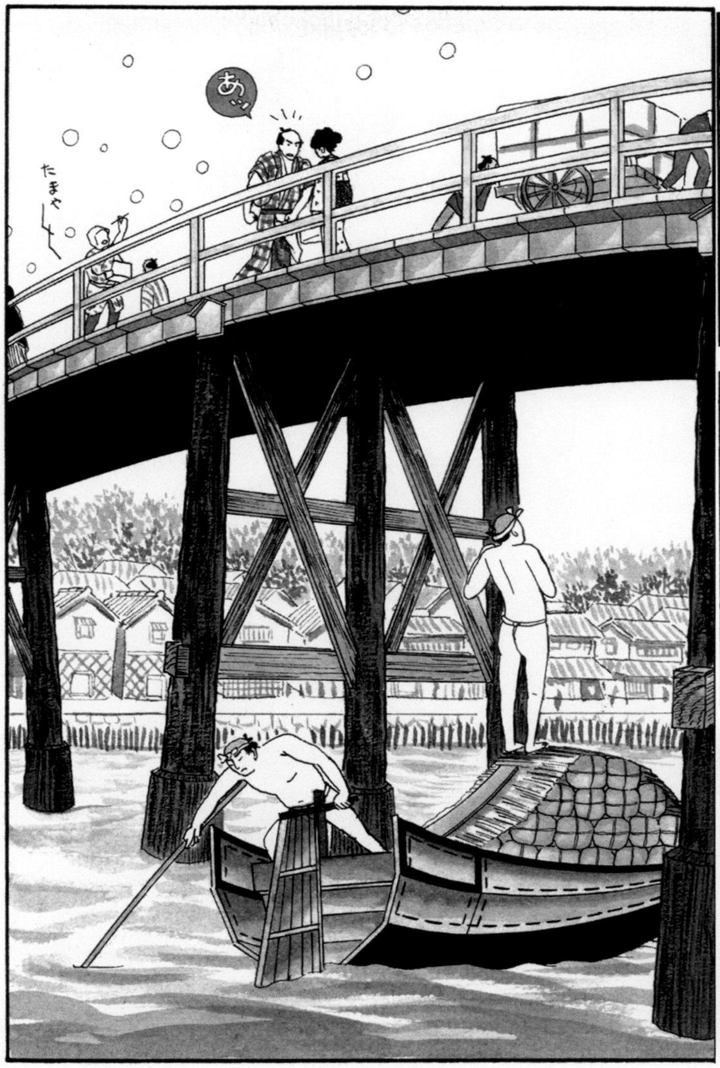
あっ
たまや

353–354
Sugiura Hinako, *Sarusuberi* (*Lagerstrœmia*).
© Suzuki Michiko, *Complete Works of Sugiura Hinako*, volume 3, Tokyo: Chikuma Shobô, 1995

The bridges, whose curved forms Sugiura Hinako shows in close-up in daylight and then at night, together with the boats drifting down the current, both evoke the passage of time.

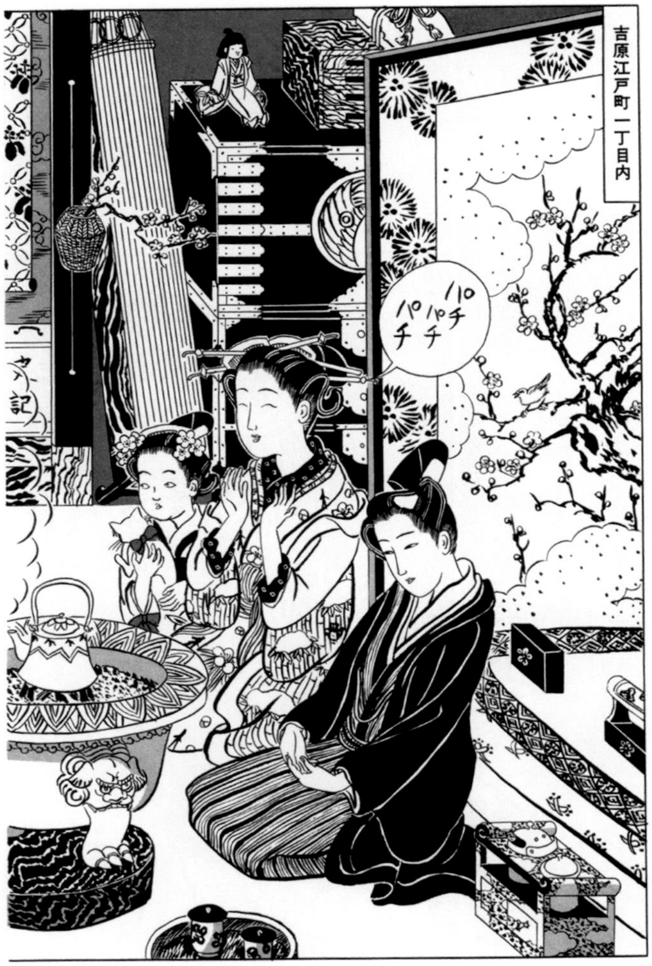
吉原江戸町一丁目内
パチパチパチ

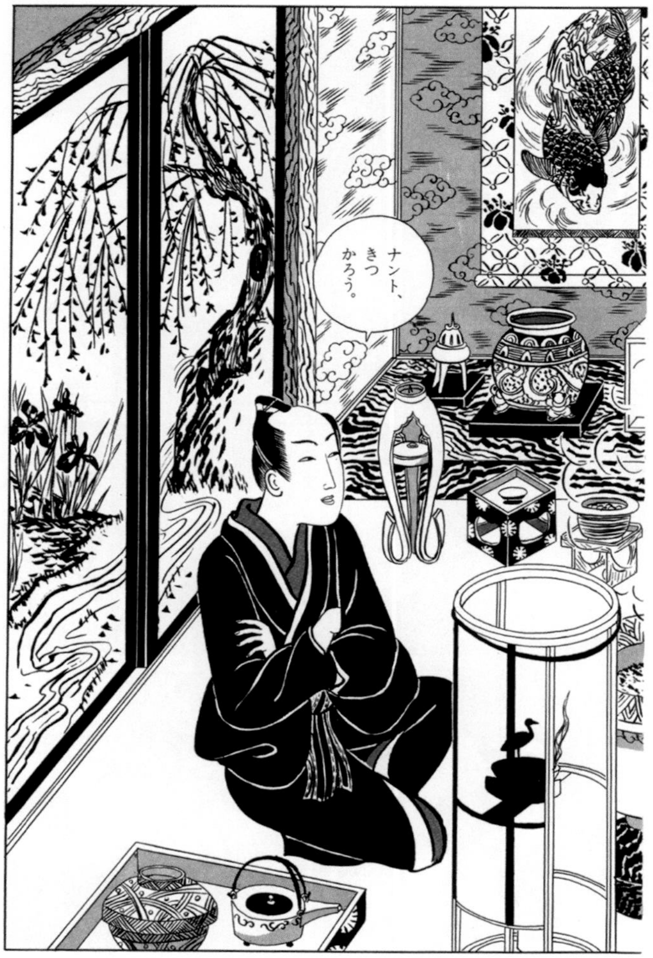
ナント、きつかろう。

355
Sugiura Hinako, *Futatsu Makura (Lacquer Pillows: Wind on the Flowers)*. © Suzuki Michiko, *Complete Works of Sugiura Hinako*, volume 1, Tokyo: Chikuma Shobô, 1995

Wealthier customers to the "green houses" were received by solicitous courtesans in lavishly decorated rooms. Precious ceramics, musical instruments, *kakemonos**, such as this one inspired by a work by Hokusai, and delicately patterned folding-screens—everything contrives to make the locale seem both sophisticated and welcoming.

356
Sugiura Hinako, *Futatsu Makura (Lacquer Pillows: Wind on the Flowers)*. © Suzuki Michiko, *Complete Works of Sugiura Hinako*, volume 1, Tokyo: Chikuma Shobô, 1995

Two details close to Utamaro's heart are visible in the privacy of the bedroom: the rear view of the delicate sweep of the courtesan's neck and the mosquito net through which the decor can be glimpsed.

よく寝たのウ。

357
Sugiura Hinako, *Futatsu Makura (Lacquer Pillows: Wind on the Flowers)*. © Suzuki Michiko, *Complete Works of Sugiura Hinako*, volume 1, Tokyo: Chikuma Shobô, 1995

Using a technique often employed by the print-masters, the figure in the foreground is drawn only partially so as to give the impression they are no more than passing by. Conversely, the wisteria that envelops the greater part of the image evokes the permanence of nature.

父の自慢である庭先の藤棚が咲きそろったのをはなむけに
私は城下を落ちました。
家を出て程なく道端に立つ者があります。
月明りでよくよく見ればかの娘でした。
ふり返るとただぽっかり闇があるのではないかとかあるいは娘が夜叉に変じているのではないかとかさまざまな事を考えながら歩きました。
ヒタ
ヒタ
ヒタ
ヒタ

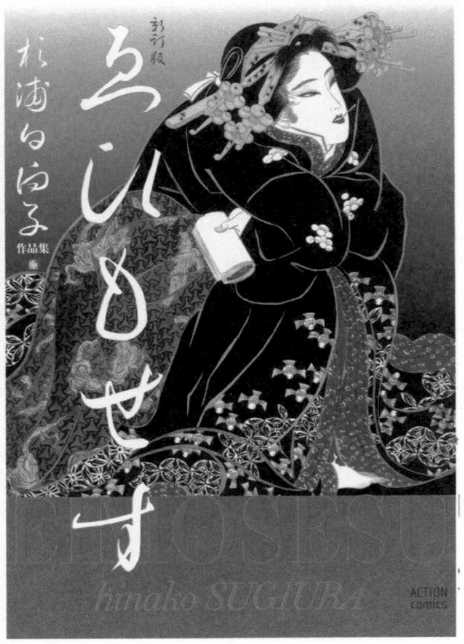
作品集
EIMOSESU
hinako SUGIURA
ACTION comics

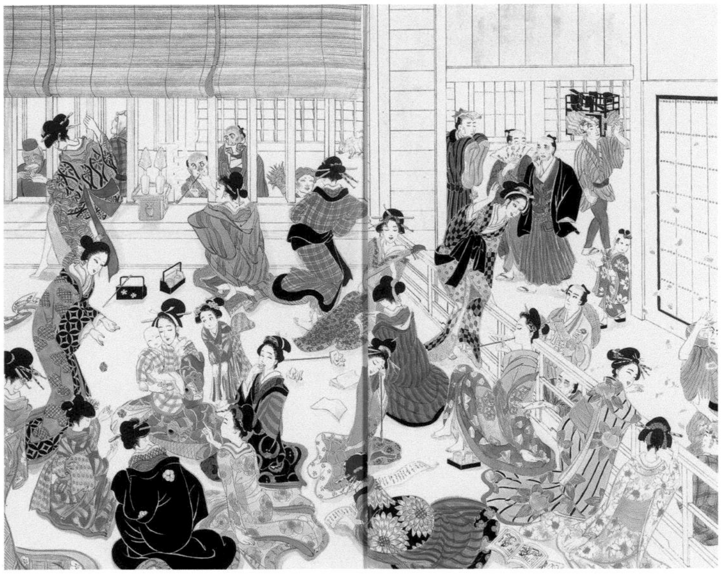

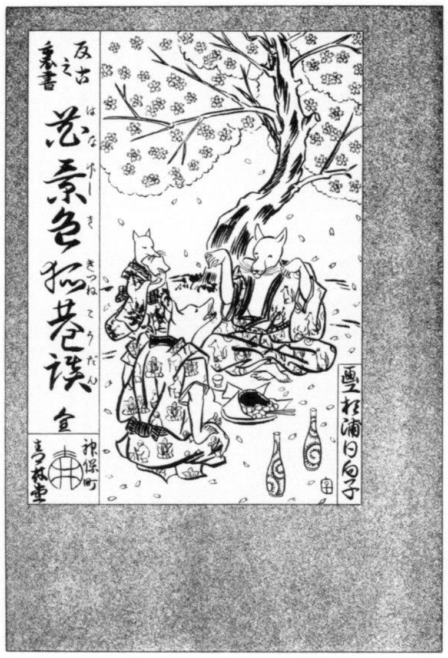

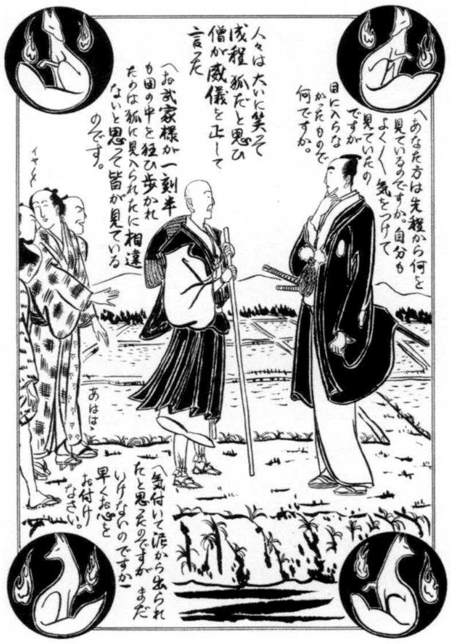
へあなた方は先程から何を見ているのですか。自分もよくく気をつけて見ていたのですが目に入らなかったもので何ですか。
人々は大いに笑って成程狐だと思ひ僧が威儀を正して言った
へお武家様が一刻半も田の中を狂ひ歩かれたのは狐に見入られたに相違ないと思って皆が見ているのです。
イヤく
あはは、
へ気付いて泥から出られたと思ったのですがまだいけないのですか
早くお心をお付けなさい。

358–362

Sugiura Hinako, *Eimosesu*.

Sugiura Hinako also produced manga in the style of the "yellow books" of the Edo period, following the traditional technique of introducing texts in between the images.

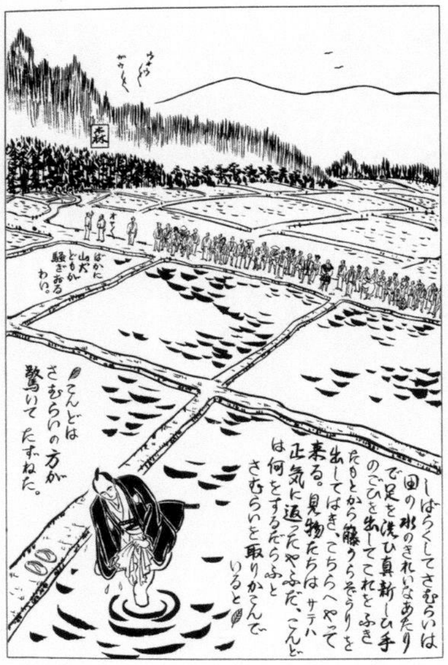
森
はかに山犬どもが騒ぎおるわい。
しばらくしてさむらいは田の水のきれいなあたりで足を洗ひ真新しひ手のごひを出してこれをふきたもとから艤うらぞうりを出してはき、こちらへやって来る。見物たちは正気に返ったやふだ、こんどは何をするだらふとさむらいを取りかこんでいると
こんどはさむらいの方が驚いてたずねた。

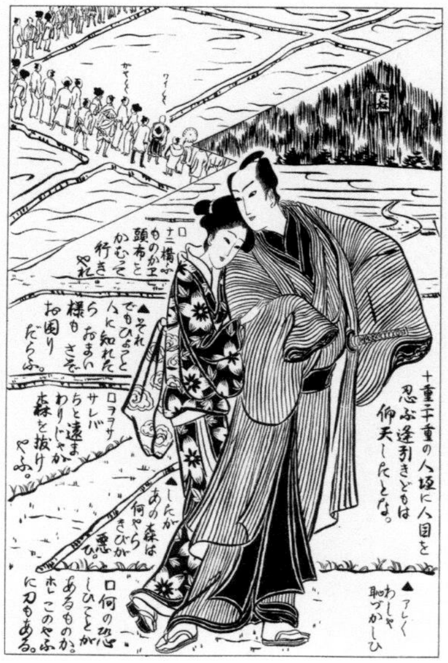
十重二十重の人垣に人目を忍ぶ逢引きどもは仰天したとな。
▲アレく わしゃ恥づかしひ
▲それでもひょっと人に知れたらおまい様もさぞお困りだらふ。
▲したがあの森は何やらきびが悪ひ。
ロ何の恐しひことがあるものか。ホレこのやふに力もある。
ロヲヲササレバちと遠まわりじゃが森を抜けやふ。

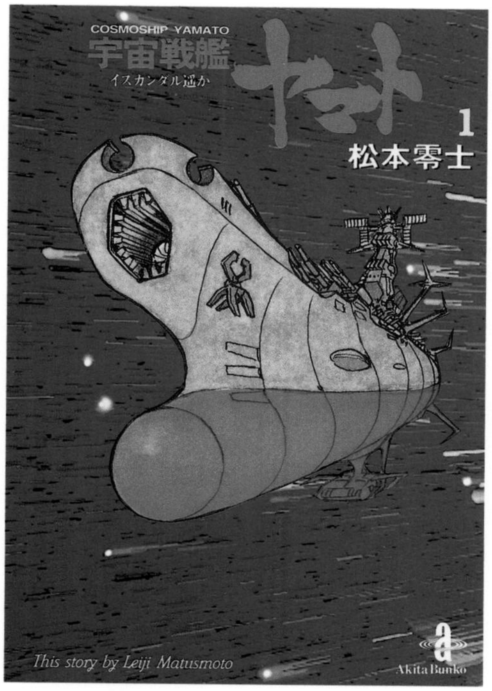
COSMOSHIP YAMATO
宇宙戦艦
イスカンダル遥か
ヤマト
1
松本零士
This story by Leiji Matusmoto
Akita Bunko

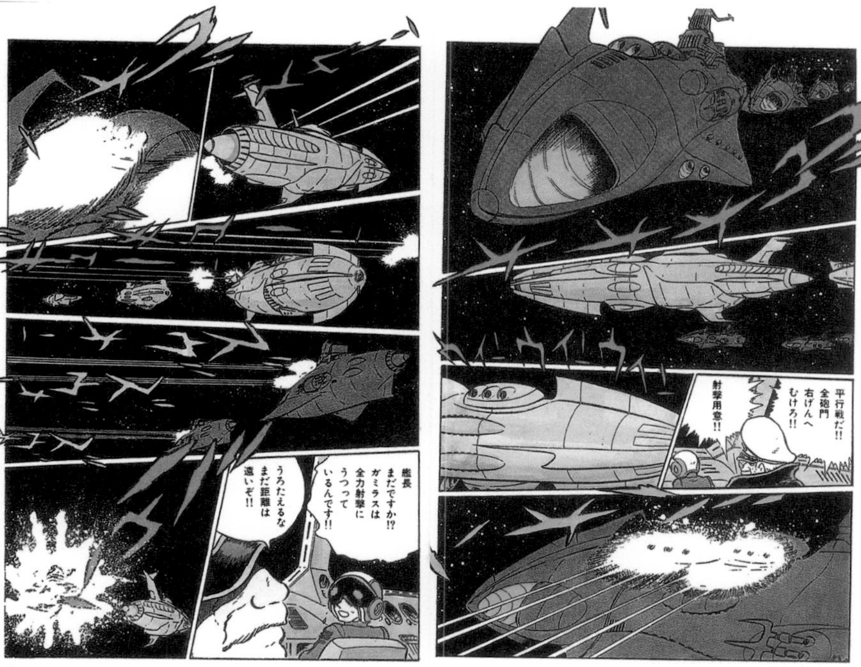
平行戦だ!! 全砲門 右げんへ むけろ!!
射撃用意!!
艦長 まだですか!? ガミラスは 全力射撃に うつって いるんです!!
うろたえるな まだ距離は 遠いぞ!!
7
6

363–364
Matsumoto Leiji, *Uchû senkan Yamato (Space Battleship Yamato)*. © Matsumoto Leiji, Akita Shoten, reprint 1994

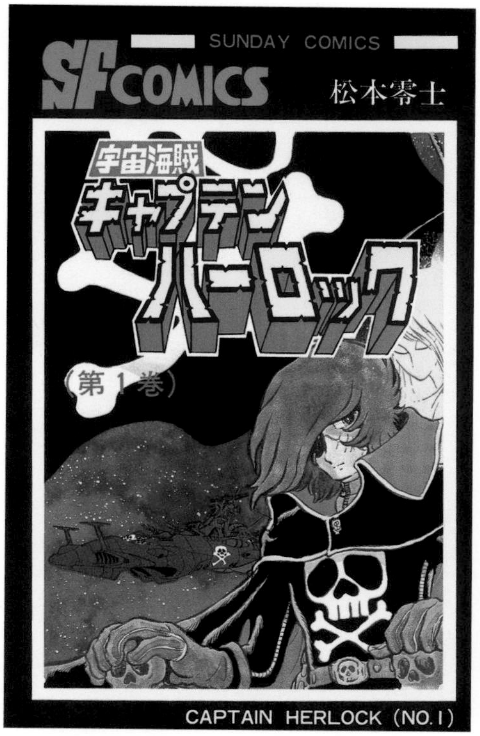
SUNDAY COMICS
SF COMICS
松本零士
宇宙海賊
キャプテン
ハーロック
(第1巻)
CAPTAIN HERLOCK (NO. 1)

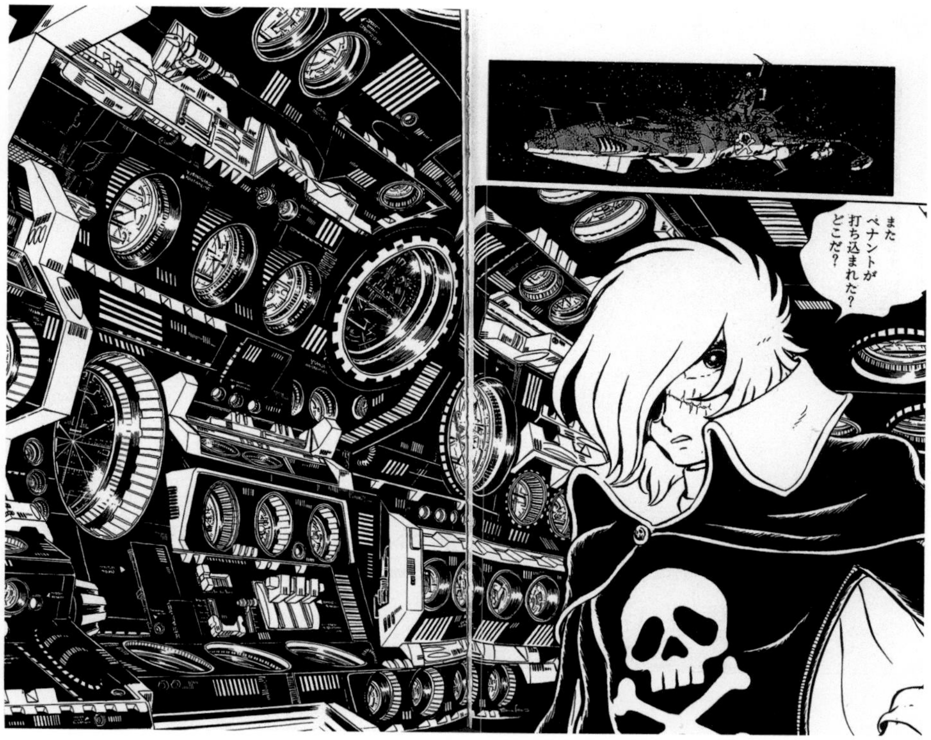
また ペナントが 打ち込まれた? どこだ?

365–366
Matsumoto Leiji, *Uchû kaizoku kyaputen hârokku (Space Pirate Captain Harlock)*.
© Matsumoto Leiji, Akita Shoten, 1977

The 1970s saw the birth of his famous character, Captain Harlock, who proved an overnight success. The action is set in the year 2977, when the Earth hovers on the brink of being invaded by the armies of the Sylvidres.

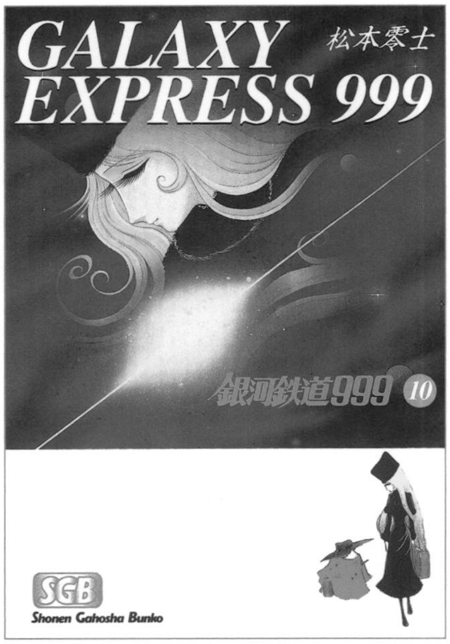
GALAXY
EXPRESS 999
松本零士
銀河鉄道999
10
SGB
Shonen Gahosha Bunko

367–368

Matsumoto Leiji, *Ginga tetsudô 999 (Galaxy Express 999).*

© Matsumoto Leiji, Shônen Gahôsha, 2003

This manga relates the life and travels of Tetsurô, a young orphan who gets on to an intergalactic train in the company of the mysterious Maetel with her wavy blonde locks. Readers are whisked away into an uplifting story of futuristic worlds in which Matsumoto Leiji describes the feelings of his characters and the atmosphere in which they live with great sensitivity and poetry.

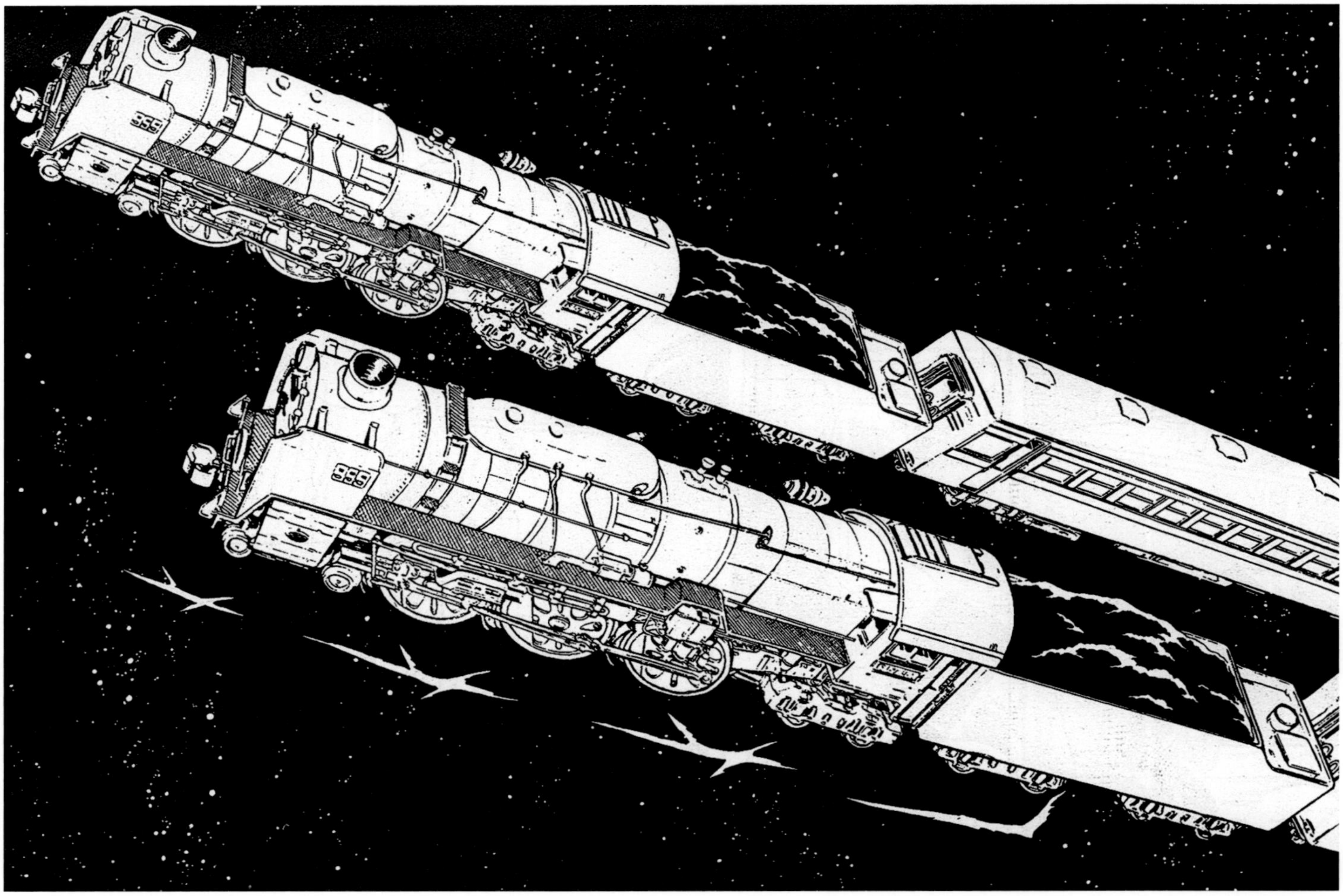

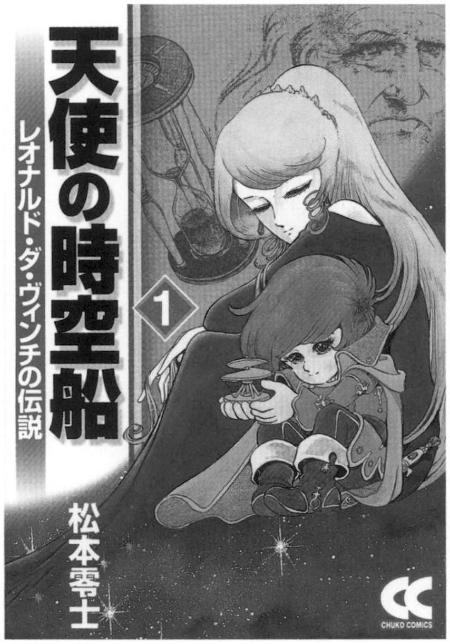
天使の時空船
レオナルド・ダ・ヴィンチの伝説
1
松本零士
CHUKO COMICS

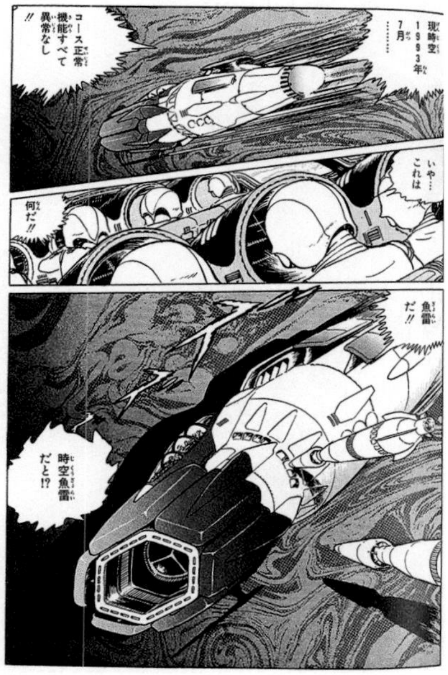
現時空 1993年 7月……
コース正常 機能すべて 異常なし!!
いや…これは
何だ!!
魚雷だ!!
時空魚雷だと!?

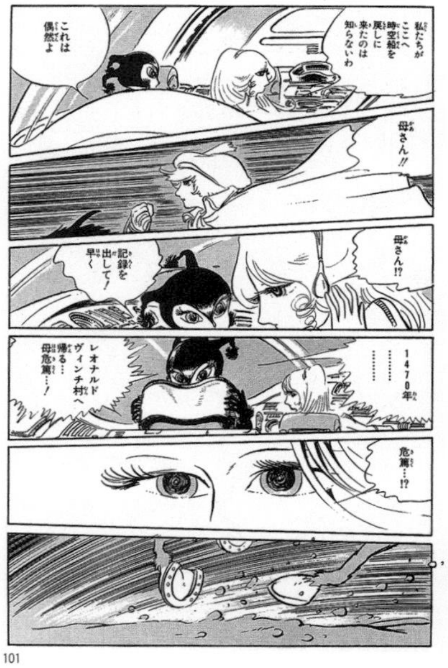
私たちがここへ時空船を戻しに来たのは知らないわ
これは偶然よ
母さん!!
母さん!?
記録を出して! 早く
1470年………
レオナルド ヴィンチ村へ帰る… 母危篤…!
危篤…!?
101

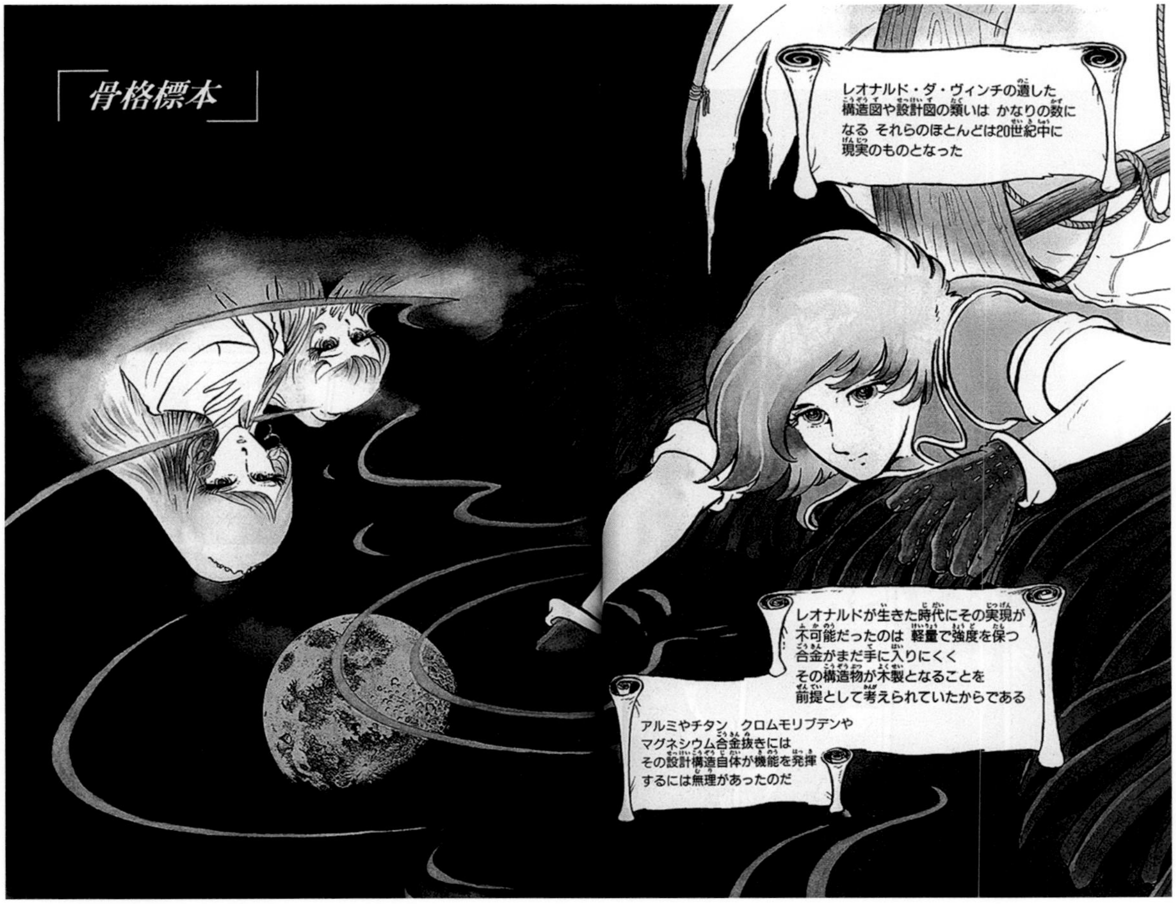
骨格標本
レオナルド・ダ・ヴィンチの遺した構造図や設計図の類いは かなりの数になる それらのほとんどは20世紀中に現実のものとなった
レオナルドが生きた時代にその実現が不可能だったのは 軽量で強度を保つ合金がまだ手に入りにくく その構造物が木製となることを前提として考えられていたからである
アルミやチタン クロムモリブデンや マグネシウム合金抜きには その設計構造自体が機能を発揮するには無理があったのだ

369–371

Matsumoto Leiji, *Tenshi no sora jikûsen Leonarudo Da Vinchi no densetsu (The Vessel of Space-time of the Angel: the Legend of Leonardo da Vinci)*. © Matsumoto Leiji, Chûokoron shinsha, 2006

This story occurs in the future but includes flashbacks that transport readers to the time of Leonardo da Vinci. With considerable talent, Matsumoto Leiji pictures the land in which the Italian artist lived, his life, passions, and visionary inventions, through the medium of a thrilling interstellar adventure.

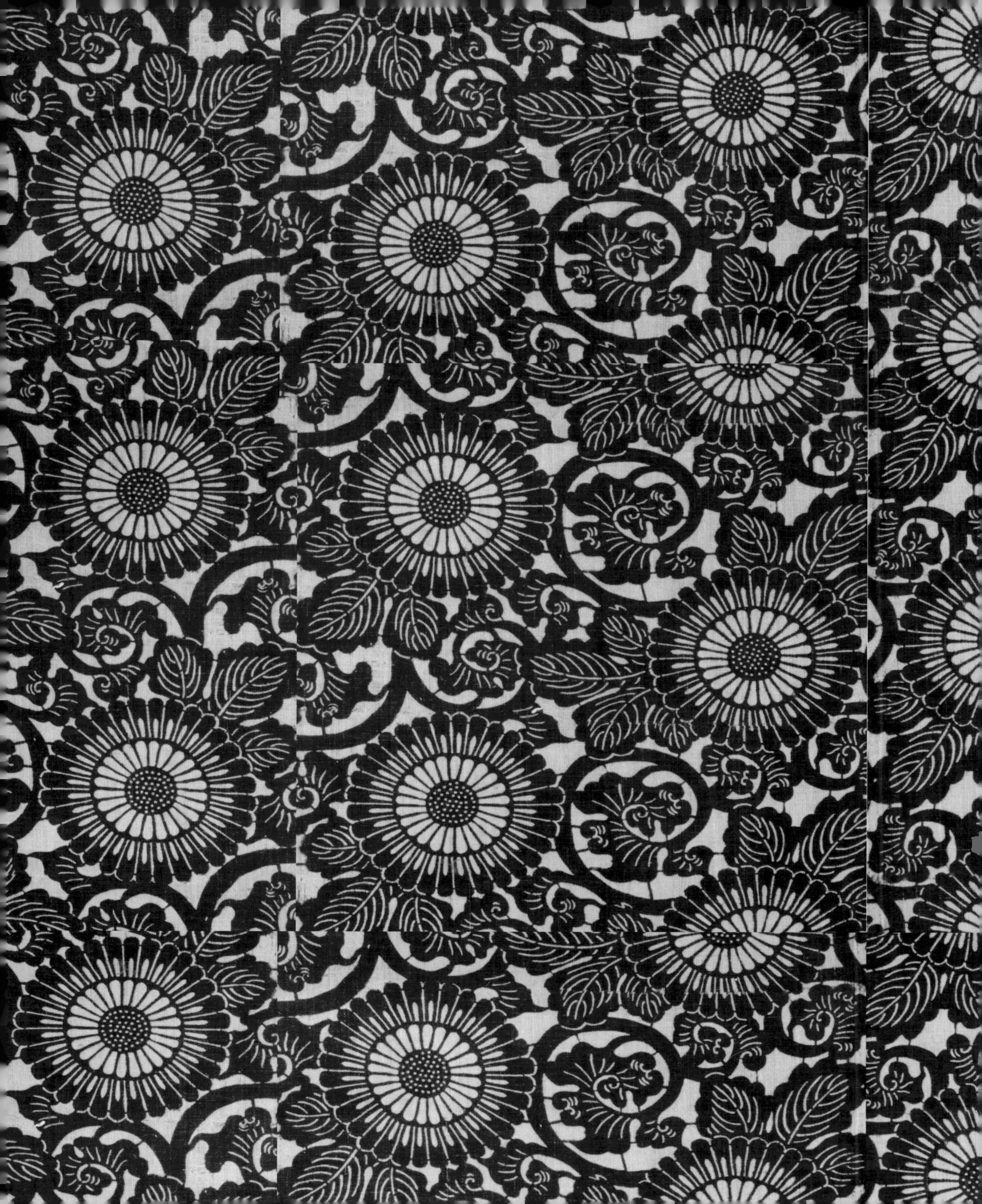

INTERVEW WITH MATSUMOTO LEIJI AND MAKI MIYAKO

On January 8, 2007, Matsumoto Leiji and his wife Maki Miyako graciously agreed to answer a few questions from me.

Brigitte Koyama-Richard: It's rare and very interesting to see a *mangaka* couple pursuing their careers in tandem. Before turning to your work, I would like to know if you ever talk about manga among yourselves?

Matsumoto Leiji: Yes, it does happen every now and again.

Maki Miyako: It's bound to.

B. K.-R.: Mrs Maki Miyako, could you tell me about your beginnings in the world of manga.

M. M.: Like my husband, I always hugely enjoyed drawing and reading. But, unlike him, in my childhood it was not my plan to make this my profession. As I grew up, I realized that writing wasn't enough to encapsulate my thoughts and that I needed to draw too. I was already holding down a job when my first work came out. I was just twenty. The manga of my youth, like *Maki no Kuchibue (Maki's Whistling)*, bring back good memories, and I'm pleased they've been reprinted.

B. K.-R.: Has the style of your characters changed much since that time?

M. M.: It's certain that one develops over time and that one's readers change too. It seems obvious that one's drawing follows a similar evolution.

B. K.-R.: The stories you write and draw are set as frequently in the past as in the present. Isn't it hard to switch period and subject like that?

M. M.: No, by reading a lot I am able to conjure up the past. Moreover, I have always adored *kabuki** and *bunraku**, which for me constitute a solid cultural foundation.

B. K.-R.: Do you ever encourage one another or give one another advice?

M. L.: Yes, sometimes, and then we don't beat around the bush!

B. K.-R.: Do you think that manga is eternal, like literature?

M. L.: Yes, I'm sure it is. For me, manga is a haven of peace.

B. K.-R.: Specialists studying manga often ask the question: "Is manga an art?"

M. L.: Certain works really are, but only time will tell which ones will be regarded as such.

B. K.-R.: I would like you to tell me about the manga you read in your childhood.

M. L.: I was born in 1938 in Kokura in the north of the island of Kyûshû, where I lived until I was eighteen. This was really lucky for me because it was a city with cinemas and many bookshops. While still really young I started buying every manga and comic strip I could get my hands on. A manga cost only from five to ten yen each, the price of a piece of candy. All the same, I preferred books to sweets. This enabled me to collect works that are now impossible to find. I also managed to get hold of some comics the American army soldiers sold off cheaply. I flicked through them with interest. I didn't always understand the meaning, but I could admire the drawings.

B. K.-R.: Did you enjoy drawing?

M. L.: I think I've always done drawings. I remember that at primary school already, I couldn't stop myself drawing manga during lessons. But my teachers and then my professors never prevented me. On the contrary, as I liked to read a lot, they encouraged my passion, feeding my imagination and introducing me to literary works from around the world, as well as to historical texts.

B. K.-R.: At what age did you begin?

M. L.: I began at fifteen years old, when I won a prize from the newspaper *Mainichi*, for which I then started to draw.

B. K.-R.: In a previous interview, you confided to me that your long-limbed and graceful female characters are inspired by the image of Western women.

M. L.: That's correct. I have been mad about the movies since I was a kid. I saw many cartoons and films from all countries and particularly enjoyed the film by Julien Duvivier, *Marianne of My Youth* (1955), with Marianne Hold, as well as Roger Vadim's *Barbarella* (1968), with Jane Fonda. I took these heroines and the fashions of the time as a starting point in drawing female characters for my manga.

B. K.-R.: Your drawings of machines of the future, spaceships in particular, are remarkably accurate.

M. L.: I am keen on machines of all kinds and study them in books and periodicals.

B. K.-R.: What are your other sources of inspiration?

M. L.: Traveling. To draw and write manga, you have to have read a great deal and travel quite a lot too. I have crisscrossed the globe and have wonderful memories of the various countries I've visited and the people I've met. A smile is the best means of communication.

B. K.-R.: Today, manga is a phenomenal success the world over. What do you think about this state of affairs?

M. L.: Manga can be understood and enjoyed everywhere. They amuse people, but also let them share in one and the same pleasure. They offer tremendous reading and their success will be lasting.

B. K.-R.: In 2006, part of your fantastic collection of manga was unveiled at the Communications Museum in Tokyo. The variety and fine state of conservation of these works were surprising. In the nineteenth century, the Japanese let the choicest examples of their prints go to the West. And now, as manga is experiencing such popularity abroad, Japan has only just opened, at the end of 2006, its first museum devoted to manga. Your collection, which includes manga by Hokusai, as well as all the important manga of the twentieth century, in addition to many foreign comic strips, thus forms a pool of cultural resources. What was your idea behind collecting it?

M. L.: My fondest desire would be to have it shown in its entirety in Japan, of course, but also abroad, so as to get the cultural importance of manga recognized and appreciated at its rightful value.

B. K.-R.: Do you have a message for the readers of this book?

M. L.: Let us live joyously and strive to make our dreams come true.

M. M.: My message is the same as my husband's. One has to look on the bright side of life and endeavor to fulfill our dreams.

372
Matsumoto Leiji, *Ginga tetsudô 999 (Galaxy Express 999)*.
© Matsumoto Leiji, Shônen Gahôsha, 2003

Taniguchi Jirô: a manga poet

Taniguchi Jirô is one of the most admired *mangaka* in Europe, especially in France and Italy. The lyricism and sensitivity that emerge from his drawings are rare in today's manga, which are centered mainly on action. In his very first illustrations, Taniguchi Jirô showed especial interest in animals, before turning to crime stories. He became better known through his manga, *Botchan*. His elegant style, which is often compared to that of Franco-Belgian graphic novelists, is imbued with great poetry. *The Walking Man*, then *Quartier Lointain*, and *The Almanac of My Father*, have gained him a devoted readership in the West. It is not an exaggeration to say that his works are a fusion of Western graphics with manga. Figs. 375–37

373–374
Taniguchi Jirô and Kusumi Masayuki, *Sanpo Mono* (adapted in French as *Quartier Lointain*).
© Taniguchi Jirô and Kusumi Masayuki, Free Style, 2006

In a spirit very close to *The Walking Man*, the recently published *Quartier Lointain* describes a man who observes, reflects on life and on his surroundings, taking the time to absorb the landscape and the atmosphere. He sets out on a search for vestiges of the past, pacing through quarters where the community spirit is far from idealized and along age-old streets where timber-built stores are proudly emblazoned with *norens**.

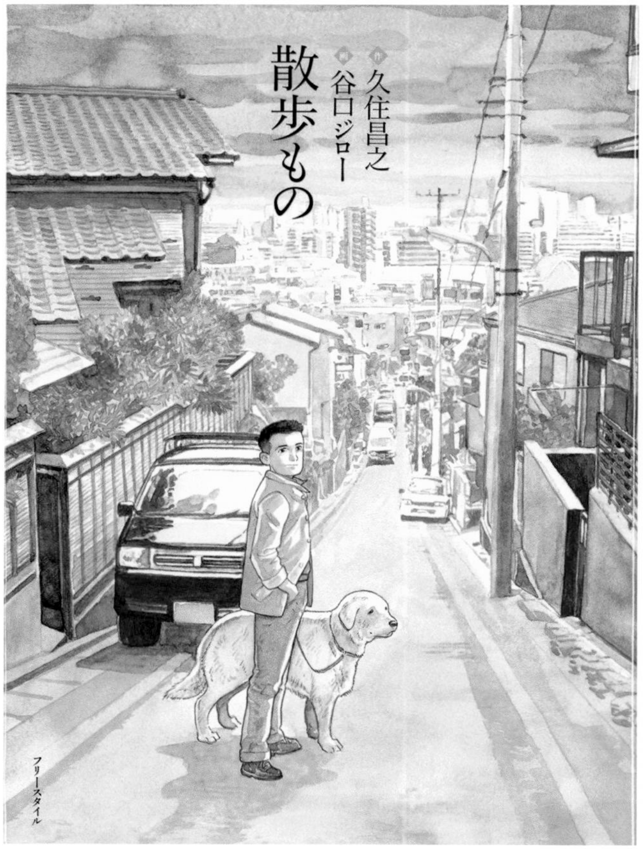
散歩もの
久住昌之
谷口ジロー
フリースタイル

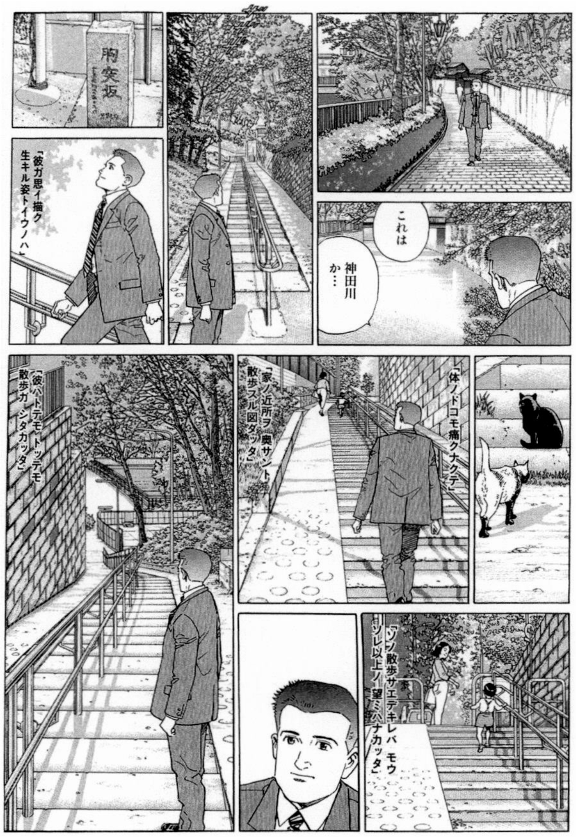
これは
神田川か…
「彼ガ思イ描ク
生キル姿トイウノハ
「体ノドコモ痛クナクテ」
「家ノ近所ヲ奥サント
散歩スル図ダッタ」
「ソノ散歩サエテキレバ モウ
ソレ以上ノ望ミハナカッタ」
「彼ハトテモトッテモ
散歩ガシタカッタ」

ワイドKCパーティー
ワイドKC 137 パーティー
ワイドKCパーティー
歩くひと
歩くひと
谷口ジロー
谷口ジロー
ISBN4-06-176637-6
講談社 P530
C0379 P530E (0)
講談社 定価530円 (本体515円)

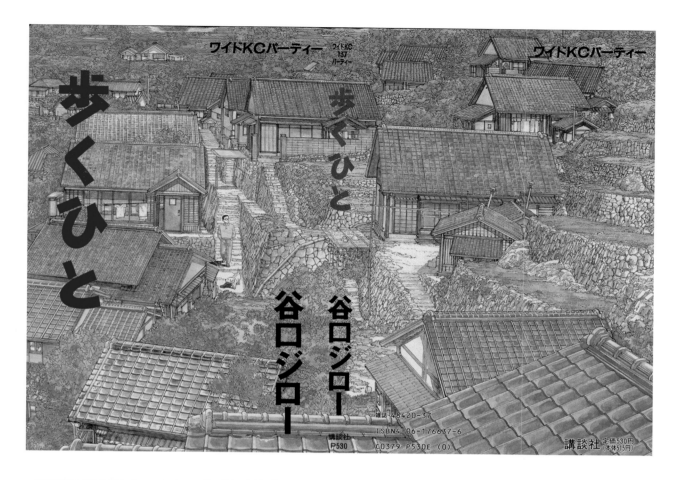

375–376

Taniguchi Jirô, *Aruku Hito (The Walking Man)*. © Taniguchi Jirô, Kôdansha, 1992

Taniguchi spirits his readers away to a poetic universe in which they share his hero's impressions of the symbiosis between nature and man, which he evokes with components of surprising simplicity.

Taniguchi Jirô's range of themes is very varied, but the artist seems to prefer narratives that allow him the opportunity of recreating details of the natural environment, the fleeting moments of everyday life, with remarkable sensitivity. Taniguchi's layouts allow for a multiplicity of viewpoints, with a preference for bird's-eye views using a type of perspective often met with in earlier prints. With a fine-lined and carefully handled drawing style, the artist tends to emphasize the architecture and landscapes, to the point, on occasion, of making them the main protagonists of the story as against the characters. Many of the works that have made him famous—especially in Europe—are imbued with a strange, often restful atmosphere. Taniguchi freely admits, moreover, to the influence of filmmaker Ozu Yaujirô for *The Walking Man* that functions on the level of introspection and thoughtfulness.

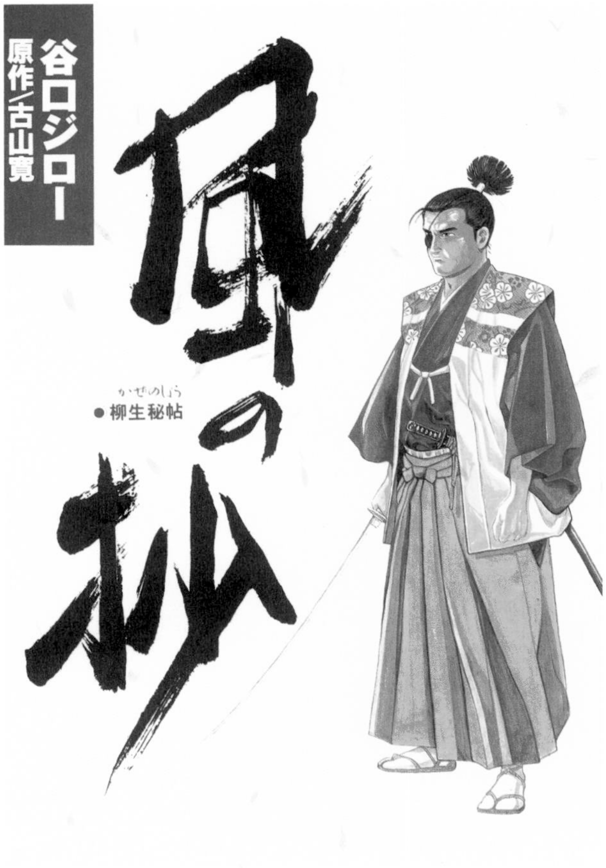
谷口ジロー
原作/古山寛
風の抄
柳生秘帖

377–378

Taniguchi Jirô, Kan Furuyama, *Kaze no shô (The Book of the Wind)*. © Taniguchi Jirô, Kan Furuyama, Akita Shoten, 1992

But Taniguchi Jirô does not forget his origins and has also participated in typically Japanese manga, such as *The Book of the Wind*, where the top-down views, in diagonal and in perspective, are reminiscent of those in Japanese prints.

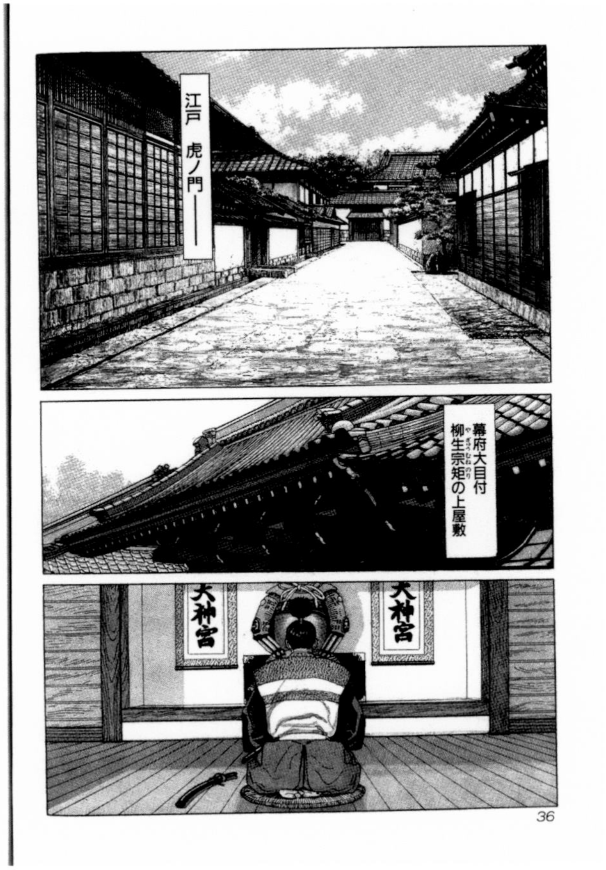
江戸 虎ノ門——
幕府大目付 柳生宗矩の上屋敷
大神宮
大神宮
36

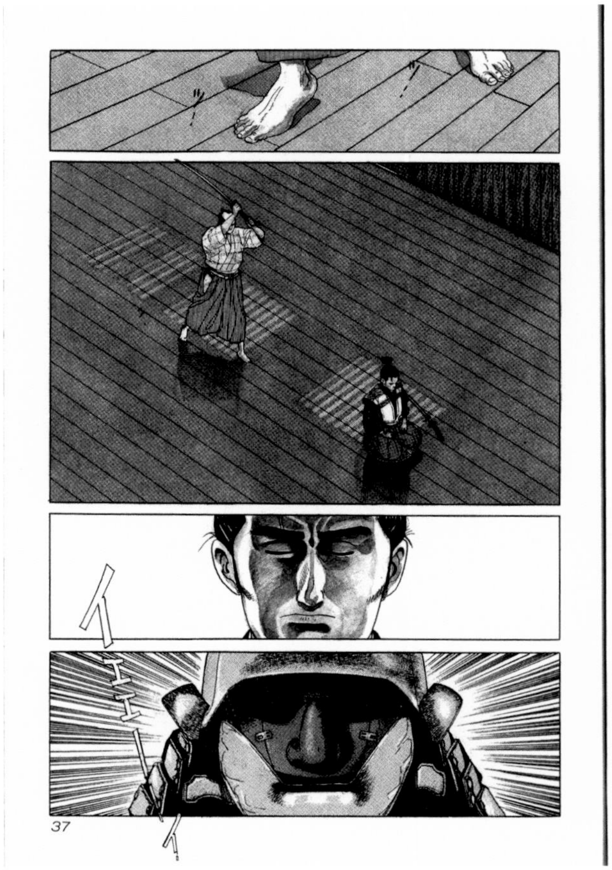
37

森へ
谷口ジロー
Jiro Taniguchi
Into the forest
KAWADE SHOBO SHINSYA

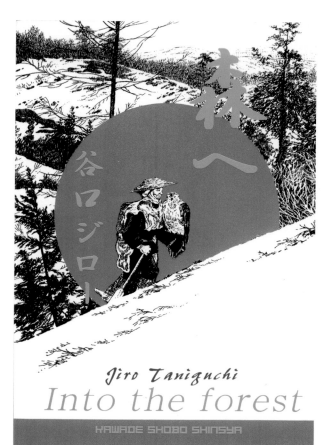

379–380

Taniguchi Jirô, Kawade Shobô, *Mori e (In the Forest)*. © Taniguchi Jirô, Kawade Shobô, 1994

In a collection that expresses his sensibility wonderfully, the author tells several stories. One about a falconer caught in a snowstorm and fighting against wind and cold is especially beautiful. The bird tries to protect its master against various predators, but the cold finally kills him. All are touched by these images of nature, of the cooperation between man and animal, and of the struggle for survival.

十日ほどたって 老人は小屋を出た
若い鷹の傷は 回復も早かった
えかったなあ ハヤテ
山の神さんの おかげだぞ
さ 村へ帰るべえ
陽ざしには もう 春のぬくもりが あった

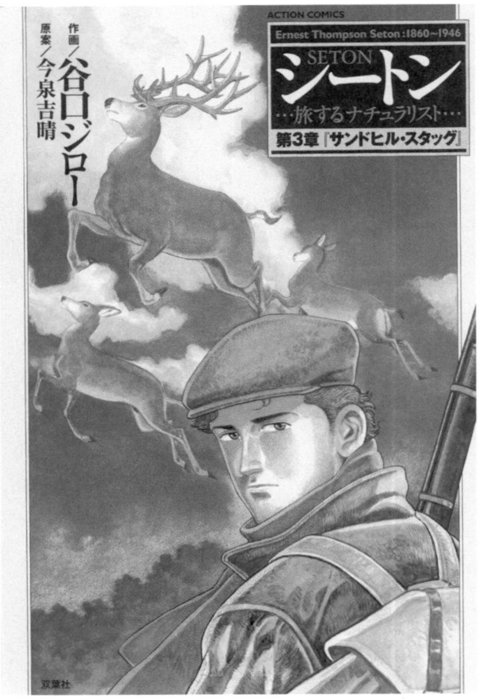
ACTION COMICS
Ernest Thompson Seton : 1860–1946
SETON
シートン
…旅するナチュラリスト…
第3章『サンドヒル・スタッグ』
作画／谷口ジロー
原案／今泉吉晴
双葉社

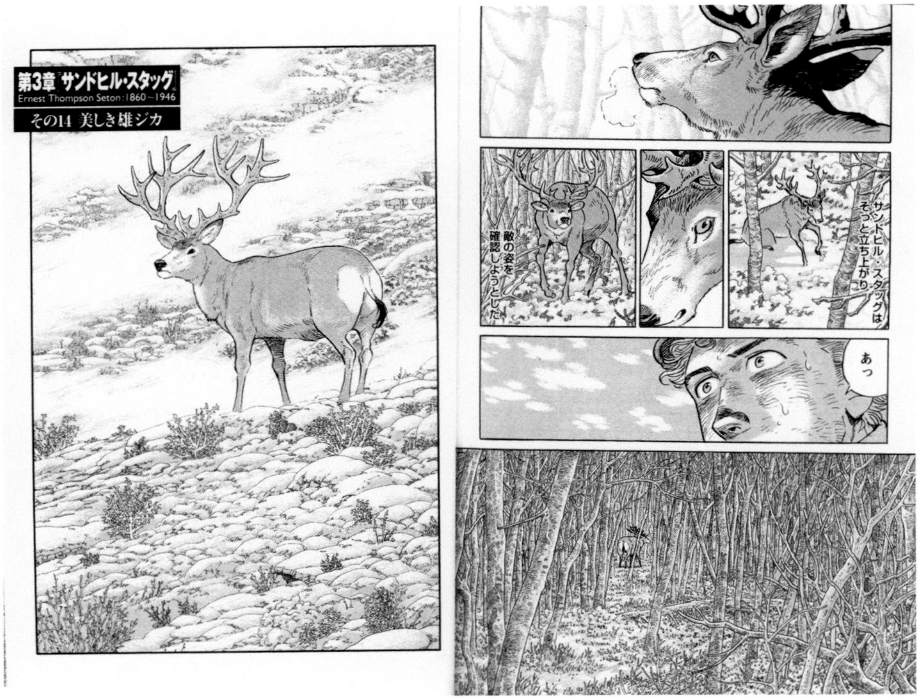
サンドヒル・スタッグは
そっと立ち上がり
敵の姿を
確認しようとした
あっ
第3章 サンドヒル・スタッグ
Ernest Thompson Seton : 1860–1946
その14 美しき雄ジカ

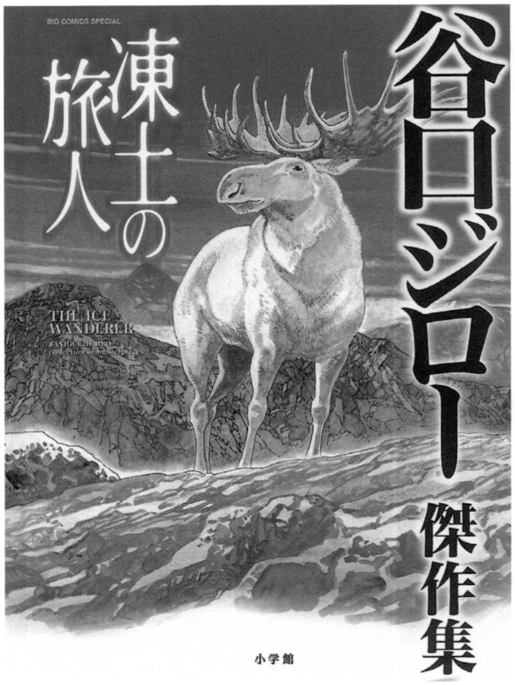
BIG COMICS SPECIAL
凍土の旅人
谷口ジロー傑作集
THE ICE WANDERER
小学館

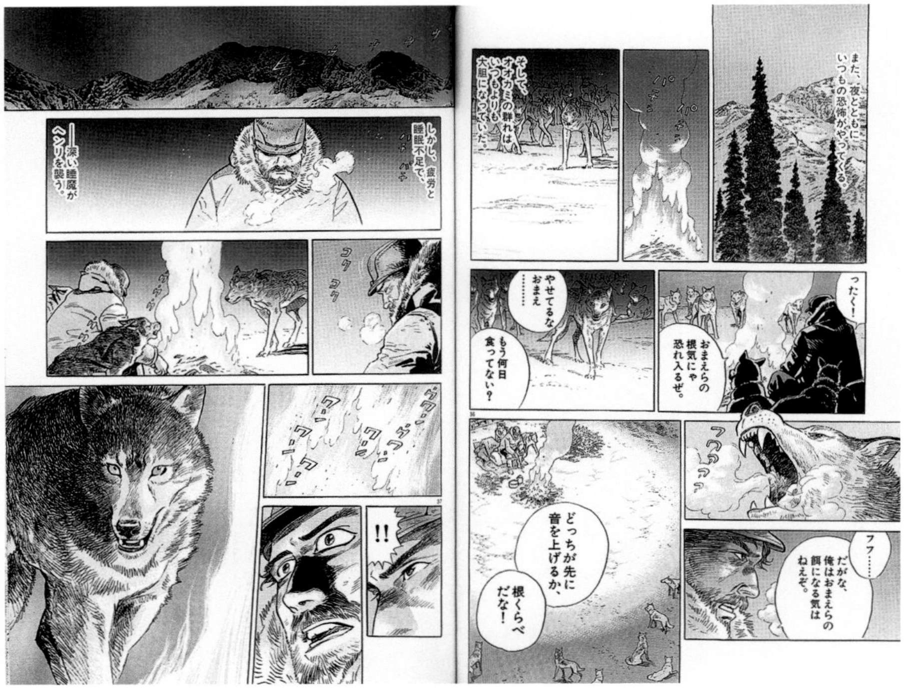
また、夜とともに
いつもの恐怖がやってくる。
パチ
パチ
そして、
オオカミの群れは
いつもよりも
大胆になっていた。
ったく!
おまえらの
根気にゃ
恐れ入るぜ。
やせてるな
おまえ
……
もう何日
食ってない?
フワァァ
フフ……
だがな、
俺はおまえらの
餌になる気は
ねえぞ。
どっちが先に
音を上げるか、
根くらべ
だな!
しかし、疲労と
睡眠不足で、
━━深い睡魔が
ヘンリを襲う。
コク
コク
!!

381–382

Taniguchi Jirô, Imaizumi Yoshiharu, *Seton*, no. 3.

© Taniguchi Jirô, Imaizumi Yoshiharu, Tokyo: Futabasha, 2005

Taniguchi is particularly fond of drawing animals in their natural habitat. The landscapes in this series, dedicated to the famous American naturalist and artist Ernest Seton (1860–1946), are especially meticulous. In this scene full of pathos, hunter and stag gaze on one another, but the young Seton will see to it that the animal escapes.

383–384

Taniguchi Jirô, *Tôdo no tabibito (The Ice Wanderer)*.

© Taniguchi Jirô, Tokyo: Shogakukan, 2005

Mountain ranges extending as far as the eye can see; a solitary man confronting animals in an untamed environment—Nature remains one of his favorite subjects.

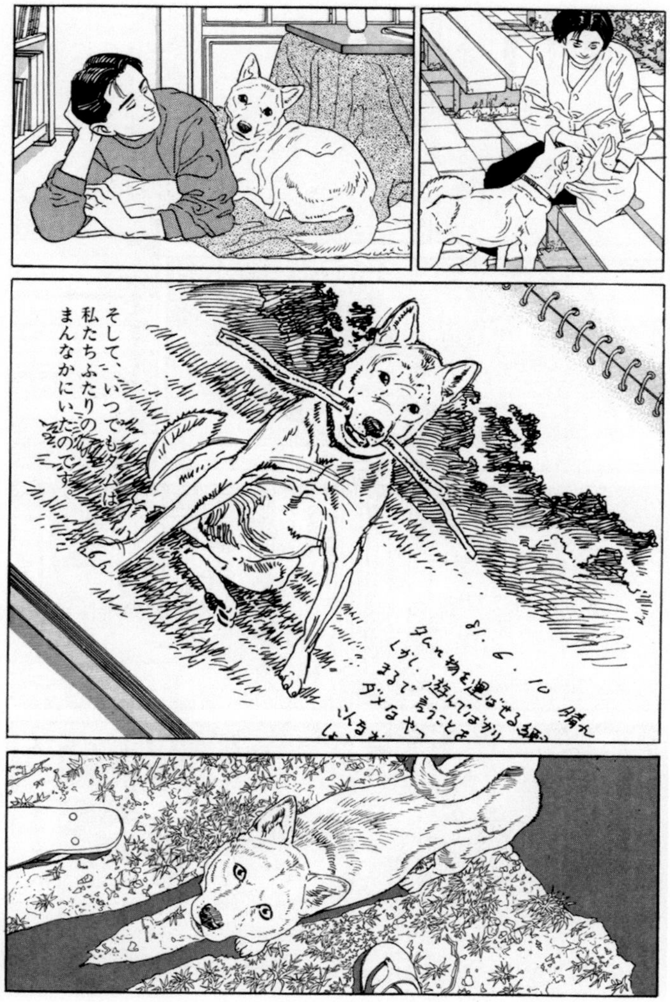
そして、いつでもタムは
私たちふたりの
まんなかにいたのです。

385
Taniguchi Jirô, *Inu o kau (Dreamland).*
© Taniguchi Jirô, Tokyo: Shogakukan, 2001

Far from the great outdoors, this manga plunges us back into daily life in Japan.

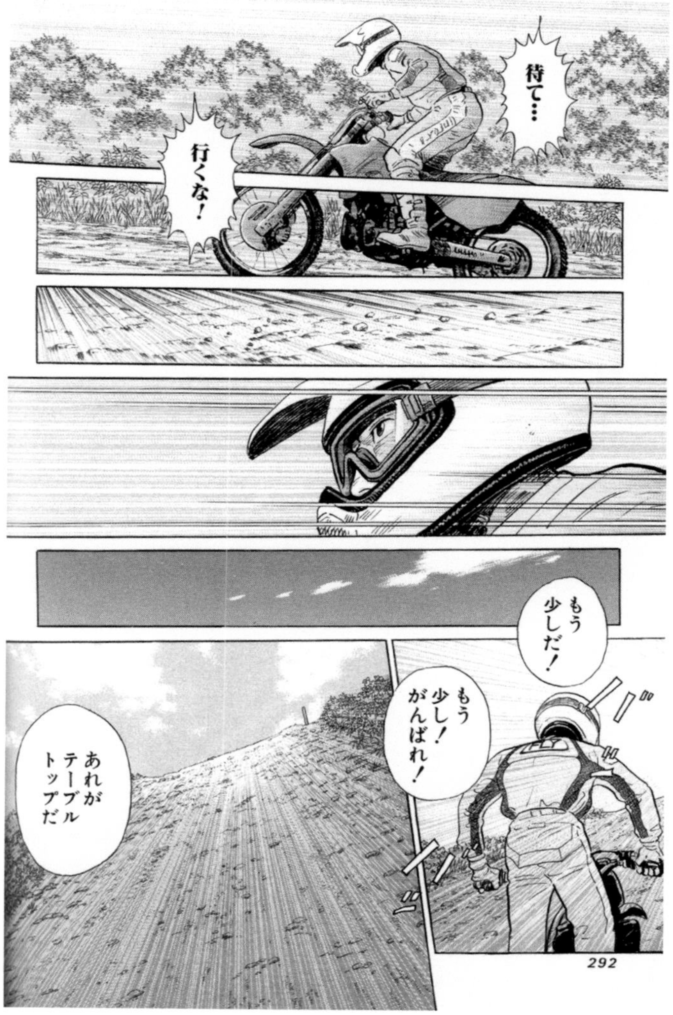
待て…
行くな！
もう少しだ！
もう少し！がんばれ！
あれがテーブルトップだ

386
Taniguchi Jirô, *Hare yuku sora (In a Glorious Sky).*
© Taniguchi Jirô, Tokyo: Shûeisha, 2005

In telling this poignant history, Taniguchi Jirô adopts a very different style. A high-school pupil on a motorbike is knocked down by a car and falls into a coma. When he comes round, he is totally amnesic, but feels inhabited by the soul of someone else. He discovers that he is haunted by the soul of the driver of the car that hit him and who lost his life in the accident. The young man doesn't know how to explain to those around him exactly what has happened to him. Only his girlfriend ends up believing him and helps him recover his own identity. But if the victim haunts his spirit, it is only because he is trying to bear witness to a social phenomenon: forced by his company to overwork, it was this that made him so tired and, in consequence, caused the accident.

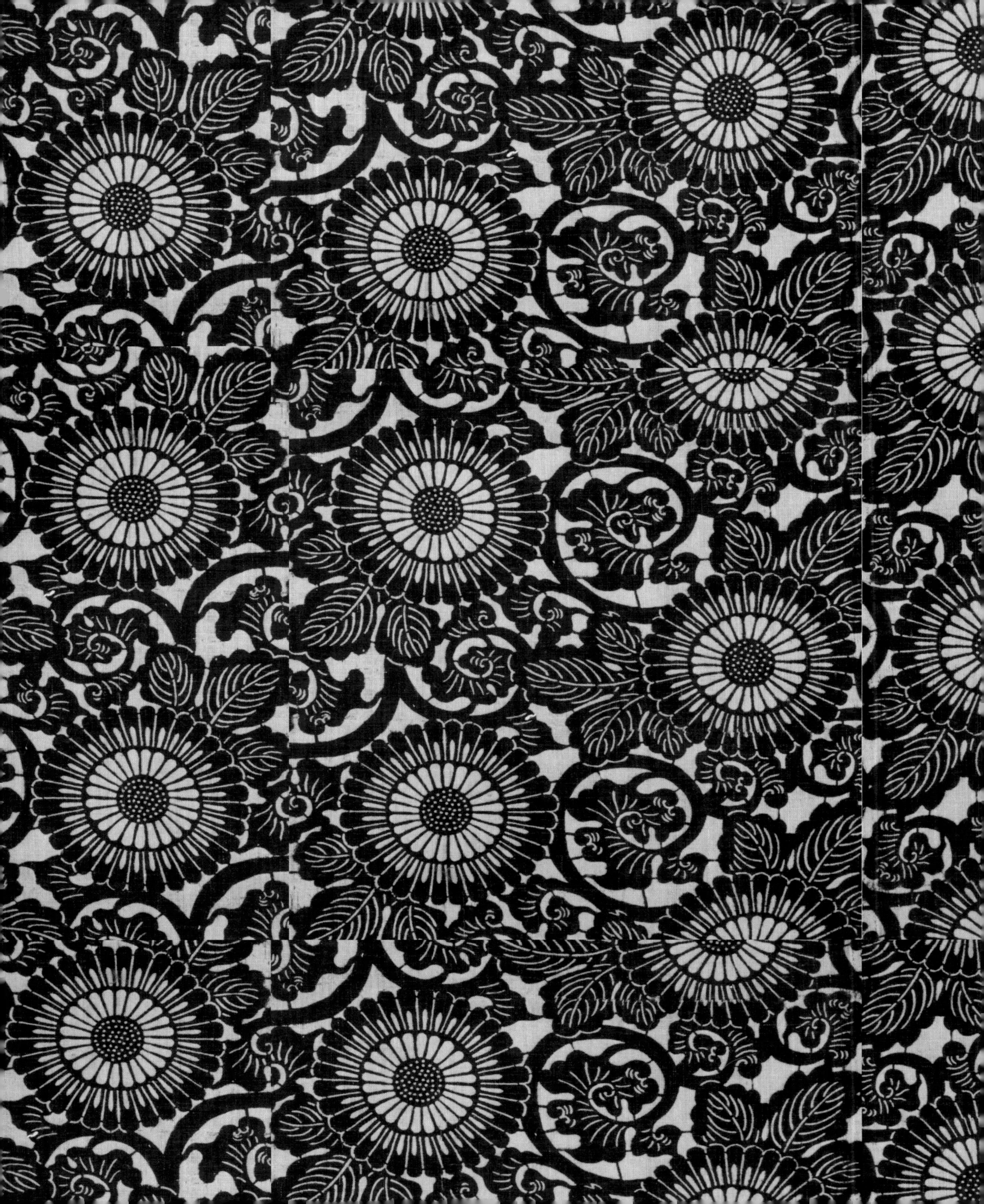

INTERVEW WITH TANIGUCHI JIRÔ

My meeting with Taniguchi Jirô in January 2007 was an enriching experience. I was charmed by the kindness and modesty of this artist, who seems not to fully understand the reasons for his success in Europe, and particularly in France. He truly does not seem to grasp what it is in his manga that so perfectly fulfills the demands of a public eager to find a vivid atmosphere as much as a good story.

Brigitte Koyama-Richard: How you explain your success in France?

Taniguchi Jirô: I'm often asked this question and I can never find an adequate answer. I myself am at once astonished and delighted by it.

B. K.-R.: Isn't it because your sensibility is so close to our own? In several of your manga, like *The Walking Man* or *Quartier Lointain*, your characters take the time to look at life around them, to gaze at an old house, a deserted building, go down some forgotten lane, or pay attention to everyone they encounter, etcetera.

T. J.: It's possible. I feel very good in France and, if I spoke the language, it seems to me I could live there—not in Paris because it's too large a city, but in the provinces—why not?

B. K.-R.: When did you discover manga?

T. J.: Like the majority of the Japanese children, I read plenty when I was young. I devoured the works of Tezuka Osamu and other Japanese artists, and then, one day, I discovered foreign comics. I couldn't read the text, but I was intrigued by the drawings. It was probably this diversity that made me want to become a *mangaka*. My idea was to produce work that looked like no other.

B. K.-R.: The graphics in your works are especially precise: the landscapes in particular are depicted very accurately.

T. J.: I like lines to be precise. I deliberately spend a great deal of time on the landscapes.

B. K.-R.: In your manga, one "walks" in the company of the characters. One recognizes the various quarters they go through. For those who have never gone to Japan, it's a lovely way of discovering Tokyo and other cities. How do you manage to depict the settings you choose as the backdrop to your stories so accurately?

T. J.: I take many photographs that enable me to provide a painstaking description of the places.

B. K.-R.: Animals also occupy a significant place in your oeuvre.

T. J.: Yes, I'm attracted by stories that take place in nature and I enjoy drawing animals.

B. K.-R.: You have collaborated with foreign artists. Do you ever think of renewing the experience?

T. J.: It was extremely enriching, so I fully intend to.

B. K.-R.: What are your plans now?

T. J.: I have a few things on hand but I want to be able to work at my own pace, to create works I can put my heart into, and to take the time to do my drawings properly.

387
Mizuki Shigeru, *Hakaba no Kitarô*
(Kitarô of the Cemetery), Kôdansha, 1965.
© Mizuki Shigeru Production

This manga, which shows little Kitarô preparing to enter hell, was subsequently adapted as an animation that proved a delight for children. In fact Mizuki Shigeru had created a new genre of manga: thanks to him, the world of the supernatural and of the famous Japanese tales of *yôkai* has become a worthy subject of study for many researchers, and even something of a fad. He himself investigated the question thoroughly, cataloging the various *yôkai* in the form of anthologies. His richly illustrated narratives always conclude on a moral note, with "good" invariably carrying the day.

Mizuki Shigeru: master of the supernatural

A stone's-throw from Fuchû Station in Tokyo, a number of multi-colored and highly sympathetic-looking little *yôkai** (the monsters that pervade Japanese folktales) inform passersby that they are approaching Mizuki Shigeru's production house.

A monster of slightly larger size at the entrance of the residence invites us in. The master works among his family, in a convivial atmosphere. All around, hundreds of fabulous beings jostle for position in showcases, creating an ambience that is a far cry from the frenetic bustle of the Japanese capital.

When the room is dappled in the half-light, there can be no doubt that one has indeed entered the supernatural world so dear to Mizuki Shigeru. Serene and gracious, he betrays nothing of the long, hard years he had to endure before his immense talent was finally recognized.

He was born in Sakai, not far from the city of Matsue where the French writer Lafcadio Hearn (1850–1904), author of many ghost stories, lived. In his infancy, Mizuki Shigeru was told many a story by an old woman who lived nearby, "Granny Non-Non," and at a very early age became a devotee of the extraordinary legends of the *yôkai*. The child, who adored sleeping and dreaming, even if this meant arriving late at school, directed his efforts towards becoming a painter, an ambition forestalled by the Second World War.

Sent to the Front in New Guinea, he there lost an arm and contracted malaria, almost dying as a result. With a raging fever, he stumbled through the forest but was taken in by some natives and saved. On his return, he drew for *kami shibai**, the strolling picture theater that was so popular after the Second World War, and then for hire shops. First published in the magazine *Garo*, his manga *Hakaba no Kitarô (Kitarô of the Cemetery)* was reissued in *Shônen Magazine* under the title *Gegege no Kitarô (Ghastly Kitarô)*, becoming a best-seller. The uncontested master of the supernatural, little by little this talented *mangaka* saw his star begin to rise. Today, there is a steady stream of interviews and TV programs about him, and spring 2007 was marked by the broadcast on TV of a new animated film taken from *Gegege no Kitarô*—and the release of a live-action movie.

Fig. 393

388
Mizuki Shigeru, original drawing for *Tobetoro no gojû nen (Tobetoro is Fifty)*, Fusosha, 1995. © Mizuki Shigeru Production

389

Mizuki Shigeru, Kashadokoro (The Big Skeleton),
published in Yôkai Gadan, Iwanami Shoten, 1992.
© Mizuki Shigeru Production

Invisible during the daylight hours, the giant
skeleton appears in the evening, making a racket
as he moves about and runs after his victims.

390

Utagawa Kuniyoshi, Sôma no kodairi, triptych
nishiki-e print, late 1840s. © Chiba City Museum of Art

This impressively realistic skeleton of terrifying
size is an illustration for a scene from a play
telling of an episode from the life of the tenth-
century warrior, Taira no Masakado, governor
of the province of Shimôsa. Power-crazed, he
assassinates his nephew, seizes his province and
makes it into an autonomous state, before he is
killed in his turn. Here his daughter conjures up
his spirit.

Frightening or sometimes just grotesque
(like the ones Kawanabe Kyôsai showed dancing), skeletons had become popular in prints
and paintings ever since the scientist and physician Sugita Genpaku (1733–1817) published the
first translation of a book of Western medicine,
Kaitai shinsho (Anatomischen Tabellen) by the
German Johannes Kulmus in 1774. Amusingly,
Mizuki Shigeru here places Kuniyoshi's skeleton in an alien context.

Illuminated *emaki** scrolls, like *nishiki-e** prints, enriched an
already fertile imagination, further nourished by works on the richly
illustrated fantastic bestiary of the past. Fueled by the art of the great
masters such as Hokusai, Kawanabe Kyôsai, Kuniyoshi, and
Hiroshige, Mizuki Shigeru has executed a series of woodblock prints
worthy of an artist of the first rank. Reworking the celebrated series
by Andô Hiroshige, *The Fifty-three Stations of the Tôkaidô**, Mizuki Figs. 398, 40
Shigeru produced a series of poetic and amusing manga, which take
us back in time: *The Fifty-three Stations on the Yôkaidô* (that is, the Figs. 128, 3
road of the *yôkai*). This large-scale work, for which the artist redraws 401–402
landscapes by his famous predecessor, adding to them a host of *yôkai*,
contains fifty-five pictures and took two years to produce.

Prints featuring journeys and landscapes appeared in the Edo era
in the wake of economic development, road improvements, and an
increase in the number of travelers, merchants, and pilgrims. These
very quickly became a huge success: pretty, colorful, inexpensive,
and of manageable size, they were ideal to take home or as a gift.
Painters would show the famous post-houses, inns, panoramas
depicted in different seasons, and other subjects. Hiroshige, with
Hokusai the unquestioned master of the landscape print, produced
many splendid series, with *The Fifty-three Stations of the Tôkaidô*
being the most famous. Mizuki Shigeru had the clever idea of having his *yôkai* travel along the Tôkaidô, just as in the Edo period.
Starting out from original drawings composed in pen, and painted
with the mineral pigments employed in traditional painting, he had
nishiki-e prints pulled in accordance with age-old methods. They
have lost nothing of their unquestionable charm.

This recent series shows Mizuki Shigeru as a marvelous story-
teller who can breathe fresh life into the tales of the past without
losing anything of his interest in the present, as he travels and
appears at many of the exhibitions devoted to him in Japan and
throughout the world.

The artist was awarded the Grand Prix at the Festival
d'Angoulême 2007 for his manga, *NonNon Bâ*.

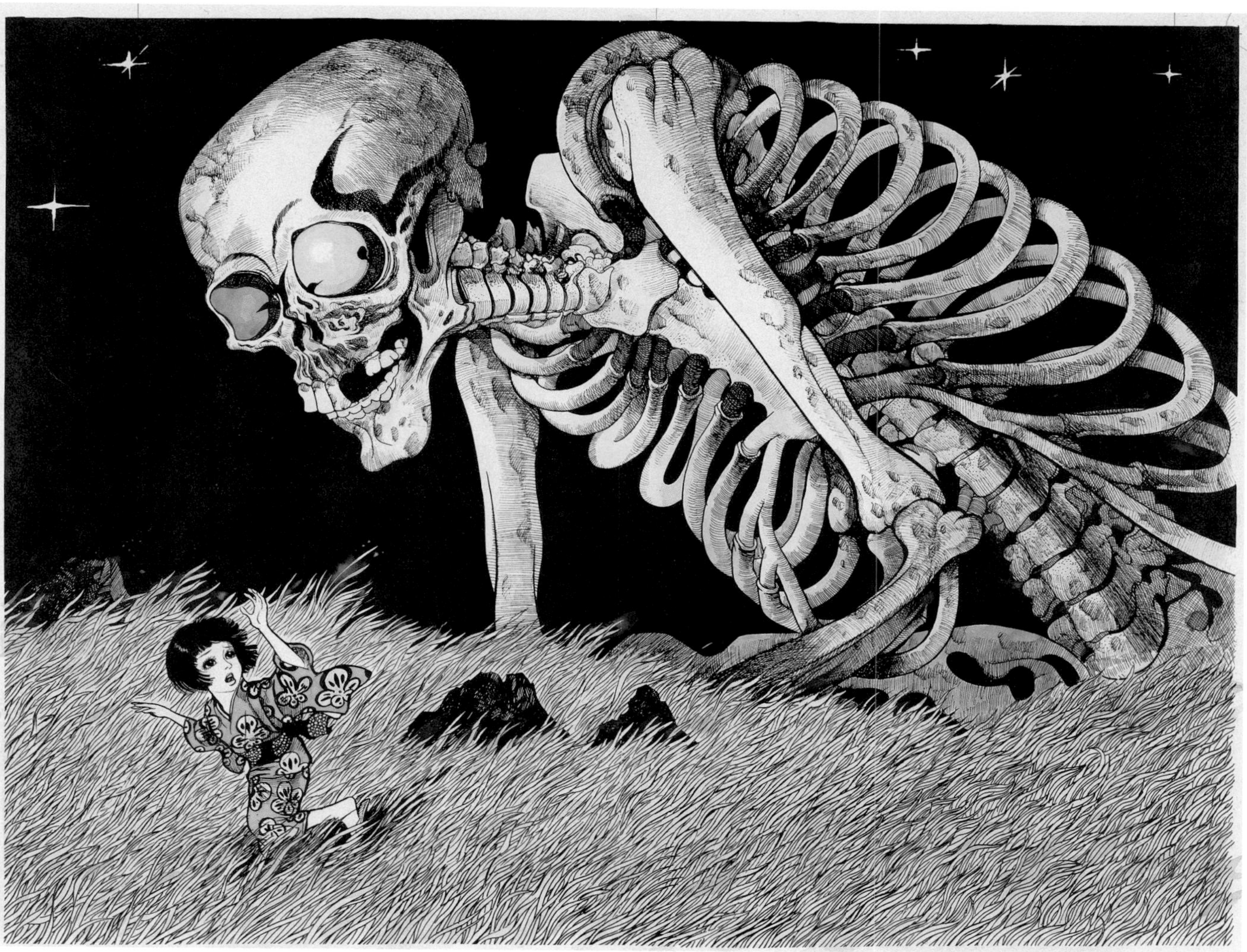

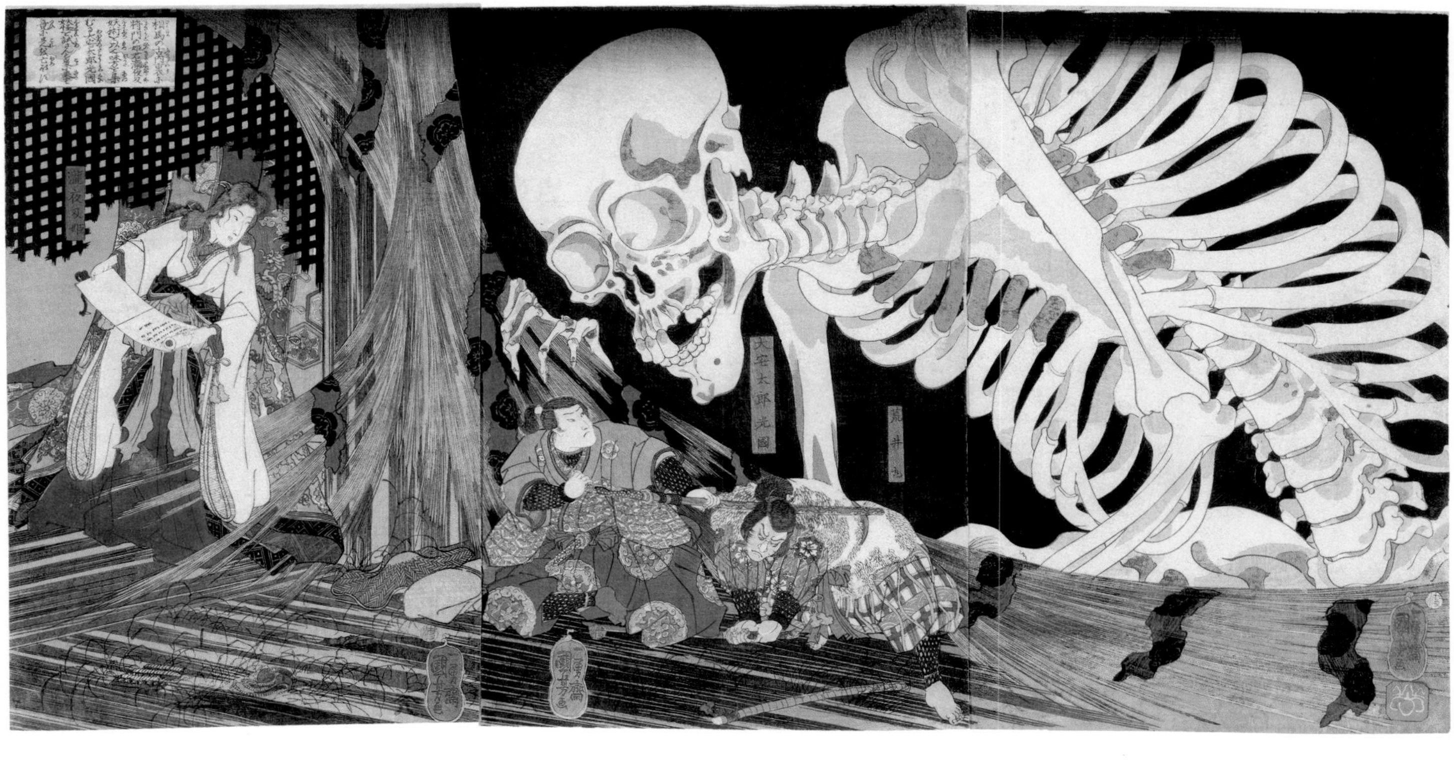
大宅太郎光圀
荒井丸

391

Utagawa Hiroshige, *Tairano Kiyomori (Looking at Ghosts)*, triptych *nishiki-e* print. © Kanagawa Prefectural Museum of Cultural History

This is one of the few prints showing *yôkai* made by the landscape painter Hiroshige. On closer inspection the charming backdrop of the snow-covered garden appears unduly strange: the branches of the trees are made up of dozens of skulls and skeletons and the hill too presents a ghastly form. They are, in fact, the ghosts of hundreds of soldiers killed in combat during the Civil War in the Hôgen era (1156–59), which have come back to haunt the spirit of Tairano Kiyomori (1118–1181), head of the Taira clan, who would massacre his opponents without a second thought. Hiroshige alludes to the painful episode with humor and subtlety.

392

Original drawing by Mizuki Shigeru, *Yôkai Hikôsen (A Yôkai Airship)*, issued in the review *Shûkan Shônen Magazine* in 1968, publisher Kôdansha. © Mizuki Shigeru Production

The making of Japanese prints

To a great extent, the making of Japanese prints remains a mystery. Figs. 396–402 The processes, however, deserve to be better known and preserved, and this is the mission of the Adachi Foundation for print preservation that worked on the series. A Japanese print, like a manga or a movie, is the work of a team, the three principal participants on the creative level being the draughtsman, *eshi*, the engraver, *horishi*, and the printer, *surishi*.

The editor orders a drawing from the painter. His goal, primarily commercial, is to sell the greatest number of prints of the highest quality and in conformity with the style criteria of the time. A print taken up by the public would be reproduced in two to three hundred copies for a first impression and subsequently, after repairing the boards or cutting new ones, up to one or two thousand.

The painter hands his drawing to the engraver, whose delicate role it is to carve the drawing in relief as accurately and as thoroughly as possible. In general, cherry-wood boards are used; that is the most suitable wood due to its relative hardness. The engraver then places the verso of the original drawing, painted in Chinese ink on very fine paper, against the previously dampened board, rubbing it gently with the end of his fingers until the lines of the drawing penetrate into the wood and are left impressed. During the rubbing process, the paper falls apart, leaving just the design, which the engraver now starts to engrave in its entirety. He then spreads some ink, *sum*, over the whole surface of the wood and prints his work (*kyôgozuri*) to see whether it has come off.

He then has to engrave as many boards as there are to be colors, the number normally being chosen by the draughtsman and printer. Mizuki Shigeru's print *Nihon bashi asa no kei* (figs. 128, 401–402), made Figs. 128, 401–402 in keeping with this tradition, employs no fewer than sixteen colors in addition to the Chinese ink base: it thus required seventeen boards.

The engraver then makes a reference mark on each board, a notch called a *kentô**, which allows the printer to apply the colors successively without the sheet of paper moving about. The boards are then passed over to the printer, who prepares the paper made using mulberry glue mixed with vegetable adhesive. This very flexible paper absorbs colors perfectly. During the Edo period, its

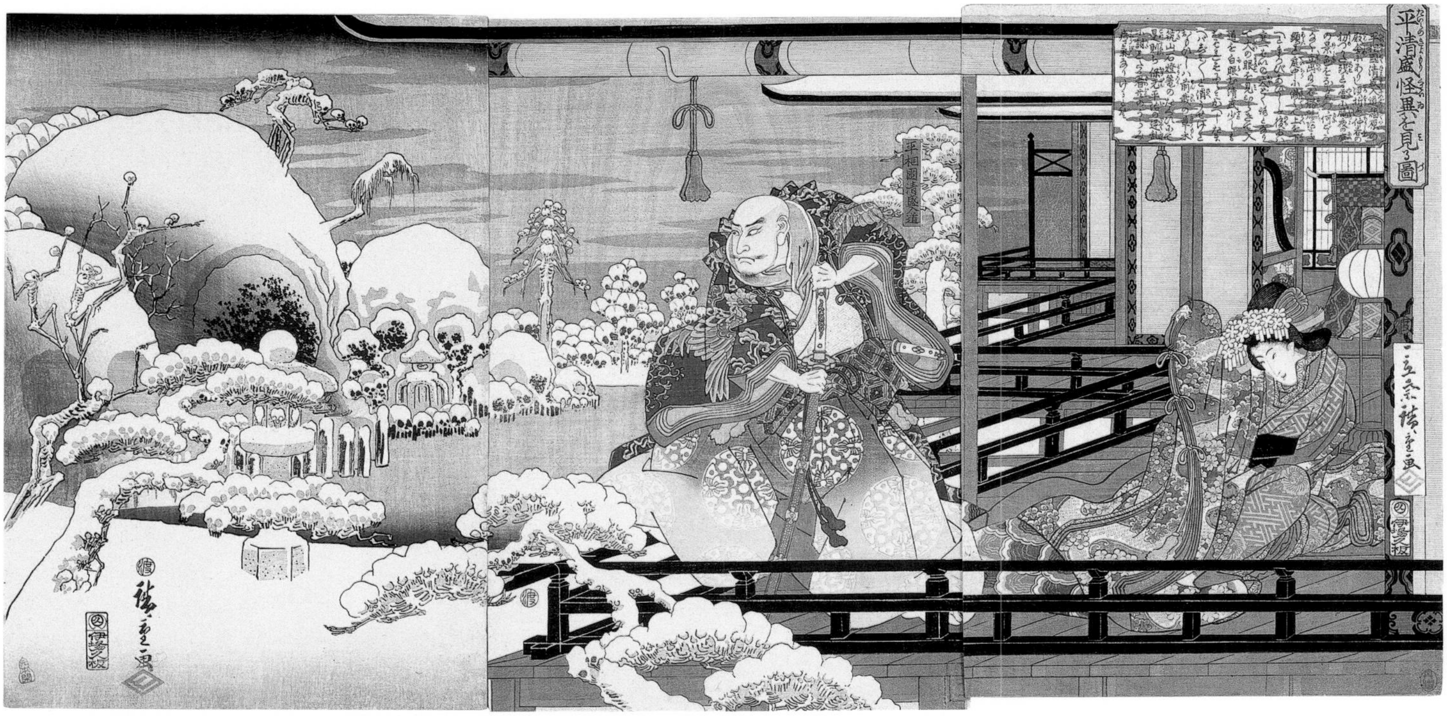
平清盛怪異を見る圖

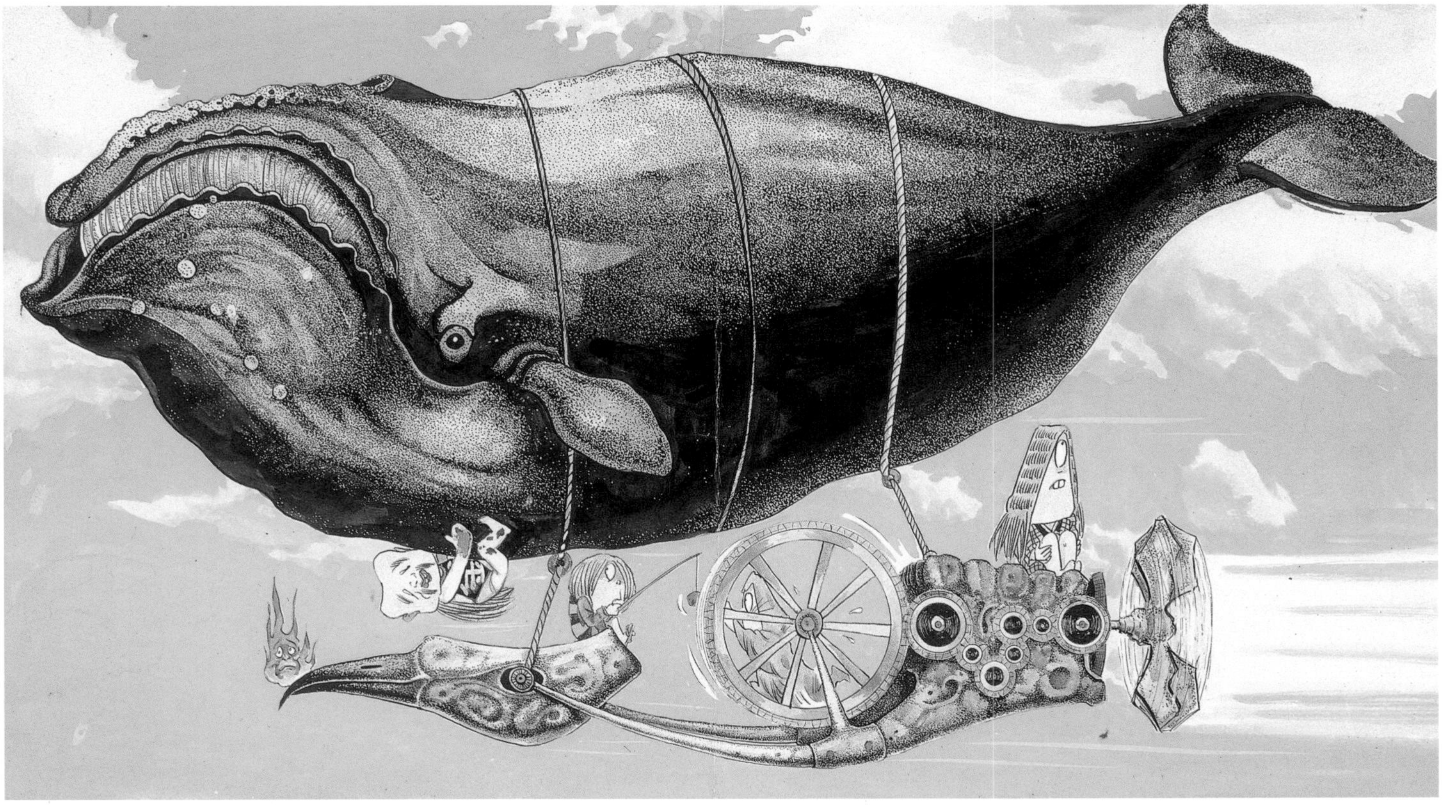

393
Mizuki Shigeru, *Gegege no Kitarô sos*,
© Mizuki Shigeru Production

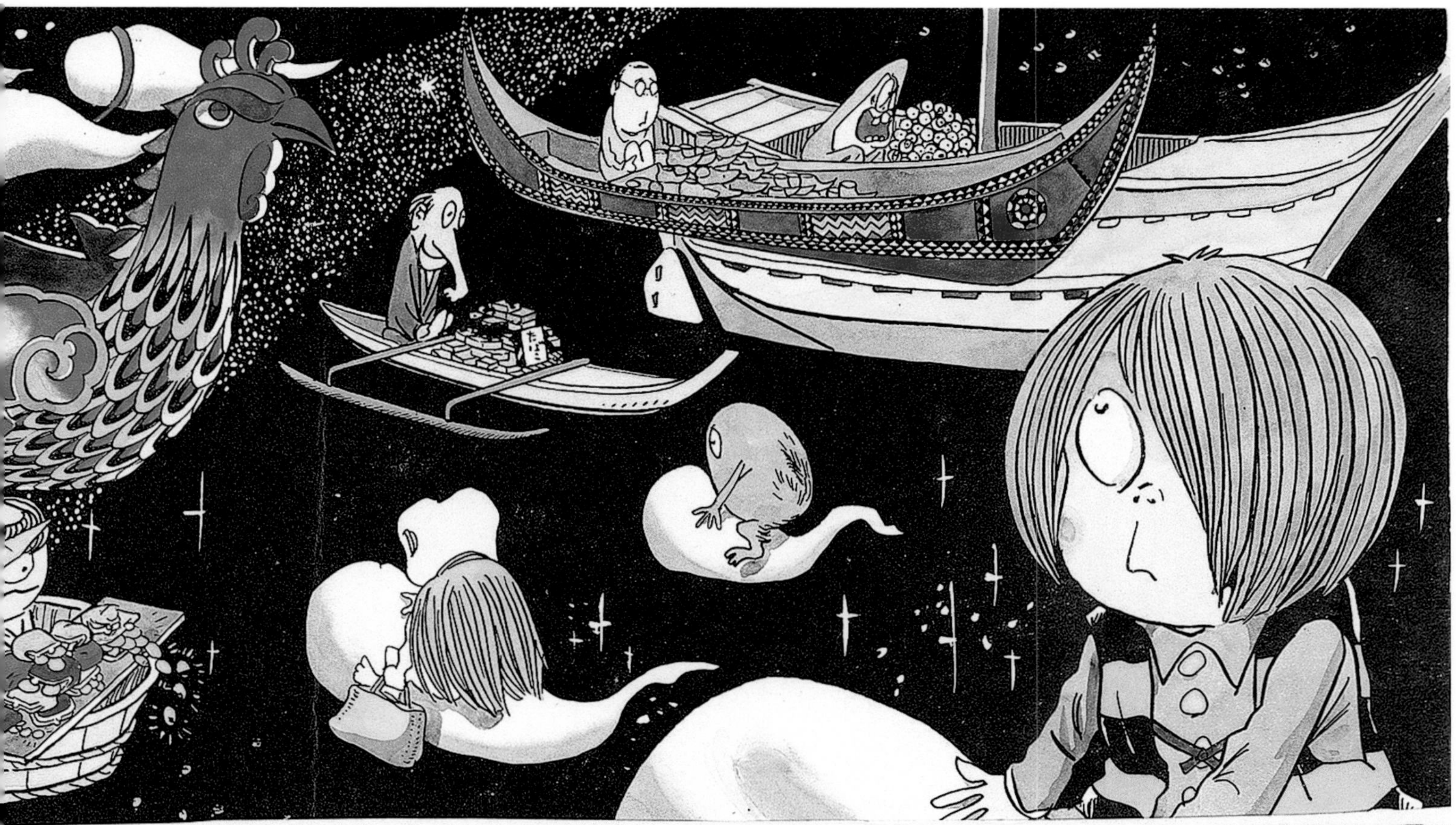

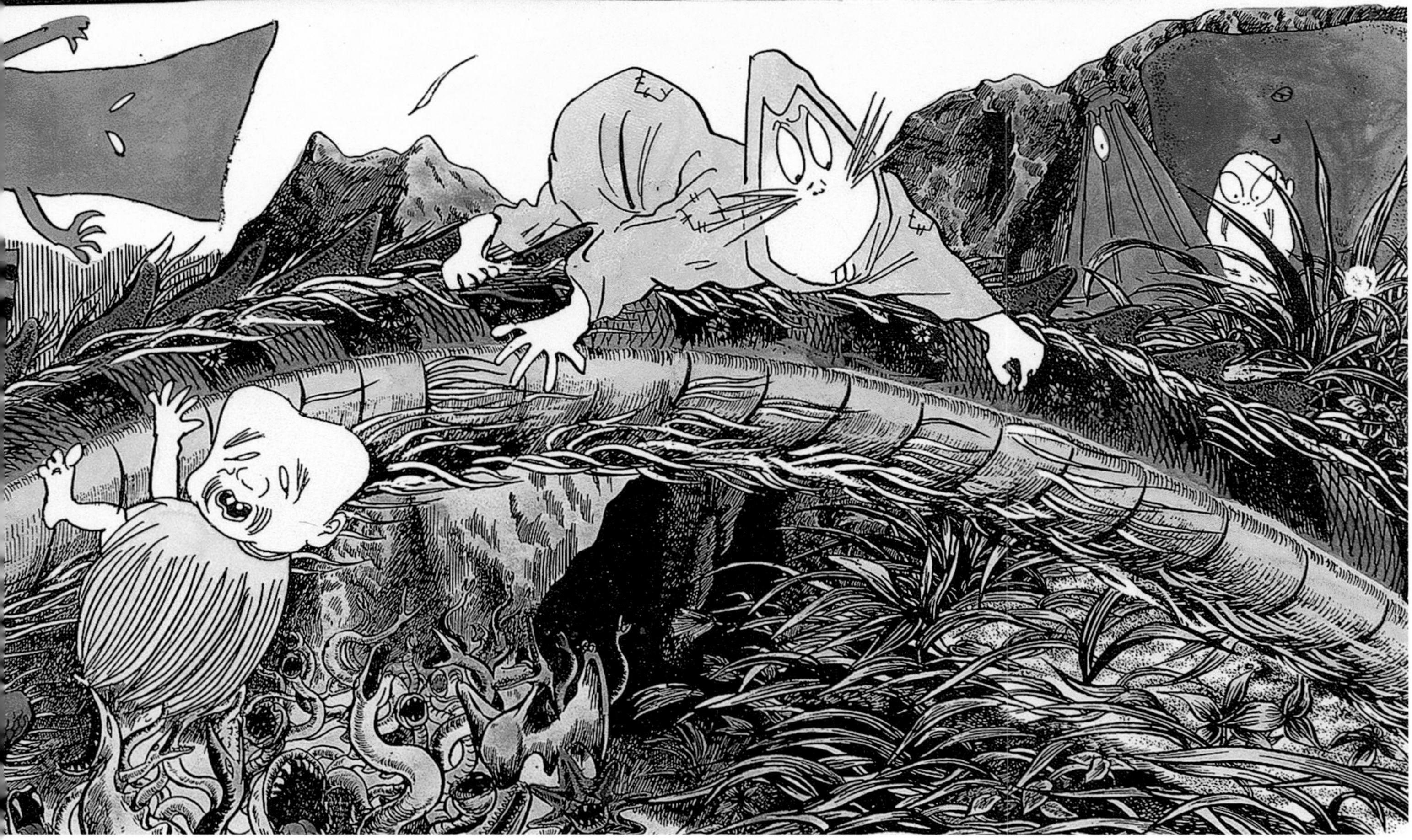

thickness and composition evolved. Only *hôshôgami** paper of the finest quality is permitted for *surimono**, which call for highly sophisticated techniques such as embossing (gauffrage), mica ground, and the most delicate pigments. The paper must always be kept moist. The printer then dampens each board on both sides using a horsehair brush, the tip of which has been scorched then rounded off with a piece of shagreen, and proceeds to print the drawing in Chinese ink; it is these lines (*sumi sen*) that form the basis of any print. He then applies each color, the lightest hues first, using a kind of pad, the *baren*, which each printer makes for himself out of bamboo leaves. In this way, the colors are printed one after the other until the final result is obtained.

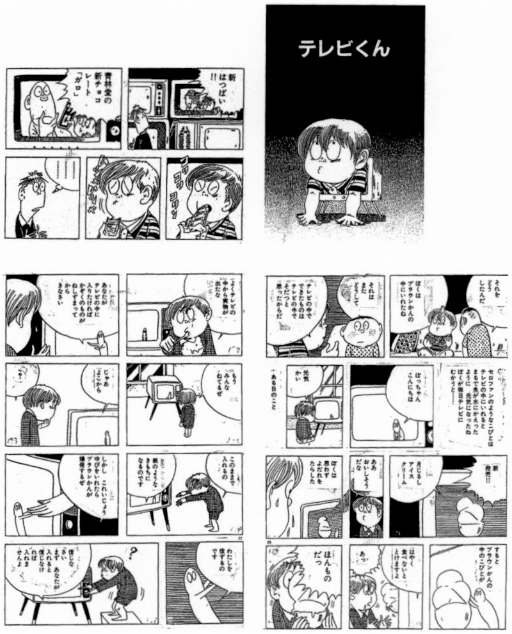
テレビくん

394
Mizuki Shigeru, *Terebi kun (Little Terebi)*, 1965, Kôdansha. © Mizuki Shigeru Production

This manga, launched by the publisher Kôdansha, tells of the adventures of a gifted little boy who has the strange ability to enter and leave a TV set *(terebi)* at will.

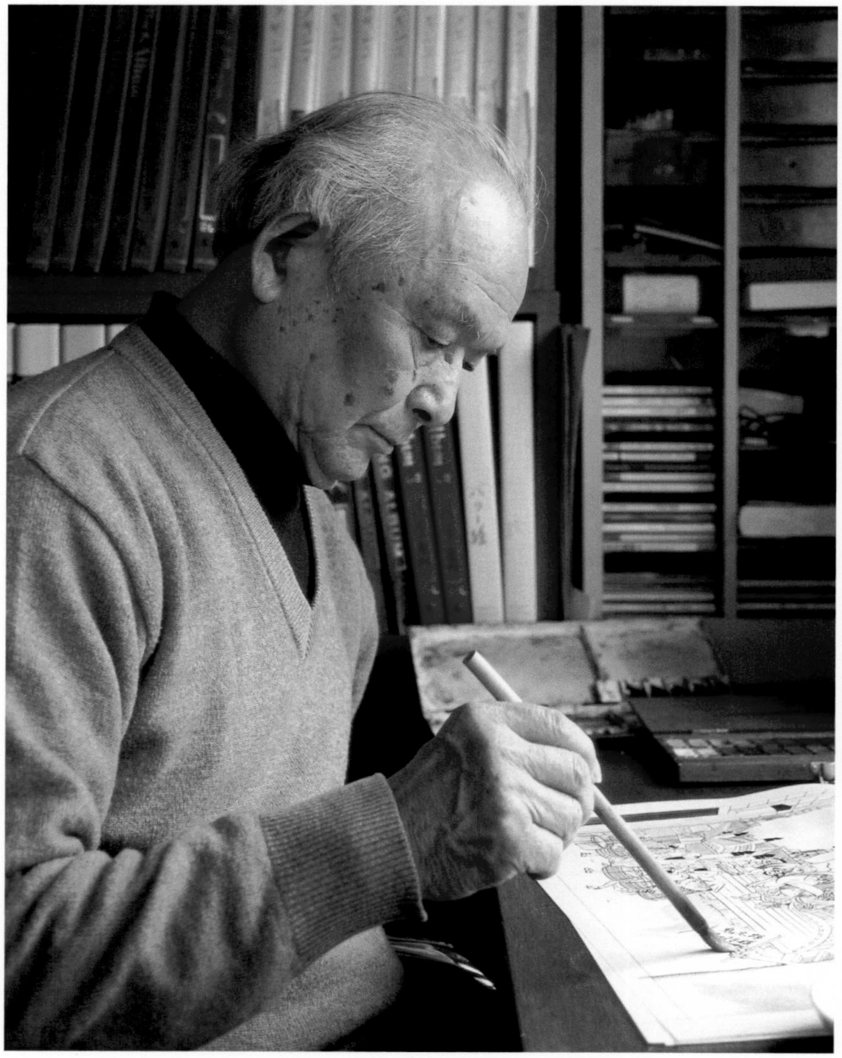

395
Mizuki Shigeru. © Mizuki Productions Co., Ltd.
© Yanoman Corporation
© Photo Kobayashi Hôji
© The Adachi Foundation for the Preservation of Woodcut Printings

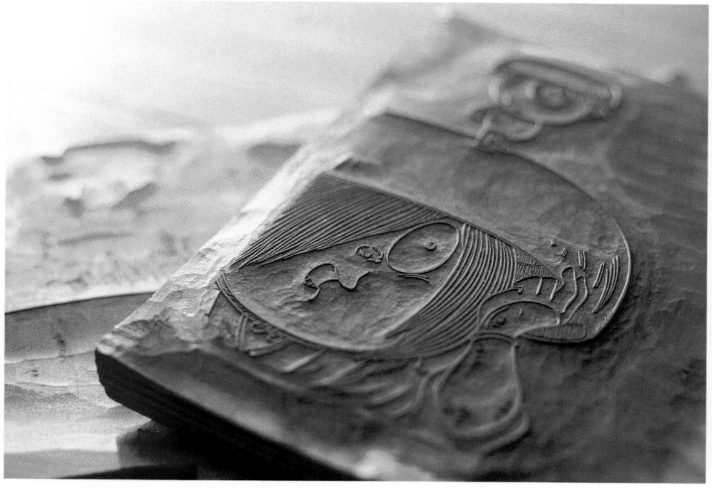

396
Wooden board for *The Fifty-three Stations on the Yôkaidô* by Mizuki Shigeru. © Mizuki Productions Co., Ltd. © Yanoman Corporation
© The Adachi Foundation for the Preservation of Woodcut Printings

This is one of the boards used for engraving the print entitled *Keishi sanjô Ôhashi*, followed by the complete print by Mizuki Shigeru, and, finally, the one by Hiroshige that he took as his starting point.

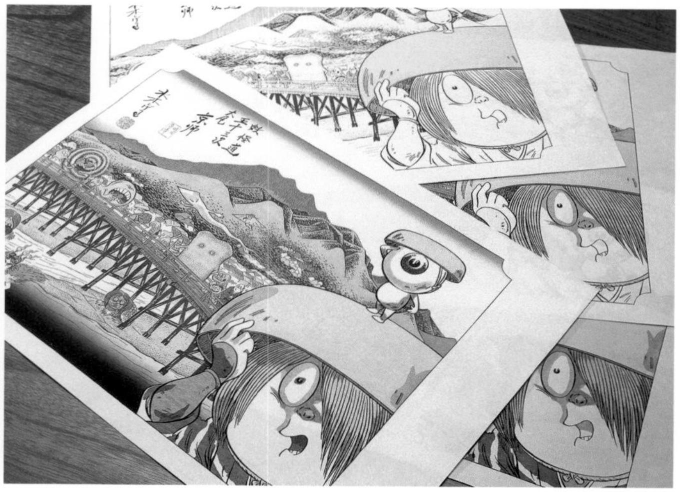

397
Mizuki Shigeru, *Keishi sanjô Ôhashi (The Great Bridge of Sanjô at Keishi).*
© Mizuki Productions Co., Ltd. © Yanoman Corporation
© The Adachi Foundation for the Preservation of Woodcut Printings

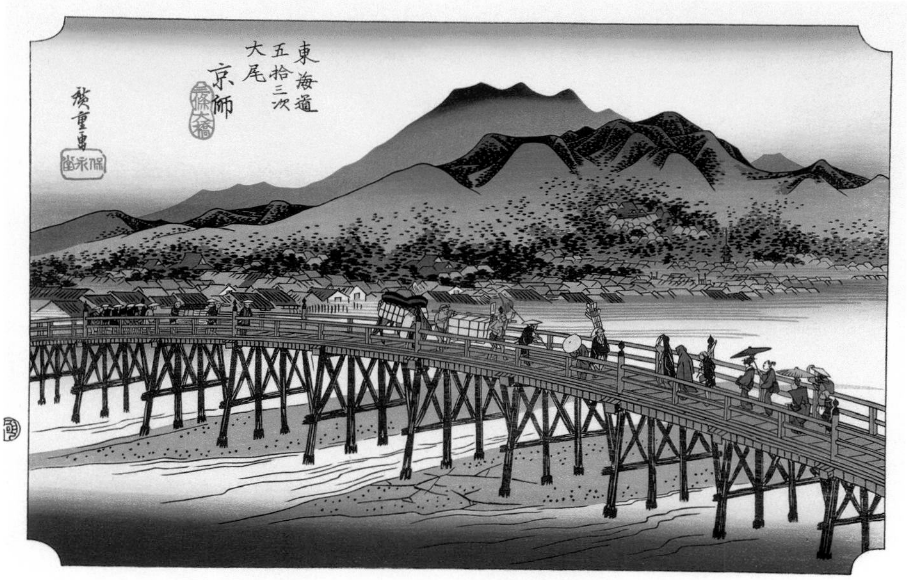
東海道
五拾三次
大尾
京師

398
Andô Hiroshige, *Keishi sanjô Ôhashi (The Great Bridge of Sanjô at Keishi).*
© The Adachi Foundation for the Preservation of Woodcut Printings

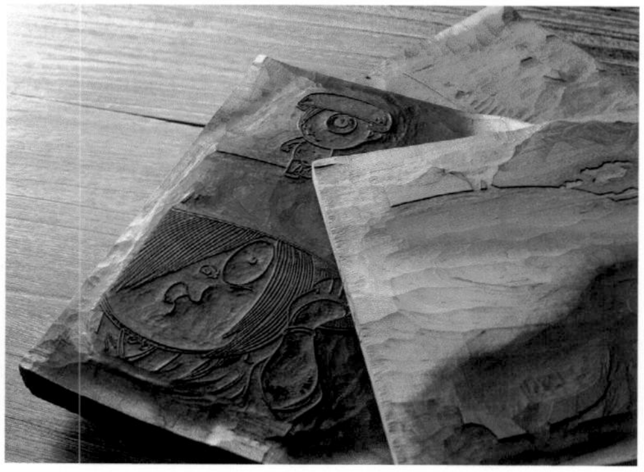

399
Wooden boards for *The Fifty-three Stations on the Yôkaidô* by Mizuki Shigeru. © Mizuki Productions Co., Ltd. © Yanoman Corporation
© The Adachi Foundation for the Preservation of Woodcut Printings

Three more of the plates used to carry out the print showing the Great Bridge of Sanjô at Keishi.

400
Andô Hiroshige, *Nihon bashi asa no kei (The Bridge at Nihon Bashi in the Morning)*. © The Adachi Foundation for the Preservation of Woodcut Printings

401
Mizuki Shigeru, *Nihon bashi asa no kei (The Bridge at Nihon Bashi in the Morning)* from the series *The Fifty-three Stations on the Yôkaidô*.
© Mizuki Productions Co., Ltd © Yanoman Corporation
© The Adachi Foundation for the Preservation of Woodcut Printings

Mizuki Shigeru likes to rework Hiroshige's series of the *The Fifty-three Stations of the Tôkaidô*, such as in this view of the bridge of Nihon bashi. The middle of the bridge is occupied by his fetish character, the sympathetic Kitarô. One sees the nobles setting forth from the city of Edo to return to their fiefdoms. The sun is just rising over the capital and in the foreground traders are busying themselves at work.

402 (facing page)
Mizuki Shigeru, *Nihon bashi asa no kei (The Bridge at Nihon Bashi in the Morning)* from the series *The Fifty-three Stations on the Yôkaidô*.
© Mizuki Productions Co., Ltd © Yanoman Corporation
© The Adachi Foundation for the Preservation of Woodcut Printings

These are six of the twenty-four boards required to pull the print.
First stage: only the Chinese ink contour lines appear.
Second stage: the printer starts by applying the lightest hues, here yellow.
Fourth stage: the color orange is introduced.
Tenth stage: the horizon is colored pink and various tones of blue and green are applied.
Sixteenth stage: the blue line in the sky is added, the gradation providing an impression of perspective.
Twenty-fourth and last stage: the complexion of the figures is given a light tint. Mizuki's print, more colorful than Hiroshige's, called for more blocks, but the art of the Edo epoch here lives again in all its splendor and originality.

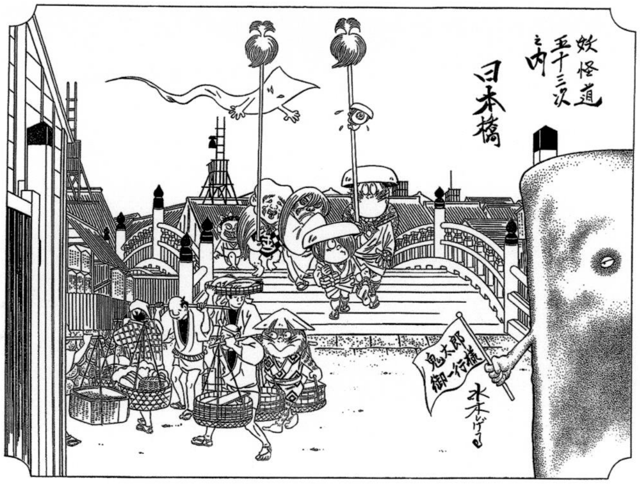
妖怪道五十三次之内
日本橋
鬼太郎御一行様
水木しげる

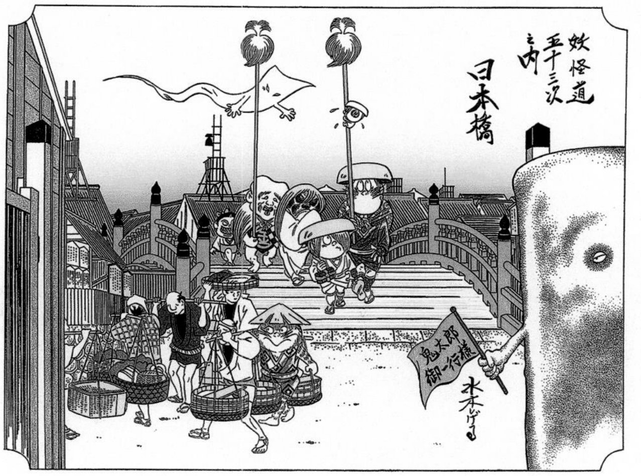
妖怪道五十三次之内
日本橋
鬼太郎御一行様
水木しげる

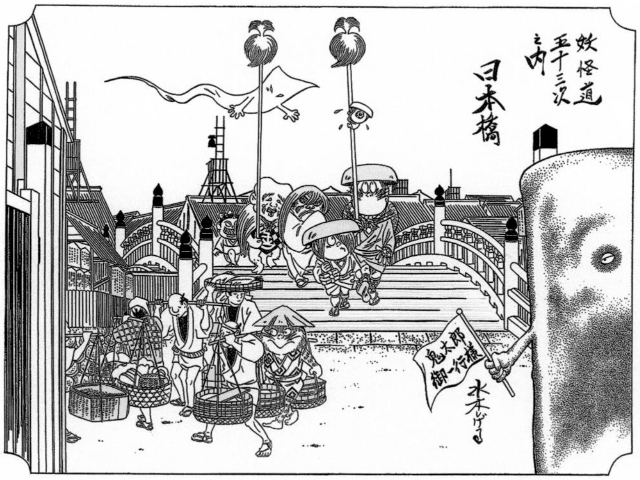
妖怪道五十三次之内
日本橋
鬼太郎御一行様
水木しげる

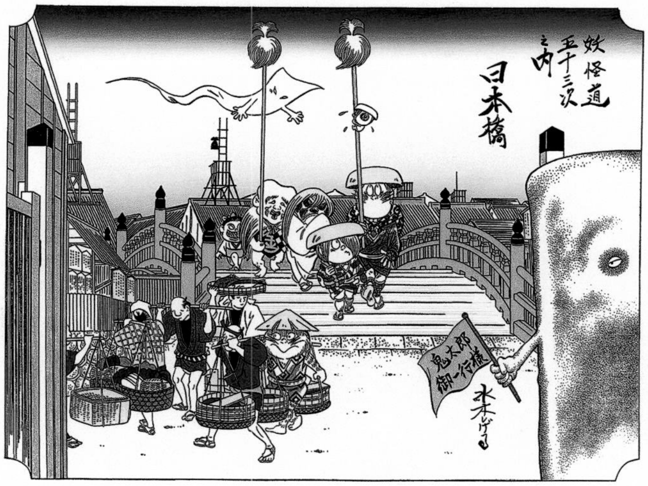
妖怪道五十三次之内
日本橋
鬼太郎御一行様
水木しげる

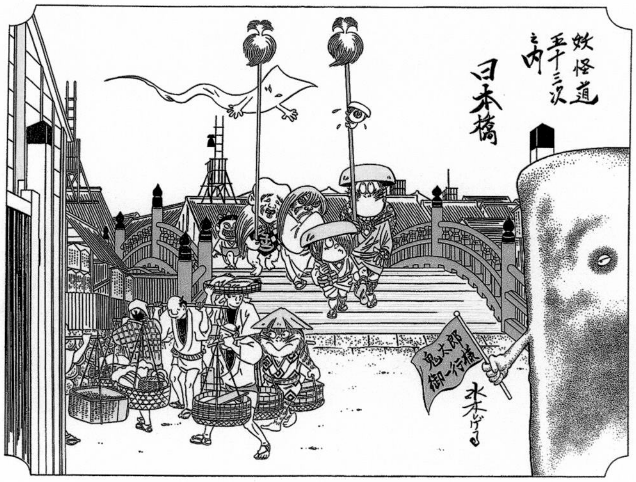
妖怪道五十三次之内
日本橋
鬼太郎御一行様
水木しげる

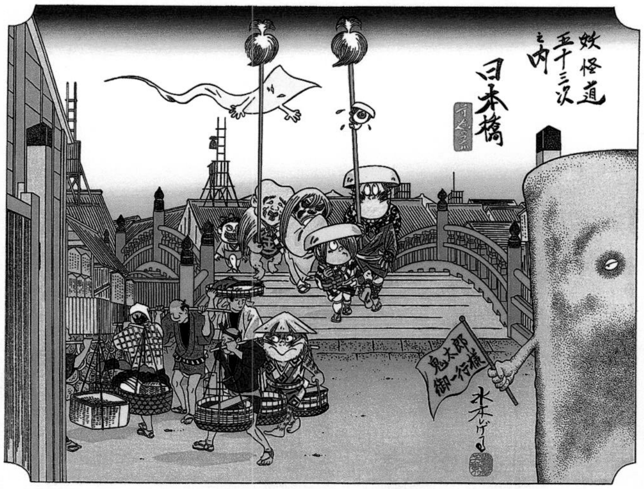
妖怪道五十三次之内
日本橋
鬼太郎御一行様
水木しげる

妖怪道五十三次

日本橋

発行 株式会社やのまん 制作年 平成一五年
限定 初摺 二〇〇部の内 第 番

403
Utagawa Hiroshige, *Hara, asa no Fuji (Mount Fuji Early in the Morning*; print from
The Fifty-three Stations of the Tôkaidô).
© The Adachi Foundation for the Preservation of Woodcut Printings

404
Mizuki Shigeru, *Hara (The Plain)*. © Mizuki Productions Co., Ltd.
© Yanoman Corporation © The Adachi Foundation for the Preservation of Woodcut Printings
For this print Mizuki once again takes inspiration from Hiroshige's famous series.

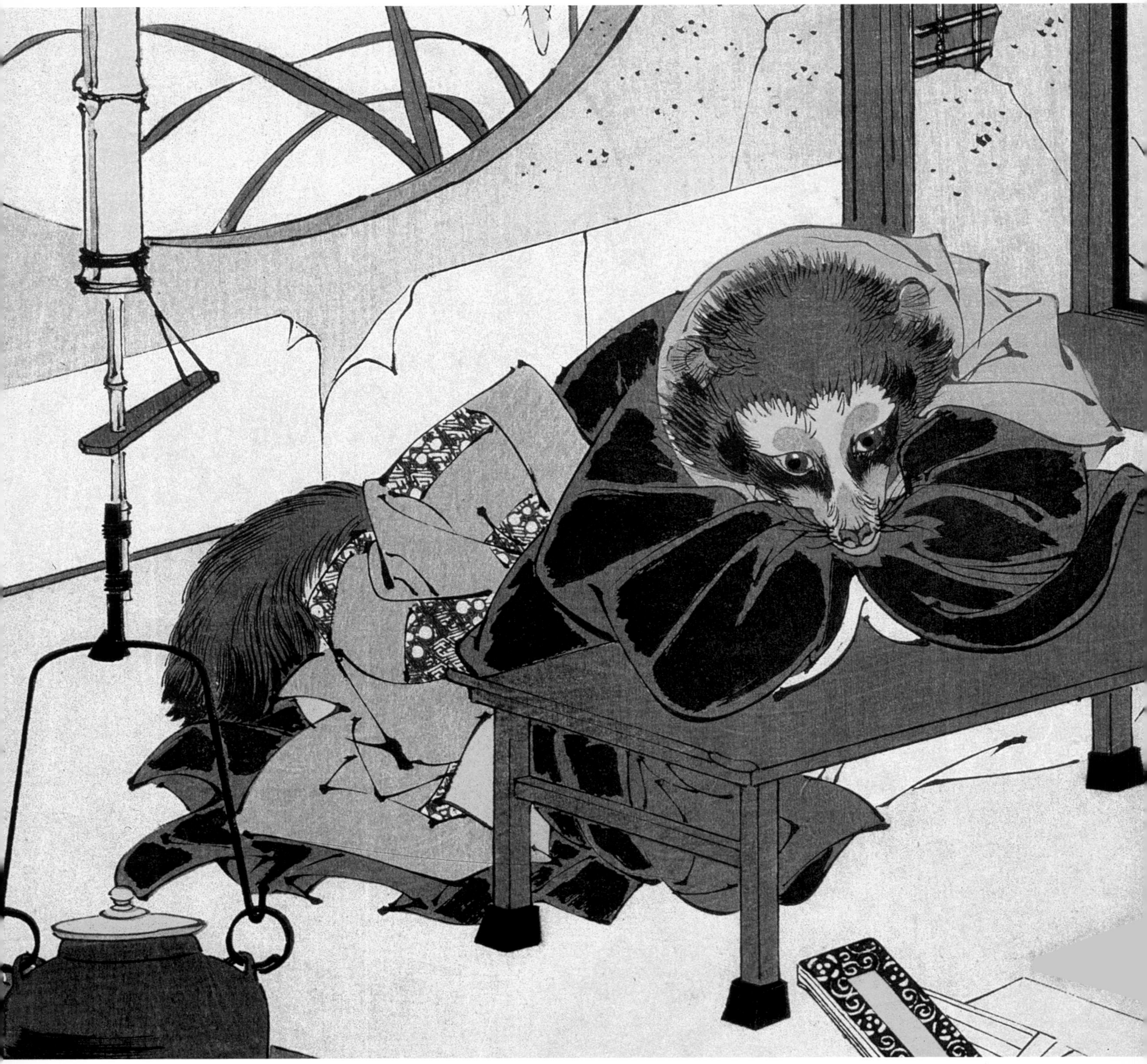

Fig. 412 (detail)

FROM MANGA TO ANIME: THE WORK OF STUDIO GHIBLI

A few years ago, European fans began discovering the wonderful animations made by Studio Ghibli, whose quality has transformed the very notion of Japanese anime*. Now every one of the studios' films is greeted as movie event, and the long-awaited release of *Heisei tanuki gassen Pompoko* (*The Battle of the Tanuki in the Heisei Era*, *Pompoko*, 1994; known as *The Raccoon War* in English) in January 2006, and of *Kaze no tani no Nausicaä (Nausicaä of the Valley of the Wind)* in August of the same year have been hailed with enthusiasm by audiences. Figs. 405–408 Fig. 409

An entire book could hardly do justice to the seminal importance of the work of Studio Ghibli, their founders, Miyazaki Hayao and Takahata Isao, and their team. The two works cited above are, however, essential in the context of the present volume.

Manga* is often criticized for its oversimplistic graphics. Nevertheless, most *mangaka** excel as much as in drawing as in storytelling. *Nausicaä* itself is a prime example of this fact. It is hardly necessary to introduce its creator, Miyazaki Hayao, an anime-maker known the world over, in particular for *Voyage of Chihiro (Spirited Away)* and *Princess Mononoke.* It is, though, often forgotten that he was also the creator of the manga *Nausicaä*, which came out for ten years in the magazine *Animage*. His supremely refined drawings pull readers into the story and its characters, almost without the need of a written text.

As we have recalled throughout this book, contemporary manga emerged from an image of ancestral Japanese culture. Its traces can be unearthed in the very first caricatures dating from 1,000 years ago, and continue in later hand scrolls and prints. Japanese thought and pictorial expression have of course evolved, yet their essence remains perceptible in today's manga and anime. Some of the most brilliant *mangaka* are fond of exploiting the rich veins of this cultural past.

If nowadays all successful manga are soon made into animations, some anime created from scratch are undeniable works of art. Takahata Isao had already deeply moved audiences with his sublime *Tomb of the Fireflies* and his nostalgia-tinged anime, *Omoide Poroporo* (a.k.a. *Only Yesterday*). *The Raccoon War* takes us into the depredations of the modern world, though it is also freighted with regular references to traditional Japanese culture. The cute *tanuki** (dog-like Figs. 405–408 raccoons) it stars have been present in folktales and legends since earliest times. Generally endowed with enormous testicles, a symbol of fertility, they are—with foxes and certain cats—the only animals able to change shape. Figs. 411–41

With his legendary sensitivity, Takahata Isao here tackles serious problems: deforestation, urban migration, industrialization of once protected zones, pollution, human indifference....

Faced with the destruction of their mountain when people come to build the city of Tama, the wretched *tanuki*, who no longer know where they are to live or to find food, decide to react. They do their utmost to halt the building work, transforming themselves into various objects, humans, and *yôkai** (monsters), but without result. With man in charge, to survive they will be forced to take on human form. Traditional culture is a constant presence in the film. The *yôkai*, which already populated scrolls and brocade prints, once again try to instill fear in man—but all in vain. Fig. 409

The fox's wedding procession also makes an appearance. Details abound that allude to ancestral Japan, and the question arises as to why the author, under the pretence of entertaining cinemagoers, marshals such references to tradition. In fact, Takahata Isao has always had a passion for literature. He had already surprised readers with his book *Jûni seiki no animehon* (Animations of the Twelfth Century), in which he explains how Japanese anime has sources in *emaki** painting scrolls. In *The Raccoon War*, Takahata Isao evokes the crystallization of culture past, present, and future.

405–408
Shots from the film *The Battle of the Tanaki in the Heisei Era, Pompoko,* 1994 © Hatake Jinusho GNH © Studio Ghibli

From top to bottom: The meeting of the *tanuki*; the *tanuki* transformed into the *yôkai* of the Procession of the Hundred Demons; a *tanuki*-transformed into a dragon; *tanuki* transformed into foxes, in a marriage procession.

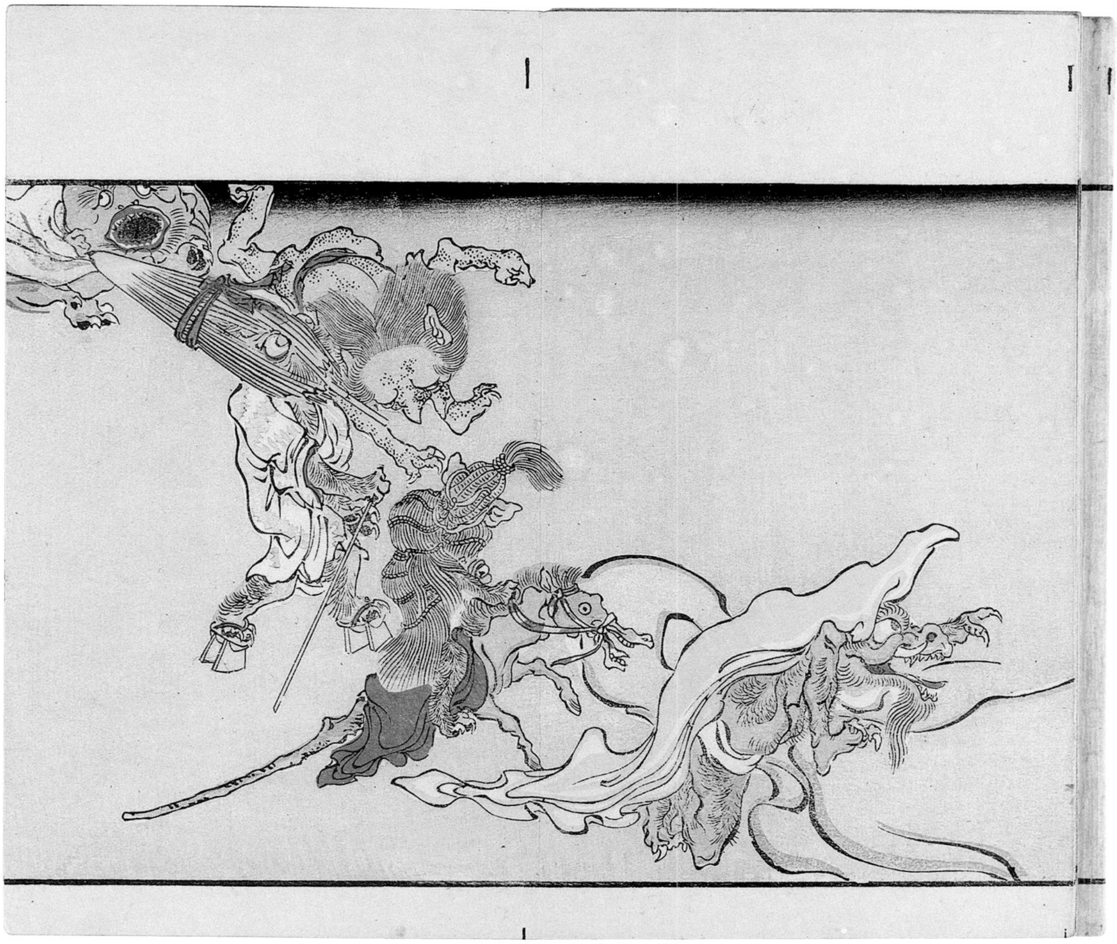

409
Kawanabe Kyôsai, *The Night Parade of One Hundred Demons* from *Pandemonium Kyôsai Hyakki Gadan* (illustrated book, 1889, signed by Kawanabe Tôiku). © Kawanabe Kyôsai Memorial Museum

The umbrella monster, *kasa yôkai*, one meets in *The Raccoon War*, had already appeared in scrolls and prints such as those of Kyôsai.

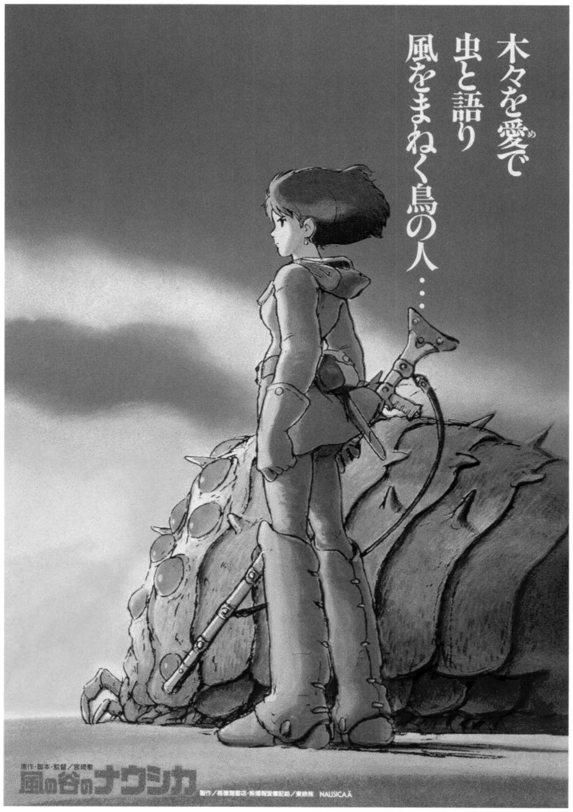
木々を愛で
虫と語り
風をまねく鳥の人……
風の谷のナウシカ
NAUSICAÄ

410
Kaze no tani no Nausicaä (Nausicaä of the Valley of the Wind), © 1984 Nibariki – GN

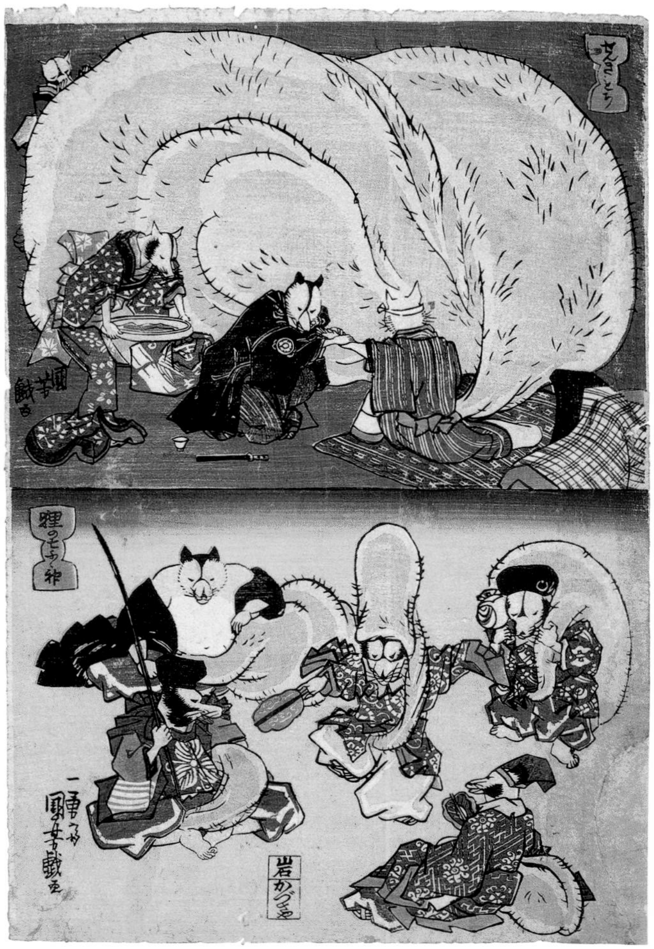

411
Utagawa Kuniyoshi, *Seven Gods of Happiness Represented by Tanuki*, no date. © Machida City Museum

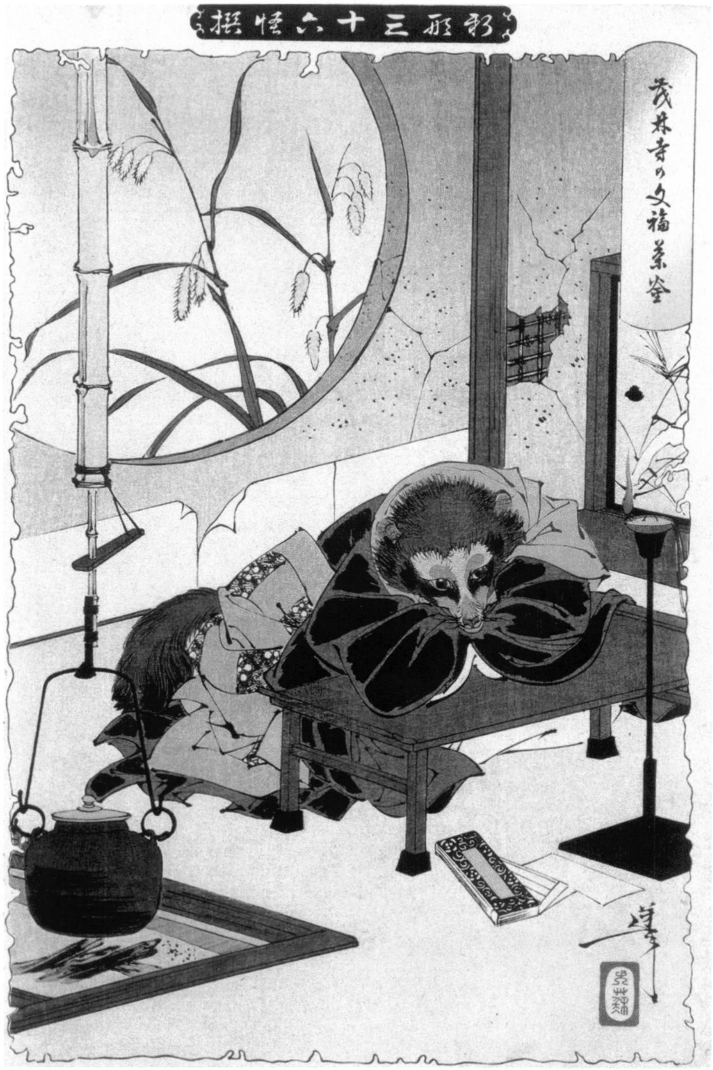
新形三十六怪撰
茂林寺の文福茶釜

412
Tsukioka Yoshitoshi, *Bumbuku Chagama* (*The Enchanted Teapot*), 1892. © Machida City Museum

An old man saves the life of a *tanuki* that, to his singular surprise, then turns into a teapot. He goes off to sell it in the temple, but each time someone touches it, it transforms into a *tanuki* and makes its way back to the old man. As the *tanuki* undergoes his myriad metamorphoses, he earns the old man a lot of money. There are several popular variants of this tale.

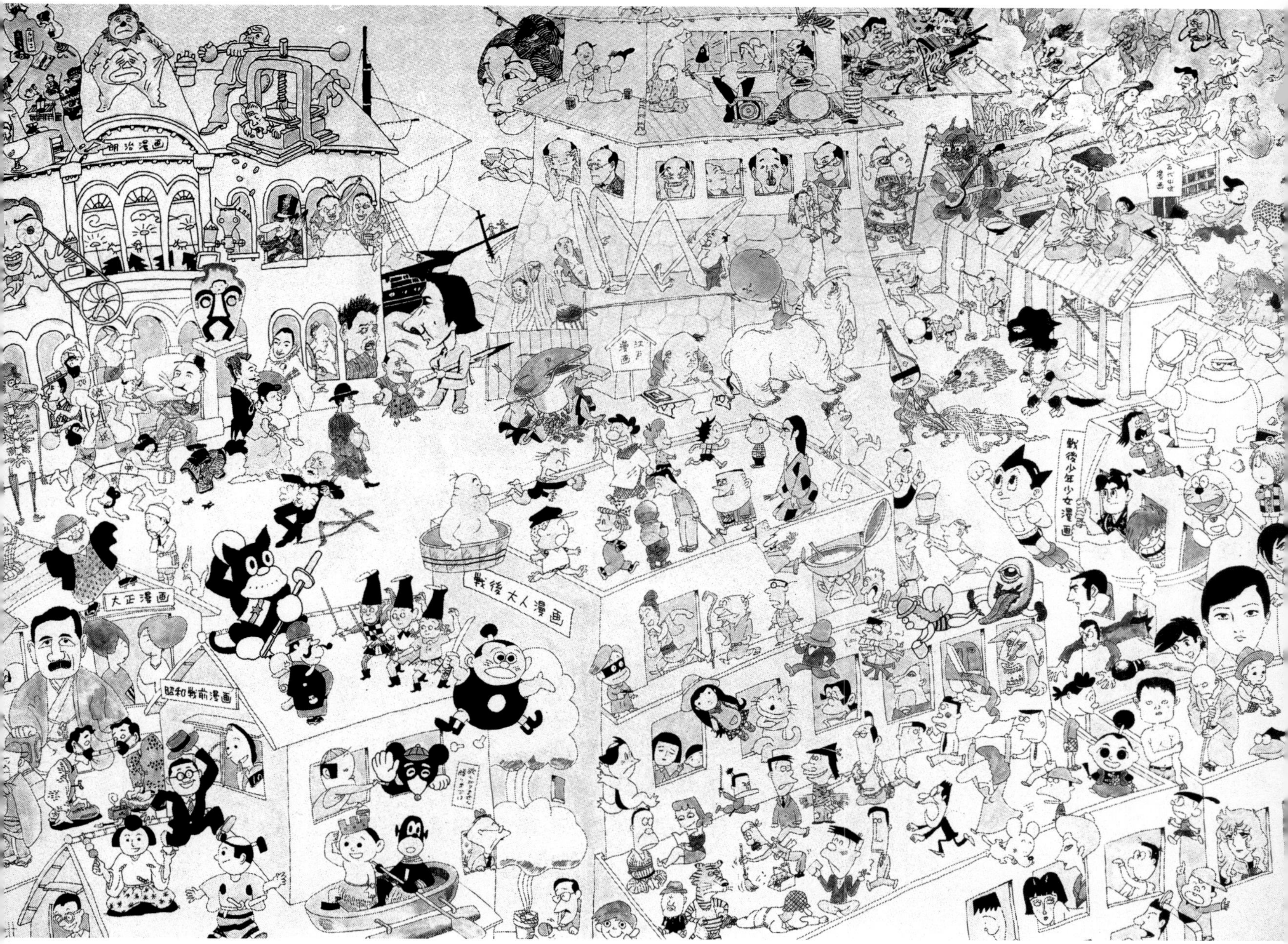
明治漫画
江戸漫画
大正漫画
戦後大人漫画
戦後少年少女漫画
昭和戦前漫画

413
Maekawa Shinsuke, *Nihon Manga no nagare*
(The Current of the Manga). © Kawasaki City Museum

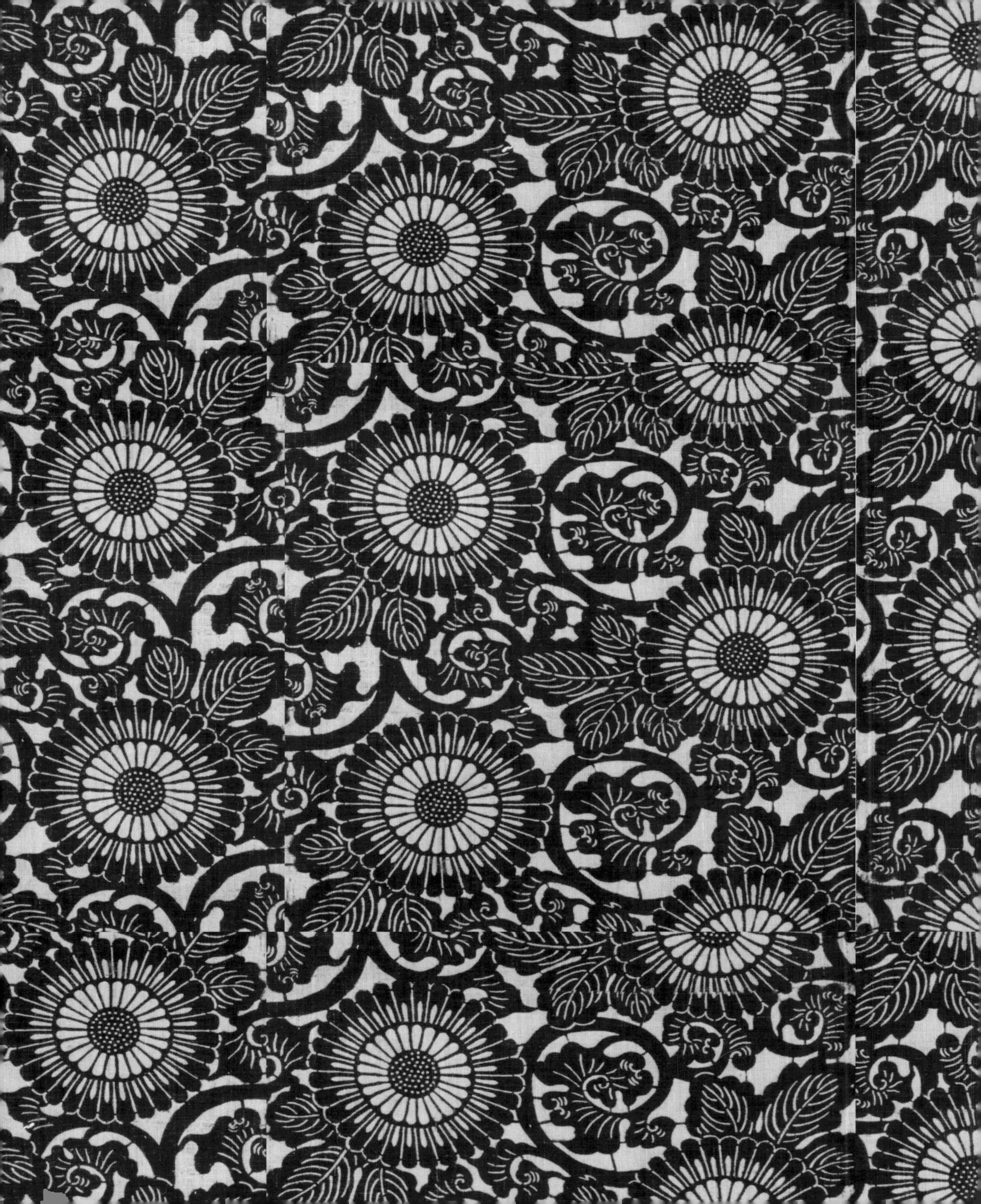

INTERVIEW WITH TAKAHATA ISAO

In December 25, 2006, Takahata Isao was kind enough to grant me an interview. He spoke to me enthusiastically of Japanese culture and of French literature, with which he is extremely conversant. Fascinated by Jacques Prévert, he made recently brought out an annotated translation of two collections of the French poet's verse and has presented a CD of his finest songs. His sensitivity comes over as much in his translations as in his animations.

Brigitte Koyama-Richard: What do you think of the Western enthusiasm for manga and Japanese animation?

Takahata Isao: It amazes me.

B. K.-R.: And what about the deserved success of your own anime?

T. I.: Obviously I'm delighted, but I would like to make clear that we never sought to produce works for a foreign public. In making them, we took inspiration from what surrounds us. We create the films we want to, and are happy to see that people like them…

B. K.-R.: On many occasions you have said and written that manga and animation are indirectly influenced by prints and *emaki* hand scrolls.

T. I.: For sure. I don't like the word "influence," however. Rather there has been continuity in Japanese painting and culture since the appearance of the *emaki* scroll. One cannot explain the existence of manga and Japanese animation solely by reference to American cartoons and comic strips, and still less by the caricatures of Hogarth, Goya, and Daumier. One has to go back well before then, to the *Scroll of Birds and Animals* and to that of *The Legends of Mount Shigi*.

B. K.-R.: What are the main characteristics of Japanese drawing?

T. I.: Its line. From the beginning, the Japanese have known about using line. Hokusai, Hiroshige, and Kuniyoshi all knew something of the chiaroscuro technique one finds in Western painting. And yet they did not employ it, and I think that their choice was a judicious one. In his series of *Hundred Views of Edo*, Hiroshige manages perfectly well to render perspective by drawing certain elements as flat tints and superimposing them towards a vanishing point. The painters of the *ukiyo-e** executed their portraits of beautiful women solely in line.

The faces of the Japanese are flatter than those of Westerners and their noses far less prominent. For that reason they were able draw faces from the front, just with line and color. You will notice how George Bigot painted his Japanese characters with noses longer and more pointed than local artists ever did. It was probably just impossible for him to draw noses that small!

It is then only natural that, in a country like Japan, where the tradition of pictures made up of lines is deeply rooted, animations where the colors are applied in blocks are much appreciated. There are no shadows in Japanese animation. I think that the tradition of the *ukiyo-e* print—having passed through works by artists such as Mucha, and Bilibine, books illustration, as well as comic books, etc.—today lives on in animation that uses cel.

B. K.-R.: I would like you to say something about *Pompoko (The Raccoon War)*. Why did you choose *tanuki* when tackling the problem of cities encroaching on the countryside?

T. I.: It's a subject very dear to my heart. Accounts of *tanuki* changing shape are ever-present in traditional culture, but it was reckoned a stupid subject and nobody took the risk of going with it. I admit the first time that I saw a real *tanuki* I was disappointed, because the ones in the folktales seemed so much more interesting. In transposing the metamorphosis of the *tanuki* to our era, I employed it in all its forms: the real animal and the shape it takes in manga and in *ukiyo-e** prints—for example, Sugiura Shigeru's manga and the *tanuki* of Kuniyoshi. As for the *yokai*, I borrowed them from the painting scroll, *The Night Parade of One Hundred Demons*, and from prints by Hokusai and Kuniyoshi.

B. K.-R.: As you see it, *emaki* hand scrolls occupy a crucial place in Japanese culture, don't they?

T. I.: Yes, absolutely. They are the predecessors of both manga and of animation. With just line and color, they manage to let a story unfold by controlling the element of time. I will not go so far as to say that they lie at its root, but I think that manga, like animation, do have a place in the current of traditional pictorial expression, just like painting scrolls and *ukiyo-e* prints.

B. K.-R.: What are your plans?

T. I.: I have so many, and only time will tell whether I'll manage to carry them all out. But, apart from our own output, we want to make works by talented foreign animators better known to Japanese audiences. Thus every year we introduce a number of artists who enrich our culture of animation. We seek to open ourselves to outsiders because there are many foreign productions that deserve the attention of a Japanese public.

B. K.-R.: Thank you for your time.

The very strength of manga and Japanese anime, which makes these two genres into a veritable pictorial culture, derives from the fact that they are anchored in Japanese ancestral civilization, in which art and literature were inextricably linked. The works of Takahata Isao serve as a magnificent example.

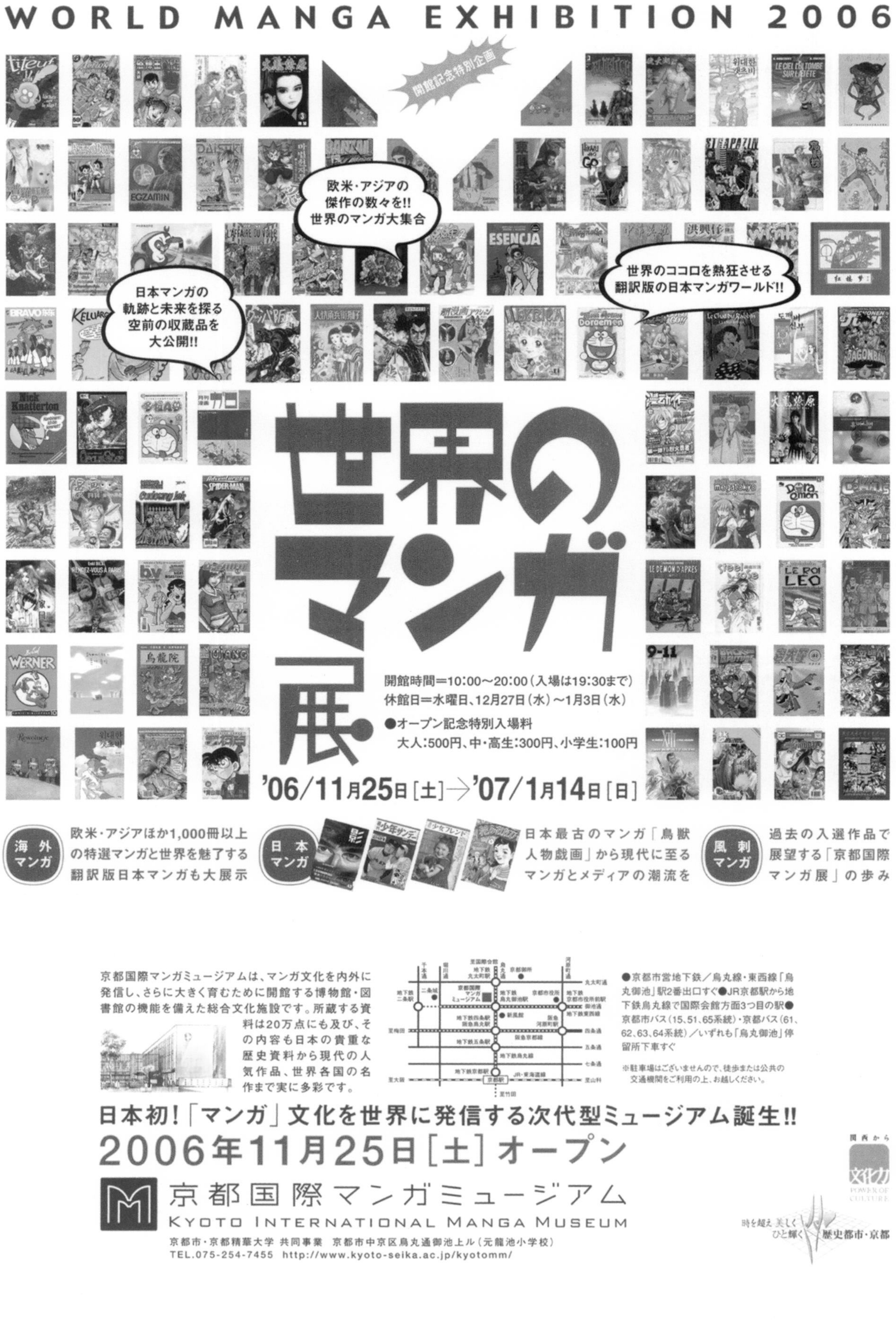
WORLD MANGA EXHIBITION 2006
開館記念特別企画
欧米・アジアの傑作の数々を!! 世界のマンガ大集合
世界のココロを熱狂させる翻訳版の日本マンガワールド!!
日本マンガの軌跡と未来を探る空前の収蔵品を大公開!!
世界のマンガ展
開館時間＝10:00～20:00（入場は19:30まで）
休館日＝水曜日、12月27日（水）～1月3日（水）
●オープン記念特別入場料
大人:500円、中・高生:300円、小学生:100円
'06/11月25日[土]→'07/1月14日[日]
海外マンガ
欧米・アジアほか1,000冊以上の特選マンガと世界を魅了する翻訳版日本マンガも大展示
日本マンガ
日本最古のマンガ「鳥獣人物戯画」から現代に至るマンガとメディアの潮流を
風刺マンガ
過去の入選作品で展望する「京都国際マンガ展」の歩み
京都国際マンガミュージアムは、マンガ文化を内外に発信し、さらに大きく育むために開館する博物館・図書館の機能を備えた総合文化施設です。所蔵する資料は20万点にも及び、その内容も日本の貴重な歴史資料から現代の人気作品、世界各国の名作まで実に多彩です。
●京都市営地下鉄／烏丸線・東西線「烏丸御池」駅2番出口すぐ●JR京都駅から地下鉄烏丸線で国際会館方面3つ目の駅●京都市バス（15、51、65系統）・京都バス（61、62、63、64系統）／いずれも「烏丸御池」停留所下車すぐ
※駐車場はございませんので、徒歩または公共の交通機関をご利用の上、お越しください。
日本初!「マンガ」文化を世界に発信する次代型ミュージアム誕生!!
2006年11月25日[土]オープン
京都国際マンガミュージアム
KYOTO INTERNATIONAL MANGA MUSEUM
京都市・京都精華大学 共同事業 京都市中京区烏丸通御池上ル（元龍池小学校）
TEL.075-254-7455 http://www.kyoto-seika.ac.jp/kyotomm/
関西から 文化力 POWER OF CULTURE
時を超え 美しく ひと輝く 歴史都市・京都

Some of the *mangaka* I had the pleasure of meeting readily explained why they looked for inspiration in the culture of the Edo* period—or even in more remote periods of their history—in choosing subjects for their works, while others expressed little awareness of the cultural rootedness that makes manga, even when imitated in other countries, a unique phenomenon.

One cannot, of course, deny the influence of Western culture on Japanese comic strips, caricatures, and manga throughout the twentieth century, but it is obvious that this influence has always been a two-way process. Those who affirm that manga owes everything to the Occident forget that Western painters and caricaturists were often, consciously or not, marked by the Japanese paintings and prints brought to Europe and the United States at the end of the nineteenth century and the beginning of the twentieth.

Subsequently the artistic movement that then developed, known by the name *japonisme*, also had an impact on comics and animations, including Walt Disney (as shown in the exhibition held at the Galeries du Grand Palais in Paris in 2006–07). In the nineteenth century, the Japanese, who had failed to appreciate the esthetic and cultural value of their brocade prints, let them leave to the West, where they were collected with a passion and snapped up by connoisseurs and artists into whose attitudes and art they fed.

In the twentieth century, Japan long hesitated to acknowledge manga as a key influence in its popular culture. One had to await the beginning of the twenty-first century to see the first museum devoted to manga open in Kyoto, in November 2006.

Astonished by the enthusiasm aroused by manga abroad, the Japanese are more and more aware of the historical and graphical richness of these thousands of volumes, which henceforth form part of their cultural heritage and which the artist Maekawa Shinsuke summarizes so well in his picture.

414

The poster for the exhibition "Cartoons [manga] of the World" that took place in 2006 at the International Museum of Manga. © International Museum of Manga

GLOSSARY

Aka-hon: "Red book." The word was forged in 1673 during the Edo period due to books of this type being issued in red covers. It was readopted after the Second World War for manga with colorful and predominantly red covers.

Akihabara: a district in Tokyo selling primarily household appliances and computer equipment which has recently turned to anime, video games, and manga merchandise.

Anime: Japanese animated films.

Anpan: small round bun filled with kidney-bean paste.

Ao-hon: "Green book." Volumes produced at the end of the eighteenth century that took their themes from the kabuki theater.

Asobi-e: term designating playful prints.

Bakufu, the: military government of the Shogun.

Baren: sort of pad wrapped in a bamboo leaf with a string made of bamboo fiber. The printer uses the *baren* to rub the sheet of paper placed on the wooden board, so printing the colors.

Bijinga: print showing female beauties.

Bishôjo: manga depicting lesbianism.

Bishônen: manga describing the experience of love between young men.

Bunraku: Traditional Japanese puppet theater founded in Osaka in the seventeenth century.

Bushi or samurai: warrior of the time of Tokugawa.

Bushidô: "Way of the Warrior." Set of laws rooted in the loyalty and faithfulness of a vassal towards his lord.

Chônin: term designating artisans and merchants in the Edo period.

Chonmage: traditional male hairstyle in which the hair is put up into a chignon or topknot and the top of the skull shaved.

Daimyô: overlord or governor of a province.

Dainagon: title given to state councilors from 702.

Daruma: or *Bodai-Daruma*: Japanese name of Bodhidharma (fifth to sixth century), an Indian Buddhist monk who is meant to have reached China at the end of the fifth century. Founder of the Zen sect.

Ecchi (see *etchi*).

Edo: today's Tokyo. It was the capital of the Tokugawa from 1603 to 1867.

Ehon: illustrated book on various themes.

Emaki or *emakimono*: painting scroll.

Emonogatari: illustrated narrative.

E-sugoroku: a sort of board game.

Etchi: erotic manga.

Ezôshiya: in the Edo period, store selling prints.

Fusuma: wall partition made of patterned Japanese paper.

Gekiga: manga that started appearing in the 1950s with themes and a graphic style rooted in reality.

Geta: traditional clogs.

Giga: humorous drawings, caricature.

Goodies: merchandise derived from manga and anime.

Hakama: broad pleated trousers resembling a divided skirt.

Hangi: board for woodcuts.

Hanmoto: publisher of prints and illustrated books.

Hashira-e: long, narrow prints, of variable size, intended to be hung on pillars around the house.

Hentai: pornographic manga with a penchant for perversity.

Hon: in Japanese, "book."

Hôshôgami: Fine-quality Japanese paper, incorporating embossing, on which the most luxurious prints are pulled.

Hyakki yagyô: procession or parade of one hundred demons that goes abroad at night.

Ichimai-e: print printed on a single sheet.

Japanimation: term of American origin designating Japanese animated films or animes.

Jidai geki: manga with an historical storyline set before the Meiji era.

Jihon donya: non-specialist publisher.

Jizô: Jizô Bosatsu, Japanese Buddhist form of the *bodhisattva* Kshitigarbha. In Japan, he is ascribed with the power of providing children and guarding roads.

Josei manga: manga for young women.

Jûni-hitoe: formal attire consisting in several (up to twelve) colored kimonos worn one over the other.

Kabuki: popular dramatic art that developed in Japan towards the end of the seventeenth century.

Kakejiku: traditional hanging scroll.

Kakemono: paint or calligraphy scroll unrolling top to bottom.

Kami: in Shintoism, the divine spirits.

Kami shibai: strolling theater for children, using pictures on paper, which attained great success following the Second World War.

Kannon: often represented in a female manifestation, Kannon Bosatsu is the most popular *bodhisattva* in Japan.

Kanô: celebrated school of painting of the Edo era whose works were intended primarily for the aristocracy.

Kappa: mythical amphibian that lives in water. The size of a young child, it possesses a human body and a tortoise's head, with short tufty hair like a crown. Although benevolent towards humans, it can play tricks on them.

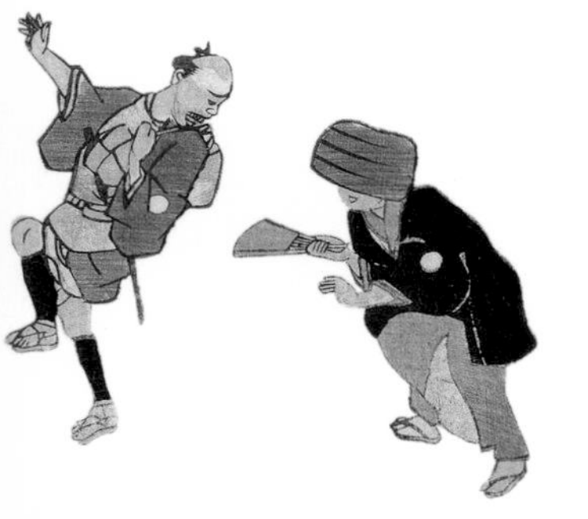

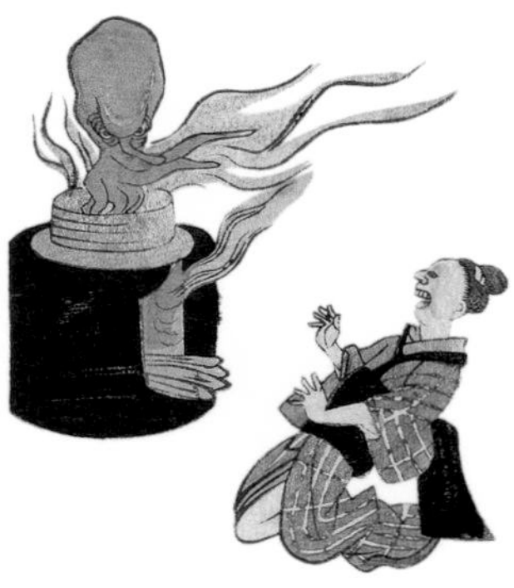

Kashihon manga: lending bookstall, hire bookshop.

Kawaii: "cute".

Kentô: a notch in the woodcut board that allows the printer to hold the sheet of paper firmly to ensure accurate registration.

Kibyôshi: chapbook with a yellow cover.

Kitsune: a fox to whom many supernatural powers were ascribed.

Koban: a currency of the Edo era.

Kokkeibon: little books of comic content that became extremely popular in the Edo period.

Kôsenga: style of landscape print that incorporates Western-style perspective.

Kuro-hon: "Black books" containing primarily kabuki plays, between 1744 and 1751.

Kusa-zôshi: illustrated books in the Edo period.

Kyôka: a poem composed of thirty-one syllables, fashionable in the Edo era.

Manga: term used for the first time by Katsushika Hokusai to designate a "collection of drawings for learning to paint." In the beginning, then, the word was synonymous with neither caricature nor comic strip. The meaning the term has today dates only from the twentieth century.

Mangaka: person who draws manga.

Manga kissa: "manga café" stocking large numbers of Manga which customers pay to read by the hour.

Miko: girl or young woman serving in a Shinto sanctuary.

Misemono: public entertainments in the Edo era.

Mitate-e: traditional subject humorously reworked and updated with a hint of parody.

Mon: insignia of a family, clan, individual, or even a store.

Namazu-e: print representing a catfish that was supposed to act as protection against serious earthquakes.

Nanga: "Southern painting." This style of landscape painting was brought by the Chinese to the city of Nagasaki in the south of Japan at the beginning of the eighteenth century and developed over the two following centuries.

Nara ehon: luxury book in the Edo period.

Nenjûgyôji: annual rites and ceremonies.

Nihon-ga: painting in the Japanese style (Nihon=Japan; ga=painting).

Ninja: person trained in espionage and assassination.

Ninjôbon: popular storybooks of the Edo era.

Nishiki-e: polychrome, so-called "brocade" prints pulled using more than three colors, created in 1765 by the painter Suzuki Harunobu.

Noren: a bolt of cloth with a slit, decorated with the insignia of the tradesman, hoisted each morning above the entrance door to a store to show that it is open.

Nozoki karakuri: images in perspective that are observed through an optical box.

Obake: phantom, ghost.

Ôban: paper format (approximately 15 x 9 ¾ in. [38 x 25 cm]) used for certain *ukiyo-e* prints.

Obi: kimono belt.

Oiran: courtesan.

Ôkubi-e: print representing a portrait bust. Utamaro's likenesses of courtesans were especially renowned, as were the portraits of actors such as those left by the enigmatic Sharaku.

Oni: a general name given to the demons of Japanese folklore.

Otaku: a "couch potato," whose enthusiasms are not necessarily confined to manga.

Ôtsu-e: popular paintings executed by Ôtsu craftsmen for pilgrimages.

Ponchi-e: word derived from "Punch," meaning caricatures.

Rangaku: "Dutch studies." This term includes the sciences and technologies in general that came from the West.

Rangakusha: a specialist in "Dutch studies" in the Edo period.

Rônin: a samurai without a master.

Ryôgoku: one of the most famous bridges in Edo over the River Sumida on which splendid firework displays were held often represented in prints.

Samurai: a warrior attached to a feudal lord.

Sankin kôtai: alternate service imposed by the government of the Tokugawa that obliged feudal nobles to reside in the city of Edo for months at a time.

Sechie-zumô: sumo bout formerly held in the presence of the emperor.

Sei-i-tai shôgun: supreme head.

Seinen manga: manga for young adult male readers.

Seppuku: ritual suicide

Shamisen: three-stringed musical instrument.

Sharebon: writings on the lives of courtesans in the Edo period.

Shinôkôshô: name given to the society of Edo divided into the four classes, warriors, peasants, artisans, and merchants.

Shogun: governor.

Shogunate: government of the Tokugawa.

Shôji: sliding partitions with a frame stretched with light paper.

Shôjo ai: see *bishôjo*.

Shôjo manga: manga for girls.

Shomotsu: anthology of religious and scholarly works.

Shônen ai: see *bishônen*.

Shônen manga: manga for boys.

Shunga: erotic print.

Sôshi: diverting book illustrated with prints.

Story manga: very long and involved manga narratives invented by Tezuka Osamu at the beginning of the 1950s.

Sugoroku: a game like backgammon or tric-trac.

Sumizuri-e: primitive print in black ink.

Sumo: ritual wrestling match between two opponents held in the center of a circular arena. Very old, it was democratized in the Edo period and today still attracts great crowds and high TV ratings. Currently increasing numbers of the best fighters, called *sumôtori*, come from abroad.

Surimono: luxury prints on the finest paper and in the rarest color pigments, made for special occasions at the request of poets' clubs and not put on sale.

Sûtra kyô: Buddhist scriptures.

Tanabata: feast day falling on the seventh day of the seventh moon according to the solar calendar that celebrates the reunion between the Herdsman and the Weaver.

Tanuki: protean animal, a kind of raccoon, a member of the Japanese folklore bestiary.

Tengu: a fantastic beast of Japanese legend. Winged but with a human body and often endowed with a long nose, it is a frightening and much-feared creature.

Tera: Buddhist temple.

Terakoya: in the Edo period, schools set up in the precincts of Buddhist temples.

Tôba-e: caricatures of the Edo era whose name comes from the monk Tôba, to whom the scroll of *Frolicking Animals and People* is ascribed.

Tokaido: road connecting Kyoto and Edo represented in many prints.

Tokonoma: a space in a dwelling serving to display a flower vase, an objet d'art, or a *kakemono*.

Tokugawa: the surname of the Shogun that seized power in 1603, keeping it until 1867.

Tsukumogami: "spirit of old objects," "artifact spirit."

Ubuyu: a newborn baby's ceremonial first bath.

Uchiwa: a fan of almost circular shape.

Uchiwa-e: print in which the contour of the fan forms the frame in the image.

Uki-e: print depicting a view in Western-type perspective.

Ukiyo-e: paintings and prints of the "Floating World." The term covers amusements, theater, teahouses, actors, courtesans, etc.; hence, an "ephemeral world."

Ukiyo-zôshi: popular tale inspired by the "Floating World."

Waka: classic thirty-one syllable poem.

Yakusha-e: prints showing half-length portraits of actors.

Yôkai: monsters, apparitions, and supernatural beasts in traditional folktales.

Yokohama: large port located close to Tokyo that fulfilled an important role in trade with the West in the time of the Meiji.

Yokohama-e: print of Yokohama portraying the opening of Japan to the West and its subsequent modernization.

Yoshiwara: pleasure quarters in the city of Edo.

TIMELINE

Prehistory: to 538 C.E.

Jomon culture: early pottery

Yayoi culture: from 600 B.C.E. to 3rd cent. C.E.

538–710 Asuka period
710–784 Nara period
794–1185 Heina period
1185–1333 Kamakura period
1336–1573 Muromachi period
1573–1598 Monoyama period
1603–1867 Edo period
1868–1912 Meiji era
1912–1926 Taishô era
1926–1989 Shôwa era
1989– Heisei era

OUR ANCESTORS THE *MANGAKA*

BIGOT, Georges Ferdinand (1860–1927). French painter and caricaturist. In 1883 he traveled to Japan where he taught painting at the Military Academy in Tokyo and produced illustrations and caricatures for many newspapers. He returned to France in 1899, having been a war correspondent during the Sino-Japanese conflict.

CONDER, Josiah (1852–1920). English architect. He designed many Western-style buildings in Japan and trained young Japanese architects. A talented artist, he also learned traditional painting techniques from Kawanabe Kyôsai.

FUJITA Tsuguharu, Leonard (known as FUJITA) (1886–1968). Japanese painter, member of the School of Paris.

FUKUZAWA Yukichi (1834–1901). Japanese man of letters, journalist, and philosopher. He set up the newspaper *Jiji Shinpô*, famous for its caricatures, and founded Keiô University in Tokyo. After a sojourn in Europe, he endeavored to make Western culture more widely known in his homeland.

HIRAGA Gennai (1728–1779). Japanese scientist, playwright, and painter. He founded the first Western-style painting school.

HIROSHIGE, see UTAGAWA Hiroshige Andô.

HOKUSAI, see KATSUSHIKA Hokusai.

ITÔ Hirobumi (1841–1909). Politician who occupied various high positions, including those of Minister of the Interior and Prime Minister.

KANAGAKI Robun (1829–1894). Writer, humorist, and journalist, author of *Seiyô dôchû hizakurige* (Shank's Mare to the Western Seas, 1870–76) and *Agura nabe* (The Beefeater, 1871–72).

KATSUSHIKA Hokusai (1760–1849). *Ukiyo-e** printmaker. He was the most widely appreciated Japanese artist in Europe in the second half of the nineteenth century and influenced many Western painters. His extremely rich and varied oeuvre comprises series such as *The Thirty-six Views of Mount Fuji*, as well as the celebrated *Manga*. In the West, Edmond de Goncourt was the first to devote a biography to him, compiled with the assistance of Hayashi Tadamasa.

KAWANABE Kyôsai (1831–1889). *Ukiyo-e* printmaker of the Kanô* school. His many-faceted talent made him a favorite with foreigners then residing in Japan. He met Guimet and Régamey, as well as the Australian painter, Menpes. His friend and disciple Josiah Conder left a book of memoirs documenting his life.

KEISAI Eisen (1790–1848). Japanese artist who produced a large number of paintings, *ukiyo-e* prints, and book illustrations. He is famous for his landscapes and *bijinga**, or pictures showing beautiful women.

KITAGAWA Utamaro (1753–1806). *Ukiyo-e* printmaker. Like Hokusai, he exerted a considerable influence on Western art in the second half of the nineteenth century. He worked with the famous publisher Tsutaya Jûzaburô, bringing out works such as *The Book of Insects, The Directory of "Green Houses,"* etc. He also painted some very fine portraits of courtesans.

KITAZAWA Rakuten (1876–1955). A pioneer of manga.

KOBAYASHI Kiyochika (1847–1915). Printmaker and engraver. He also learned the technique of oil painting and photography, and created a new style called "*kôsenga*" ("images of light"), designed to translate chiaroscuro effects and variations in hue. He was active during the opening up of Japan, producing many cartoons for newspapers and reviews.

KÛKAI (Kôbô Daishi) (774–835). Buddhist monk considered as the intellectual mentor of the aristocracy of the time, and as the forefather of classic Japanese culture.

NAKAE Chômin (1847–1901). Japanese philosopher. He learned French and, in 1871, left for France to study literature and philosophy there. He also founded *Tôyô jiyû shinbun* (The Free Newspaper of the Orient) as well as a political periodical.

NATSUME Sôseki (1867–1916). The foremost Japanese writer and thinker of modern times.

ÔKUMA Shigenobu (1838–1922). Politician who actively supported the imperial cause at the time of the Meiji Restoration. Well read, he studied English and Dutch. He occupied high political posts and founded Waseda University in Tokyo.

SHIBA Kôkan (1747–1818). Japanese painter. In the 1780s, he traveled to Nagasaki where he worked with Hiraga Gennai and became

acquainted with Western science. His paintings were inspired by Western theories of perspective and geometry. He also produced copperplate engravings and prints.

SHIKITEI Sanba (1776–1822). Japanese playwright. *Ukiyoburo* (1809–13) is one of his best-known works.

SUZUKI Harunobu (1725?–1770). *Ukiyo-e* printmaker. He was the first to produce multicolored woodblock prints.

TOKIWA Mitsunaga (active towards the end of the Heian period). Court painter. The scroll *Ban dainagon emaki* (now listed as a National Treasure) is ascribed to him.

TOKUGAWA Ieyasu (1542–1616). Warrior and founder of the hereditary dynasty of the Tokugawa Shogun*. Having overcome his enemies at the battle of Sekigahara in 1600, he became the most powerful *daimyo**, in 1603 accepting the title of *sei-i-tai shôgun** to the emperor. Unchallenged, he established a new capital at Edo*, which was to take the name Tokyo in 1868.

TOMO no Yoshio (809–868). Minister at the court of the emperor. Exposed as having set on fire the door to the Ôtenmon Imperial Palace at Kyôto in 866, and having deflected the guilt for his act onto his political enemy, Minamoto no Makoto, he was sent into exile.

TOYOTOMI Hideyori (1593–1615). Son of Toyotomi Hideyoshi and his favorite, Yodogimi. After a fruitless bid for power, he was defeated by Tokugawa Ieyasu and committed suicide.

TOYOTOMI Hideyoshi (1536–1598). Japanese warrior. In 1587, he banned Christianity and paved the way for the unification of Japan completed by Tokugawa Ieyasu.

UTAGAWA Hiroshige Andô (1797–1858). Japanese painter. He was a pupil of the artist Utagawa Toyohiro (1773–1828). His work is devoted primarily to landscape, including world-famous series such as *The Fifty-three Stations of the Tokaido*, *The Hundred Views of Edo*, etc.

UTAGAWA Kuniyoshi (1797–1861). *Ukiyo-e* printmaker also known as Ichiyûsai Kuniyoshi. His disciples included Kawanabe Kyôsai.

UTAGAWA Yoshimori (1830–1885). Printmaker and disciple of Utagawa Kuniyoshi.

UTAMARO, see KITAGAWA Utamaro.

CHRONOLOGY

Seventh century: Caricatures of the Hôryûji.

Twelfth century: Many painting scrolls such as the *Scroll of Frolicking Birds and Animals*, and the *Scrolls of the Legends of Mount Shigi*, etc. are made by artists.

Twelfth to seventeenth century: Painting scrolls, folding-screens and paintings are essentially aimed at the aristocracy or monks. The merchant and artisan classes will have to wait until the Edo* period to benefit from a fledgling culture of their own.

Edo period (1603–1867): Illuminated books, then volumes printed by woodblock. Hand-tinted woodblock prints; followed by appearance of brocade prints in about 1765. In these prints, one finds the first evidence of "wood bubbles," and of all kinds of pictorial expressions that will reappear in manga* proper. Ôtsu images, the *Ôtsu-e**, are all the rage.

1720: Several publications of *Tôba-e**.

1794: Sharaku paints numerous portraits of *kabuki** actors.

1814: The publication of the first volume of *Manga* by Hokusai.

1848: Utagawa Kuniyoshi paints his famous "recomposed" faces.

1855: Terrible earthquake in Edo—prints representing a catfish are sold.

1862: Charles Wirgman founds *The Japan Punch*.

1874: Publication of the review, *E Shinbun Nipponchi*, and *Kyôsai rakuga*, thumbnail sketches by Kawanabe Kyôsai.

1877: The review *Marumaru Chinbun* first comes out.

1881: *Kiyochika Punch*, periodical by Kobayashi Kiyochika.

1882: Arrival in Japan of the French painter and caricaturist Georges Bigot.

1887: Publication of Bigot's review, *Tobae*.

1901: Miyatake Gaikotsu sets up the magazine *Kokkei Shinbun*.

1902: The newspaper *Jiji Shinpô* starts a satirical comic-strip column on political and social life, *Jiji manga*, in its Sunday numbers.

1905: Kitazawa Rakuten founds the review *Tokyo Puck*.

1906: Publication of the review *Osaka Puck*.

1907: Following the fad for postcards, Miyatake Gaikotsu founds *The World of Postcards*, which includes cut-out humorous postcards.

1912: Kitazawa Rakuten sets up the reviews *Rakuten Puck* and *Katei Puck*.

1915: Okamoro Ippei establishes The Tokyo manga kai, or Association of Tokyo Manga.

1921: *Jiji Shinpô* includes a whole Sunday supplement with manga dealing with political stories.

1923: The review *Asahi Gurafu* publishes serial manga, like the *Adventures of Shôchan, Nonki ni tôsan* (A Careless Father).

1924: Publication of the first real review for children, *Kodomo Puck*.

1929: Kitazawa Rakuten leaves on a journey to Europe and the United States.

1931: Publication of the manga *Nora Kuro* by Tagawa Suiko in *Shônen Kurabu*.

1944–1946: For the most part, newspapers cease featuring manga.

1947: *Aka-hon* Manga*, manga with red covers, flourish.

1949: *Sazae san*, one of the most popular post-war manga, appears. Its author, Hasegawa Machiko, is the first woman *mangaka** to have her talent recognized.

1950: Tezuka Osamu settles in Tokyo and publishes *Kimba the Lion*.

1952: Tezuka Osamu's *Tetorwan Atomu (Astro Boy)* begins publication in the review, *Shônen*.

1953: Launch of the NHK television channel.

1955: Publication of several manga magazines: *Bokura, Nakayoshi, Ribon*, etc.

1961: Tezuka Osamu founds his animation company, Mushi Production.

1963: *Astro Boy* becomes the first twenty-minute TV animation series. Publication of the magazines *Shôjo Friend* and *Margaretto*.

1964: Publication of *Obake no Q-Tarô (Q-Taro)* by Fujiko Fujio in the magazine, *Shonen Sunday*.

1966: *Shônen Magazine* exceeds a print run of a million. Opening of the Ômiya Museum of Manga on the site of Kitazawa Rakuten's house.

1968: Publication of the magazine, *Garo*.

1970: Public funeral of Riki-ishi Tôru, a character from the manga *Ashita no Joe*, by Chila Tetsuya and Kajiwara Ihki.

1972: Beginning of the publication of *The Rose of Versailles* by Ikeda Riyoko in *Margaretto*.

1973: Tezuka Osamu's *Black Jack*.

1975: *Candy* by Igarashi Yumiko.

1976: *Comiket*, a new fanzine market, starts in Tokyo.

1977: Publication of the complete works of Tezuka Osamu by Kôkenda publishing. Matsumoto Leiji creates *Captain Harlock*.

1980: First manga for women: *Be in Love*. The combined sales of the five weekly magazines: *Shônen Magazine, Shônen Sunday, Shônen King, Shônen Jump, Shônen Champion* exceed ten million for the special New Year's Day number.

1982: Ôtomo Katsuhiro's *Akira*. *Nausicaä of the Valley of the Wind* by Miyazaki Hayao

1985: *Dragon Ball* by Toriyama Akira.

1986: Beginning of the publication of *Chibi Marukochan* in the magazine *Ribon*, and of *Introduction to the Japanese Economy*, a manga by Ishinomori Shôtarô.

1988: *Shônen Jump's* print run exceeds five million.

1989: Death of Tezuka Osamu.

1990: Exhibition dedicated to Tezuka Osamu at the Museum of Modern Art of the City of Tokyo. The same year, a show in honor of Wirgman on the hundredth anniversary of his death in Kobe and Yokohama. CLAMP publishes *RG Veda*.

1992: Takeuchi Nasko's *Sailor Moon* becomes a huge success.

1994: The Tezuka Osamu Museum opens.

1996: Beginning of *Pocket Monster*.

1997: Publication of Oda Eiichirô's *One Piece*. Appearance of *manga kissa*, cafés where manga are available to read.

1999: Success of Yazawa Ai's *Nana*. *Naruto* by Kishimoto Masashi.

2000: Classical music becomes fashionable as a manga topic thanks to *Nodame no Cantabile* by Ninomiya Tomoko. The University of Seika in Kyoto opens the first department for comic strips.

2002: Beginning of the review *Manga Kenkyû* ("Manga Studies"), published by Nihon Manga gakkai, the Japanese Manga Association. Publication of the monthly magazine *Shônen Jump* in English. *One Piece* reaches 2.6 million copies for the first run, a record.

2003: *Pluto* by Urasawa Naoki. *Adventures of Shôchan* reprinted. The Mizuki Shigeru Museum opens. Many events celebrate the fictional date of birth of *Astro Boy*.

2004: *Death Note* by Ôba Tsugumi, Olata Takeshi.

2005: The teaching of manga and anime develops in Japanese universities.

2006: Opening of the Kyoto International Manga Museum.

2007: January 16, 2007, launch of *Gumbo*, the first free manga magazine, published by Dijima. On April 18, a funeral for Raôh, a celebrated character from the manga *Hokuto no Ken* (*Ken the Survivor*) takes place at the Kôyasan temple, Tokyo. More than three thousand people attend the ceremony in driving rain. This marks the first time that a temple has agreed to hold a funeral for a manga character. The International Manga Prize, created in 2007 in Japan, was awarded for the first time in July 3, 2007 to Lee Chi Ching, a *mangaka* from Hong Kong, for his work as a whole.

RECENT STATISTICS FROM JAPAN

The most recent statistics pertaining to the state of the manga market in Japan in 2006 are provided by *Shuppan geppô*: a monthly publication report, *Komikku ichiba* (The Manga Market, 2006) Tokyo: Shuppan Kagaku Kenkyûjo, February 2007.

- Manga turnover fell 4.2 percent in 2006, with book sales dropping by 2.7 percent and reviews by 5.9 percent. "Media Mix" are on the upturn.
- Only the five largest publishing companies (Kôdansha, Shûeisha, Shogakukan, Akita Shoten, and Hakusuisha) kept pace. All the others have fallen by 10 percent.
- Over the last thirteen years, the market leader has been Detective Conan.
- The number of copies of manga has fallen by a record 7.4 percent.
- Sales of monthly reviews for children have fallen by 8.5 percent and for adults by 6 percent; weeklies for children have fallen by 7.4 percent, and for adults by 1.1 percent.
- In 2006, manga book sales represent 24,100,000,000 yen in 59,000,000 copies; there were 1,459 new titles, 59 more than in 2005. The average selling price of a manga is 408 yen, that is 2 yen more than in 2005.
- Manga Internet sales (for mobile telephones, etc.) has risen to 3,400,000,000 yen.

SELECTED BIBLIOGRAPHY

On the Japanese print and the Edo period, one may refer to the bibliography provided in Brigitte Koyama-Richard, *La Magie des estampes japonaises*, Paris: Hermann, 2003.

Works in Western languages

Amano, Masanao, and Julius Wiedeman, *Manga*, Cologne: Taschen, 2004.

Bande dessinée et figuration narrative, Musée des Arts Décoratifs/Palais du Louvre, Paris, March 1967.

Bastide, Julien and Anthony Prezman, *Guide des manga*, Paris: Bordas, 2006.

Bouquillard, Jocelyn and Christophe Marquet, *Hokusai Manga*, Paris: Bibliothèque Nationale de France/Seuil, 2007.

Calza, Gian Carlo (gen. ed.) *Hokusai*, London: Phaidon, 2005.

Du pinceau à la typographie. Regards japonais sur l'écriture et le livre, Études thématiques no. 20, École Française d'Extrême-Orient, Paris, 2006.

Gaumer, Patrick, *Larousse de la B.D.*, Paris: Larousse, 2004.

Goncourt, Edmond de, *Outamaro, Hokousaï*, Paris: 10/18 ("Fin de siècle"), 1986.

Gravett, Paul, *Manga. Sixty Years of Japanese Comics*, London: Laurence King, 2004.

Groensteen, Thierry, *L'Univers des mangas. Une introduction à la bande dessinée japonaise*, Paris: Casterman, 1996.

Groensteen, Thierry, *The System of Comics* (tr. N. Nyguen & B. Beaty), University of Mississippi Press, 1999.

Hu-Sterk, Florence, *La Beauté autrement. Introduction à l'esthétique chinoise*, Paris: Éditions You-Feng, 2004.

Koyama-Richard, Brigitte, *Japon rêvé : Edmond de Goncourt et Hayashi Tadamasa*, Paris: Hermann, 2001.

Koyama-Richard, Brigitte, *La Magie des estampes japonaises*, Paris: Hermann, 2003.

Koyama-Richard, Brigitte, *Kodomo-e: l'estampe japonaise et l'univers des enfants*, Paris: Hermann, 2004.

Linhartová, Véra, *Sur un fond blanc*, Paris: Éditions Le Promeneur/Gallimard, 1996.

Moliterni, Claude and Philippe Mellot, *Chronologie de la bande dessinée*, Paris: Flammarion ("Tout l'art"), 1996.

Nagata, Seiji, *Hokusai, Genius of the Japanese Ukiyo-e*, Tokyo: Kôdansha. Intl., 1999.

Petrucci, Raphael, *La Philosophie de la nature dans l'art d'Extrême-Orient*, Paris: Éditions You-Feng, 1998.

Schodt, Frederik L., *Manga! Manga! The World of Japanese Comics*, Tokyo: Kodansha, 1983.

Tillon, Fabien, *Les Manga*, Éditions Nouveau Monde ("Les Petits Illustrés"), 2005.

Reviews, catalogs

Animeland, le petit monde de la japanim et du manga, special number no. 5, June 2003.

Animeland, le petit monde de la japanim, vol. 2, special number no. 10, July–August 2006.

Le Guide Phénix du manga 2005–2006, Paris: Asuka, 2005 (the reference source for manga).

Exposition d'œuvres sur les us et coutumes japonais, tableaux de M. Rakuten Kitazawa de Tokio (exh. cat.), Salon d'Art Japonais at the Musée du Jeu de Paume, Paris, June 1929.

Catalogue of Paintings East and West by Rakuten Kitazawa of Tokyo, The Fine Art Society, Ltd., London, 1930.

Maîtres de la bande dessinée européenne, Bibliothèque Nationale de France, Paris: Seuil, 2000.

Oikawa, Shigeru, "Les dessins humoristiques de Georges Bigot, un peintre populaire au Japon et en France," *Humoresques*, January 23, 2006.

Tezuka. The Marvel of Manga (exh. cat.), published under the general editorship of Philip Brophy in partnership with Tezuka Productions, National Gallery of Victoria, Melbourne, 2006.

Selected works in Japanese

Hosogaya Atushi (gen. ed.), *Nihon Manga o shiru tame no bukku gaido* (A Guide to Books on Japanese Manga), Tokyo: Asian Manga Summit Japan Executive Committee, 2002.

Ichikawa Hiroaki and Ishikawa Hidekazu, *Edo no manabi, Apprendre à l'époque d'Edo*. Tokyo: Kawade shobô shinsha, 2006.

Ishiko Jun (illustrations by Tezuka Osamu), *Tezuka Osamu mirai kara no shisha* (Tezuka Osamu, the Messenger of the Future), Four Bunko B 200, Production Tezuka, Tokyo: Dôshin-sha, 2002.

Ishiko Jun (illustrations by Tezuka Osamu), *Tezuka Osamu Part 2, shônen manga no sekai* (Tezuka Osamu Part Two: the World of Manga for Boys), Four Bunko B 230, Tokyo: Dôshin-sha, 2000.

Ishiko Jun (illustrations by Tezuka Osamu), *Tezuka Osamu Part 3, Shôjo no manga no sekai* (Tezuka Osamu Part Two: the World of Manga for Girls), Four Bunko B 247, Tokyo: Dôshin-sha, 2002.

Kumon (gen. ed.), *Ukiyo-e no naka no kodomotachi* (*Children of the Edo Period as seen in Ukiyoe*), Tokyo: Kumon Publishing, Co., Ltd, 1993.

Matsumoto Leiji, Hidaka Bin, *Manga Dai hakubutsukan* (The Great Museum of Manga), Tokyo: Shogakukan Creative, 2004.

Minami Kazuo, *Edo no fûshi ga* (Caricatures in the Edo Period), Yoshikawa Kôbunkan, 1997.

Minami Kazuo, *Bakumatsu Edo no bunka Ukiyo-e to fûshiga* (Culture in the Bakufu [government] of Edo, *Ukiyo-e* [Prints] and Caricatures), Hanawa Shobô, 1998.

Miyahara Kojirô and Ogino Masahiro, *Manga no shakai gaku* (Sociology of the Manga), Tokyo: Sekai shisôsha, 2001.

Mizuki Shigeru, *Yôkaidô gojûsan tsugi* (The Fifty-three Views of the Yôkaidô), Tokyo: Yanoman, 2006.

Nagata Seiji, *Katsushika Hokusai*, Tokyo: Yoshikawa Kôbunkan, 2000.

Nagatani Kunio, *Manga no kôzôgaku* (study of the structure of manga, index), Tokyo, 2000.

Nakano Haruyuki, *Manga sangyô ron* (Theory of the Industry of Manga), Tokyo: Chikuma shobô, 2004.

Natsume Fusanosuke, *Manga no fukayomi otona yomi* (An Analytical Reading of Mangas for Adults), Tokyo: I-suto Puresu, 2004.

Natsume Fusanosuke, *Manga gaku e no chôsen, shinka suru hihyô chizu* (Tentative Research on Mangas, Plans, and Graphs on the Evolution of their Reception), Tokyo: NTT shuppan, 2004.

Natsume Fusanosuke, *Manga wa ima dô natte oru no ka ?* (What Is the Present Situation in Manga?), Tokyo: Media Selekuto, 2005.

Oikawa Shigeru, *Furansu no ukiyo-e shi Bigot, Bigot to epina-ru hanga* (The French Painter of *Ukiyo-e* Prints, Bigot; Bigot and Images d'Épinal"), Tokyo: Kodama-sha, 1998.

Okudaira Hideo, *Emakimono saihakken* (The Rediscovery of the *Emakimono*), Tokyo: Kadokawa Shoten, 1987.

Rakuten manga shû taisei, Taishô hen (General Collection of the Manga of Rakuten, Taishô Era), Ômiya: Kitazawa Rakuten Kenshôkai, 1973.

Rakuten manga shû taisei, Meiji hen (General Collection of the Manga of Rakuten, Meiji Era), Ômiya: Kitazawa Rakuten Kenshôkai, 1974.

Rakuten manga shû taisei, Shôwa hen (General Collection of the Manga of Rakuten, Shôwa Era), Ômiya: Kitazawa Rakuten Kenshôkai, 1976.

Shimizu Isao, *Koramu Manga kan, fûshi to asobi* (The Museum of Mangas, Caricatures, and Games), Tokyo: Shinshindô, 1984.

Shimizu Isao et al., *Kindai Manga Zen rokkan* (Modern Manga in Six Volumes), Tokyo: Chikuma Shobô, 1985.

Shimizu Isao, *Bigot: nihon sobyôshû* (Georges Bigot*:* Anthology of Drawings), Tokyo: Iwanami Bunko, Iwanami shoten, 1986.

Shimizu Isao, *Manga shonen to akahon Manga sengo Manga no tanjô* (Mangas for Boys and Mangas with Red Covers), Tokyo: Tôsui Shobô, 1989.

Shimizu Isao, *Ôsaka manga shi Manga bunka hasshin toshi 300 nen* (The History of Ôsaka Manga*:* 300 Years Since the City Launched the Culture of the Manga), Tokyo: Nyûton Puresu, 1998.

Shimizu Isao, *Manga tanjô Taishô demokurashi-kara no shuppatsu* (The Birth of Manga from the Democracy of Taishô"), Rekishi bunka raiburary, Tokyo: Yoshikawa Kôbunkan, 1999.

Shimizu Isao, *Manga no rekishi* (History of Manga), Tokyo: Kawade shobô, 1999.

Shimizu Isao, *Bigot-ga mita nihonjin* (The Japanese Seen by Bigot), Tokyo: Kôdansha (Kôdansha gakujutsu bunko), 2001.

Shimizu Isao, *Nihon kindai manga no tanjô* (The Birth of Modern Manga*)*, Tokyo: Yamakawa, 2001.

Shimizu Isao, *Edo no Manga* (Edo Period Manga), Tokyo: Kôdansha gakujutsu Bunkô, 2003.

Shimizu Isao, *Nenpyô Nihon manga shi* (Chronology of the History of Japanese Manga), Tokyo: Kinsen shoten, 2007.

Sugiura Hinako, *Edo e yôkoso* (Welcome to Edo), Chikuma Shobô, 1989.

Sugiura Hinako, *Ichinichi Edojin* (A Day in a Person's Life in the Edo Era), Tokyo: Shinchôsha, 1998.

Takahata Isao, *Eiga o tsukurinagara kangaeta koto 1955–91* (My Thoughts When Making My Films 1955-91), Tokyo: Tokuma Shoten, 1991.

Takahata Isao, *Heisei tanuki gassen Pompoko* (*Pompoko, Tanuki* Combat in the Heisei Era), Tokyo: Tokuma Shoten, Hatake jimusho, 1994.

Takahata Isao, *Eiga o tsukurinagara kangaeta koto 1991–99* (My Thoughts When Making My Films 1991–99), Tokyo: Tokuma Shoten, Studio Ghibli, 1999.

Takahata Isao, *Jûni seiki no anime-shon, kokuhô emakimono ni miru eigateki animeteki narumono* (Cartoons in the Twelfth Century. Aspects Evocative of the Cinema and Animation in Twelfth-century Painting Scrolls Listed as National Treasures), Tokyo: Studio Ghibli Company, Tokuma Shoten, 1999.

Takeuchi Osamu, *Manga hyôgengaku nyûmon* (Introduction to Expression in Manga), Tokyo: Chikuma Shobô, 2005.

Takeuchi Osamu et al. (gen. ed.), *Gendai Manga Hakubutsukan 1945–2005* (The Encyclopedia of Contemporary Manga), Tokyo: Shogakukan Creative, 2006.

Tezuka Osamu, *Boku no manga jinsei* (My Life in Manga), Iwanami Shinsho, no. 509, Tokyo, 1997 (2nd ed. 2006).

Tezuka Setsuko, *Otto Tezuka Osamu to tomoni komorebi ni ikiru* (My Life with My Husband Tezuka Osamu: a Sunbeam between the Trees"), Tokyo: Kôdansha, 1995.

CATALOGS AND PERIODICALS

Âto Manga wa geijutsuka ? Shinka suru manga hyôgen no yukue (Art: Is Manga an Art? Concerning the Evolution of Expression in Manga), *Bijutsu techô*, vol. 58, no. 876, 2, 2006.

Edo jidai no insatsu bunka Ieyasu wa katsuji ningen data (Printing in the Edo Period Ieyasu: Typographic Man) (exh. cat.), Tokyo: Printing Museum, 2000.

Emakimono anime no genryû (Illustrated Narrative Hand Scrolls: Origin of Animation) (exh. cat.), Chiba shi Museum, October 1999.

Kaikan 25 shûnen kinen Ôta kinen bijutsukan meihin ten (The 25th Anniversary Exhibition Masterpieces of the Ôta Memorial Museum of Art) (exh. cat.), Ôta Memorial Museum of Art 2005.

Kindai Manga tsukuriageta Kiyochika, Rakuten to jûnin no fûshi gaka ten (Exhibition of the Ten Caricaturists, including Kiyochika and Rakuten, Who Created the Modern Comic Strip) (exh. cat.), Ukiyo-e Ôta Memorial Museum of Art, Tokyo, 1984.

Kindai manga no so Kitazawa Rakuten zuroku (The Father of Modern Manga, Kitazawa Rakuten) (exh. cat.) published by the cultural and international section of the city of Ômiya, 1991.

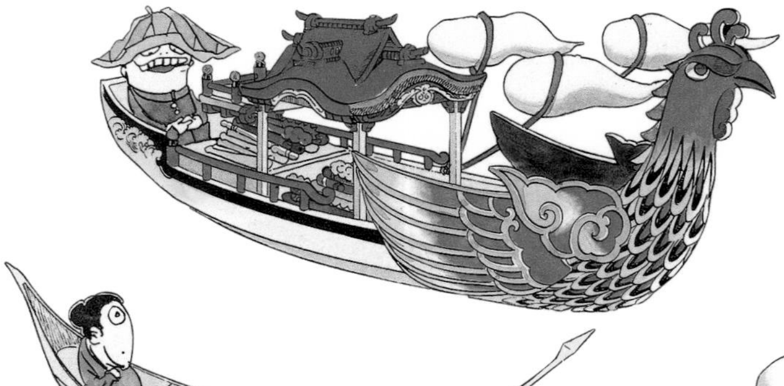

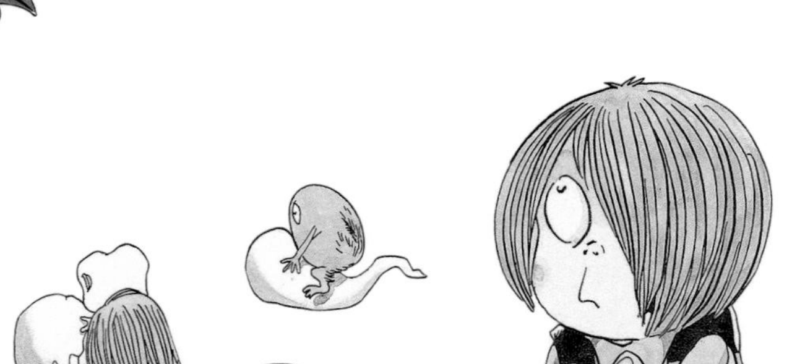

Manga bunka no genryû Fûshi to asobi kokoro (The Origin of Manga, Caricatures and Humor) (exh. cat.), Museum of the Prefecture of Fukushima, 1992.

Manga kindai jiken ten, exh. cat. of manga concerned with events from the modern period, Tamachi City Museum, 1994.

Meiji no omokage furansujin gaka Bigô no sekai (Images of the Meiji Era, the World of Georges Bigot, a French Artist in Japan), Kawasaki City Museum, 2002.

Nihon no manga 300 nen (300 Years of Manga in Japan) (exh. cat.), Kawasaki City Museum, 1996.

Ô Mizuki Shigeru ten (The Great Exhibition of the Work of Mizuki Shigeru), (exh. cat.) Edo-Tokyo Museum et al., Tokyo: Asahi Shuppansha, 2004.

Ô Mizuki Shigeru ten (The Great Exhibition of the Work of Mizuki Shigeru) (exh. cat.), traveling exhibition from April 2004 to September 2005, Tokyo: Mizuki Production—Asahi shinbunsha, 2004–2005.

Ôtsu-e (exh. cat.), Machida City Museum, 2006.

Shôwa no manga ten (Showa Period Manga) (exh. cat.), Asahi Shinbunsha, 1989.

Translated from the French by David Radzinowicz

Editorial consultant
Xavier Hébert

Design
Philippe Ducat

PH. DVX

Hare yuku sora

Cover Design
Nicolas Weil

Copyediting
Penny Isaac

Proofreading
Helen Woodhall

Typesetting
Claude Olivier-Four

Color Separation
Les Artisans du Regard, Paris

The text was set in Janson and Gill.

Dépôt légal: 01/2008
08 09 10 3 2 1
Printed in Singapore by Imago

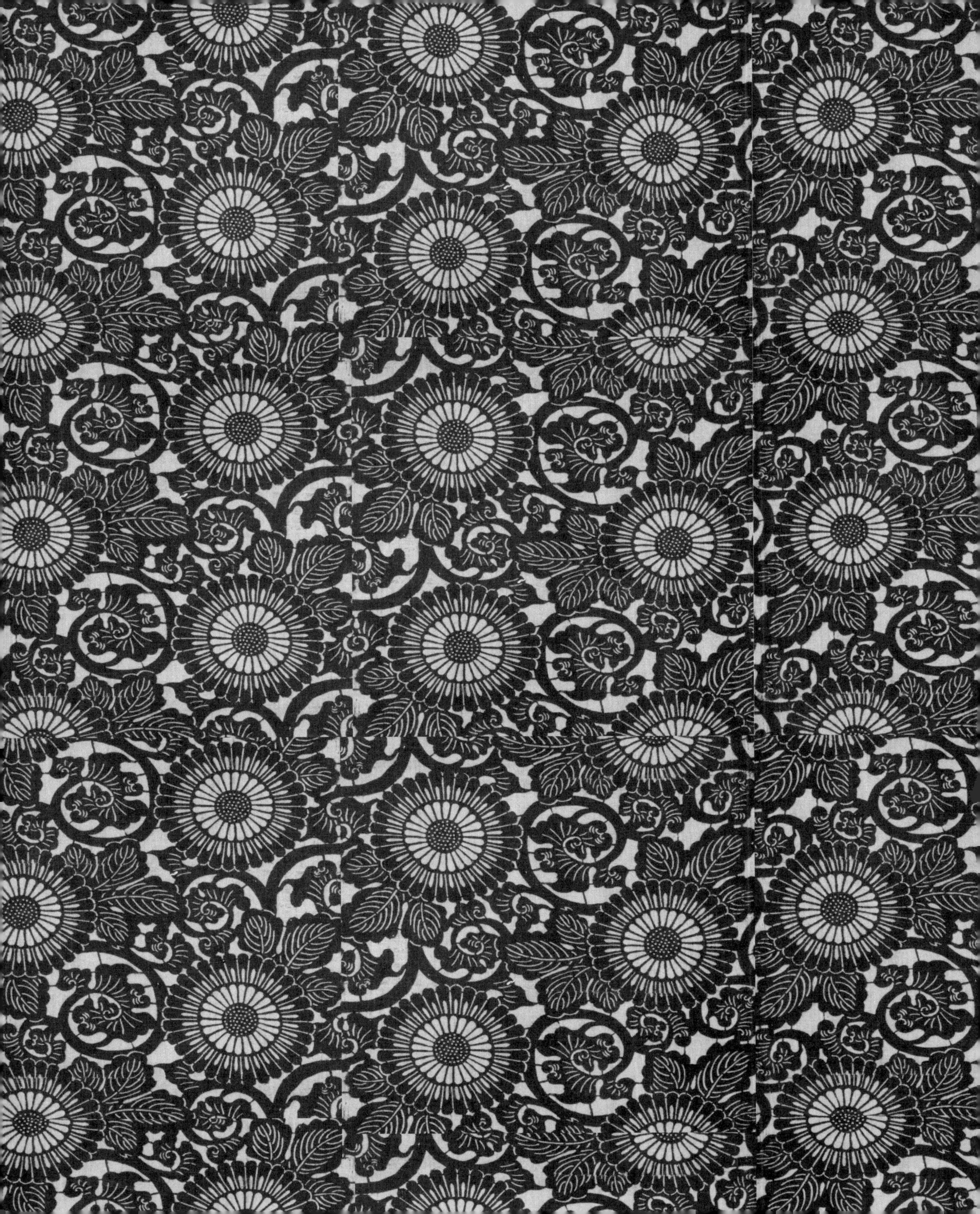

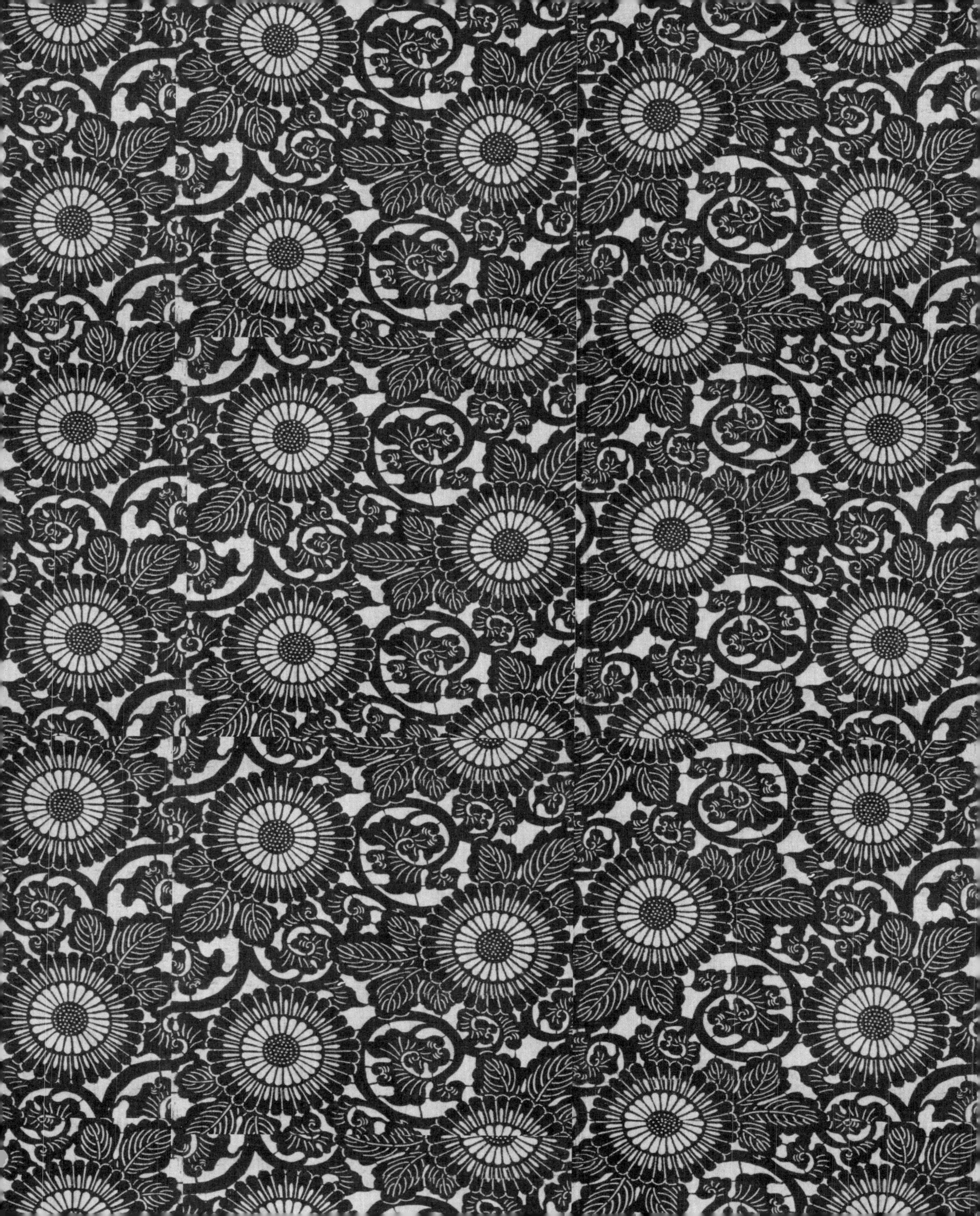